Linux Internals

Moshe Bar

McGraw-Hill
New York   San Francisco   Washington, D.C.
Auckland   Bogotá   Caracas   Lisbon   London   Madrid
Mexico City   Milan   Montreal   New Delhi   San Juan
Singapore   Sydney   Tokyo   Toronto

McGraw-Hill

A Division of The McGraw·Hill Companies

Copyright © 2000 by The McGraw-Hill Companies, Inc. All rights reserved. Printed in the
United States of America. Except as permitted under the United States Copyright Act
of 1976, no part of this publication may be reproduced or distributed in any form or by
any means, or stored in a data base or retrieval system, without the prior written permission
of the publisher.

1 2 3 4 5 6 7 8 9 0   DOC/DOC   0 5 4 3 2 1 0

P/N 0-07-212596-9

Part of ISBN 0-07-212598-5

The sponsoring editor for this book was Michael Sprague and the production manager
was Clare Stanley. It was set in New Century Schoolbook by Patricia Wallenburg.

Printed and bound by R.R. Donnelley & Sons.

To Yehoshua

May God bless you and give you peace.

Contents

Preface

In the last two years, first with version 2.0, then 2.2. and soon 2.4, Linux has undergone amazing progress to what now constitutes probably one of the most advanced operating systems for servers and workstations alike.

Especially with the upcoming 2.4 series, much effort have been put by us developers into making the kernel highly scalable and able to efficiently handle and manage huge quantities of memories, many concurrent CPUs, and a vast array of modern peripherals.

If somebody until a few years ago could go read the kernel source code and understand the main concepts by herself, it has become very hard indeed today. Not only has the size of the source code grown significantly, but as the core developers themselves learned new techniques and technologies, the algorithms and source code have become increasingly complex and hard-to-understand.

Moshe Bar's work in bringing the intricacies of the Linux kernel 2.3.xx and 2.4 closer to the enthusiast, the system administrator, and system programmer is important to bridge the gap between kernel developers and users.

During the making of this book, I was in close contact with Moshe and had to face and answer dozens of questions. He never accepted an answer as such until he fully understood the algorithm or functionality.

As a core kernel developer, I have found this book to be a good introduction as well as a reference work to be used to look up the Linux kernel concepts.

Moshe Bar has over the years written a great deal of articles, papers, and treatises on OS principles and his involvement with prior OS projects, such as MVS, VM, and bsd shows in his thorough approach and clear technical language.

Ingo Molnar

Introduction

Linux Internals was written to enhance the general understanding of the inner workings of Linux. Most of these "internals" happen to be in a kernel inside the Linux operating system kernel. This book is, however, not a full source code commentary in the common sense of the term. Certainly a lot of the code is commented, but the emphasis is rather on the functionality of the code, rather than on the code itself.

The Linux kernel contains the code that controls a system's resources, user processes, data I/O, and extended functions, such as the Linux kernel-space web server kHTTPd.

The Linux Kernel

A *kernel* is operating system software that runs in protected mode and has access to the hardware's privileged registers. Some operating systems employ a *microkernel architecture*, where device drivers and other code are loaded and executed on demand, and do not necessarily reside always in memory.

The kernel is not a separate process running on the system. It is the guts of the operating system, which controls the scheduling of processes to achieve multitasking and provides a set of routines, constantly in memory, to which every user-space process has access.

By contrast, a *monolithic architecture*, in which all device drivers are part of the kernel proper, is more common among UNIX implementations, and is the design employed by classics such as BSD. The Linux kernel, too is a mostly monolithic kernel—all device drivers are part of the kernel proper—but unlike BSD, a Linux kernel's device drivers also can be *loadable*, that is, they can be loaded and unloaded from memory through user commands.

This book primarily references the 2.4.x series of kernels for the Intel x86 architecture (at the time of this writing, still called 2.3.51). All code samples used throughout this book are based on the 2.3.49 kernel, although sometimes, a preview on the 2.5 kernel series is used.

Who Should Read This Book

Linux Internals is targeted at system and network administrators, developers, and capacity planning managers. It will also appeal to Linux enthusiasts who have a good general understanding of hardware and software.

In the chapters that follow, system administrators will learn how to adapt a kernel to specific needs and hardware environments. In addition, by tuning the kernel in the appropriate places, system throughput can be increased considerably. The File Systems section of this book discusses choosing, installing, and correctly configuring a file system. Linux developers will learn which programming techniques yield the best performance for their programs and debugging will be easier after reading this book because external factors to the user programs will be better understood.

Finally, Linux enthusiasts in general, will learn to appreciate their favorite kernel even more after discovering its hidden gems of technical design.

What You Should Know Before Reading This Book

No previous kernel knowledge is necessary, but it helps to have a good understanding of the general concepts of hardware and software. It addition, it helps if you have a working knowledge of the Linux interface and a rudimentary understanding of what's involved in basic system administration.

It also helps to be able to read C programs, although most of the code provided is explained. For a good introduction to C, I always strongly advise *The C Programming Language*, by Kernighan/Ritchie, the designers of C.

What This Book Contains

This book begins with an introduction to OS theory and kernel concepts in general and relative to UNIX in detail.

The next chapters are dedicated to the five pillars of every kernel:

- Processes
- Inter-process communication
- Signals (interrupts) handling
- Virtual memory
- File systems

Each chapter is structured the same way; it first gives a detailed explanation of the inner workings of the kernel pertinent to the subject. Then, a few coding examples are provided to show how to change the functionality of the kernel. Finally, the relevant kernel data structures (the C include files) are listed for easy reference. Together with the algorithms listed in the main body of the chapter, the reader has a complete aggregation of code and data, as well as the necessary explanations. There is no attempt to present an exhaustive commentary on the Linux kernel source code, rather we focus on the most important subjects and on performance-relevant issues of the kernel. Appendices are included at the end of the book for system calls, the GPL license, and other useful information.

You can read straight through the chapters to learn more about the Linux kernel, or you might choose to go straight to a chapter of interest and use this book as a reference. Whenever a code snippet is shown in the text, the corresponding data structures can be found at the end of the chapter.

Where to Find More Information

The most up-to-date information on Linux kernels can be found on the Internet. It is, however, essentially raw data. Gathering this information, assembling it, and putting it into a coherent format is not a trivial task. This is the biggest value of *Linux Internals*—it provides a coherent, researched, and formatted source of information that is otherwise available to the public through scattered web sites, source code, and articles.

One good source of information on the kernel is, of course, the kernel source code itself. There is a site with an excellent source code navigator for all available architectures and Linux versions at **http://lxr.linux.no/source/**.

At **http://www.linuxhq.com** you can find information on all kernel versions, and particularly, on the version currently under development. For a full list of GNU tools, visit **www.gnu.org**.

Finally, keeping up with the kernel developer mailing list is informative, although the sheer volume of this mailing list and the poor signal-to-noise ratio make it difficult at times to extract any useful information.

Suggestions, Comments

Any suggestions or comments are very welcome and can be addressed either to **moshe_bar@hotmail.com** or to Moshe Bar, c/o McGraw-Hill, Professional Book Group, Two Penn Plaza, New York, NY 10121.

Acknowledgments

First of all, it is my duty to thank God for giving me all I needed to write this book.

This book could not have been done without the help of some star developers of the Linux Kernel Hacking fraternity. People like Ingo Molnar, Andrea Arcangeli, Stephen Tweedie, Hans Reiser, and Steve Best contributed greatly to this book.

Joe Pranevich's article "The Wonderful World of 2.4 Kernels" gave me important ideas on how to generally describe the advances made in the 2.4 kernel. Thank you, Joe.

Matthew Dillon, of FreeBSD fame, wrote an important paper describing general virtual memory concepts that inspired the description of Linux general VM concepts in this book. Thank you, Matt.

A few angels watched over the creation and completion of this book: Patricia Campbell, Scott Fallin, Tom Syroid, Philip Courier and wife Patricia Lambert, and Brad Dixon all voluntarily contributed many hours out of their little available time to help me edit this book. Patricia Campbell and Brad Dixie's technical expertise pointed to many embarrassing mistakes before they found their way to print. Scott Fallin, my long-time partner in the development of a gpl'd Kha0s OS, highlighted many difficult to understand text sections and helped me to make them better. Philip Courier and Patricia Lambert, often with a lot of humor, greatly ameliorated the style and consistency of the individual chapters. My friend, author Tom Syroid, helped make this book a reality by sharing his authoring experience with me. To him I am especially indebted.

During the editing process, a mailing list was used (Linux-based, obviously) to discuss topics such as C coding style, the correct definition of terms, etc. among the editors. This proved to be a savvy move and greatly contributed to the spirit of the team and to the quality of this book. Thank you all.

Robo-chan, my soul brother, pushed my spirit up when it was down. Thank you, Roberto.

Many thanks as well to TopTier Israel and the Baan group for providing me with a sysadmin/consultant job during the writing of this book to keep the revenue stream flowing and for providing machinery to test what I write about.

Open Source— Implications for a Modern Operating System

Without doubt, the main reason for the unusual success of Linux is its General Public License (GPL). The concept of Open Source, though, or freeware as it is sometimes called, is actually quite old. The first proponent of freeware was Richard Stallman, of the Free Software Foundation (FSF), who designed the GPL license for some excellent and now-widespread software he wrote—most prominently the Emacs editing environment and the GCC compiler for C and C++. Richard Stallman has also been working for a long while now on a full GNU operating system, a project called *GNU Hurd*. Under development for nearly a decade, this OS is still not a reality, but the many powerful technologies that have emerged from this project have found their way to other OSs, such as Linux, BSD, and others.

Operating systems benefit from having an Open Source approach to development in two ways: reliability and performance. The reliability of Linux stems in large part from the scrutiny of hundreds of thousands of developers auditing the code, improving it, changing it, and trying it out. As Eric Raymond stated in his famous paper "The Cathedral and the Bazaar," "Given a large enough beta-tester and co-developer base, almost every problem will be characterized quickly and the fix obvious to someone."

Linux' performance benefits much for the same reasons; public scrutiny of the code leads to continuous improvement of the overall efficiency of kernel execution path. Furthermore, many academic institutions have adopted the Linux operating system for their research and have been able to use advanced techniques such as hardware profiling and virtual machine tracers to find hitherto hidden performance bottle-necks in the code.

Finally, through the porting of the Linux kernel to a great variety of processor platforms, certain parts had to be adapted or re-written. Through this process of comparison and adaptation, better code emerged that was soon back-ported to other platforms.

Having so many eyes scrutinizing the Linux code base makes for a better Quality Assurance (QA) department than any closed model software development organization could ever afford. This in turn, makes for better quality software.

A mere development model such as Open Source, cannot by itself replace proper design and coding methods. But here again, the Open Source model excels proprietary models by great lengths. Consider the example of a kernel improvement in Linux. For as long as hackerdom has existed, great emphasis has been put on elegant design, proper data structure design, and performance-related issues. Even in the most hidden code snippets, you sometimes find beautiful and superbly crafted yet stunningly efficient design.

History of Linux

Linux began, as do most successful projects, as a project sprung from necessity, in Finland in 1991. Linus B. Torvalds, then a student at the University of Helsinki, bought himself a PC based on the i386, the first Intel CPU to have on-chip support for virtual memory management. Not entirely satisfied with the MS/DOS operating system, Torvalds decided to implement the Minix OS (need to amplify the origins and nature of Minix) on his PC instead.

When AT&T in the seventies began to realize that their UNIX operating system was becoming a valuable commercial product it decided with version 7 to prohibit the distribution of the source code together with the binary as was previously the practice. Many universities as a result had to drop the study of UNIX and reverted back to studying only theory.

Unfortunately, studying theory does not provide the student the confidence with OS theory that could be achieved when actually applying the concepts to a real OS. Therefore, Andrew Tanenbaum decided to develop an OS that included all of the concepts and features of UNIX but from completely new source code. This way he could avoid the strict licensing restrictions of AT&T and still teach his students about UNIX. Minix was from the beginning designed to run on PCs and was based originally on the feature set of AT&T UNIX Version 7. Soon, however, Tanenbaum significantly enhanced Minix until it came to include all the functions and feature of a modern OS. Minix is still used today as a pedagogic tool but also in production system at selected sites. For a comprehensive overview of Minix, it is advisable to study Andrew S. Tanenbaum's and Albert S. Woodhull's seminal work (*Operating Systems* by Prentice Hall).

Soon he was enhancing Minix to provide the functions and features that he needed for his study. He decided that Minix was too much an academic OS; he began to create an operating system from scratch. Torvalds' most important decision was to make his new OS's source code freely available over the Internet—which is to say, Open Source—under the name of Linux, a contraction of Linus and UNIX.

The first version, version 0.01, was made available for download on the Internet in August 1991. In October of the same year, Torvalds made an official announcement of the availability of version 0.02. This version already could execute such UNIX-user-land programs as the bash shell, the GNU gcc compiler, and other basic utilities, but not much more.

Because of the Open Source nature of the project, and with the source code immediately available all over the globe, soon many hackers, computer freaks, and PC enthusiasts began looking at the code and enhancing it. Many began to send their suggestions to Torvalds, who inaugurated the "official" reference Linux source code development tree. Looking through their code suggestions, he rejected most, but some he incorporated into Linux. Development continued this way for three more years before a first production version was announced.

In 1992 and 1993, the first Linux distributions appeared. Distributions, the primary way to obtain a fully functional OS, include the Linux kernel, the X windowing system, and a comprehensive package of application programs and utilities, which can number in the hundreds or more. Distributions also include an installer, which prepares the binary image of the OS and the boot/shutdown scripts, and makes sure that all components are compatible with and tuned for each other. Last but not least, distributions also provide documentation. Today many distributions exist, the most successful being RedHat, SuSE, and Caldera.

In March 1994, version 1.0 was made available. It still showed the occasional erratic behavioral quirk, as I fondly remember, but it was quite usable. Linux 1.0 featured TCP/IP, SLIP, and printer support, and had enough drivers to support a wide range of the PC equipment then available. After that, the Linux boom really began, and millions of enthusiasts in all corners of the world started using the system.

The highlights of the steady ascent of Linux to its status as the major power in the IT market today are shown in Table 1.1.

TABLE 1.1 Timeline of Linux develpment	August 1991	Version 0.01
	October 1991	Official announcement 0.02
	November 1993	First Slackware Distribution with kernel 0.99
	March 1994	Version 1.0
	June 1995	First port to the Alpha architecture
	October 1996	Debian Linux is used on the space shuttle in orbit (on an IBM laptop)
	January 1999	Version 2.2.0
	March 2000	Version 2.3.49 (pre 2.4.0)

Linux Functionality

Linux has come a long way from its humble beginning in 1991. As the phenomenon of Open Source has spread far and wider, more and more people have contributed to the Linux kernel and to its subsystems. At the same time, thousands upon thousands of userspace packages have been added at ever-increasing frequency. With the concurrent rise of the World Wide Web, some Web sites are devoted solely to the purpose of daily announcements about new software versions available for Linux.

Linux is available on many platforms, including Intel, Sparc, Alpha, MIPS, the Motorola 68000 family, and PowerPC. Early on, Linux was brought into conformance with the Portable Operating System Interface (POSIX) standard. Its POSIX compliance allows applications developed under Linux to be very easily ported to other POSIX-compliant OSs. On Intel CPU-based systems, the Linux binaries conform to iBSCS standards. This allows, for example, a statically linked program to run under FreeBSD or Solaris without recompilation.

Technically, Linux provides (among others) the following functions:

- Multi-user environment
- Multi-process, multi-processor (SMP) environment
- Inter-Process communication (IPC, pipes, sockets)
- Process control
- POSIX-style terminal management
- TCP/IP, Ipv4, Ipv6 support
- Support for a wide variety of hardware
- Demand paging with optional Least Recently Used (LRU) algorithms and page coloring
- Swapping
- Buffer cache
- Dynamic and shared libraries
- Support for many file systems (ext2fs, UFS, NTFS, HPFS, MS/DOS, ISO9660, coda, and many more)

Novelties in the 2.4 Kernel

Linux 2.2 was a major improvement over Linux 2.0 and the Linux 1.x series. It supported many new file systems, a new system of file caching, and it was much more scalable. Linux 2.4 builds on these improvements and more, to be the best Linux kernel yet in a wide variety of situations.

The Linux kernel is a collection of modular components and subsystems, including device drivers, protocols, and other types of component. These are glued to the core of the Linux kernel by Application Programming Interfaces (APIs), which provide a standard method by which the Linux kernel can be expanded. Most of this book focuses on these components of the Linux OS, the components that do the most work.

- In the 2.4 kernel series Linux has vastly improved its ability to handle a large number of processes and tasks. The task limit now numbers beyond 4,090. The scheduler's efficiency has been improved somewhat, and Linux 2.4 can better handle systems with a large number of concurrent processes than could earlier versions.
- Linux 2.4 can also handle much larger "enterprise-class" hardware than could previous Linux kernel revisions. For example, Linux 2.4, with appropriate patches, can address beyond 4GB of RAM. (One machine I have seen is configured with 12GB of RAM and has one address space of 8.3GB resident size.)
- Scalability on SMP systems is now comparable to proprietary OSs and in some instances even better.
- Support for other processor platforms has been increased, too. In addition to the traditional architectures mentioned earlier, Linux 2.4 now supports the new Transmeta Crusoe processor directly. The 3Com PalmPilot as well as Psion5, both run Linux natively. The new Intel IA64 (next generation, 64-bit successor to the venerable Intel x86 architecture), will probably be ready in 2000, but is not yet included directly with the kernel.
- New file system support has been added (the Irix efs file system and the UDF standard used on DVD disks), while certain other support has been made obsolete (QNX and ext1).
- The introduction of *tasklets*, a revolutionary way of handling low-level interrupts[1], makes the TCP/IP stack (along with other subsystems and userprograms) much more efficient. New networking protocol software is capable of handling the DECNet standard.
- Linux 2.2 and Linux 2.0 include built-in support for starting a Java interpreter (if present) whenever a Java application is executed. (Linux was one of the first OSs to do this at the kernel level.) Linux 2.4 still includes support for loading Java interpreters as necessary,

---

1 We will see how tasklets work in Chapter 3.

but the specific Java driver has been removed and users must upgrade their configurations to use the "Misc." driver.

- The first OS to so, the Linux 2.4 kernel includes a kernel web daemon, or kHTTPd. This facility allows the handling of more efficient static web pages.

In the chapters ahead, we will explore in detail these and many other features of the Linux kernel.

Compiling a Kernel

Most system administrators configure a new Linux server by first installing a base system from one of the widespread distributions, such as RedHat, SuSE, or TurboLinux. This installation fulfills two basic purposes. It conveniently installs a coherent, compatible set of compilers, kernel source files, file management utilities, and other utilities and subsystems. It also installs a bootable kernel on the server or workstation with which the administrator can then create the desired configuration.

Once the base system is installed, the diligent system administrator should then compile the kernel as needed. Most system administrators will want to change the processor support for their kernels. Many distributions still install a kernel for the most common denominator, the i486 type of CPU. By compiling his or her own kernel, the system administrator can tell the kernel configurator to prepare the kernel for a specific type of CPU, which nowadays—especially on servers—is often a Pentium II or Pentium III. Some administrators might want to have SCSI support in the kernel, or ISDN if needed.

The prospect of having to compile and install a new kernel seems a dangerous and daunting task to many. You might be afraid of doing something wrong, and making it impossible to boot the machine. It is true that there is a certain risk of doing things the wrong way, as there is with all system administrator tasks. This is why it is best to compile the new kernel immediately after installation. If something goes wrong, the system can be reinstalled from scratch, without wasting too much of your time. Making such a mistake later on, after you have installed additional software (such as a database manager), would prove much more painful. There is no need to worry, however. Compiling a kernel and installing it is simpler than many might think.

WARNING

*Careful! Apply all necessary kernel source patches before compiling the kernel. The links to obtain generic kernel patches are at **www.linuxhq.com**.*

Source Code Tree Structure

To patch a kernel and compile it, as well as to help you better understand the information in upcoming chapters, it is helpful to have a good overview of the source code tree structure.

```
|-- Documentation
|   |-- arm
|   |   `-- nwfpe
|   |-- cdrom
|   |-- fb
|   |-- filesystems
|   |-- i386
|   |-- isdn
|   |-- kbuild
|   |-- m68k
|   |-- networking
|   |   `-- ip_masq
|   |-- powerpc
|   |-- sound
|   |-- sysctl
|   `-- video4linux
|       `-- bttv
|-- arch
|   `-- i386
|       |-- boot
|       |   |-- compressed
|       |   `-- tools
|       |-- kernel
|       |-- lib
|       |-- math-emu
|       `-- mm
|-- configs
|-- drivers
|   |-- acorn
|   |   |-- block
|   |   |-- char
|   |   |-- net
|   |   `-- scsi
|   |-- ap1000
|   |-- block
|   |   `-- paride
|   |-- cdrom
|   |-- char
|   |   |-- ftape
|   |   |   |-- compressor
|   |   |   |-- lowlevel
|   |   |   `-- zftape
|   |   |-- hfmodem
|   |   |-- ip2
|   |   `-- joystick
|   |-- dio
|   |-- fc4
|   |-- isdn
|   |   |-- act2000
|   |   |-- avmb1
|   |   |-- divert
|   |   |-- eicon
|   |   |-- hisax
```

```
|    |    |-- icn
|    |    |-- isdnloop
|    |    |-- pcbit
|    |    `-- sc
|    |-- macintosh
|    |-- misc
|    |-- net
|    |    |-- fc
|    |    |-- hamradio
|    |    |    `-- soundmodem
|    |    `-- irda
|    |-- nubus
|    |-- pci
|    |-- pnp
|    |-- sbus
|    |    |-- audio
|    |    `-- char
|    |-- scsi
|    |    `-- aic7xxx
|    |-- sgi
|    |    `-- char
|    |-- sound
|    |    `-- lowlevel
|    |-- tc
|    |-- usb
|    |    `-- maps
|    |-- video
|    `-- zorro
|-- fs
|    |-- adfs
|    |-- affs
|    |-- autofs
|    |-- coda
|    |-- devpts
|    |-- efs
|    |-- ext2
|    |-- fat
|    |-- hfs
|    |-- hpfs
|    |-- isofs
|    |-- lockd
|    |-- minix
|    |-- msdos
|    |-- ncpfs
|    |-- nfs
|    |-- nfsd
|    |-- nls
|    |-- ntfs
|    |-- proc
|    |-- qnx4
|    |-- romfs
|    |-- smbfs
|    |-- sysv
|    |-- ufs
```

```
|   |-- umsdos
|   `-- vfat
|-- ibcs
|   |-- Doc
|   |-- PROD.Patches
|   |-- Patches
|   |-- Tools
|   |-- VSYS
|   |-- devtrace
|   |-- iBCSemul
|   |   `-- maps
|   |-- include
|   |   `-- ibcs
|   `-- x286emul
|-- include
|   |-- asm -> asm-i386
|   |-- asm-generic
|   |-- asm-i386
|   |-- linux
|   |   |-- byteorder
|   |   |-- lockd
|   |   |-- modules
|   |   |-- modules-BOOT
|   |   |-- modules-smp
|   |   |-- modules-up
|   |   |-- nfsd
|   |   |-- raid
|   |   `-- sunrpc
|   |-- net
|   |   `-- irda
|   |-- scsi
|   `-- video
|-- init
|-- ipc
|-- kernel
|-- lib
|-- mm
|-- modules
|-- net
|   |-- 802
|   |   |-- pseudo
|   |   `-- transit
|   |-- appletalk
|   |-- ax25
|   |-- bridge
|   |-- core
|   |-- decnet
|   |-- econet
|   |-- ethernet
|   |-- ipv4
|   |-- ipv6
|   |-- ipx
|   |-- irda
|   |   |-- compressors
```

```
|    |    |-- ircomm
|    |    |-- irlan
|    |    `-- irlpt
|    |-- lapb
|    |-- netlink
|    |-- netrom
|    |-- packet
|    |-- rose
|    |-- sched
|    |-- sunrpc
|    |-- unix
|    |-- wanrouter
|    `-- x25
|-- pcmcia-cs-3.0.14
|    |-- cardmgr
|    |-- clients
|    |    `-- patches
|    |-- debug-tools
|    |-- doc
|    |-- etc
|    |    `-- cis
|    |-- flash
|    |-- include
|    |    |-- linux
|    |    `-- pcmcia
|    |-- man
|    `-- modules
`-- scripts
     |-- ksymoops
     `-- lxdialog
```

Notice how nicely Linux organizes the source code into architecture-dependent and independent code. About 95 percent of the kernel source is independent code, and thus will be exactly the same on all porting sets of Linux. The remaining 5 percent is usually assembler code or minor details, such as clock timer frequency.

The arch/ Directory

Architecture-dependent code resides in the arch/ directory. Under this directory, for each existing porting set of Linux, there are three more subdirectories: kernel/, lib/, and mm/.

The kernel/ subdirectory contains architecture-dependent implementations of general kernel features, such as signals handling, clock handling, and so forth. The lib/ subdirectory contains local implementations of library functions that run faster if compiled from architecture-dependent source code. The mm/ subdirectory contains local memory handling implementations.

The drivers/ Directory

Perhaps unsurprisingly, all drivers source code resides in the drivers/ directory. Because of the great variety of devices supported by Linux 2.4, there is a lot of source code here; actually, more than 50 percent of all the kernel source resides within the drivers/ directory.

The fs/ Directory

The fs/ directory is the location for all supported file systems. Those experimenting with new file systems, such as IBM's JFS or Hans Reiser's reiserfs, will have to patch this directory to contain the source code for those file systems.

The include/ Directory

Before a new kernel is actually compiled, it must be configured. Configuring in this context means telling the make utility which drivers, features, and modules to compile into the kernel. By default, most standard distributions come with a uniprocessor kernel. To implement the standard SMP features of the kernel, configuration with SMP is required.

The ipc/ Directory

All the code necessary for handling interprocess communication is in the ipc/ directory. The all-important semaphores-handling C code is here (sem.c). Nevertheless, this directory contains only 3,751 lines of code.

The init/ Directory

Main.c, which contains a lot of very important code, like the code to implement fork() and that most-often-executed code, the cpu_idle() loop, resides in the init/ directory.

The code that produces the bogomips reading at boot is here for those who are still looking at it for an indication of speed. You will find that it does not actually measure processor speed. The BogoMips reading has become somewhat of an indicator of a computer's speed. What it does in fact is measure the time it takes the processor to perform an noop (no operation) which does not at all indicate the system's performance.

```
void __init calibrate_delay(void)
{

    unsigned long ticks, loopbit;
    int lps_precision = LPS_PREC;

    loops_per_sec = (1<<12);

    printk("Calibrating delay loop... ");
    while (loops_per_sec <<= 1) {
        /* wait for "start of" clock tick */
        ticks = jiffies;
        while (ticks == jiffies)
            /* nothing */;
        /* Go .. */
        ticks = jiffies;
        __delay(loops_per_sec);
        ticks = jiffies - ticks;
        if (ticks)
            break;
    }
```

The lib/ Directory

The lib/ directory holds code that is often needed by other parts of the kernel. For instance, inflate.c can be found here; this code can decompress a kernel at boot and load it into memory. It also knows how to decompress standard PKZIP 8-bit compression algorithms.

The kernel/ Directory

Some of the most frequently called kernel functions reside in the kernel/ dirctory. The scheduler, fork(), and timer.c are found here. You will also find printk.c in this directory. Throughout the kernel source code, printk() is used instead of printf(), because the printf() function is not SMP-capable when called from within the kernel. If it were, various tasks running on different CPUs might write to the console or to the syslog at the same time and garble the output.

The mm/ Directory

The mm/ directory contains the source code to implement the virtual memory manager in the Linux kernel.

The net/ Directory

All the code for networking support is in the `net/` directory. TCP/IP, Netware, and Appletalk are all in here.

Compiling It

Before you can actually compile the kernel, you must tell the compilation utilities which functionalities you want, and whether to include those functionalities built into the kernel or configured as a dynamically loadable module (we will see later how the kernel handles loadable modules).

Table 2.1 shows the commands used to configure the kernel.

TABLE 2.1

Commands used to configure the kernel

Type	Command (as root)
Text prompt	`make config`
Text menus (ncurses style)	`make menuconfig`
GUI (requires X to run)	`make xconfig`

As you can see in the table above there are three ways to configure a kernel. The make config simply opens a character mode dialog that will ask one question after the other on the terminal until all questions are answered. For each question there are three possible answers: Yes, No or Module. Module here tells the kernel configuration to use a loadable module dynamically at execution time instead of statically linking the function into the kernel. This will somewhat slow down the first calling of the particular function at execution time, it is however compensated by a significantly smaller kernel. If you need to fit your kernel onto a diskette this is often the only way to do it.

`make menuconfig` opens up a colourful (on a color terminal) menu-based utility that will allow you to configure the kernel as needed. Most people use to configure their kernels this for the ease of use it offers. The functionaliy is obviously the same as with the other two commands.

The third way to configure a kernel, is make xconfig. This works only if you have a correctly configured and running X Window environment. It will allow to use the mouse to select items and set them as needed.

The command `make config` stores your previous choices, so you can always start it again and just change what you need.

Once you have configured your kernel to your satisfaction, you can proceed with the compilation.

```
root@ maguro /usr/src #   make dep; make clean; make bzImage; make modules-install
```

The directive `make bzImage` compiles the kernel and leaves a file in `arch/i386/boot` called `bzImage` (among other things). The above compilation code might take some time to execute. On a dual PIII 700 MHz with 512MB RAM, this code takes about 4 minutes to run. On a slower computer, compile time will be longer.

Now it's time to install the new kernel. Most people use LILO (the Linux Loader) for this. The command `make bzlilo` installs the kernel, runs LILO on it, and gets you all ready to boot, *but only* if LILO is configured in the following way on your system: kernel is /vmlinuz, (no, you're right, lilo) is in `/sbin`, and your lilo config (`/etc/lilo.conf`) agrees with this.

Otherwise, you need to use LILO directly. It's a fairly easy package to install and work with, but it has a tendency to confuse people with its configuration file. Look at the config file (either `/etc/lilo/config` for older versions or `/etc/lilo.conf` for new versions), to determine the current setup. The config file looks like this:

```
image = /vmlinuz
    label = Linux
    root = /dev/hda1
    ...
```

The `image =` is set to the currently installed kernel. Most people use `/vmlinuz`. The command `label` is used by LILO to determine which kernel or operating system to boot, and `root` is the `/directory` of that particular operating system.

Make a backup copy of your old kernel and copy the bzImage that you just made into place (`cp bzImage /vmlinuz` if you use `/vmlinuz`).

Rerun LILO. You have now added the kernel to your boot manager. Alternatively, if you wanted to make a boot disk, to check things out before you actually commit your new kernel to the LILO configuration, you could use the `mkbootdisk` utility shipped with most distributions.

The GNU gcc Compiler

The Linux kernel is written for the GNU gcc compiler. Trying to compile it with any other C compiler will result in complete failure. The source code is full of gcc-specific directives that prevent using anything but the gcc compiler. Because of this gcc affinity, the kernel source code might look strange to people who are used to developing for other C compilers. One such common idiosyncrasy is the use of *inline functions*. An inline function is a directive to the gcc compiler to fully expand the called function in each recurrence, instead of executing a function call each time to a single referenced instance of the called function (which requires expensive stack operations).

Some might object that this precludes achieving truly portable code. This is, however, really not the case. Because the gcc compiler exists on all platforms (inherently so) to which Linux has been ported, the code is portable across those architectures. It is, of course, not portable in the sense of being able to compile correctly under other C compilers. On the other hand, a kernel is not something that requires portability across architectures and compilers. The Linux kernel is optimized for reliability and efficiency, and these two goals are certainly much more important than portability.

Coding Conventions

After reading this book, you may feel ready to contribute to the Linux kernel. You are obviously welcome to do so, as long as you respect certain conventions.

- Commentaries are always /* */ style, even for one-line comments. The // comment is not acceptable.
- Most often, function-opening brackets ({) are on a separate line.
- If statements are coded this way:

```
if (str[0] >= '0' && str[0] <= '9') {
      strcpy(name, "ttyS");
      strncpy(name + 4, str, sizeof(name) - 5);
    } else
      strncpy(name, str, sizeof(name) - 1);
    name[sizeof(name) - 1] = 0;
```

▪ Single-line `if` statements are acceptable:

```
if (!strcmp(str, "ttya")) strcpy(name, "ttyS0");ne ifs are
quite OK:
```

▪ Kernel source, since the earliest times, has always contained a lot of `gotos`. Linux is no exception. It contains a `goto` for about every 80 lines of code. This is not because of sloppy programming style, but rather a requirement dictated by the craving for speedy code. In a next'ed `while` statement, it is just much easier to use `goto` to get out of the code rather than `break`.

Architecture Dependencies

Linux runs on a wide variety of processor platforms. Almost every month, you can read about a new successful porting to another architecture. Just remember that Linux originated on the i386 processor. This is clearly visible everywhere in the kernel code.

Table 2.2 illustrates the ports achieved so far:

TABLE 2.2

Ports achieved so far

Processor Type	Bite size	Maintainer
Intelx86	32	Linus Torvalds
Crusoe	32	Linus Torvalds
MIPS	32/64	Alan Cox
IA64	64	The Trillian Project
PA-RISC	64	The Puffin Group
Alpha	64	Richard Henderson
ARM	32	Russell King
Sparc	32/64	David S. Miller
PPc	32	Cort Dougan
M68000	32	Jes Sorensen

Linux
Kernel Base
Functions

This chapter is essential before proceeding further because it deals with the common functionality of the Linux kernel. This common functionality includes CPU management, device handling, interrupts handling, clock and time handling, and boot and shutdown issues. The reader is well advised to refer back to the concepts detailed in this chapter whenever he or she encounters them again in later chapters. (Throughout this chapter, whenever source is referenced it alludes to the 2.3.99 (2.4) source, unless otherwise specified. Sometimes, a preview of the 2.5 series is given.)

The sections on interrupts handling and clock handling are certainly the most technically challenging. It helps to have a good C reference book on hand when reading through these sections.

As discussed in Chapter 2, the operating system's main job is to provide a set of extended instructions. These extended instructions are called *system calls*. In the Microsoft Windows® world they are called *Application Programming Interfaces* or APIs. In many ways what we perceive of an operating system is really just its set of system calls. You can, for instance, run a program that was written for MS Windows95 under Linux, as long as you can provide the MS Windows' system calls (or APIs). (And provided it runs on the same CPU architecture, obviously.) This is exactly what the Open Source WINE[1] project does; it allows applications such as Microsoft Word97 to run under Linux natively.

What's an OS Anyway?

According to Andrew Tanenbaum, the function of an operating system is primarily to provide its users with a convenient interface (this refers not only to the graphical user interface, but also to the Application Programming Interface) to the real hardware. In this respect, an operating system is an extension of the hardware. It presents the user with the equivalent of an extended machine or virtual machine that is easier to program than the underlying hardware.

Operating systems are therefore interfaces between applications and the machine. This is why all physical processes (access to external or internal peripherals, memory, and other hardware resources) are transferred to the operating system. The virtualization of the physical layer, and its diversity, frees the developer from the complexity of managing all the existing peripherals.

---

1 WINE's home page is at **www.wine.org**.

The OS also avoids exposing to the user the limitations of a particular machine. If the system is available on several machine architectures, the user interface and programs will be the same and won't need to be adapted to the new architecture.

Resource Management

Modern computers contain a multitude of components, such as processors, memory, clocks, timers, disks, network interfaces, and many others. It is the job of the operating system to provide for an orderly and controlled allocation of the processors, memory, and I/O devices among the various programs competing for them.

Because in a modern OS many programs and users can access or share the computer's resources at the same time, some means of protection from competing demands is needed. User A should not be able to modify User B's data without User B's prior consent. Likewise, a misbehaving program should not be able to overwrite the memory reserved to the operating system itself, because this would invariably lead to a system crash; this is exactly what happens when users see the dreaded "blue screen of death" on Microsoft Windows operating systems. Finally, a modern OS should also be able to keep an account of the use of the computer's resources and provide statistics or the raw data for the charging of the resources to its various users.

CPU Management

Before we enter kernel details and Linux-specific implementation, it is important to see how CPUs actually work. This will help later in the book to understand why the Linux kernel insists on doing things in an unorthodox way for the sake of performance.

RISC-style CPUs, such as the MIPS[2] series or the PA-RISC[3], execute a data processing instruction (e.g. add, subtract, multiply, etc.) and send the result to the CPU registers. RISC-style CPUs typically use one or two instructions to handle what CISC processors do in five, six, or more instructions. Obviously, there is no magic involved. The CISC CPU needs to store temporary results somewhere, usually in internal registers not visible to the assembler programmer. Sometimes, CISC CPUs also use *immediate constants* instead of registers, which are commonly used for a fixed value (e.g. "1") in instructions such as `r0=1` or `MOV r0,#1`.

Suppose we have the following two instructions:

```
MOV r0,#0;
ADD r1,r2,r3;
```

The first one is typically executed first, but because the second instruction has no data dependencies on the first instruction (i.e. it does not use the `r0` register), from a logical point of view, the CPU could just as well execute both at the same time. This is *instruction-level parallelism* or *ILP*.

Now, suppose the program instead had the following instructions:

```
MOV r0,#0;
ADD r1,r0,r2;
```

In this case, the second instruction could only execute after the first had completed, because it depends on the first instruction's moving 0 to register `r0`. These two operations cannot be executed in parallel, because of the data dependency on `r0`. Needless to say, the compiler generating this assembler code should be shot dead, because it could just as well have directly added the constant 0 in the second instruction, thereby allowing the CPU to run both in parallel.

Memory Load Latency

Load latency is the delay in CPU cycles (on today's CPUs one cycle is typically around 1.5 nanoseconds; 1 nanosecond = 1 one-billionth of a second) between executing the load operation (to fetch data from memory) and being able to perform an operation on the data just loaded. The concept of load latency pertains to access to the RAM modules. Access to the CPU-internal memory (the registers) has no load latency.

---

2 The MIPS CPU is produced by MIPS Inc., a subsidiary of Silicon Graphics, Inc. (SGI). MIPS CPUs are generally 64-bit and very fast, while still featuring modest requirements for electricity and space. Next to the SGI workstations and servers, many embedded systems run MIPS processors. There has been a Linux port available for MIPS for quite some time now.

3 The PA-RISC is manufactured by Hewlett-Packard and is mainly used for their workstations and servers. A Linux port to this processor is available from the Puffin Group, a group of hackers financed by HP.

A latency of 0 implies the possibility of combining another operation in the same cycle, such as a load and add in one cycle. A load latency of 1 implies that an operation on the data obtained can only start in the next cycle, and so on.

Minimum load latency is when the data is in the Level 1 cache, which for Intel Pentium CPUs is on the processor die. A bad case of load latency happens when the system has to fetch data from the RAM banks. On modern systems this is generally takes in the neighborhood of 120 cycles, and worsens as CPUs get faster and RAM makes little progress in speed.

From the point of view of the CPU, the worst case of all happens when a *page fault* occurs and the OS has to page-in a page of virtual memory from the hard drive. For somebody used to seeing the world in terms of nanoseconds, waiting 50 or more milliseconds for a page to be brought in from disk and correctly processed by the OS is an eternity.

Obviously, the greater the latency the more the ILP is reduced, because a parallelized instruction might not execute before the CPU resets after a fetch from memory.

Most floating-point–heavy programs tend to store data in an array structure and thus tend to have a rather high potential for ILP, which is probably why floating-point (FP) performance has increased faster than integer performance, although another reason is that CPU designers have been able to allocate more transistors on the die to FP operations.

To store data about the status of the system's virtual memory, tasks, and many other things, the Linux kernel makes heavy use of *linked lists*; (sometimes also called an *array*). A linked list or array is an arrangement of data within a contiguous group of cells of all the same size. The location of any element in the array is simply:

```
"index0_location + index_number * cell_size"
```

For a linked list, each cell is separate, and contains a pointer to the location of the next cell in memory (or 0 if it's the last cell in the list) and the actual data. Not only does this take up much more memory, but it is much slower to jump to a random position, because you have to go through every single previous cell in the list, which causes a lot of CPU stalls to reset after a fetch from the RAM banks. There are some advantages to linked lists, though, and we're stuck with them.

Code to search for the end of a linked list

Label	Assembler instruction	Comments
Loop	LOAD r0,r0	Load the pointer to the next cell (Often written like "LOAD r0,[r0]" though)
	CMP r0,#0	Compare the pointer to 0
		Do a "branch" back to the "Loop" label if the last compare was Not Equal
	BNE Loop	branch = jump = goto = set the Program Counter (PC) register. The PC register points to the next instruction to load and execute.

The above three instructions make up the core of a code loop that searches for the end of a linked list. The only register being used is r0, so you would think that parallelism is impossible. But the CPU can actually start executing the second iteration of the loop at the same time as the compare instruction. The load writes r0 at the end of the cycle, so it doesn't affect the compare, and the branch doesn't use r0. You could do this by specially compiling the loop (a bit like "loop unrolling"), or by using out-of-order execution, if available. This is illustrated below.

Possible ILP for linked-list loop

CPU cycle	Iteration 1	Iteration 2	Iteration 3
1	LOAD r0,r0		
2	CMP r0,#0	LOAD r0,r0	
3	BNE Loop	CMP r0,#0	LOAD r0,r0
4		BNE Loop	CMP r0,#0
5			BNE Loop

Here, the row for each "CPU cycle" is executed during that cycle. On a 600MHz CPU, this cycle lasts a mere 1.667 nanoseconds. The CPU is actually executing three instructions per cycle. However, the above example assumes a load latency of 1. The Intel Pentium, Pentium II, and Pentium III processors have a load latency of 3 for the primary cache. Here is how the instruction flow would look in that case:

ILP for linked-list loop, when load latency is 3

CPU cycle	Iteration 1	Iteration 2	Iteration 3
1	LOAD r0,r0		
2	load 1		
3	load 2		
4	CMP r0,#0	LOAD r0,r0	
5	BNE Loop	load 1	
6		load 2	
7		CMP r0,#0	LOAD r0,r0
8		BNE Loop	load 1
9			load 2
10			CMP r0,#0
11			BNE Loop

As you can see, a higher latency reduces the average instructions per cycle.

Table 3.1 illustrates how load latency affects the average number of instructions per cycle (the achieved level of ILP):

TABLE 3.1

Load latency affects ILP

Load latency (CPU cycles)	Average ILP (Instructions per Cycle)
1	3
2	1.5
3	1
4	0.75
5	0.6

These examples are very much simplified. In the real world, the calculation is further complicated by the fact that modern PCs and servers usually have a three-tier memory model, with Level 1 (L1) cache, Level 2 (L2) cache, and RAM, on top of the CPU registers. All have different load latencies. Therefore, you need to calculate the average hit or miss ratio for each memory layer and apply it to the equation for the table above.

Caches

A cache is a subset of main memory, used to make memory access faster. When a memory access is issued, the caches are checked first; if the data are not already cached, then main memory is to be accessed. Given that a cache will hold thousands of memory addresses, it is not possible to check every single cache line quickly, so compromises are made. The fastest type of cache is *direct-mapped* or *one-way associative*. For each possible memory request, there is only one place to check. Although it is very simple and very fast, it is not very efficient. Imagine that you only have 10 cache locations (10 "lines") for each address in memory; the cache line to check would be the memory address "modulus 10"—0, 10, 20, etc. (goto position 0, 1, 11, 21 etc.; goto position 1, and so on). Most Level 1 caches are *two-way* or *four-way associative* caches. This means that each memory location can be in two or four possible places. This is slower. The larger a cache is, the harder it is to make it fast, which is why most really massive Level 2 caches are direct-mapped. The choice of size, speed, and associativity depends on speed requirements and transistor budget. You can't have them both, although it gets easier as you make the fabrication process smaller.

The most important factor in dealing with caches is the cache *hit rate*, which is the percentage of found items versus searched items. Different programs and different data sets have higher or lower hit rates. Regardless of how you increase the achieved ILP, the cache hit rates also have an impact on the final speed of a program. It is up to the kernel designer to make sure that a processor makes effective use of the caches available on it. In this respect, again, the Linux kernel always tries to avoid cache misses through clever algorithm and data structure design.

Branch Prediction

The instruction stream going through execution seldom goes beyond four instructions without a branch. As we saw, modern CPUs execute more than one instruction at a time—even out of order, sometimes. However, every branch in the code will stop this parallelism if the CPU doesn't know which instruction comes at a branch. That's because branches usually happen based on a condition.

You might have code like this:

```
LOAD r0,r0
CMP r0,#0
BNE Loop
```

where BNE means Branch Not Equal. Out-of-order execution here, as we saw before, is not possible, because the destination of the branch is dependent on a previous result.

Modern CPUs however, can predict branches. A smart compiler knows how to order assembler code to facilitate the branch prediction of the CPU. It is also up to the C programmer to give hints to the compiler, to allow it to generate assembler code that takes branch prediction into consideration.

Software Issues

In a system with just one CPU, keeping track of that CPU is quite easy. Because Linux is a Symmetric Multi-Processor (SMP)-capable operating system, the kernel also needs to keep track of all CPUs present and schedule work among them. Even the simplest form of an SMP computer, one with two CPUs, gives many new possibilities and difficulties. For one, making two CPUs work with the same kernel image and the same (shared) hardware is a rather complex task. A kernel that might be suitable for a one-CPU system will fail miserably when executed by two or more CPUs concurrently.

To make Linux SMP-aware, the user must recompile the kernel with the SMP option set to yes. For a step-by-step tutorial on recompiling and installing a new Linux kernel, refer to Chapter 2.

On a uniprocessor kernel, all SMP-related code is empty and does nothing. Therefore, a uniprocessor kernel and an SMP kernel are quite different in Linux. Unlike proprietary operating systems, like WinNT or Solaris, the uniprocessor version of the Linux kernel is much lighter than the SMP version, because it is not slowed down by unnecessary SMP code. Under SMP conditions, there are certain operations within the kernel that must be serialized. In other words, certain kernel transactions on certain data structures need to be executed by just one CPU at a time to avoid chaos.

Let's take an example of a data structure that indicates if an interrupt has been serviced yet, irq_served. If irq_served is greater than zero, then the kernel knows there is work to do. Now, let's assume that while CPU 0 checks for the value, finds 1, and wants to begin execution,

CPU 1 has also found a value of 1 and also starts execution. Because CPU 0 was briefly interrupted, CPU 1 has time to finish serving the interrupt. Now, when CPU 0 comes back to handle the interrupt it will find nothing to do (because CPU 1 already handled it), and will fail with an error. This might seem like an innocuous example, but there are hundreds of more dangerous code parts that will wreak havoc with your system if not properly serialized. In the parlance of kernels, these serialization mechanisms are called *spinlocks* or *mutexes*.

Spinlocks (Mutexes)

With version 2.0, the Linux kernel became, for the first time, SMP-aware and scaled, if not excellently, at least well up to a limited number (at best maybe 4) of CPUs. Version 2.4 and the forthcoming version 2.5, scale even better on systems with many CPUs.

The graph below (Figure 3.1) illustrates how kernels can only scale up to a certain limit before adversely impacting performance.

Figure 3.1
Please provide figure caption.

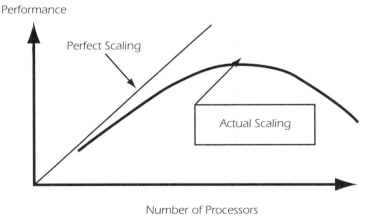

The Linux kernel developer's main concern is how to make Linux work well on large, multiprocessor servers.

Serialization is the main constraint in an OS on multiprocessor hardware. Systems implementing an SMP architecture have a single physical address space and kernel virtual address space. A single image of the operating system is shared by all the processors installed on the system. The symmetry is due to the peer-to-peer relationship between the processors; there is no master processor that executes all kernel code and handles interrupts. All the processors can process interrupts, execute kernel functions, and so on, as seen in Figure 3.2.

Figure 3.2
Please provide figure caption.

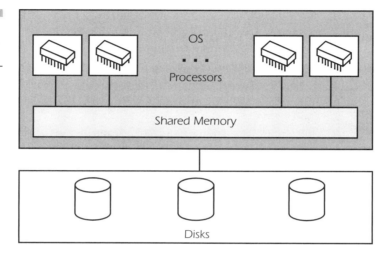

To understand spinlocks (we will also use the term "mutex," which stands for "mutual exclusion;" the terms are interchangeable) better, it may help to use another example. Let's assume the kernel needs to add a new process to its list of processes. The kernel must traverse the list of all processes, obtain the last process ID number (the PPID), and insert a new entry in the list. If, at the very moment the kernel is adding an entry, but just before it finishes doing so, a second processor executes the very same code section of the kernel, trying to add yet another process, the second processor gets the same new process ID number, and the list of processes might end up corrupted. Therefore, the whole section that inserts a new process has to be "mutexed." The kernel does this by setting a variable to −1 just before it enters the critical code section; after finishing it adds +1 to the variable to indicate end of a spinlock/mutex. The data structure, with its definitions, is appended at the end of this section:

```
linux/smp_lock.h
linux/smp.h
```

If another processor wants to execute the same code section, it will test the variable before entering; this second processor will see that the variable is now set to −1; as long as the variable stays negative, the second processor will have to wait before it can enter the critical code section. Once the first processor exits the region it adds 1 to the variable. Now the value is 0 and the second processor can enter the region and immediately set the variable to −1 again, so that other processors are prevented from executing that region.

There are two flavors of spinlocks, *adaptive* and *spin*. When a kernel code segment attempts to acquire a mutex lock, and the lock is being held, the thread can do one of two things: spin or *block*. Spinning on a spinlock means simply executing a tight loop, with lock acquisition attempted in each pass through the loop. Blocking means putting the thread to sleep.

There are pros and cons to both approaches. Spinning has the advantage of not requiring a context switch in the processor, such that, once the lock is acquired, execution continues. Saving a context switch is important for performance. Upon context switching, the task that was executing might not find its cache lines still in the primary or secondary caches, and would thus cause an access to the much slower RAM modules through the bus. The downside is that a processor is consumed during the spin.

Blocking frees up the processor, because the blocked task is put into a sleep state and the processor switches context to another task, thus freeing it up for other work. Blocking does, however, require the overhead of context-switching the thread back in once the lock is available, and the general overhead of dealing with a wakeup mechanism.

Adaptive spinlocks deal with these choices in a dynamic fashion. If a spinlock is currently owned by another task when a kernel task attempts to acquire the lock, the state of the task is checked. If the task holding the lock is running, the kernel task trying to get the lock will spin, assuming that the running task will release the lock shortly. If the holder of the lock (its owner task) is sleeping, then the task wanting the lock will also block (sleep), because it doesn't make sense to consume a processor spinning and waiting for the holder to wake up and release the lock. Most mutex locks in the Linux kernel are adaptive. Spinlocks are used only for locks where context switching is not allowed, such as in the top-half interrupts of the highest priority, like timers. In the event of a kernel task's blocking on a mutex lock or a *reader/writer lock* (reader/writer locks are not adaptive—a held write lock always results in a sleep), sleep queues with expirations are used (see the text on interrupts handling later in this chapter) and these synchronize the wakeup when the lock is available.

There are thousands of such critical code regions in a UNIX kernel. Developing a sound, optimized locking strategy for all these regions is crucial for good SMP performance. Over the years, Linux has developed excellent SMP ability. The coming 2.5 series of kernels will undoubtedly further improve this capability.

Data Structures—linux/smp.h

```
1    #ifndef  LINUX SMP H
2    #define  LINUX SMP H
3
4    /*
5     *        Generic SMP support
6     *              Alan Cox. <alan@redhat.com>
7     */
8
9    #ifdef __SMP__
10
11   #include <asm/smp.h>
12
13   /*
14    * main cross-CPU interfaces, handles INIT, TLB flush, STOP, etc.
15    * (defined in asm header):
16    */
17
18   /*
19    * stops all CPUs but the current one:
20    */
21   extern void  smp send stop (void);
22
23   /*
24    * sends a 'reschedule' event to another CPU:
25    */
26   extern void FASTCALL (smp send reschedule (int CPU));
27
28
29   /*
30    * Boot processor call to load the other CPU's
31    */
32   extern void smp_boot_cpu (void);
33
34   /*
35    * Processor call in. Must hold processors until ..
36    */
37   extern void smp callin (void);
38
39   /*
40    * Multiprocessors may now schedule
41    */
42   extern void smp commence (void);
43
```

```
44      /*
45       * Call a function on all other processors
46       */
47      extern int smp call function (void (*func) (void * info), void *info,
48                                  int retry, int wait);
49
50      /*
51       * True once the per process idle is forked
52       */
53      extern int smp threads ready;
54
55      extern int smp_num_cpu;
56
57      extern volatile unsigned long smp msg data;
58      extern volatile int smp src cpu;
59      extern volatile int smp msg id;
61      #define MSG ALL BUT SELF          0x8000    /* Assume <32768 CPU's */
62      #define MSG ALL                   0x8001
63
64      #define MSG INVALIDATE TLB        0x0001    /* Remote processor TLB invalidate */
65      #define MSG STOP CPU              0x0002    /* Sent to shut down slave CPU's
66                                                   * when rebooting
67                                                   */
68      #define MSG RESCHEDULE            0x0003    /* Reschedule request from master CPU*/
69     #define MSG CALL FUNCTION          0x0004    /* Call function on all other CPUs */
70
71      #else
72
73      /*
74       *          These macros fold the SMP functionality into a single CPU system
75       */
76
77      #define smp num cpus                                1
78      #define smp processor id ()                         0
79      #define hard smp processor id ()                    0
80      #define smp threads ready                           1
81      #define kernel lock ()
82      #define cpu logical map (cpu)                       0
83      #define cpu number map (cpu)                        0
84      #define smp call function (func, info, retry, wait) ({ 0; })
85
86      #endif
87      #endif
88
```

Data Strutures linux/smp_lock.h

```
1      #ifndef  LINUX SMPLOCK H
2      #define  LINUX SMPLOCK H
3
4      #ifndef__SMP__
```

```
5
6       #define lock kernel()                       do { } while(0)
7       #define unlock kernel()                     do { } while(0)
8       #define release kernel lock(task, cpu)      do { } while(0)
9       #define reacquire kernel lock(task)         do { } while(0)
10
12
13      #include <asm/smplock.h>
14
15      #endif /* __SMP__ */
16
17      #endif
18
```

Device Handling

All device handling within the Linux kernel happens through *special
files*. A special file appears in the file system tree structure as a normal
file under /dev. These special files, however, use no space. Rather, these
special files are links to device drivers. The device drivers are either
included within the kernel or else called on demand by means of the kernel modules mechanism. It is usually up to the system administrator to
decide whether to compile a driver into the kernel or make it a loadable
module. Having a driver compiled inside the kernel slightly increases
the size of the kernel binary image until it might not fit onto a single
diskette. Using loadable modules, however, increases response time for
the first-ever access to the device, because the kernel must first locate
the module and append it to itself.

Because this book addresses servers rather than smaller installations, the issue of having a slightly bigger kernel is not considered. It is
unheard of for a server to boot from diskettes, except for testing and/or
kernel-maintenance tasks. Adding a few kilobytes to a kernel is not a
cause of concern. On a machine with 1GB of memory, the kernel easily
takes up to 50MB for the complete complement of kernel structures, as
we will see later.

When a process opens a special file, the kernel redirects all read and
write requests to the appropriate device driver. The driver in turn executes the original read or write operation on behalf of the process. There
are two types of special files, the *block mode device* and the *character
mode device*. All such devices share the same meta-information:

- Type (block or character).

- Major number (number identifying the controller of the device, e.g. the IDE controller for disks).
- Minor number (number identifying the actual device within the controller).

Block Device Handling

All devices that structure the data they contain into blocks, such as disks, floppies, and CDROMs, read or write that data in chunks, or more appropriately, in blocks. The kernel buffer cache optimizes reading and writing from and to blocks.

Because it is necessary for the understanding of concepts covered later, we must discuss the basic concepts of disk device access.

Components of Disk Access Time: The Path of a Disk I/O Operation

We will examine SCSI disks here, because IDE disks are really not worth putting in a self-respecting Linux server; IDE controllers don't disconnect from the bus while waiting for completion from disk I/O. In a multi-user, multi-tasking environment like Linux, this is clearly detrimental to performance—to put it mildly.

A simple SCSI subsystem consists of four main components: the host computer, the SCSI host adapter, the embedded target controller, and the disk mechanism itself. When the OS receives an I/O request from the user, it converts the request into an SCSI command sequence. The requesting process is blocked, pending the completion of the I/O operation, unless the request was issued synchronously (there are certain application where this makes sense). The command sequence is then transferred across the host's I/O bus (PCI, ISA, SBUS, Channels, etc.) to the SCSI host adapter. The host adapter then accepts responsibility for interacting with the target controllers and their devices.

Next, the host adapter selects the target by asserting its control line on the SCSI bus when the bus is available; this period is known as the *selection phase*. When the target responds to the selection, the host adapter transfers the command to the target; this period is called the *command phase*.

If the target is able to satisfy the command immediately (maybe from its cache), it returns the requested data or status. If the operation is a read, the data are not usually available, so the target disconnects, thus freeing the SCSI bus for other operations. If the operation is a write, a *data phase* immediately follows the command phase on the bus; the data are transferred to the target's cache, and the target disconnects.

Writes are *not* acknowledged until the data is actually put on the disk platter. This is because the target controller's cache is subject to power failure. On some units an uninterruptible power supply (UPS) is available, and the disk's controller can be told to acknowledge writes as soon as they are in the cache. This greatly improves performance.

Mechanical Disk Operations

Moving the disk arm radially (seeking) costs between 0.5 and 40 milliseconds, depending on how far the arm must actually travel. The other mechanical operation, waiting for the platter to rotate until the block flies under the head, costs 4.2 to 8.6 milliseconds. This delay is called *rotational latency*. The actual time to transfer data from the platter to the disk RAM or vice versa is called the *internal transfer time*, and is dependent upon the rotational speed and the density at which these data are recorded onto the platter. Although rotational speed is constant for any given disk, recording density is usually variable. For typical disk drives, the internal transfer speed varies between 2MB/sec and 7MB/sec. The data are transferred from the disk platter to the intelligent disk controller embedded in all SCSI disks. For the typical I/O request of 8KB, internal transfer consumes 1 to 4 milliseconds. In addition, I/O requests spend 0.5 to 2 milliseconds (depending on the speed of the host processor) being processed in the OS. Finally, the data must be transferred over the SCSI bus. At the 20MB/sec of a fast/wide SCSI bus, the typical I/O takes an additional 0.39 milliseconds. Thus, in the average case, an I/O takes about 28 to 30 milliseconds, assuming all paths are clear of contention. In a multi-user, multi-tasking environment such as UNIX, essentially all I/O behaves randomly; that is, it is spread among the whole disk and disk units.

RAID Comes to the Rescue

The best performance can be achieved by *striping* (RAID 0 and 1) and *mirroring*. If you stripe a database among several disks and additionally mirror it, the logic in the RAID controller makes sure to distribute the I/O among as many disks as possible, therefore returning the desired data to the user process more quickly.

It can never be stressed enough: do not store too much data on one disk. It is tempting to use one 18GB disk instead of installing and maintaining three or four smaller disks. The professional system administrator must resist this temptation. Do we need to say why? Well, let's repeat it just for the sake of comprehensive reporting. On a disk of, say, 2GB you have x I/O that go through the whole chain as described above. On a 18GB disk, you will have 9x I/O through the same bus, same controller, and same disk device. No matter how fast the new 18GB or 31GB disks are, they will never make up for the linear increase of access compared to a small device.

Character Device Handling

All devices that require the kernel to send or receive data from them one byte at a time are *character devices*. Terminals, modems, and printers all belong to this device type. On PC systems (be they workstations or servers), the primary mechanism to access devices (sound cards, SCSI controllers, graphic adapters) is *direct memory access* (DMA). The DMA is actually an area of memory within these devices mappable through RAM. This allows access to the registers of these devices, by writing to a certain RAM location. The proper handling of DMA is thus of primary importance for the kernel to be able to recognize and manage those devices attached to DMA controllers (most devices).

DMA Operation

Most 64-bit platforms have special hardware that translates bus addresses (DMA addresses) to physical addresses, similar to how page tables and/or *translation lookaside buffers* (TLBs) translate virtual addresses to physical addresses. This is necessary so that PCI devices, for example, can access with a single address cycle (32-bit DMA address) any page in the 64-bit physical address space.

Previously in Linux, 64-bit platforms—such as the Alpha—had to set artificial limits on the maximum RAM size in the system, so that the `virt_to_bus()` static scheme would work (the DMA address translation tables were filled on bootup to map each bus address to the physical page `__pa(bus_to_virt())`.

For Linux to use dynamic DMA mapping, it needs some help from the drivers. It must take into account that DMA addresses should be mapped only for the time that they are actually used, and unmapped after the DMA transfer. The following API will work, of course, even on platforms where no such hardware exists.

First of all, one needs to make sure that

```
#include <linux/pci.h>
```

is in the driver code. This file will obtain the definition of the dma_addr_t type, which should be used everywhere you hold a DMA (bus) address returned from the DMA mapping functions.

DMA Addressing Limitations

Devices can have DMA addressing limitations. For example, some devices are only capable of driving the low-order 24 bits of address on the PCI bus for DMA transfers. For correct operation, the driver must interrogate the PCI layer in your device probe routine to see if the PCI controller on the machine can properly support the DMA addressing limitation of the device. This query is performed via a call to pci_dma_supported():

```
int pci_dma_supported(struct pci_dev *pdev, dma_addr_t device_mask)
```

Here, pdev is a pointer to the PCI device struct of the device, and device_mask is a bitmask describing which bits of a PCI address the device supports. It returns non-zero if the adapter card can perform DMA properly on the machine. If it returns zero, the device cannot perform DMA properly on this platform, and attempting to do so will result in undefined behavior. In the failure case, there are two options:

1. Use some non-DMA mode for data transfer, if possible.
2. Ignore this device and do not initialize it.

It is recommended that the driver print a kernel KERN_WARN message to the Syslog indicating which of the options was chosen. This facilitates the debugging process.

So if, for example, your device can only drive the low 24 bits of address during PCI bus mastering, you might do something like:

```
if (! pci_dma_supported(pdev, 0x00ffffff))
    goto ignore_this_device;
```

Types of DMA Mapping

There are two types of DMA mapping, *consistent* and *streaming*.

Consistent DMA mappings are usually mapped at driver initialization and unmapped at the end of driver initialization. The hardware should guarantee that the device and the CPU can access the data in parallel and will see updates made by each other without any explicit software flushing.

Good applications of consistent mappings are:

- Network card DMA ring descriptors.
- SCSI adapter mailbox command data structures.
- Device firmware microcode executed out of main memory.

The invariant these examples all require is that any CPU store-to-memory is immediately visible to the device, and vice versa. Consistent mappings guarantee this.

Streaming DMA mappings, which are usually mapped for one DMA transfer, are unmapped right after it (unless you use `pci_dma_sync`, as below). Hardware can optimize streaming mapping for sequential accesses.

Good applications of streaming mappings are:

- Networking buffers transmitted or received by a device.
- Filesystem buffers written or read by a SCSI device.

The interfaces for streaming mapping were designed in such a way that an implementation can make whatever performance optimizations the hardware allows. To this end, when using such mappings you must be explicit about what you want to happen.

Using Consistent DMA Mappings

To allocate and map a consistent DMA region, you should enter:

```
dma_addr_t dma_handle;
cpu_addr = pci_alloc_consistent(dev, size, &dma_handle);
```

where `dev` is a struct `pci_dev` *. You should pass NULL for PCI-like buses where devices don't have struct `pci_dev` (like ISA and EISA). This argument is needed because the DMA translations may be bus specific (and often may be private to the bus to which the device is attached).

The `size` parameter is the length of the region the driver needs to allocate.

This routine allocates RAM for that region, so it acts similarly to `__get_free_pages`, but takes size instead of a page order. It returns two values: the virtual address, which you can use to access it from the CPU, and the `dma_handle`, which you pass to the card.

The CPU return address and the DMA bus master address are both guaranteed to be aligned to the smallest `PAGE_SIZE` order that is greater than or equal to the requested size. This invariant exists (for example) to guarantee that if you allocate a chunk that is smaller than or equal to 64 kilobytes, the extent of the buffer you receive will not cross a 64K boundary.

To unmap and free such a DMA region, the driver calls:

```
pci_free_consistent(dev, size, cpu_addr, dma_handle);
```

where `dev`, `size` are the same as in the above call and `cpu_addr` and `dma_handle` are the values `pci_alloc_consistent` returned to you.

DMA Direction

The interfaces described below take a DMA direction argument, which is an integer that takes on one of the following values:

- `PCI_DMA_BIDIRECTIONAL`
- `PCI_DMA_TODEVICE`
- `PCI_DMA_FROMDEVICE`
- `PCI_DMA_NONE`

Provide the exact DMA direction if you know it.

The value `PCI_DMA_TODEVICE` means "from main memory to the PCI device"; `PCI_DMA_FROMDEVICE` means "from the PCI device to main memory." Device driver developers are strongly encouraged to specify this as precisely as possible.

If you absolutely cannot know the direction of the DMA transfer, specify `PCI_DMA_BIDIRECTIONAL`. This means that the DMA can go in either direction. The platform guarantees that you may legally specify this and that it will work, but this may be at the cost of performance.

The value PCI_DMA_NONE is used for debugging. It is possible to hold this in a data structure before you come to know the precise direction of the DMA transfer. This helps catch cases where direction tracking logic has failed to set things up properly.

Another advantage to specifying this value precisely (outside of potential platform-specific optimizations) is for debugging. Some platforms actually have a write permission Boolean flag, with which DMA mappings can be marked, much like page protections in a user program. Such platforms can and do report errors in the kernel logs when the PCI controller hardware detects violation of the permission setting.

Only streaming mappings specify a direction; consistent mappings implicitly have a direction attribute setting of PCI_DMA_BIDIRECTIONAL.

The SCSI subsystem provides mechanisms for you to easily obtain the direction to use, in the SCSI command:

```
scsi_to_pci_dma_dir(SCSI_DIRECTION)
```

where SCSI_DIRECTION is obtained from the sc_data_direction member of the SCSI command on which your driver is working. The interface mentioned above returns a value suitable for passing to the streaming DMA mapping interfaces below.

For networking drivers, it's a rather simple affair. For transmit packets, map and unmap them with the PCI_DMA_TODEVICE direction specifier. For receive packets, just the opposite: map and unmap them with the PCI_DMA_FROMDEVICE direction specifier.

Using Streaming DMA Mappings

The streaming DMA mapping routines can be called from an interrupt context. There are two versions of each map/unmap, one of which will map or unmap a single memory region, the other of which will map or unmap a scatterlist.

To map a single region, enter:

```
dma_addr_t dma_handle;
dma_handle = pci_map_single(dev, addr, size, direction);
```

To unmap it, enter:

```
pci_unmap_single(dev, dma_handle, size, direction);
```

You should call `pci_unmap_single` when the DMA activity is finished, for example, when interrupt status tells you the DMA transfer is done.

Similarly, with scatterlists, map a region gathered from several regions by entering:

```
int i, count = pci_map_sg(dev, sglist, nents, direction);
struct scatterlist *sg;
for (i = 0, sg = sglist; i < count; i++, sg++) {
    hw_address[i] = sg_dma_address(sg);
    hw_len[i] = sg_dma_len(sg);
}
```

where `nents` is the number of entries in the `sglist`.

The implementation is free to merge several consecutive `sglist` entries into one, and returns the actual number of sg entries to which it mapped them. For example, if DMA mapping is done with `PAGE_SIZE` granularity, any consecutive `sglist` entries can be merged into one—provided the first one ends and the second one starts on a page boundary. In fact this is a huge advantage for cards which either cannot do scatter-gather, or have a very limited number of scatter-gather entries.

In these cases, you should loop count times (this can be less than `nents` times) and use `sg_dma_address()` and `sg_dma_length()` macros where you previously accessed `sg->address` and `sg->length`, as shown above.

To unmap a scatterlist, just call:

```
pci_unmap_sg(dev, sglist, nents);
```

Make sure DMA activity has finished.

NOTE

The `nents` *argument to the* `pci_unmap_sg` *call must be the same one you passed into the* `pci_map_sg` *call; it should not be the count value returned by the* `pci_map_sg` *call.*

Every `pci_map_{single,sg}` call should have its `pci_unmap_{single,sg}` counterpart, because the bus address space is a shared resource (although in some ports the mapping is per each *bus*, so less devices contend for the same bus address space). You could render the machine unusable by eating all bus addresses.

If you need to use the same streaming DMA region multiple times and touch the data in between the DMA transfers, just map the region with `pci_map_{single,sg}`. After each DMA transfer, call either:

```
                pci_dma_sync_single(dev, dma_handle, size, direction);
```

or:

```
                pci_dma_sync_sg(dev, sglist, nents, direction);
```

and after the last DMA transfer, call one of the DMA unmap routines
pci_unmap_{single,sg}. If you don't touch the data from the first
pci_map_*, call pci_unmap_*, then you don't have to call the
pci_sync_* routines at all.

Here is some pseudocode that shows a situation in which you would
need to use the pci_dma_sync_*() interfaces.

```
my_card_setup_receive_buffer(struct my_card *cp, char *buffer, int len)
{
    dma_addr_t mapping;

    mapping = pci_map_single(cp->pdev, buffer, len, PCI_DMA_FROMDEVICE);
    cp->rx_buf = buffer;
    cp->rx_len = len;
    cp->rx_dma = mapping;
    give_rx_buf_to_card(cp);
}

...

my_card_interrupt_handler(int irq, void *devid, struct pt_regs *regs)
{
    struct my_card *cp = devid;
    ...
        if (read_card_status(cp) == RX_BUF_TRANSFERRED) {
            struct my_card_header *hp;

            /* Examine the header to see if we wish
             * to except the data. But synchronize
             * the DMA transfer with the CPU first
             * so that we see updated contents.
             */
            pci_dma_sync_single(cp->pdev, cp->rx_buf, cp->rx_len,
                    PCI_DMA_FROMDEVICE);

            /* Now it is safe to examine the buffer. */
            hp = (struct my_card_header *) cp->rx_buf;
            if (header_is_ok(hp)) {
                pci_unmap_single(cp->pdev, cp->rx_buf, cp->rx_len,
                        PCI_DMA_FROMDEVICE);
                pass_to_upper_layers(cp->rx_buf);
                make_and_setup_new_rx_buf(cp);
            } else {
                /* Just give the buffer back to the card. */
```

```
                        give_rx_buf_to_card(cp);
              }
          }
      }
```

Drivers fully converted to this interface should not use `virt_to_bus` any longer, nor should they use `bus_to_virt`. Some drivers must be changed a little, because there is no longer an equivalent to `bus_to_virt` in the dynamic DMA mapping scheme; you must always store the DMA addresses returned by the `pci_alloc_consistent` and `pci_map_single` calls (`pci_map_sg` stores them in the scatterlist itself if the platform supports dynamic DMA mapping in hardware) in your driver structures and/or in the card registers.

Interrupts Handling

Interrupts are major and unpleasant facts of life for an OS developer. One has to be extremely careful when writing interrupt-handling code. The complete and profound understanding of the dynamics of a running system is paramount here as perhaps nowhere else in the code. They are ugly, they are complex, and they should really be hidden away from the OS developer in hardware or somewhere else. Because this is not possible, the best the OS developer can do is hide the interrupt handling routines deep down in the bowels of the kernel, so that no other part of the kernel ever has to deal with interrupts. This is exactly what the Linux kernel does.

For instance, the Linux device drivers do not have any notion of interrupts; they just issue their I/O request and let the kernel take care of servicing the interrupts generated from that I/O operation.

As a good example, it serves to look at the source code for the timer interrupt handler. A *timer* is just like your alarm clock next to your bed. It is set with a time value in microseconds, and returns when that value has counted down to zero.

The kernel timer interrupt handler is `do_timer()`, in `kernel/timer.c`:

```
void do_timer(struct pt_regs * regs)
{
        (*(unsigned long *)&jiffies)++;
        lost_ticks++;
        mark_bh(TIMER_BH);
        if (!user_mode(regs))
```

```
                        lost_ticks_system++;
            if (tq_timer)
                    mark_bh(TQUEUE_BH);
}
```

This code first increases the global `jiffies` variable by one, then it marks the appropriate timer *bottom-half handler* to be run. *Jiffie* is the Linux name for the unit of execution. On an IA32 (i386) machine it is usually 10 milliseconds. The bottom-half handler is run right after the IRQ routine returns. Bottom-half handlers are special *soft interrupt routines*, similar to NT's (deferred procedure call DPC[4]) concept.

The timer interrupt also takes care of *lost interrupts*. If, for example, the timer bottom half takes too long to execute (e.g., because there is a very high interrupt load reaching the system), then it could happen that a new timer interrupt arrives before the timer bottom half finishes execution. This does not happen on faster machines, but on slower systems it is a possibility which must be taken into account.

The timer bottom-half handler is where the real time and timer handling job is done. The function `timer_bh()` actually runs all kernel timers and their callback functions:

```
kernel/timer.c
void timer_bh(void)
{
        update_times();
        run_old_timers();
        run_timer_list();
}
```

The `update_times()` takes care of the time of day calculations, system load calculations, and per-process time and processor usage statistics.

The snippet `run_old_timers()` is just ancient Linux code; it will probably be removed in 2.5. It's a simple timer implementation that is still used in a few places.

The actual Linux timer code resides in `run_timer_list()`.

Linux timers are highly scalable. On busy Internet servers, more than a 100,000 timers can run at once. The Linux timer implementation is a very clever trick, written by Arne Gangstad, which has also been copied by proprietary OS vendors. The trick consists in keeping *exponential* timeout values, instead of *absolute* timeout values. The code for its

---

4 A deferred procedure call (DPC) is a kernel task which can be executed in a deferred and asynchronous fashion, and/or with a low priority.

implementation resides in `timer vectors` (`kernel/timer.c`) and looks like this:

```
struct timer_vec {
        int index;
        struct timer_list *vec[TVN_SIZE];
};

struct timer_vec_root {
        int index;
        struct timer_list *vec[TVR_SIZE];
};

static struct timer_vec tv5 = { 0 };
static struct timer_vec tv4 = { 0 };
static struct timer_vec tv3 = { 0 };
static struct timer_vec tv2 = { 0 };
static struct timer_vec_root tv1 = { 0 };
```

Each timer vector is an array of timer ringlists. Timers are ordered by timeout value relative to the present time. Short-term timers are placed into `tv1`, timers with big timeouts are placed into `tv2`, `tv3`, and so on. The addressing of timer vectors is exponential: the timeout value is divided into bitfields, and the highest order non-zero bitfield shows which timer vector is used.

Now comes the juicy part. On every timer interrupt all timers have to be advanced, because their timeout value is decreased by 1. We obviously do not want to do this for, say, 100,000 timers, so the following trick is used. The timer vectors have a *current pointer* (index), which is increased by 1 if the previous time vector overflows. This is, the index of `tv1` advances from 0 to 255; once it reaches 256 we advance `tv2` by one, and the index of `tv1` is set to 0. If `tv2` overflows to 64, then `tv3` is advanced by one and `tv2` index is set to zero. If `tv3` has overflowed to 64 then `tv4` is advanced, and so on. As you can see, the `tv1` index increases on every timer tick (jiffy), `tv2` index increases every 256 ticks, the `tv3` index increases every 256×64 ticks, the `tv4` index increases every 256×64×64 ticks, and so on. Short-term timers are so common that `tv1` was increased to hold 256 timerlist entries.

Additionally, if the current index (which has just been increased) has an entry that is non-zero, then the entry has to be "expired":

```
static inline void run_timer_list(void)
{
    spin_lock_irq(&timerlist_lock);
    while ((long)(jiffies - timer_jiffies) >= 0) {
            struct timer_list *timer;
```

```
                    if (!tv1.index) {
                            int n = 1;
                            do {
                                    cascade_timers(tvecs[n]);
                            } while (tvecs[n]->index == 1 && ++n <
                            NOOF_TVECS);
                    }
                    while ((timer = tv1.vec[tv1.index])) {
                            void (*fn)(unsigned long) = timer->function;
                            unsigned long data = timer->data;
                            detach_timer(timer);
                            timer->next = timer->prev = NULL;
                            spin_unlock_irq(&timerlist_lock);
                            fn(data);
                            spin_lock_irq(&timerlist_lock);
                    }
                    ++timer_jiffies;
                    tv1.index = (tv1.index + 1) & TVR_MASK;
            }
       spin_unlock_irq(&timerlist_lock);
}
```

In the case of `tv1` expiry. all timers must be run (the timer functions must be executed). For `tv2`, `tv3`, and others, "expiry" means that all timers in that timer list must be moved into a one-lower timer vector. This is done by `cascade_timers()`.

What is the advantage of this approach? The advantage is that `add_timer()`, `del_timer()`, and `modify_timer()` execute in constant time, independent of the number of timers in the system. I have found that a large percentage of long-term timers are deleted prior to their expiration, especially in the network code. In that case no penalty is paid for handling the expiration.

Cascading and expiring timers is very fast as well. There are Linux SMP system demos with more than 4 million timers running and expiring, and the kernel keeps up with them easily.

The timer expiration part is especially interesting from the SMP scalability point of view:

```
while ((timer = tv1.vec[tv1.index])) {
      void (*fn)(unsigned long) = timer->function;
      unsigned long data = timer->data;
      detach_timer(timer);
      timer->next = timer->prev = NULL;
      spin_unlock_irq(&timerlist_lock);
      fn(data);
      spin_lock_irq(&timerlist_lock);
}
```

Note how the timerlist spinlock is unlocked before executing the (user-provided) timer function. This greatly increases SMP scalability, and is the most scalable IRQ handling code in any UNIX-style OS.

As a good kernel-based example for the above code, it makes sense to implement measurement mechanisms for expiring timers. To measure the rate of timer expires in a system, you must write a simple kernel module and use add_timer(). In this example we use a 10-second timer:

```
DECLARE_WAITQUEUE_HEAD(timer_sleep);
void your_handler (unsigned long private_data)
{

    printk("timer expired, data got: %08lx.\n", private_data);
    wake_up(&timer_sleep);
}

int init_module(void)
{
    struct timer_list *timer;

    timer = kmalloc(sizeof(*timer));
    memset(timer, 0, sizeof(*timer));

    timer->function = your_handler;
        timer->expires = jiffies + 10*HZ;
        add_timer(timer);

    printk("waiting for timer ...\n");
    sleep_on(&timer_sleep);
    printk("timer finished, good.\n");
    del_timer(timer);

    return -1; // fake error, thus the module wont stay
}

int cleanup_module (void)
{
    // doesnt actually get called
    return 0;
}
```

Another good example of network IRQ handling, where IRQs happen at very high rates, especially for gigabit gear, is where network drivers on packet arrival unqueue the packet from the networking hardware's structures, acknowledge the IRQ, and return. The bottom-half handler NET_BH processes the packet, calculates the checksums (if the hardware did not calculate the checksum directly), queues the packet to sockets handlers, and changes the socket status. The total processing time of NET_BH is probably a few milliseconds, while the hardware interrupts themselves continue to arrive at high frequency. If we did everything in the IRQ handler, then we'd stall the hardware with unacknowledged IRQs, and we'd also stall the arrival of new packets.

In the latest kernel versions (2.3.48), Ingo Molnar and other developers have introduced the concept of *tasklets*, which are the SMP-scalable equivalent of bottom-half handlers. Right now one type of bottom-half handler assumes SMP exclusivity. Other types may execute in parallel just fine, but not the bottom-half handler of the same type (and IRQ handlers can run in parallel with bottom-half handlers as well.) The code for these tasklets entered the Linux kernel as of version 2.3.48.

Data Structure—linux/interrupt.h

```
/* Tasklets --- multithreaded analogue of BHs.

   Main feature differing them of generic softirqs: tasklet
   is running only on one  simultaneously.

   Main feature differing them of BHs: different tasklets
   may be run simultaneously on different CPUs.

   Properties:
   * If tasklet_schedule() is called, then tasklet is guaranteed
     to be executed on some cpu at least once after this.
   * If the tasklet is already scheduled, but its excecution is still not
     started, it will be executed only once.
   * If this tasklet is already running on another CPU (or schedule is called
     from tasklet itself), it is rescheduled for later.
   * Tasklet is strictly serialized with regard to itself, but not
     with regard to other tasklets. If client needs some intertask synchronization,
     it makes it with spinlocks.
 */

struct tasklet_struct
{
    struct tasklet_struct *next;
    unsigned long state;
    atomic_t count;
    void (*func)(unsigned long);
    unsigned long data;
};
```

Another novelty in the latest kernels is SMP IRQ affinity, designed and implemented by Ingo Molnar. The output from `cat /proc/irq/IRQ#/smp_affinity` specifies which target CPUs are permitted for a given IRQ source.

This feature is implemented through a bitmask of allowed CPUs. It cannot actually turn off all CPUs, and if an IRQ controller does not support IRQ affinity, then the value will not change from the default 0xffffffff.

Here is an example of restricting IRQ44 (eth1) to CPUs 0 to 3, then restricting the IRQ to CPUs 4 to 8 (in an 8-CPU SMP box):

```
root@hatta# cat smp_affinity
ffffffff
root@hatta# echo 0f > smp_affinity
root@hatta# cat smp_affinity
0000000f
root@moon# ping -f h
PING ika (192.168.1.199): 56 data bytes
...
--- ika ping statistics ---
29 packets transmitted, 29 packets received, 0% packet loss
round-trip min/avg/max = 0.1/0.1/0.4 ms
root@hatta# cat /proc/interrupts | grep 44:
 44:         0      1785        1785       1783        1783            1
1        0   IO-APIC-level  eth1
root@hatta# echo f0 > smp_affinity
root@hatta# ping -f h
PING ika (192.168.1.199): 56 data bytes
..
--- hell ping statistics ---
2779 packets transmitted, 2777 packets received, 0% packet loss
round-trip min/avg/max = 0.1/0.5/585.4 ms
root@hatta#]# cat /proc/interrupts | grep 44:
 44:      1068      1785        1785       1784        1784         1069       1070       1069
IO-APIC-level  eth1
root@hatta#
```

Linux Time-Keeping Functions

The system's awareness of time and dates is a software abstraction and thus not kept anywhere in hardware. For the system to maintain a consistent date across reboots, obviously hardware must be used to store and update the time and date. This is done at the lowest hardware levels, maintaining hardware registers used for interval timing (counting processor clock ticks), along with larger hardware register spaces to store detailed date information (i.e., year, month, day, hour, minute, second). Some software functions in the OS simply use the interval counter, along with a known starting point, and convert the tick count into something that has meaning to mere mortals and is relevant to computer software.

Of course, determining the date and time based on some integer count is impossible without a point of reference and knowledge of the count unit (seconds, milliseconds, and so on). Most UNIX systems available today use January 1, 1970, 00:00:00 as an *epoch*, or point of reference for time counters. In other words, clock counter values maintain the number of seconds since the epoch, and, with a reference date and interval, the kernel can do the necessary arithmetic to convert a counter value to the correct date and time. The reason for the year 2038 problem in UNIX systems is due to this use of January 1, 1970 as a reference date. Using a 32-bit data type, counting the number of seconds since the epoch causes the kernel to overflow sometime around January 19, 2038. This problem goes away on a 64-bit kernel, where there is a 64-bit data type to count the seconds since the epoch—so we're good for about 10 billion years or so.

All Intel MP-compliant SMP boards have the so-called *IO-APIC*, which is actually an enhanced interrupt controller. It enables us to route hardware interrupts to multiple CPUs, or to CPU groups.

Linux supports all variants of compliant SMP boards, including those with multiple IO-APICs. (Multiple IO-APICs are used in high-end servers to distribute IRQ load further).

There are (a few) known breakages in certain older boards, whose bugs are usually worked around by the kernel. If your MP-compliant SMP board does not boot Linux, then consult the linux-smp mailing list archives first.

If your box boots fine with enabled IO-APIC IRQs, then your `/proc/interrupts` will look like this:

```
root @ hatta:~> cat /proc/interrupts
         CPU0
  0: 1360293  IO-APIC-edge   timer
  1:       4  IO-APIC-edge   keyboard
  2:       0  XT-PIC  cascade
 13:       1  XT-PIC  fpu
 14:    1448  IO-APIC-edge   ide0
 16:   28232  IO-APIC-level  Intel EtherExpress Pro 10/100 Ethernet
 17:   51304  IO-APIC-level  eth0
NMI:       0
ERR:       0
```

The clock and timer facilities are used by the kernel for general housekeeping chores that must be done at regular intervals. The kernel (software) sets up the computer clock (hardware) to generate a clock interrupt at regular intervals. An interrupt handler is entered with every clock interrupt, and this handler code does interval processing for the kernel (we'll take a closer look at this in a moment). The kernel can also use the hardware clock for real-time profiling or other time- and interval-related functions. Solaris provides command-line and programming interfaces to timer and date functions, including, of course, the basic date(1) command, which sets or retrieves the kernel's notion of the date and time.

System Clock

All computer systems—from desktop PCs to high-end multiprocessor systems—have a clock circuit of some sort.

All PCs have a *real-time clock* (RTC) built into them. Usually, and RTC is built into the chipset of the computer, but some may actually have a Motorola MC146818 (or clone) on the board. This is the clock that keeps the date and time while your computer is turned off. This same clock chip can also be used to generate signals, from a slow 2Hz to a relatively fast 8192Hz, in increments of powers of two. The clock can also work like an alarm, raising IRQ 8 when it has counted down to a previously stored value. The alarm can also be programmed only to check any subset of the three programmable values, meaning that it could be set to ring on the 30th second of the 30th minute of every hour, for example.

The driver controlling the real clock is /dev/rtc (major 10, minor 135, read-only character device) and it reports the current value in the form of an unsigned long. The low byte contains the type of interrupt (update-done, alarm-rang, or periodic) that was raised; the remaining bytes contain the number of interrupts since the last read. Status information is reported through the pseudo-file /proc/driver/rtc if the /proc filesystem is enabled. A user process can monitor these interrupts by doing a read(2) or a select(2) on /dev/rtc.

Under heavy IRQ load, sometimes the interrupts pile up because they get processed together by the bottom-half IRQ handler of the kernel. It is up to the user program to check the number of interrupts received since the last read. On modern hardware these IRQ jams typically start to happen for frequencies above 4096Hz and more. Programming and/or enabling interrupt frequencies greater than 64Hz is only allowed by root. This was done to prevent a misbehaving user program from generating lots of IRQs that impact overall system performance.

Also, if the kernel time is synchronized with an external time source, the kernel will write the time back to the CMOS clock every 11 minutes. In the process of doing this, the kernel briefly turns off RTC periodic interrupts, so be aware of this if you are doing serious work.

The alarm and/or interrupt frequency are programmed into the RTC via `ioctl(2)` calls, as listed in `include/linux/mc146818rtc.h` (see the data structure below).

The following user program (supplied with the kernel documentation with RedHat's distribution) best illustrates how to use `ioctls` to control the real time clock:

```c
/*
 *    Real Time Clock Driver Test/Example Program
 *
 *    Compile with:
 *        gcc -s -Wall -Wstrict-prototypes rtctest.c -o rtctest
 *
 *    Copyright (C) 1996, Paul Gortmaker.
 *
 *    Released under the GNU General Public License, version 2,
 *    included herein by reference.
 *
 */

#include <stdio.h>
#include <linux/mc146818rtc.h>
#include <sys/ioctl.h>
#include <sys/time.h>
#include <sys/types.h>
#include <fcntl.h>
#include <unistd.h>
#include <errno.h>

void main(void) {

int i, fd, retval, irqcount = 0;
unsigned long tmp, data;
struct rtc_time rtc_tm;

fd = open ("/dev/rtc", O_RDONLY);

if (fd ==  -1) {
    perror("/dev/rtc");
    exit(errno);
}

fprintf(stderr, "\n\t\t\tRTC Driver Test Example.\n\n");

/* Turn on update interrupts (one per second) */
retval = ioctl(fd, RTC_UIE_ON, 0);
if (retval == -1) {
    perror("ioctl");
    exit(errno);
}

fprintf(stderr, "Counting 5 update (1/sec) interrupts from reading /dev/rtc:");
```

```
fflush(stderr);
for (i=1; i<6; i++) {
    /* This read will block */
    retval = read(fd, &data, sizeof(unsigned long));
    if (retval == -1) {
        perror("read");
        exit(errno);
    }
    fprintf(stderr, " %d",i);
    fflush(stderr);
    irqcount++;
}

fprintf(stderr, "\nAgain, from using select(2) on /dev/rtc:");
fflush(stderr);
for (i=1; i<6; i++) {
    struct timeval tv = {5, 0}; /* 5 second timeout on select */
    fd_set readfds;

    FD_ZERO(&readfds);
    FD_SET(fd, &readfds);
    /* The select will wait until an RTC interrupt happens. */
    retval = select(fd+1, &readfds, NULL, NULL, &tv);
    if (retval == -1) {
        perror("select");
        exit(errno);
    }
    /* This read won't block unlike the select-less case above. */
    retval = read(fd, &data, sizeof(unsigned long));
    if (retval == -1) {
        perror("read");
        exit(errno);
    }
    fprintf(stderr, " %d",i);
    fflush(stderr);
    irqcount++;
}

/* Turn off update interrupts */
retval = ioctl(fd, RTC_UIE_OFF, 0);
if (retval == -1) {
    perror("ioctl");
    exit(errno);
}

/* Read the RTC time/date */
retval = ioctl(fd, RTC_RD_TIME, &rtc_tm);
if (retval == -1) {
    perror("ioctl");
    exit(errno);
}

fprintf(stderr, "\n\nCurrent RTC date/time is %d-%d-%d, %02d:%02d:%02d.\n",
    rtc_tm.tm_mday, rtc_tm.tm_mon + 1, rtc_tm.tm_year + 1900,
```

```
        rtc_tm.tm_hour, rtc_tm.tm_min, rtc_tm.tm_sec);

/* Set the alarm to 5 sec in the future, and check for rollover */
rtc_tm.tm_sec += 5;
if (rtc_tm.tm_sec >= 60) {
    rtc_tm.tm_sec %= 60;
    rtc_tm.tm_min++;
}
if (rtc_tm.tm_min == 60) {
    rtc_tm.tm_min = 0;
    rtc_tm.tm_hour++;
}
if (rtc_tm.tm_hour == 24)
    rtc_tm.tm_hour = 0;

retval = ioctl(fd, RTC_ALM_SET, &rtc_tm);
if (retval == -1) {
    perror("ioctl");
    exit(errno);
}

/* Read the current alarm settings */
retval = ioctl(fd, RTC_ALM_READ, &rtc_tm);
if (retval == -1) {
    perror("ioctl");
    exit(errno);
}

fprintf(stderr, "Alarm time now set to %02d:%02d:%02d.\n",
    rtc_tm.tm_hour, rtc_tm.tm_min, rtc_tm.tm_sec);

/* Enable alarm interrupts */
retval = ioctl(fd, RTC_AIE_ON, 0);
if (retval == -1) {
    perror("ioctl");
    exit(errno);
}

fprintf(stderr, "Waiting 5 seconds for alarm...");
fflush(stderr);
/* This blocks until the alarm ring causes an interrupt */
retval = read(fd, &data, sizeof(unsigned long));
if (retval == -1) {
    perror("read");
    exit(errno);
}
irqcount++;
fprintf(stderr, " okay. Alarm rang.\n");

/* Disable alarm interrupts */
retval = ioctl(fd, RTC_AIE_OFF, 0);
if (retval == -1) {
    perror("ioctl");
    exit(errno);
```

```
}

/* Read periodic IRQ rate */
retval = ioctl(fd, RTC_IRQP_READ, &tmp);
if (retval == -1) {
    perror("ioctl");
    exit(errno);
}
fprintf(stderr, "\nPeriodic IRQ rate was %ldHz.\n", tmp);

fprintf(stderr, "Counting 20 interrupts at:");
fflush(stderr);

/* The frequencies 128Hz, 256Hz, ... 8192Hz are only allowed for root. */
for (tmp=2; tmp<=64; tmp*=2) {

    retval = ioctl(fd, RTC_IRQP_SET, tmp);
    if (retval == -1) {
        perror("ioctl");
        exit(errno);
    }

    fprintf(stderr, "\n%ldHz:\t", tmp);
    fflush(stderr);

    /* Enable periodic interrupts */
    retval = ioctl(fd, RTC_PIE_ON, 0);
    if (retval == -1) {
        perror("ioctl");
        exit(errno);
    }

    for (i=1; i<21; i++) {
        /* This blocks */
        retval = read(fd, &data, sizeof(unsigned long));
        if (retval == -1) {
            perror("read");
            exit(errno);
        }
        fprintf(stderr, " %d",i);
        fflush(stderr);
        irqcount++;
    }

    /* Disable periodic interrupts */
    retval = ioctl(fd, RTC_PIE_OFF, 0);
    if (retval == -1) {
        perror("ioctl");
        exit(errno);
    }
}

fprintf(stderr, "\n\n\t\t\t *** Test complete ***\n");
fprintf(stderr, "\nTyping \"cat /proc/interrupts\" will show %d more events on IRQ
```

```
8.\n\n",                                         irqcount);

close(fd);

} /* end main */
```

As with many (but not all) UNIX-based operating systems, the kernel at boot time sets this clock chip to interrupt the kernel every n hundredths of a second. Usually, UNIX machines set this value to 100 times per second. In operating systems like Solaris, this value is a tunable parameter. Although it doesn't make sense in fast hardware to let the clock interrupt the kernel less than 100 times per second, it may make sense to let it do so more often (say 1,000 times per second).

Human-readable timekeeping is kernel based and managed with the `gettimeofday()` and `settimeofday()` system calls (e.g. `arch/i386/kernel/timer.c`). At bootup, the kernel aligns itself to the BIOS (CMOS) clock and subsequently updates its time of day based on the timer interrupt.

Accurate time of day is extremely important in this globalized Internet world; thus the kernel also has a *Network Time Protocol* (NTP) facility, which in conjunction with `xntpd` enables Linux to keep up with high-precision atomic clocks scattered around the world and accessible through the Internet. The very complex and very accurate NTP protocol itself is implemented by `xntpd`. The kernel provides functionality to speed up and slow down the flow of time without introducing user-visible time warps or time jumps. An example of such a Linux system coupled to an atomic clock is:

```
[mingo@s]$ date
Tue Jan  4 13:22:19 CET 2000
[mingo@s]$ ntptrace
localhost: stratum 4, offset -1.113059, synch distance 0.15135
goliat.eik.bme.hu: stratum 3, offset -1.039804, synch distance 0.05267
maze.bme.hu: stratum 2, offset -1.134906, synch distance 0.06520
hora.cs.tu-berlin.de: stratum 1, offset -1.132075, synch distance
0.00023, refid 'GPS'
```

The Linux box above is synchronized over multiple NTP servers with an atomic clock that sends it an interrupt every n milliseconds. On the i386 architecture, this value is usually set to 10 milliseconds. In other words, the kernel will wake up 100 times per second. The accuracy of NTP is to within 100 microseconds.

To be able to handle housekeeping tasks such as setting the clock, the Linux kernel asks the timer to send it an IRQ at regular intervals. The exact place where this value is set is in the architecture-specific part of the kernel. Because each architecture may have different needs, it makes sense to do it this way.

For i386, everything related to the timer is in `linux/arch/i386/kernel/time.c` but the real clock initialization happens in `linux/arch/i386/kernel/irq.c` in the function `init_IRQ()`:

```
__initfunc(void init_IRQ(void))
{
    [..]
    /*
     * Set the clock to 100 Hz, we already have a valid
     * vector now:
     */
    outb_p(0x34,0x43);          /* binary, mode 2, LSB/MSB, ch 0 */
    outb_p(LATCH & 0xff , 0x40);      /* LSB */
    outb(LATCH >> 8 , 0x40);  /* MSB */

    [..]
}
```

where LATCH is a macro defined in `linux/include/linux/timex.h`:

```
/* LATCH is used in the interval timer and ftape setup. */
   #define LATCH  ((CLOCK_TICK_RATE + HZ/2) / HZ)
   /* For divider */
```

and `CLOCK_TICK_RATE` is provided by `linux/include/asm-i386/timex.h`:

```
#define CLOCK_TICK_RATE 1193180 /* Underlying HZ */
```

Basically the formula is:

```
[1]   CLOCK_TICK_RATE / HZ -> downcount
```

and then the kernel writes the `downcount` in the timer chip. HZ is the frequency of the timer interrupt that we want to achieve.

On the i386 architecture Linux uses a 100Hz timer mainly because the earliest Linux development was done with the obsolete standards of the time where a hundredth of a second was a significant amount of time for a processor. Now, with processors such as the Alpha chip, which are orders of magnitude faster, architectures use a 1024Hz timer in Linux.

As you can see by the above formula the only thing that we need to change to make the IA32 (Intel x86) port using a, say, 1000Hz timer is the HZ define, which is the only input of the formula.

```
root@hirame:~/kernel > find 2.2.13/include/asm-* -type f -exec
    egrep '# *define *HZ' {} /dev/null \;
2.2.13/include/asm-alpha/param.h:# define HZ     1024
2.2.13/include/asm-arm/arch-ebsa110/param.h:#define HZ 100
2.2.13/include/asm-arm/arch-ebsa285/param.h:#define HZ 100
2.2.13/include/asm-arm/arch-nexuspci/param.h:#define HZ 100
2.2.13/include/asm-arm/arch-rpc/param.h:#define HZ 100
2.2.13/include/asm-arm/proc-armo/param.h:#define HZ 100
2.2.13/include/asm-i386/param.h:#define HZ 100
2.2.13/include/asm-m68k/param.h:#define HZ 100
2.2.13/include/asm-mips/param.h:#define HZ 100
2.2.13/include/asm-ppc/param.h:#define HZ 100
2.2.13/include/asm-sparc/param.h:#define HZ 100
2.2.13/include/asm-sparc64/param.h:#define HZ 100
```

There is a preferred HZ definition for each architecture.

Although changing HZ to 1,000 will just allow the kernel to use a 1,000 timer, you should bear in mind that any program running in user space (if not adapted accordingly) will continue to think that the kernel is running with a 100Hz timer. In other words, some user space programs such as top could break. This happens because some data are still exported from kernel space to user space in jiffy units (100 per second).

This "visibility" problem inside the kernel could be solved by splitting the currently unique HZ into an internal HZ and a user space-exported HZ. There are patches that do just that. They have not been integrated into the kernel yet, simply because the 100Hz timer seems not to hurt too much.

It's also interesting to note that the timer IRQ in an IA32-SMP system only manages the system time and starts the software interrupts (bottom-half handlers). All the scheduling accounting is triggered instead by an SMP-timer interrupt generated by the IO-APIC in broadcast to all CPUs (as opposed to the timer IRQ, which is a unicast IRQ on the IA32-SMP port). So, if the purpose of the timer frequency increase was to make scheduling more fine-grained, in a IA32-SMP system we should instead only change the frequency of the SMP timer interrupt by reprogramming the IO-APIC. That frequency of the IO-APIC local timer IRQ is set in linux/arch/i386/kernel/smp.c within the function setup_APIC_timer().

Data Structure—linux/mc146818rtc.h

```
1     /* mc146818rtc.h - register definitions for the Real-Time-Clock / CMOS RAM
2      * Copyright Torsten Duwe <duwe@informatik.uni-erlangen.de> 1993
3      * derived from Data Sheet, Copyright Motorola 1984 (!).
4      * It was written to be part of the Linux operating system.
5      */
6     /* permission is hereby granted to copy, modify and redistribute this code
7      * in terms of the GNU Library General Public License, Version 2 or later,
8      * at your option.
9      */
10
11    #ifndef  MC146818RTC H
12    #define  MC146818RTC H
13    #include <asm/io.h>
14    #include <linux/rtc.h> /* get the user-level API */
15
16    #ifndef RTC PORT
17    #define   RTC PORT (x)      (0x70 + (x))
18    #define   RTC ALWAYS BCD  1
19    #endif
20
21    #define CMOS READ (addr) ({ \
22    outb p ((addr) ,RTC PORT (0)); \
23    inb p (RTC PORT (1)); \
24    })
25    #define CMOS WRITE (val , addr) ({ \
26    outb p ((addr) ,RTC PORT (0)); \
27    outb p ((val) ,RTC PORT (1)); \
28    })
29
30    /*************************************************************************
31     * register summary
32     *************************************************************************/
33    #define RTC SECONDS           0
34    #define RTC SECONDS ALARM     1
35    #define RTC MINUTES           2
36    #define RTC MINUTES ALARM     3
37    #define RTC HOURS             4
38    #define RTC HOURS ALARM       5
39    /* RTC_*_alarm is always true if 2 MSBs are set */
40    # define RTC ALARM DONT CARE   0xC0
41
42    #define RTC DAY OF WEEK       6
43    #define RTC DAY OF MONTH      7
44    #define RTC MONTH             8
45    #define RTC YEAR              9
46
47    /* control registers - Moto names
48     */
49    #define RTC REG A             10
50    #define RTC REG B             11
51    #define RTC REG C             12
```

```
52      #define RTC REG D                    13
53
54      /*******************************************************************
55       * register details
56       *******************************************************************/
57      #define RTC FREQ SELECT RTC REG A
58
59      /* update-in-progress  - set to "1" 244 microsecs before RTC goes off the bus,
60       * reset after update (may take 1.984ms @ 32768Hz RefClock) is complete,
61       * totalling to a max high interval of 2.228 ms.
62       */
63      # define RTC UIP                      0x80
64      # define RTC DIV CTL                  0x70
65          /* divider control: refclock values 4.194 / 1.049 MHz / 32.768 kHz */
66      #   define RTC REF CLCK 4MHZ          0x00
67      #   define RTC REF CLCK 1MHZ          0x10
68      #   define RTC REF CLCK 32KHZ         0x20
69          /* 2 values for divider stage reset, others for "testing purposes only" */
70      #   define RTC DIV RESET1             0x60
71      #   define RTC DIV RESET2             0x70
72          /* Periodic intr. / Square wave rate select. 0=none, 1=32.8kHz,... 15=2Hz */
73      # define RTC RATE SELECT              0x0F
74
75      /*******************************************************************/
76      #define RTC CONTROL       RTC REG B
77      # define RTC SET 0x80                 /* disable updates for clock setting */
78      # define RTC PIE 0x40                 /* periodic interrupt enable */
79      # define RTC AIE 0x20                 /* alarm interrupt enable */
80      # define RTC UIE 0x10                 /* update-finished interrupt enable */
81      # define RTC SQWE 0x08                /* enable square-wave output */
82      # define RTC DM BINARY 0x04           /* all time/date values are BCD if clear */
83      # define RTC 24H 0x02                 /* 24 hour mode - else hours bit 7 means pm */
84      # define RTC DST EN 0x01              /* auto switch DST - works f. USA only */
85
86      /*******************************************************************/
87      #define RTC INTR FLAGS   RTC REG C
88      /* caution - cleared by read */
89      # define RTC IRQF 0x80                /* any of the following 3 is active */
90      # define RTC PF 0x40
91      # define RTC AF 0x20
92      # define RTC UF 0x10
93
94      /*******************************************************************/
95      #define RTC VALID         RTC REG D
96      # define RTC VRT 0x80                 /* valid RAM and time */
97      /*******************************************************************/
98
99      /* example: !(CMOS_READ(RTC_CONTROL) & RTC_DM_BINARY)
100      * determines if the following two #defines are needed
101      */
102     #ifndef BCD TO BIN
103     #define BCD TO BIN (val) ((val)=((val)&15) + ((val)>>4)*10)
104     #endif
105
```

```
106    #ifndef BIN TO BCD
107    #define BIN TO BCD (val) ((val)=(((val)/10)<<4) + (val)%10)
108    #endif
109
110    #endif /* _MC146818RTC_H */
111
```

Real-Time Profiling

Sometimes, a developer who wants to speed up his program and/or eliminate redundant or unused code might want to measure the number of times each stretch of his code gets executed. To do this, use a feature called *real-time profiling*, where the kernel keeps a set of real-time time stamps of the execution of the program and writes these into a log file for later analysis. Real-time profiling needs the help of hardware to do its job. Intel architectures provide such functions by default. It is up to the operating system to know how to make use of them. Windows OSs do not provide for real-time profiling.

For real-time profiling with the 2.2.x and 2.3.x kernels, you only need to boot the kernel with the parameter `profile=4`, for example. The 4 is the granularity of the profile map I use normally. In other words, to every 4-byte-long stretch of code, an integer count variable is allocated. Thus, the raw statistics for a code-stretch-usage histogram will be generated.

On the IA 32 (Intel i386) architecture, the profiler is run by the timer IRQ on UP and by the SMP local APIC timer IRQ in SMP (so both CPUs are profiled). Say we have the kernel image ranging from `0xc0100000` to `c0154321`. The kernel profiler profiles on this EIP range. For every profiler interrupt (`IRQ0` typically) we know the interrupted EIP. The logic is this:

```
/*
 * Only measure the CPU's specified by /proc/irq/prof_cpu_mask.
 * (default is all CPUs.)
 */
if (!((1<<smp_processor_id()) & prof_cpu_mask))
        return;

if (prof_buffer) {
        eip -= (unsigned long) &_stext;
        eip >>= prof_shift;
        /*
         * Don't ignore out-of-bounds EIP values silently,
         * put them into the last histogram slot, so if
```

```
  * present, they will show up as a sharp peak.
  */
 if (eip > prof_len-1)
        eip = prof_len-1;
 atomic_inc((atomic_t *)&prof_buffer[eip]);
}
```

The `prof_cpu_mask` is new. It can be set through `/proc/irq/prof_cpu_mask`. (We can pick individual CPUs to be profiled. Even though Linux SMP is completely symmetric, sometimes we do want to see only one CPU's profiling hits.)

In the above histogram, `prof_shift` is the *granularity* of the histogram; that is, if granularity is 4, then all EIPs within $x+0$ and $x+15$ bytes count as a single histogram array entry. (where x is a multiple of 16).

The profile information can be read via `/proc/profile` (which exports to user space the kernel profiling buffer). A utility exists to parse the profile buffer. The `prof` buffer can also be reset:

```
root@hirame:~ > readprofile -m /boot/System.map-2.2.13aa4 | sort
-nr | head -5
    369 total                 0.0005
    133 do_wp_page            0.1614
     24 ccpy_page_range       0.0480
     19 ext2_alloc_block      0.0552
     16 startup_32            0.0976
```

where `133` is the number of times the timer IRQ was raised inside the function `do_wp_page`. The size ratio 0.1614 is compared to the size of the function being analyzed.

The only downside of kernel profiling is that functions that run with IRQ disabled won't have any way to be profiled. In 2.3.x, the kernel also includes an *Non-Maskable Interrupt* (NMI) IRQ at HZ frequency (to automatically unlock and to get stack traces from lockups occurring with IRQ disabled). In 2.3.x we may choose to do the kernel profiling inside the NMI code, as there are no possible traces in the profiling code.

Another way to profile the kernel is by incrementing the profile count not at each timer IRQ but before each function. This can be done using `gcc` compiler features. This kind of profiling obviously is not usable for production, as it slows down the system too much, but it may be interesting to learn about the most called functions in the kernel.

For user space, the GNU `gcc` compiler provides profiling support by using the `-pg` option at compile time. A utility called `gprof` can be used to read the profiling information after a program has been executed. The

GNU `gcc` profiling is based both on the function call traces of the program and on the `PROF` timer, which is supplied by the kernel via a special `SIGPROF` signal. The `PROF` timer can be set via the `setitimer` interface.

Time of Day (TOD) Functions

There is a syscall called `gettimeofday`. It provides to user space the current system and OS time with microsecond resolution. The kernel keeps account of the system time in a variable called `xtime`, which is a normal variable and is increased at each timer IRQ. To get resolution finer than 0.01 sec, we can use two techniques on IA32:

- If the CPU is a 486 or a 386, at `gettimeofday` time we read the down-count or latch register from the timer chip and then calculate how much time passed since the last timer IRQ. The maximum TOD resolution is bound to the maximum frequency of the timer chip.
- On Pentiums and newer chips, we save the time-stamp counter value at each timer IRQ. Then, at `gettimeofday` time, we discover how much time passed since the last timer IRQ by comparing the last saved time-stamp counter with the current time-stamp counter. We know the frequency of the CPU, so we can translate from CPU cycles to an interval of real-world time through straightforward multiplication. This gives us the best TOD resolution possible on these recent chips. It's much more precise than microseconds, but the `gettimeofday` interface doesn't allow us to return information in nanoseconds.

Let's see now what happens when the timer IRQ interrupt handling routine is entered in the kernel.

Some operating systems—here we use the example of Solaris—set the free memory level that is present in the system. Linux does not do this for several reasons. The most important one is that in generating some free memory we may need to swapout, yet we can't wait for I/O completion from an IRQ handler.

NOTE

Although swapout is almost always asynchronous, sometimes we may need to wait for completion of swap I/O, to be sure that there is some free memory before we try new allocation of memory. A pool of atomic free memory is instead kept free by a proper kernel daemon (`kswapd`).

Then, obviously, the IRQ handler needs to check and adjust the clock for possible jitter. At regular intervals the i386 port flushes the system time to the hardware clock (also known as CMOS, real time clock [RTC]) inside the timer IRQ.

The IRQ handler then proceeds to calculate the percentages spent busy, waiting, and running during the previous time-unit of execution (jiffy). Note that the per-CPU and per-process accounting only tells if each CPU or process passed the last timer tick in `user/nice(?)/system/idle` modes. You don't know if the last tick has been passed in the network code, for example.

Some time ago Andrea Arcangeli wrote code to provide information about how many ticks the CPU and the current process spend in kernel SMP locks. This is quite interesting, because if you see that one CPU is spending all its time in kernel locks, it means that the code is not SMP-threaded enough for your purposes.

The `loadavg` accounting also is done within the timer IRQ.

Basically, we can repeat the timer IRQ path in these steps:

1. Save current time stamp counter and current latch count in static variables for `gettimeofday`.
2. Enter the common code for all architectures calling `do_timer()`.
3. Because `do_timer()` increases jiffies and accounts the tick as `lost_ticks`, the next update on the system clock will read and reset `lost_ticks`. `lost_ticks` is a trick necessary not to race (a race is a situation of contention with other tasks accessing the same resource; usually this occurs in poorly designed code running on am SMP system) with `gettimeofday` and to be allowed to do the update of the system clock inside the bottom-half handlers.
4. Mark the timer bottom-half queue, so that before returning from the timer IRQ we'll run it (or some other IRQ returning before us will be allowed to start it also on another CPU).
5. Update the kernel profiling with the information about the interrupted code (only if it was kernel code, of course).
6. If it's UP we also update the per-CPU and per-process profiling variables (because there's no IO-APIC SMP timer IRQ in UP).
7. Check to see whether it's time to flush the system clock to the RTC (we do this about each 11 minutes).
8. Return.

Now the IRQ code (before effectively running `iret` and so still in IRQ context) will try to execute bottom-half handlers and will notice that the bottom-half queue bitfield is set (we marked it at point 4). We'll enter `timer_bh()`, which will update the system time (according to `lost_ticks`) and run the timers (both old and new timers). All these operations will run from bottom-half context, which from a hardware point of view is still an IRQ context.

When `timer_bh` returns (after all timers have been executed and rotated), we'll effectively return from the timer interrupt.

The difference between uniprocessing (UP) and symmetric multiprocessing (SMP) is that in UP the point (6) is executed within the timer IRQ. On IA-32 SMP, point (6) is *not* executed within the timer interrupt handler; the timer IRQ skips it completely. We instead broadcast a special SMP timer IRQ to all CPUs and we run only point (6) within the ioapic local timer IRQ.

System Initialization and Boot

Most Linux distributions boot by means of the `initrd` facility, which adds the capability to load a RAM disk by the boot loader. This RAM disk can then be mounted as the root file system and programs can be run from it. Afterwards, a new root file system can be mounted from a different device. The previous root (from `initrd`) is then either moved to the directory `/initrd` or it is unmounted. This is how Linux bootstraps the kernel image into memory and then mounts the real file system.

The `initrd` utility is mainly designed to allow system startup to occur in two phases, the first where the kernel comes up with a minimum set of compiled-in drivers, and the second where additional modules are loaded from `initrd`.

When using `initrd`, the system boots as follows:

1. The boot loader loads the kernel and the initial RAM disk.
2. The kernel converts `initrd` into a "normal" RAM disk and frees the memory used by `initrd`.
3. `initrd` is mounted read-write as root.
4. The `/linuxrc` is executed (this can be any valid executable, including shell scripts; it is run with `uid 0` and can do basically everything init can do).
5. When `linuxrc` terminates, the "real" root file system is mounted.
6. If a directory `/initrd` exists, the `initrd` is moved there. Otherwise, `initrd` is unmounted.

7. The usual boot sequence (e.g. invocation of `/sbin/init`) is performed on the root file system.

Note that moving `initrd` from `/` to `/initrd` does not involve unmounting it through the `umount()` call. It is therefore possible to leave processes running on `initrd` (or leave file systems mounted, but see below) during that procedure. However, if `/initrd` doesn't exist, `initrd` can only be unmounted if it is not used by any other process. If it can't be unmounted, it remains in memory.

Also note that filesystems mounted under `initrd` continue to be accessible, but their `/proc/mounts` entries are not updated any longer. Also, if `/initrd` doesn't exist, `initrd` can't be unmounted and it will "vanish," taking those filesystems with it, thereby preventing them from being remounted properly. It is therefore strongly suggested to generally unmount all filesystems (except of course the root file system, but including `/proc`) before switching from `initrd` to the "normal" root filesystem. To deallocate the memory used for the initial RAM disk, you have to execute `freeramdisk` (see Resources, below) after unmounting `/initrd`.

Sequence of Kernel Tables Creation at Boot

Upon boot, the kernel must create and properly populate all the tables needed for the normal functioning of the system. They are almost all allocated statically and initialized at compile time in the data section. `task_struct`, `init_mm`, and `pg_data_t` array, which is in the data structure, contain all the information on the state of the memory in the machine. In previous kernels (2.2.x and prior) this information was stored in kernel-global variables. Today, with clustered Linux servers, these variables are per node.

In 2.3.49 `/include/linux/mmzone.h`, the only node of an IA32 (Intel x86) non-NUMA machine is called `contig_page_data`. The `contig_page_data->node_mem_map` is the old `mem_map_t` array of 2.2.x, with all the `struct page *` in it. The `node_mem_map` array gets allocated dynamically at boot, as soon as the number of pages in the system is known.

Hardware Recognition at Boot

In the 2.2.x versions, the kernel was used to recall the initialization callback of each subsystem configured in the kernel. Then, each subsystem called the initialization code for the devices for each low-level driver configured into the kernel. This procedure was called *hierarchical initialization* and worked fine for simple systems with a limited number of devices.

In 2.3.x the hardware recognition procedure changed considerably. Previously it was necessary to change the init callback of the higher layer to add something like:

```
#ifdef CONFIG_MY_DRIVER
    init_my_driver();
#endif
```

This is no longer necessary, because we include a pointer to init_my_driver() in a special ELF section, and the higher layer parses each special file (device driver) init section and recalls all the init callback without any need to write code outside the .c file of the low-level driver. This has simplified initialization at boot time.

It is interesting to note that, with this new hardware recognition strategy or sequence, the linking order at device driver compile time has become significant, because the information is in the ELF header of the objects. Consequently, special cases may still need explicit calling of the initialization function. For most cases, however, that's not necessary. The dynamic kernel structures in the early stage (for example, while setting up the console or the virtual memory manager) are allocated via a new bootmem allocator, which can return big chunks of physically contiguous memory. In 2.2.x we used to advance a pointer to keep track of the memory allocated by hand in the early stage, but with newer machines tables can be allocated in the middle of the memory; therefore an allocator (bootmem) was needed that was also aware of memory holes in the early stage of the boot process. The bootmem allocator also makes sure to return non-DMA memory when possible. This way, we avoid wasting the first 16MB of memory with kernel structures that don't need to be there.

Once the virtual memory manager is booted and initialized and get_pages and get_free_pages get the appropriate pointers from bootmem, all further allocations of memory are handled by the VM directly.

Shutdown

All the hard work is done in user space. The halt -f only tells the init process that the machine will halt soon via a SIGTSTP. Then, shutdown executes sys_reboot(SYS-HALT) and later will call exit(2) on an IA32 computer. In fact if you run `halt -f` you will still be able to run your machine fine; however `init` will stop forking login sessions, because it received the SIGTSTP from the `halt` process.

The common code at halt time recalls a per-architecture function called `machine_halt()`. On IA32 this function is a noop. On Alpha, for example, it sends an IPI to all CPUs so that they all call the palcode HALT function and the SRM can get control of them later.

The reboot works basically the same way, but instead of `machine_halt`, another function (`machine_restart`) gets recalled. On IA32, it reboots, sending a stop to all CPUs and disabling IO-APIC in SMP and then writing a special value to an I/O address. If that isn't enough, we load a bogus interrupt table into the Interrupt Table Descriptor (ITD) of the CPU. Then we call an `int3` (soft interrupt), which causes a triple fault; the CPU reboots the machine.

There are also kernel parameter options that force the kernel to reboot using BIOS functions instead of the above technique.

Data Structures—linux/reboot.h

```
1    #ifndef LINUX REBOOT H
2    #define LINUX REBOOT H
3
4    /*
5     * Magic values required to use _reboot() system call.
6     */
7
8    #define LINUX REBOOT MAGIC1      0xfee1dead
9    #define LINUX REBOOT MAGIC2      672274793
10   #define LINUX REBOOT MAGIC2A     85072278
11   #define LINUX REBOOT MAGIC2B     369367448
12
13
14   /*
15    * Commands accepted by the _reboot() system call.
16    *
17    * RESTART      Restart system using default command and mode.
18    * HALT         Stop OS and give system control to ROM monitor, if any.
19    * CAD_ON       Ctrl-Alt-Del sequence causes RESTART command.
20    * CAD_OFF      Ctrl-Alt-Del sequence sends SIGINT to init task.
21    * POWER_OFF    Stop OS and remove all power from system, if possible.
22    * RESTART2     Restart system using given command string.
23    */
24
25   #define LINUX REBOOT CMD RESTART        0x01234567
26   #define LINUX REBOOT CMD HALT           0xCDEF0123
27   #define LINUX REBOOT CMD CAD ON         0x89ABCDEF
28   #define LINUX REBOOT CMD CAD OFF        0x00000000
29   #define LINUX REBOOT CMD POWER OFF      0x4321FEDC
```

```
30      #define LINUX REBOOT CMD RESTART2        0xA1B2C3D4
31
32
33      #ifdef KERNEL
34

35      #include <linux/notifier.h>
36
37      extern struct notifier block *reboot notifier list;
38      extern int register reboot notifier(struct notifier block *);
39      extern int unregister reboot notifier(struct notifier block *);
40
41
42      /*
43       * Architecture-specific implementations of sys_reboot commands.
44       */
45
46      extern void machine restart(char *cmd);
47      extern void machine halt(void);
48      extern void machine power off(void);
49
50      #endif
51
52      #endif /* _LINUX_REBOOT_H */
53
```

Data Structure—linux/mmzone.h

```
1       #ifndef LINUX MMZONE H
2       #define LINUX MMZONE H
3
4       #ifdef KERNEL
5       #ifndef __ASSEMBLY__
6
7       #include <linux/config.h>
8       #include <linux/spinlock.h>
9       #include <linux/list.h>
10
11      /*
12       * Free memory management - zoned buddy allocator.
13       */
14
15      #define MAX ORDER 10
16
17      typedef struct free area struct {
18              struct list head free list;
19              unsigned int * map;
20      } free area t;
21
22      struct pglist data;
23
```

```
24    typedef struct zone struct {
25            /*
26             * Commonly accessed fields:
27             */
28            spinlock t lock;
29            unsigned long offset;
30            unsigned long free pages;
31            int low_on_memory;
32            unsigned long pages_min, pages_low, pages_high;
33
34            /*
35             * free areas of different sizes
36             */
37            free area t free area[MAX_ORDER];
38
39            /*
40             * rarely used fields:
41             */
42            char * name;
43            unsigned long size;
44            /*
45             * Discontig memory support fields.
46             */
47            struct pglist data *zone pgdat;
48            unsigned long zone_start_paddr;
49            unsigned long zone_start_mapnr;
50            struct page * zone_mem_map;
51    } zone t;
52
53    #define ZONE DMA                    0
54    #define ZONE NORMAL                 1
55    #define ZONE HIGHMEM                2
56    #define MAX NR ZONES                3
57
58    /*
59     * One allocation request operates on a zonelist. A zonelist
60     * is a list of zones, the first one is the 'goal' of the
61     * allocation, the other zones are fallback zones, in decreasing
62     * priority.
63     *
64     * Right now a zonelist takes up less than a cacheline. We never
65     * modify it apart from boot-up, and only a few indices are used,
66     * so despite the zonelist table being relatively big, the cache
67     * footprint of this construct is very small.
68     */
69    typedef struct zonelist struct {
70            zone t * zones [MAX NR ZONES+1]; // NULL delimited
71            int gfp_mask;
72    } zonelist t;
73
74    #define NR GFPINDEX                 0x100
75
76    struct bootmem data;
77    typedef struct pglist data {
```

```
78              zone t node_zones[MAX NR ZONES];
79              zonelist t node_zonelists[NR GFPINDEX];
80              struct page *node_mem_map;
81              unsigned long *valid addr bitmap;
82              struct bootmem data *bdata;
83              unsigned long node_start_paddr;
84              unsigned long node_start_mapnr;
85              unsigned long node_size;
86              int node_id;
87      } pg data t;
88
89      extern int numnodes;
90
91      #define memclass (pgzone, tzone) (((pgzone)->zone_pgdat == (tzone)->zone_pgdat)
\
92                              && (((pgzone) - (pgzone)->zone_pgdat->node_zones) <= \
93                              ((tzone) - (pgzone)->zone_pgdat->node_zones)))
94
95      /*
96       * The following two are not meant for general usage. They are here as
97       * prototypes for the discontig memory code.
98       */
99      extern void show free areas core (int);
100     extern void free area init core (int nid,  pg data t *pgdat, struct page **gmap,
101                     unsigned long *zones_size, unsigned long paddr);
102
103     #ifndef CONFIG_DISCONTIGMEM
104
105     extern pg data t contig page data;
106
107     #define NODE DATA(nid)              (&contig page data)
108     #define NODE MEM MAP(nid)           mem map
109
110     #else /* !CONFIG_DISCONTIGMEM */
111
112     #include <asm/mmzone.h>
113
114     #endif /* !CONFIG_DISCONTIGMEM */
115
116     #define MAP ALIGN(x)    ((((x) % sizeof (mem map t)) == 0) ? (x) : ((x) + \
117                     sizeof (mem map t) - ((x) % sizeof (mem map t))))
118
119     #endif /* !__ASSEMBLY__ */
120     #endif /* __KERNEL__ */
121     #endif /* _LINUX_MMZONE_H */
122
```

Data Structures—linux/timer.h

```
1       #ifndef LINUX TIMER H
2       #define LINUX TIMER H
3
```

```
4     /*
5      * Old-style timers. Please don't use for any new code.
6      *
7      * Numbering of these timers should be consecutive to minimize
8      * processing delays. [MJ]
9      */
10
11    #define BLANK TIMER        0       /* Console screen-saver */
12    #define BEEP TIMER         1       /* Console beep */
13    #define RS TIMER           2       /* RS-232 ports */
14    #define SWAP TIMER         3       /* Background pageout */
15    #define BACKGR TIMER       4       /* io_request background I/O */
16    #define HD TIMER           5       /* Old IDE driver */
17    #define FLOPPY TIMER       6       /* Floppy */
18    #define QIC02 TAPE TIMER 7         /* QIC 02 tape */
19    #define MCD TIMER          8       /* Mitsumi CDROM */
20    #define GSCD TIMER         9       /* Goldstar CDROM */
21    #define COMTROL TIMER      10      /* Comtrol serial */
22    #define DIGI TIMER         11      /* Digi serial */
23    #define GDTH TIMER         12      /* Ugh - gdth scsi driver */
24
25    #define COPRO TIMER        31      /* 387 timeout for buggy hardware (boot only) */
26
27    struct timer struct {
28            unsigned long expires;
29            void (*fn)(void);
30    };
31
32    extern unsigned long timer active;
33    extern struct timer struct timer table [32];
34
35    /*
36     * This is completely separate from the above, and is the
37     * "new and improved" way of handling timers more dynamically.
38     * Hopefully efficient and general enough for most things.
39     *
40     * The "hardcoded" timers above are still useful for well-
41     * defined problems, but the timer-list is probably better
42     * when you need multiple outstanding timers or similar.
43     *
44     * The "data" field is in case you want to use the same
45     * timeout function for several timeouts. You can use this
46     * to distinguish between the different invocations.
47     */
48    struct timer list {
49            struct timer list *next; /* MUST be first element */
50            struct timer list *prev;
51            unsigned long expires;
52            unsigned long data;
53            void (*function)(unsigned long);
54            volatile int running;
55    };
56
57    extern void add timer (struct timer list * timer);
```

```
58    extern int  del timer (struct timer list * timer);
59
60    /*
61     * mod_timer is a more efficient way to update the expire field of an
62     * active timer (if the timer is inactive it will be activated)
63     * mod_timer(a,b) is equivalent to del_timer(a); a->expires = b; add_timer(a)
64     */
65    int mod timer (struct timer list *timer, unsigned long expires);
66
67    extern void it real fn (unsigned long);
68
69    extern inline void init timer (struct timer list * timer)
70    {
71            timer->next = NULL;
72            timer->prev = NULL;
73    #ifdef __SMP__
74            timer->running = 0;
75    #endif
76    }
77
78    extern inline int timer pending (const struct timer list * timer)
79    {
80            return timer->prev != NULL;
81    }
82
83    #ifdef __SMP__
84    #define timer exit (t) do { (t)->running = 0; mb(); } while (0)
85    #define timer set running (t) do { (t)->running = 1; mb(); } while (0)
86    #define timer is running (t) ((t)->running != 0)
87    #define timer synchronize (t) while (timer is running (t)) barrier()
88    extern int del timer sync (struct timer list *  timer);
89    #else
90    #define timer exit (t) do { } while (0)
91    #define timer set running (t) do { } while (0)
92    #define timer is running (t) (0)
93    #define timer synchronize (t) barrier()
94    #define del timer sync (t) del timer (t)
95    #endif
96
97    /*
98     *        These inlines deal with timer wrapping correctly. You are
99     *        strongly encouraged to use them
100    *        1. Because people otherwise forget
101    *        2. Because if the timer wrap changes in future you wont have to
102    *           alter your driver code.
103    *
104    * Do this with "<0" and ">=0" to only test the sign of the result. A
105    * good compiler would generate better code (and a really good compiler
106    * wouldn't care). Gcc is currently neither.
107    */
108   #define time after (a,b)          ((long)(b) - (long)(a) < 0)
109   #define time before (a,b)         time after (b,a)
110
111   #define time after eq (a,b)       ((long)(a) - (long)(b) >= 0)
```

```
112     #define time before eq (a,b)        time after eq (b,a)
113
114     #endif
115
```

Data Structures—linux/time.h

```
1       #ifndef LINUX TIME H
2       #define LINUX TIME H
3
4       #include <asm/param.h>
5       #include <linux/types.h>
6
7       #ifndef STRUCT TIMESPEC
8      #define STRUCT TIMESPEC
9       struct timespec {
10              time t  tv_sec;              /* seconds */
11              long    tv_nsec;             /* nanoseconds */
12      };
13      #endif /* _STRUCT_TIMESPEC */
14
15      /*
16       * Change timeval to jiffies, trying to avoid the
17       * most obvious overflows..
18       *
19       * And some not so obvious.
20       *
21       * Note that we don't want to return MAX_LONG, because
22       * for various timeout reasons we often end up having
23       * to wait "jiffies+1" in order to guarantee that we wait
24       * at _least_ "jiffies" - so "jiffies+1" had better still
25       * be positive.
26       */
27      #define MAX JIFFY OFFSET ((~0UL >> 1)-1)
28
29      static __inline__ unsigned long
30      timespec to jiffies (struct timespec * value)
31      {
32              unsigned long sec = value->tv_sec;
33              long nsec = value->tv_nsec;
34
35              if (sec >= (MAX JIFFY OFFSET /  HZ))
36                      return MAX JIFFY OFFSET;
37              nsec += 1000000000L / HZ - 1;
38              nsec /= 1000000000L / HZ;
39              return HZ * sec + nsec;
40      }
41
42      static __inline__ void
43      jiffies to timespec (unsigned long  jiffies, struct timespec *value)
44      {
45              value->tv_nsec = (jiffies % HZ) * (1000000000L / HZ);
```

```
46                  value->tv_sec = jiffies / HZ;
47       }
48
49       struct timeval {
50               time t          tv_sec;         /* seconds */
51               suseconds t     tv_usec;        /* microseconds */
52       };
53
54       struct timezone {
55               int     tz_minuteswest; /* minutes west of Greenwich */
56               int     tz_dsttime;     /* type of dst correction */
57       };
58
59       #define NFDBITS                 NFDBITS
60
61       #ifdef KERNEL
62       extern void do gettimeofday (struct  timeval *tv);
63       extern void do settimeofday (struct timeval *tv);
64       extern void get fast time (struct timeval *tv);
65       extern void (*do get fast time)(struct  timeval *);
66       #endif
67
68       #define FD SETSIZE              FD SETSIZE
69       #define FD SET (fd,fdsetp)       FD SET (fd,fdsetp)
70       #define FD CLR (fd,fdsetp)       FD CLR (fd,fdsetp)
71       #define FD ISSET (fd,fdsetp)     FD ISSET (fd,fdsetp)
72       #define FD ZERO (fdsetp)         FD ZERO (fdsetp)
73
74       /*
75        * Names of the interval timers, and structure
77        */
78       #define ITIMER REAL     0
79       #define ITIMER VIRTUAL  1
80       #define ITIMER PROF     2
81
82       struct  itimerspec {
83               struct  timespec it_interval;   /* timer period */
84               struct  timespec it_value;      /* timer expiration */
85       };
86
87       struct  itimerval {
88               struct  timeval it_interval;    /* timer interval */
89               struct  timeval it_value;       /* current value */
90       };
91
92       #endif
93
```

Data Structures—linux/irq.h

```
1        #ifndef irq h
2        #define irq h
```

```
3
4      #include <asm/irq.h>
5      /*
6       * IRQ line status.
7       */
8      #define IRQ INPROGRESS  1        /* IRQ handler active - do not enter! */
9      #define IRQ DISABLED    2        /* IRQ disabled - do not enter! */
10     #define IRQ PENDING     4        /* IRQ pending - replay on enable */
11     #define IRQ REPLAY      8        /* IRQ has been replayed but not acked yet */
12     #define IRQ AUTODETECT  16       /* IRQ is being autodetected */
13     #define IRQ WAITING     32       /* IRQ not yet seen - for autodetection */
14
15     /*
16      * Interrupt controller descriptor. This is all we need
17      * to describe about the low-level hardware.
18      */
19     struct hw interrupt type {
20             const char * typename;
21             unsigned int (*startup)(unsigned int irq);
22             void (*shutdown)(unsigned int irq);
23             void (*enable)(unsigned int irq);
24             void (*disable)(unsigned int irq);
25             void (*ack)(unsigned int irq);
26             void (*end)(unsigned int irq);
27     };
28
29     typedef struct hw interrupt type  hw irq controller;
30
31     /*
32      * This is the "IRQ descriptor", which contains various information
33      * about the irq, including what kind of hardware handling it has,
34      * whether it is disabled etc etc.
35      *
36      * Pad this out to 32 bytes for cache and indexing reasons.
37      */
38     typedef struct {
39             unsigned int status;      /* IRQ status
40                                         - IRQ_INPROGRESS, IRQ_DISABLED */
41             hw irq controller *handler;    /* never derefed in arch
42                                              independent code */
43             struct irqaction *action;           /* IRQ action list */
44             unsigned int depth;                 /* Disable depth for nested irq
disables */
45     } cacheline aligned irq desc t;
46
47     #include <asm/hw irq.h> /* the arch dependent stuff */
48
49     extern irq desc t irq desc[NR IRQS];
50
51     extern int handle IRQ event (unsigned int, struct  pt regs *, struct irqaction
*);
52     extern spinlock t irq controller lock;
53     extern int setup irq (unsigned int , struct irqaction * );
```

```
54
55    extern hw irq controller no irq type;    /* needed in every arch ? */
56
57    #endif /* __asm_h */
58
59
```

The Linux Process Model

Up to now we have seen how the Linux kernel manages the hardware and the resources it has under its control. We are now about to embark on a detailed study of how the Linux kernel deals with user programs. The Linux kernel understands a user program to be everything that runs in a processor abstraction ring and has no direct access to processor registers and other vital hardware.

Processes

The most central concept in any operating system is the user process: an abstraction of a running program.[1]

As we saw earlier, Linux is a multitasking operating system and is therefore able to run several such user processes at once, even on a uniprocessor system. Every operating system with this capability needs a system to keep track of the various processes. The system makes sure that the processes get all the resources they need on time, but on a fair basis and without jeopardizing overall system stability. It also needs to do this efficiently, to reduce the impact of this managing activity to the lowest level possible. That model and its uses are the subject of this chapter.

The fundamental data structure within the kernel, controlling all processes, is the *process structure*, which grows and shrinks dynamically as processes are forked and finish or are killed. The process structure (called `task_struct` in the kernel source code) is around 1k in size. On a system with 1,300 processes, the `task_struct` table takes about 1,300 KB of real memory. You can get the exact size of the structure with the following simple C program:

```
#define __KERNEL__
#include <linux/sched.h>
main()
{
printf("sizeof(struct task_struct) -> %d\n", sizeof(struct task_struct));
}
```

On IA32 (i386) machines the process structure is exactly 960 bytes in size. The data structure of `task_struct` is reported at the end of this chapter for reference. Unlike other UNIX implementations, however,

---

1 Andrew S. Tanenbaum and Albert S. Woodhull, *Operating Systems*, 2nd edition, Prentice Hall, 47.

please note that this process structure does not occupy space in the real sense of the world. How is this possible?

Since the advent of Linux kernel 2.2.x, the `task_struct` is allocated at the bottom of the kernel stack. It is therefore possible to overlap the `task_struct` on the kernel stack because the `kernel_struct` is a per-task structure exactly as the `task_struct` is.

The kernel stack has a fixed size of 8,192 bytes (on the IA32). If the kernel recurses on the stack for only $8192 - 960 = 7232$ bytes, then the `task_struct` is overwritten and corrupted (and the kernel will crash soon).

Basically, what the kernel does is decrease the size of the "usable" kernel stack to around 7,232 bytes, by allocating the task structure in the bottom of the stack. It has to do this because 7Kbytes are more than enough for the kernel stack, the rest can be used for the `task_struct`.

There are a few advantages in doing so. The kernel reaches the kernel structure without any memory accesses, thus reducing the memory usage and avoiding an additional dynamic allocation at task creation time. The `task_struct` always starts on a PAGE_SIZE boundary, so the cache line is always aligned on most hardware on the market. Aligning on page boundaries (in Linux usually sized at 4KB) is important to avoid unnecessary page faults and a reduction in overall performance.

At any given moment, once Linux is in kernel mode, you can get the address of the `task_struct` with this very fast pseudo-code:

```
task_struct = (struct task_struct *) STACK_POINTER & 0xffffe000;
```

This is exactly how the above pseudo-code is implemented in C under Linux, in `linux/include/asm-i386/current.h`:

```
static inline struct task_struct * get_current(void)
{
struct task_struct *current;
__asm__("andl %%esp,%0; ":"=r" (current) : "0" (~8191UL));
return current;
}
```

For example, on a PentiumII, recalculating the `task_struct` from scratch starting from the stack pointer is much faster than passing the `task_struct` address through the stack across function calls, as is done in some other operating systems like Solaris 7. In other words, by checking only the value of the stack pointer (no memory accesses at all) the kernel can derive the address of the `task struct`. This is a big performance booster, and it shows once again that fine engineering is not only reserved to big-buck companies.

The kernel stack is set by the CPU automatically when entering kernel mode (the CPU loads the kernel stack pointer address from the CPU task segment state that is set at fork time). This is the layout of the x86 kernel stack:

```
----- 0xXXXX0000 (bottom of the stack and address of the task_struct)
TASK_STRUCT
----- 0xXXXX03C0 (last byte usable from the kernel as real kernel stack)
KERNEL_STACK
----- 0xXXXX2000 (top of the stack, first byte used as kernel stack)
```

Note also that in i386 Linux 2.4 the size of the task_struct is exactly 960 bytes. This is subject to change across kernel revisions, because every variable removed from or inserted in the task structure will change its size. And in turn, the high limit of the kernel stack will change with the size of the task_struct.

The memory for the process data structure is, as we said before, allocated dynamically during execution of the Linux kernel. More precisely the kernel doesn't allocate the task_struct at all, but only allocates the two-pages-wide kernel stack; the kernel uses a part of the kernel stack for the task_struct.

In the following diagram (Figure 4.1) you can see how the task_struct manages tasks.

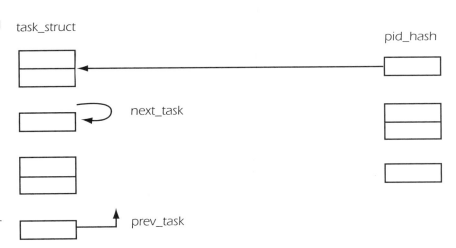

Figure 4.1
Tasks are managed through a doubly linked circular list, with pointer to the previous task and the next task. The pid_hash structure has each allocated entry point to a certain task, or more, if they are of the same process.

In many UNIX machines there is a max processes parameter for the kernel. In commercial OSs like Solaris, it is a self-tuned parameter that adjusts itself according to the amount of RAM found at boot time. (In

Solaris you can, however, still adjust this parameter in `/etc/system`.) In Linux 2.4 the max processes parameter is a run-time tunable parameter, as well. In 2.2.x, it's a compile-time tunable parameter.

In 2.2.x, to change the maximum number of tasks, the system administrator needed to change the `NR_TASKS` preprocessor definition in `Linux/include/linux/tasks.h`:

```
#define NR_TASKS 512 /* On x86 Max 4092, or 4090 w/APM configured. */
```

In 2.4, instead, it is a tunable parameter set as default to:

```
size-of-memory-in-the-system / kernel-stack-size / 2
```

Supposing you have 512MB of RAM, the default high limit of available process will be:

```
512×1024×1024 / 8192 / 2 -> 32768
```

Now, 32,768 processes might sound like a lot, but for an enterprise-wide Linux server with a database and many connections to it from a LAN or from the Internet, it is a very reasonable number. Here again, the system administrator must tune this parameter according to his requirements.

In 2.4, it also possible to increase the maximum number of tasks via a `sysctl` system call at runtime. If the administrator wants to increase the number of concurrent tasks to 40,000, he will only have to enter (as root):

```
echo 40000 > /proc/sys/kernel/threads-max
```

Forking

In the beginning there was a freshly loaded kernel and it was good. But a kernel alone is good for nothing if user programs can't run. That is why, upon boot, the kernel loads `init` as the first user program. From then on, `init` is the mother of all user programs. In UNIX parlance the parent of a process is actually called a *father*, not a mother. So, `init` is the father of all user programs. `Init` is called during boot with the following code from `linux/init/main.c`:

```
        static int init(void * unused)
{
    lock_kernel();
    do_basic_setup();

    /*
     * Ok, we have completed the initial bootup, and
     * we're essentially up and running. Get rid of the
     * initmem segments and start the user-mode stuff..
     */
    free_initmem();
    unlock_kernel();

    if (open("/dev/console", O_RDWR, 0) < 0)
        printk("Warning: unable to open an initial console.\n");

    (void) dup(0);
    (void) dup(0);

    /*
     * We try each of these until one succeeds.
     *
     * The Bourne shell can be used instead of init if we are
     * trying to recover a really broken machine.
     */

    if (execute_command)
        execve(execute_command,argv_init,envp_init);
    execve("/sbin/init",argv_init,envp_init);
    execve("/etc/init",argv_init,envp_init);
    execve("/bin/init",argv_init,envp_init);
    execve("/bin/sh",argv_init,envp_init);
    panic("No init found.  Try passing init= option to kernel.");
}
```

Here, init is entered as a kernel task and goes to create a user space process called, unsurprisingly, init. The init function is declared *unused* because it is not passed any arguments; it just reads the code for the user space program from disk and launches it.

Init is always assigned the process ID (PID) number 1. Why not 0, as counting is usually done in the computer industry? Because 0 is already taken by the idle process that is created at boot time.

In the above code, you can also see from where the console message indicating that some memory has been freed during boot comes: free_initmem. This function releases the no longer needed function in the .text.init section of the kernel. This is a typical message generated on a 512MB RAM system (here named hatta) at boot:

```
Mar 19 09:14:35 hatta kernel: Freeing unused kernel memory: 72k freed
```

Init, the father, creates children by forking them. As such, init is androgynous, being able to procreate by itself, without help of a female counterpart. Seriously though, user programs are created either from init or from a child process of init. The system call to create a child process is called fork, although in Linux there is a second way to create child processes, __clone(). The double underscore prefixing the name of the system call is there to show that it should usually be called from library functions that wrap it in more user-friendly clothing.

Forking is a means for a father process to duplicate itself into an exact copy, except for the PID. The fork() function at one point must add the newly created task to the task_struct. The kernel function used to add and remove tasks is add_to_runqueue and del_from_ runqueue. You can find it in linux/kernel/sched.c:

```
static inline void add_to_runqueue(struct task_struct * p)
{
    list_add(&p->run_list, &runqueue_head);
    nr_running++;
}
```

From the point when the new task comes to life it is totally independent.

As we saw earlier, Linux also introduced another means to create user processes, __clone. Unlike fork(), __clone allows the child process to share parts of its execution context with its parent process, such as the memory space, the table of file descriptors, and the table of signal handlers. The main use of __clone is to implement *threads*. These are multiple threads of control in a program, which run concurrently in a shared memory space. Be careful when using __clone, because it is a Linux-specific feature and thus not portable to other operating systems; fork(), is a standard function and exists on many platforms, including Windows.

Let's see how the all-important PIDs are assigned in the kernel. The actual function is get_pid() in, obviously, fork.c in linux/kernel/:

```
static int get_pid(unsigned long flags)
{
    static int next_safe = PID_MAX;
    struct task_struct *p;

    if (flags & CLONE_PID)
        return current->pid;

    spin_lock(&lastpid_lock);
```

```
    if((++last_pid) & 0xffff8000) {
        last_pid = 300;                 /* Skip daemons etc. */
        goto inside;
    }
    if(last_pid >= next_safe) {
inside:
        next_safe = PID_MAX;
        read_lock(&tasklist_lock);
repeat:
        for_each_task(p) {
            if(p->pid == last_pid   ||
               p->pgrp == last_pid  ||
               p->session == last_pid) {
                if(++last_pid >= next_safe) {
                    if(last_pid & 0xffff8000)
                            last_pid = 300;
                    next_safe = PID_MAX;
                }
                goto repeat;
            }
            if(p->pid > last_pid && next_safe > p->pid)
                next_safe = p->pid;
            if(p->pgrp > last_pid && next_safe > p->pgrp)
                next_safe = p->pgrp;
            if(p->session > last_pid && next_safe > p->session)
                next_safe = p->session;
        }
        read_unlock(&tasklist_lock);
    }
    spin_unlock(&lastpid_lock);

    return last_pid;
}
```

The code here may strike you as very difficult to understand. because the developer tried to make the code (and therefore overall process creation) as fast as possible.

If speed is of concern, why didn't the programmer just use the index number of the process in the task structure? Because many user space programmers still assume that the same PID will not occur soon after a process used it. They believe the PIDs rotate in the numbering space for PIDs. Although nobody ever made this guarantee, the kernel has to be compatible with these poorly designed programs. The function does keep a pointer to the next probable or safe PID, here called next_safe. Every time a process is created, and therefore the last_pid field is incremented beyond the next_safe PID, the above function must traverse the whole task list to search for another PID candidate.

Two tasks might share the same PID if they are threads within the same process. In that case the following code section:

```
if (flags & CLONE_PID)
            return current->pid;
```

returns the same PID immediately.

Once the `last_pid` has wrapped around the numbering space for PID (32,767), the code above starts looking for new PIDs. It will, however, jump to the next number after 300, because most numbers below 300 are usually taken by system daemons and programs started at boot and continuing run for the full life of the system. Those PIDs are hardly ever returned to the free list. To gain a few precious ticks, the kernel just skips them.

On a system configured for a maximum number of tasks beyond 32,767, it might theoretically occur that no PID slots are available. The task creation would therefore fail with a negative return code.

Obviously, the programmer does not always want to launch a copy of the original program, but rather wants to launch a totally different program at some point during program execution. For these cases, she must use `exec()`.

The only way for a user program to pass execution to another program is to

1. Fork to another instance of itself using `fork()`.
2. Then load another binary program image and pass execution to it using `exec()`.

The kernel to implement the `exec()` call is in `linux/fs/exec.c`. The program is too long to be included here (almost a thousand lines in 2.3.52). Here is what it does upon being called:

1. The code for `prepare_binprm` locates the file with the binary image and reads the first 128 bytes into the `buf` variable of `brpm` structure. (See the data structure at the end of this chapter.)

```
int prepare_binprm(struct linux_binprm *bprm)
{
    int mode;
    int retval,id_change,cap_raised;
    struct inode * inode = bprm->dentry->d_inode;

    mode = inode->i_mode;
    if (!S_ISREG(mode))             /* must be regular file */
        return -EACCES;
    if (!(mode & 0111))             /* with at least _one_ execute bit set */
        return -EACCES;
    if (IS_NOEXEC(inode))           /* FS mustn't be mounted noexec */
```

```
        return -EACCES;
if (!inode->i_sb)
        return -EACCES;
if ((retval = permission(inode, MAY_EXEC)) != 0)
        return retval;
/* better not execute files which are being written to */
if (atomic_read(&inode->i_writecount) > 0)
        return -ETXTBSY;

bprm->e_uid = current->euid;
bprm->e_gid = current->egid;
id_change = cap_raised = 0;

/* Set-uid? */
if (mode & S_ISUID) {
        bprm->e_uid = inode->i_uid;
        if (bprm->e_uid != current->euid)
            id_change = 1;
}

/* Set-gid? */
/*
 * If setgid is set but no group execute bit then this
 * is a candidate for mandatory locking, not a setgid
 * executable.
 */
if ((mode & (S_ISGID | S_IXGRP)) == (S_ISGID | S_IXGRP)) {
        bprm->e_gid = inode->i_gid;
        if (!in_group_p(bprm->e_gid))
            id_change = 1;
}

/* We don't have VFS support for capabilities yet */
cap_clear(bprm->cap_inheritable);
cap_clear(bprm->cap_permitted);
cap_clear(bprm->cap_effective);

/*  To support inheritance of root-permissions and suid-root
 *  executables under compatibility mode, we raise the
 *  effective and inherited bitmasks of the executable file
 *  (translation: we set the executable "capability dumb" and
 *  set the allowed set to maximum). We don't set any forced
 *  bits.
 *
 *  If only the real uid is 0, we only raise the inheritable
 *  bitmask of the executable file (translation: we set the
 *  allowed set to maximum and the application to "capability
 *  smart").
 */

if (!issecure(SECURE_NOROOT)) {
        if (bprm->e_uid == 0 || current->uid == 0)
            cap_set_full(bprm->cap_inheritable);
        if (bprm->e_uid == 0)
```

```
                    cap_set_full(bprm->cap_effective);
        }

        /* Only if pP' is _not_ a subset of pP, do we consider there
         * has been a capability related "change of capability".  In
         * such cases, we need to check that the elevation of
         * privilege does not go against other system constraints.
         * The new Permitted set is defined below -- see (***). */
        {
            kernel_cap_t working =
                cap_combine(bprm->cap_permitted,
                        cap_intersect(bprm->cap_inheritable,
                                current->cap_inheritable));
            if (!cap_issubset(working, current->cap_permitted)) {
                cap_raised = 1;
            }
        }
    }

    if (id_change || cap_raised) {
        /* We can't suid-execute if we're sharing parts of the executable */
        /* or if we're being traced (or if suid execs are not allowed)     */
        /* (current->mm->mm_users > 1 is ok, as we'll get a new mm anyway)   */
        if (IS_NOSUID(inode)
            || must_not_trace_exec(current)
            || (atomic_read(&current->fs->count) > 1)
            || (atomic_read(&current->sig->count) > 1)
            || (atomic_read(&current->files->count) > 1)) {
            if (id_change && !capable(CAP_SETUID))
                return -EPERM;
            if (cap_raised && !capable(CAP_SETPCAP))
                return -EPERM;
        }
    }

    memset(bprm->buf,0,sizeof(bprm->buf));
    return read_exec(bprm->dentry,0,bprm->buf,128,1);
}
```

2. Set up the arguments to be passed to the newly called program and its argument (`argc`, `argv`, `envp`).

3. Select the appropriate binary handler according to the binary file's magic number. As we saw in earlier chapters, Linux is able to execute a variety of binary formats, including a.out, ELF, Java, iBCS, and EM86. The function `search_binary_handler` recognizes the binary image according to the magic number contained in the header information.

Here is the function `search_binary_handler` from `fs/exec.c`:

```
int search_binary_handler(struct linux_binprm *bprm,struct pt_regs *regs)
{
    int try,retval=0;
    struct linux_binfmt *fmt;
#ifdef __alpha__
```

```
    /* handle /sbin/loader.. */
    {
        struct exec * eh = (struct exec *) bprm->buf;
        struct linux_binprm bprm_loader;

        if (!bprm->loader && eh->fh.f_magic == 0x183 &&
         (eh->fh.f_flags & 0x3000) == 0x3000)
        {
         int i;
         char * dynloader[] = { "/sbin/loader" };
         struct dentry * dentry;

         lock_kernel();
         dput(bprm->dentry);
         unlock_kernel();
         bprm->dentry = NULL;

            bprm_loader.p = PAGE_SIZE*MAX_ARG_PAGES-sizeof(void *);
            for (i = 0 ; i < MAX_ARG_PAGES ; i++)          /* clear page-table */
                    bprm_loader.page[i] = NULL;

         lock_kernel();
         dentry = open_namei(dynloader[0], 0, 0);
         unlock_kernel();
         retval = PTR_ERR(dentry);
         if (IS_ERR(dentry))
             return retval;
         bprm->dentry = dentry;
         bprm->loader = bprm_loader.p;
         retval = prepare_binprm(bprm);
         if (retval<0)
             return retval;
         /* should call search_binary_handler recursively here,
            but it does not matter */
        }
    }
#endif
    for (try=0; try<2; try++) {
        for (fmt = formats ; fmt ; fmt = fmt->next) {
            int (*fn)(struct linux_binprm *, struct pt_regs *) = fmt->load_binary;
            if (!fn)
                continue;
            retval = fn(bprm, regs);
            if (retval >= 0) {
                if (bprm->dentry) {
                    lock_kernel();
                    dput(bprm->dentry);
                    unlock_kernel();
                }
                bprm->dentry = NULL;
                current->did_exec = 1;
                return retval;
            }
            if (retval != -ENOEXEC)
```

```
                        break;
            if (!bprm->dentry) /* We don't have the dentry anymore */
                        return retval;
        }
        if (retval != -ENOEXEC) {
            break;
#ifdef CONFIG_KMOD
        }else{
#define printable(c) (((c)=='\t') || ((c)=='\n') || (0x20<=(c) && (c)<=0x7e))
            char modname[20];
            if (printable(bprm->buf[0]) &&
                printable(bprm->buf[1]) &&
                printable(bprm->buf[2]) &&
                printable(bprm->buf[3]))
                break; /* -ENOEXEC */
            sprintf(modname, "binfmt-%04x", *(unsigned short *)(&bprm->buf[2]));
            request_module(modname);
#endif
        }
    }
    return retval;
}
```

4. Finally, control is passed over the binary image read in from the file.

Obviously, the `fork()`, `__clone()`, and `exec()` kernel functions have serious implications for the virtual memory manager. The VM has to set up the virtual address space for the new program. It does so by creating an exact copy of each VM page each time it is referenced. On reference, the addressing hardware generates a page fault (because it is a nonexistent VM address) and calls the VM code. The VM recognizes the situation and copy-creates the new page. We shall, however, have a much closer look at VM workings in the chapter on the Linux VM manager.

Threads

In the last 10 years or so, there has been a general move from heavyweight processes to a threaded model. The reason is clear: the creation and maintenance of a full process with its own address space takes up a lot of time (in terms of milliseconds). Threads, instead, run within the same address space as the father process and therefore require much less time in creation. With the enormous importance of Web servers and the e-commerce wave, having efficient and responsive task creation and shutdown is a primary concern. In fact, for some time now, Web server developers have tried to include all programming functionality within a single address space. Apache, for instance, includes a Perl module to enable Web developers to execute Perl code without exiting the address space.

What's the difference between process and thread under Linux? And, more important, what is the difference from a scheduler's point of view? In short: nothing.

The only worthwhile difference between a thread and a process is that the threads share completely the same address space. All the threads run in the same address space so a context switch is basically just a jump from one location of code to another location of code.

The simple check to avoid the translation look-aside buffer (TLB)— the mechanism within the CPU that translates virtual memory addresses to real RAM addresses—flush and the memory manager context switch is found in linux/arch/i386/kernel/process.c:

```
/* Re-load page tables */
{
unsigned long new_cr3 = next->tss.cr3;
if (new_cr3 != prev->tss.cr3)
asm volatile("movl %0,%%cr3": :"r" (new_cr3));
}
```

The above check is in the core of the Linux kernel context switch. It checks if the address of the page-directory of the current process and the one of the to-be-scheduled-process are the same. If they are, it means they are sharing the same address space (or in other words, they are two threads) and the kernel avoids writing to the %%cr3 register, so that the userspace page tables won't be invalidated. This happens because the cr3 register just contains the data to which the kernel would write (and writing to it would mean invalidating the TLB). With the above two-line check Linux defines a difference between a kernel process switch and a kernel thread switch. This is the *only* noteworthy difference.

Because there is no difference at all between threads and processes, the Linux scheduler is written in very clean code. Only a few places related to signal handling make differences between threads and processes. This is very much contrary to, say, Solaris where the process is greatly disadvantaged compared to the thread and lightweight processes. The code below finds a measurement on a Solaris server, an Ultra 2 desktop 167-MHz processor, running Solaris 2.6:

```
orion> ftime
Completed 100 forks
Avg. Fork Time: 1.137 milliseconds
```

```
orion> ttime
Completed 100 Thread Creates
Avg. Thread Time: 0.017 milliseconds
```

In the above example, `ftime` is executing 100 forks and measuring the time elapsed. As you can see, the average fork took 1.137 milliseconds, while the average thread created (ttime code) took .017 milliseconds (17 microseconds). In this example, thread creation was about 67 times faster. Also, my test case for threads does not include flags in the thread create call to tell the kernel to create a new lightweight process (LWP) with the thread and bind the thread to the LWP. This would have added additional weight to the call, bringing it closer to the fork time.

Even if LWP creation closes the gap in creation times between processes (forks) and threads, user threads still offer advantages in resource utilization and scheduling—as we will see shortly.

Of course the Linux SMP (and even the uniprocessor variant) scheduler is clever enough to optimize the scheduling of the threads on the same CPU. This happens because by rescheduling a thread, there won't be any TLB flush and basically no context switch at all. Said differently, the virtual memory addressing won't change. A thread switch is very lightweight compared to a process switch and the scheduler is aware of that. The only things that Linux does while switching between two threads (not in strict order) are:

- Enter `schedule()`.
- Restore all the registers of the new thread (stack pointer and FP included).
- Update the TSS with the data of the new thread.
- Jump to the old EIP of the new thread.

The TLB is not touched, and the address space and all the page tables remain the same. And the big advantage is that Linux does it all very fast. Other UNIX systems are bloated by SMP locks, and so the kernel loses time getting to the task switch point. For this reason the Solaris kernel threads are slower than the userspace kernel threads. Of course, the kernel-based threads scale the load across multiple CPUs, but operating systems like Solaris pay a big fixed cost on systems with few CPUs for the benefit of scaling well with lots of CPUs.

Basically, there is no technical reason why Solaris kernel threads should be lighter than Linux kernel threads, because Linux is just doing the minimum possible operations in the context switch path (and it's doing them quickly).

The 2.4 Threaded Kernel

Linux kernel threading is constantly improving. Let's look at the different versions again:

2.0.x	No kernel threading
2.2.x	Yes
2.3.x very	SMP threaded

In 2.2.x many places are still single threaded but 2.2.x kernels scale very well on two-way SMPs. In 2.2.x, IRQ and timer handling, for example, is completely SMP threaded and the IRQ load is distributed across multiple CPUs.

In 2.4, most worthwhile code sections within the kernel are rewritten for SMP threading. In 2.4, all the virtual memory (VM) is SMP threaded, for example. The most interesting paths have a much finer granularity and are scaled very well in 2.4.

Performance Limitations

For the sake of the system's stability, a kernel has to react well in stress situations. It must, for instance, reduce priorities and resources to process that misbehave. How does the scheduler handle a (stupid) program looping tightly and forking at each turn of the loop—therefore forking off thousands of processes in a few seconds?

Obviously, the scheduler can't limit the creation of processes time-wise—say, a process every 0.5 seconds or something—because time has a very funny meaning from the CPU point of view. Thus, at one point, 0.5 seconds would be enough to accommodate the wild forking of a program, while at another point it would endanger the stability of the system.

In the 2.4 kernel, however, after a fork, the runtime priority of the process is divided between the parent and the child. This means that the parent or child will be penalized compared to the other tasks, and the other tasks will continue to run well up to the first recalculation of priorities. This enables the system not to stall during a fork flooding. This is the relevant code section in `linux/kernel/fork.c`:

```
/*
 * "share" dynamic priority between parent and child, thus the
 * total amount of dynamic priorities in the system doesnt change,
 * more scheduling fairness. This is only important in the first
 * timeslice, on the long run the scheduling behaviour is unchanged.
 */
current->counter >>= 1;
p->counter = current->counter;
```

Additionally, there is a per-user limit of threads that can be set from `init` before spawning the first user process. It can be set with `ulimit -u` on bash. You can tell it that user `moshe` can run at max 10 concurrent tasks (obviously the shell and every process must stay within these 10 tasks). In Linux the `root` user always has some spare tasks to herself. So if a user spawns tasks in loop, the administrator can just login and `killall` all the tasks of the offending user.

Because the *runtime priority* (`current->counter` in the source code) of the task is divided between the parent and the child, the kernel reacts smoothly enough to handle these situations.

If you wanted to amend the kernel to allow only one `fork()` per processor tick (a jiffy—usually one every 1/100 seconds, but this parameter, too, is tunable), you would have to patch the kernel in `linux/kernel/fork.c` like this:

```
--- 2.3.52/kernel/fork.c
+++ /tmp/fork.c     Tue Nov  9 01:34:36 1999
@@ -591,6 +591,14 @@
    int retval = -ENOMEM;
    struct task_struct *p;
    DECLARE_MUTEX_LOCKED(sem);
+   static long last_fork;
+
+   while (time_after(last_fork+1, jiffies))
+   {
+       __set_current_state(TASK_INTERRUPTIBLE);
+       schedule_timeout(1);
+   }
+   last_fork = jiffies;

    if (clone_flags & CLONE_PID) {
        /* This is only allowed from the boot up thread */
```

This is the beauty of OpenSource. If you don't like something, just change it!

Data Structures—linux/sched.h

```
ifndef _LINUX_SCHED_H
2 #define _LINUX_SCHED_H
3
4 #include <asm/param.h>  /* for HZ */
5
6 extern unsigned long event;
7
8 #include <linux/binfmts.h>
9 #include <linux/personality.h>
10 #include <linux/threads.h>
11 #include <linux/kernel.h>
12 #include <linux/types.h>
13 #include <linux/times.h>
14 #include <linux/timex.h>
15
16 #include <asm/system.h>
17 #include <asm/semaphore.h>
18 #include <asm/page.h>
19 #include <asm/ptrace.h>
20
21 #include <linux/smp.h>
22 #include <linux/tty.h>
23 #include <linux/sem.h>
24 #include <linux/signal.h>
25 #include <linux/securebits.h>
26
27 /*
28  * cloning flags:
29  */
30 #define CSIGNAL         0x000000ff  /* signal mask to be sent at exit */
31 #define CLONE_VM        0x00000100  /* set if VM shared between processes */
32 #define CLONE_FS        0x00000200  /* set if fs info shared between processes */
33 #define CLONE_FILES     0x00000400  /* set if open files shared between processes
                                           */
34 #define CLONE_SIGHAND   0x00000800  /* set if signal handlers shared */
35 #define CLONE_PID       0x00001000  /* set if pid shared */
36 #define CLONE_PTRACE    0x00002000  /* set if we want to let tracing continue on
                                           the child too */
37 #define CLONE_VFORK     0x00004000  /* set if the parent wants the child to wake
                                           it up on mm_release */
38 #define CLONE_PARENT    0x00008000  /* set if we want to have the same parent as
                                           the cloner */
39
40 /*
41  * These are the constant used to fake the fixed-point load-average
42  * counting. Some notes:
43  *  - 11 bit fractions expand to 22 bits by the multiplies: this gives
44  *    a load-average precision of 10 bits integer + 11 bits fractional
45  *  - if you want to count load-averages more often, you need more
46  *    precision, or rounding will get you. With 2-second counting freq,
47  *    the EXP_n values would be 1981, 2034 and 2043 if still using only
```

```
48   *      11 bit fractions.
49   */
50 extern unsigned long avenrun[];          /* Load averages */
51
52 #define FSHIFT          11               /* nr of bits of precision */
53 #define FIXED_1         (1<<FSHIFT)       /* 1.0 as fixed-point */
54 #define LOAD_FREQ       (5*HZ)            /* 5 sec intervals */
55 #define EXP_1           1884             /* 1/exp(5sec/1min) as fixed-point */
56 #define EXP_5           2014             /* 1/exp(5sec/5min) */
57 #define EXP_15          2037             /* 1/exp(5sec/15min) */
58
59 #define CALC_LOAD(load,exp,n) \
60         load *= exp; \
61         load += n*(FIXED_1-exp); \
62         load >>= FSHIFT;
63
64 #define CT_TO_SECS(x)   ((x) / HZ)
65 #define CT_TO_USECS(x)  (((x) % HZ) * 1000000/HZ)
66
67 extern int nr_running, nr_threads;
68 extern int last_pid;
69
70 #include <linux/fs.h>
71 #include <linux/time.h>
72 #include <linux/param.h>
73 #include <linux/resource.h>
74 #include <linux/timer.h>
75
76 #include <asm/processor.h>
77
78 #define TASK_RUNNING            0
79 #define TASK_INTERRUPTIBLE      1
80 #define TASK_UNINTERRUPTIBLE    2
81 #define TASK_ZOMBIE             4
82 #define TASK_STOPPED            8
83 #define TASK_EXCLUSIVE          32
84
85 #define __set_task_state(tsk, state_value)               \
86         do { (tsk)->state = (state_value); } while (0)
87 #ifdef __SMP__
88 #define set_task_state(tsk, state_value)                 \
89         set_mb((tsk)->state, (state_value))
90 #else
91 #define set_task_state(tsk, state_value)                 \
92         __set_task_state((tsk), (state_value))
93 #endif
94
95 #define __set_current_state(state_value)                      \
96         do { current->state = (state_value); } while (0)
97 #ifdef __SMP__
98 #define set_current_state(state_value)          \
99         set_mb(current->state, (state_value))
100 #else
101 #define set_current_state(state_value)              \
```

```
102              __set_current_state(state_value)
103 #endif
104
105 /*
106  * Scheduling policies
107  */
108 #define SCHED_OTHER              0
109 #define SCHED_FIFO               1
110 #define SCHED_RR                 2
111
112 /*
113  * This is an additional bit set when we want to
114  * yield the CPU for one re-schedule.
115  */
116 #define SCHED_YIELD              0x10
117
118 struct sched_param {
119         int sched_priority;
120 };
121
122 #ifdef __KERNEL__
123
124 #include <linux/spinlock.h>
125
126 /*
127  * This serializes "schedule()" and also protects
128  * the run-queue from deletions/modifications (but
129  * _adding_ to the beginning of the run-queue has
130  * a separate lock).
131  */
132 extern rwlock_t tasklist_lock;
133 extern spinlock_t runqueue_lock;
134
135 extern void sched_init(void);
136 extern void init_idle(void);
137 extern void show_state(void);
138 extern void cpu_init (void);
139 extern void trap_init(void);
140 extern void update_one_process( struct task_struct *p,
141         unsigned long ticks, unsigned long user, unsigned long system, int cpu);
142
143 #define MAX_SCHEDULE_TIMEOUT     LONG_MAX
144 extern signed long FASTCALL(schedule_timeout(signed long timeout));
145 asmlinkage void schedule(void);
146
147 /*
148  * The default fd array needs to be at least BITS_PER_LONG,
149  * as this is the granularity returned by copy_fdset().
150  */
151 #define NR_OPEN_DEFAULT BITS_PER_LONG
152
153 /*
154  * Open file table structure
155  */
```

```
156 struct files_struct {
157         atomic_t count;
158         rwlock_t file_lock;
159         int max_fds;
160         int max_fdset;
161         int next_fd;
162         struct file ** fd;          /* current fd array */
163         fd_set *close_on_exec;
164         fd_set *open_fds;
165         fd_set close_on_exec_init;
166         fd_set open_fds_init;
167         struct file * fd_array[NR_OPEN_DEFAULT];
168 };
169
170 #define INIT_FILES { \
171         ATOMIC_INIT(1), \
172         RW_LOCK_UNLOCKED, \
173         NR_OPEN_DEFAULT, \
174         __FD_SETSIZE, \
175         0, \
176         &init_files.fd_array[0], \
177         &init_files.close_on_exec_init, \
178         &init_files.open_fds_init, \
179         { { 0, } }, \
180         { { 0, } }, \
181         { NULL, } \
182 }
183
184 struct fs_struct {
185         atomic_t count;
186         int umask;
187         struct dentry * root, * pwd;
188 };
189
190 #define INIT_FS { \
191         ATOMIC_INIT(1), \
192         0022, \
193         NULL, NULL \
194 }
195
196 /* Maximum number of active map areas.. This is a random (large) number */
197 #define MAX_MAP_COUNT    (65536)
198
199 /* Number of map areas at which the AVL tree is activated. This is arbitrary. */
200 #define AVL_MIN_MAP_COUNT       32
201
202 struct mm_struct {
203         struct vm_area_struct * mmap;        /* list of VMAs */
204         struct vm_area_struct * mmap_avl;    /* tree of VMAs */
205         struct vm_area_struct * mmap_cache;  /* last find_vma result */
206         pgd_t * pgd;
207         atomic_t mm_users;                   /* How many users with user
                                                    space? */
```

```
208            atomic_t mm_count;                           /* How many references to
                                                               "struct mm_struct" (users
                                                               count as 1) */
209            int map_count;                              /* number of VMAs */
210            struct semaphore mmap_sem;
211            spinlock_t page_table_lock;
212            unsigned long context;
213            unsigned long start_code, end_code, start_data, end_data;
214            unsigned long start_brk, brk, start_stack;
215            unsigned long arg_start, arg_end, env_start, env_end;
216            unsigned long rss, total_vm, locked_vm;
217            unsigned long def_flags;
218            unsigned long cpu_vm_mask;
219            unsigned long swap_cnt; /* number of pages to swap on next pass */
220            unsigned long swap_address;
221            /*
222             * This is an architecture-specific pointer: the portable
223             * part of Linux does not know about any segments.
224             */
225            void * segments;
226 };
227
228 #define INIT_MM(name) {                                      \
229                &init_mmap, NULL, NULL,                       \
230                swapper_pg_dir,                               \
231                ATOMIC_INIT(2), ATOMIC_INIT(1), 1,            \
232                __MUTEX_INITIALIZER(name.mmap_sem),           \
233                SPIN_LOCK_UNLOCKED,                           \
234                0,                                            \
235                0, 0, 0, 0,                                   \
236                0, 0, 0,                                      \
237                0, 0, 0, 0,                                   \
238                0, 0, 0,                                      \
239                0, 0, 0, 0, NULL }
240
241 struct signal_struct {
242        atomic_t                count;
243        struct k_sigaction      action[_NSIG];
244        spinlock_t              siglock;
245 };
246
247
248 #define INIT_SIGNALS { \
249                ATOMIC_INIT(1), \
250                { {{0,}}, }, \
251                SPIN_LOCK_UNLOCKED }
252
253 /*
254  * Some day this will be a full-fledged user tracking system.
255  * Right now it is only used to track how many processes a
256  * user has, but it has the potential to track memory usage etc.
257  */
258 struct user_struct;
259
```

```
260 struct task_struct {
261 /* these are hardcoded - don't touch */
262         volatile long state;    /* -1 unrunnable, 0 runnable, >0 stopped */
263         unsigned long flags;    /* per process flags, defined below */
264         int sigpending;
265         mm_segment_t addr_limit;       /* thread address space:
266                                          0-0xBFFFFFFF for user-thead
267                                          0-0xFFFFFFFF for kernel-thread
268                                       */
269         struct exec_domain *exec_domain;
270         volatile long need_resched;
271
272         cycles_t avg_slice;
273         int lock_depth;           /* Lock depth. We can context switch in and out
                                         of holding a syscall kernel lock... */
274 /* begin intel cache line */
275         long counter;
276         long priority;
277         unsigned long policy;
278 /* memory management info */
279         struct mm_struct *mm, *active_mm;
280         int has_cpu;
281         int processor;
282         struct list_head run_list;
283         struct task_struct *next_task, *prev_task;
284         int last_processor;
285
286 /* task state */
287         struct linux_binfmt *binfmt;
288         int exit_code, exit_signal;
289         int pdeath_signal;  /*  The signal sent when the parent dies  */
290         /* ??? */
291         unsigned long personality;
292         int dumpable:1;
293         int did_exec:1;
294         pid_t pid;
295         pid_t pgrp;
296         pid_t tty_old_pgrp;
297         pid_t session;
298         /* boolean value for session group leader */
299         int leader;
300         /*
301          * pointers to (original) parent process, youngest child, younger sibling,
302          * older sibling, respectively.  (p->father can be replaced with
303          * p->p_pptr->pid)
304          */
305         struct task_struct *p_opptr, *p_pptr, *p_cptr, *p_ysptr, *p_osptr;
306
307         /* PID hash table linkage. */
308         struct task_struct *pidhash_next;
309         struct task_struct **pidhash_pprev;
310
311         wait_queue_head_t wait_chldexit;         /* for wait4() */
312         struct semaphore *vfork_sem;             /* for vfork() */
```

```
313           unsigned long rt_priority;
314           unsigned long it_real_value, it_prof_value, it_virt_value;
315           unsigned long it_real_incr, it_prof_incr, it_virt_incr;
316           struct timer_list real_timer;
317           struct tms times;
318           unsigned long start_time;
319           long per_cpu_utime[NR_CPUS], per_cpu_stime[NR_CPUS];
320 /* mm fault and swap info: this can arguably be seen as either mm-specific or
       thread-specific */
321           unsigned long min_flt, maj_flt, nswap, cmin_flt, cmaj_flt, cnswap;
322           int swappable:1;
323 /* process credentials */
324           uid_t uid,euid,suid,fsuid;
325           gid_t gid,egid,sgid,fsgid;
326           int ngroups;
327           gid_t   groups[NGROUPS];
328           kernel_cap_t   cap_effective, cap_inheritable, cap_permitted;
329           struct user_struct *user;
330 /* limits */
331           struct rlimit rlim[RLIM_NLIMITS];
332           unsigned short used_math;
333           char comm[16];
334 /* file system info */
335           int link_count;
336           struct tty_struct *tty; /* NULL if no tty */
337 /* ipc stuff */
338           struct sem_undo *semundo;
339           struct sem_queue *semsleeping;
340 /* CPU-specific state of this task */
341           struct thread_struct thread;
342 /* filesystem information */
343           struct fs_struct *fs;
344 /* open file information */
345           struct files_struct *files;
346 /* signal handlers */
347           spinlock_t sigmask_lock;          /* Protects signal and blocked */
348           struct signal_struct *sig;
349           sigset_t signal, blocked;
350           struct signal_queue *sigqueue, **sigqueue_tail;
351           unsigned long sas_ss_sp;
352           size_t sas_ss_size;
353
354 /* Thread group tracking */
355           u32 parent_exec_id;
356           u32 self_exec_id;
357 /* Protection of fields allocatio/deallocation */
358           struct semaphore exit_sem;
359 };
360
361 /*
362  * Per process flags
363  */
364 #define PF_ALIGNWARN    0x00000001        /* Print alignment warning msgs */
365                                          /* Not implemented yet, only for 486*/
```

```
366 #define PF_STARTING        0x00000002      /* being created */
367 #define PF_EXITING         0x00000004      /* getting shut down */
368 #define PF_PTRACED         0x00000010      /* set if ptrace (0) has been called */
369 #define PF_TRACESYS        0x00000020      /* tracing system calls */
370 #define PF_FORKNOEXEC      0x00000040      /* forked but didn't exec */
371 #define PF_SUPERPRIV       0x00000100      /* used super-user privileges */
372 #define PF_DUMPCORE        0x00000200      /* dumped core */
373 #define PF_SIGNALED        0x00000400      /* killed by a signal */
374 #define PF_MEMALLOC        0x00000800      /* Allocating memory */
375 #define PF_VFORK           0x00001000      /* Wake up parent in mm_release */
376
377 #define PF_USEDFPU         0x00100000      /* task used FPU this quantum (SMP) */
378 #define PF_DTRACE          0x00200000      /* delayed trace (used on m68k, i386) */
379
380 /*
381  * Limit the stack by to some sane default: root can always
382  * increase this limit if needed..   8MB seems reasonable.
383  */
384 #define _STK_LIM           (8*1024*1024)
385
386 #define DEF_PRIORITY       (20*HZ/100)       /* 200 ms time slices */
387
388 /*
389  *   INIT_TASK is used to set up the first task table, touch at
390  * your own risk!. Base=0, limit=0x1fffff (=2MB)
391  */
392 #define INIT_TASK(name) \
393 /* state etc */ { 0,0,0,KERNEL_DS,&default_exec_domain,0, \
394 /* avg_slice */ 0, -1, \
395 /* counter */   DEF_PRIORITY,DEF_PRIORITY,SCHED_OTHER, \
396 /* mm */        NULL, &init_mm, \
397 /* has_cpu */   0,0, \
398 /* run_list */  LIST_HEAD_INIT(init_task.run_list), \
399 /* next_task */ &init_task,&init_task, \
400 /* last_proc */ 0, \
401 /* binfmt */    NULL, \
402 /* ec,brk... */ 0,0,0,0,0,0, \
403 /* pid etc.. */ 0,0,0,0,0, \
404 /* proc links*/ &init_task,&init_task,NULL,NULL,NULL, \
405 /* pidhash */   NULL, NULL, \
406 /* chld wait */ __WAIT_QUEUE_HEAD_INITIALIZER(name.wait_chldexit), NULL, \
407 /* timeout */   0,0,0,0,0,0,0, \
408 /* timer */     { NULL, NULL, 0, 0, it_real_fn }, \
409 /* utime */     {0,0,0,0},0, \
410 /* per CPU times */ {0, }, {0, }, \
411 /* flt */       0,0,0,0,0,0, \
412 /* swp */       0, \
413 /* process credentials */                                    \
414 /* uid etc */   0,0,0,0,0,0,0,0, \
415 /* suppl grps*/ 0, {0,}, \
416 /* caps */      CAP_INIT_EFF_SET,CAP_INIT_INH_SET,CAP_FULL_SET, \
417 /* user */      NULL, \
418 /* rlimits */   INIT_RLIMITS, \
419 /* math */      0, \
```

```
420  /* comm */        "swapper", \
421  /* fs info */      0,NULL, \
422  /* ipc */          NULL, NULL, \
423  /* thread */       INIT_THREAD, \
424  /* fs */           &init_fs, \
425  /* files */        &init_files, \
426  /* signals */      SPIN_LOCK_UNLOCKED, &init_signals, {{0}}, {{0}}, NULL,
                        &init_task.sigqueue, 0, 0, \
427  /* exec cts */     0,0, \
428  /* exit_sem */     __MUTEX_INITIALIZER(name.exit_sem),       \
429  }
430
431  #ifndef INIT_TASK_SIZE
432  # define INIT_TASK_SIZE 2048*sizeof(long)
433  #endif
434
435  union task_union {
436          struct task_struct task;
437          unsigned long stack[INIT_TASK_SIZE/sizeof(long)];
438  };
439
440  extern union task_union init_task_union;
441
442  extern struct   mm_struct init_mm;
443  extern struct task_struct *init_tasks[NR_CPUS];
444
445  /* PID hashing. (shouldnt this be dynamic?) */
446  #define PIDHASH_SZ (4096 >> 2)
447  extern struct task_struct *pidhash[PIDHASH_SZ];
448
449  #define pid_hashfn(x)    ((((x) >> 8) ^ (x)) & (PIDHASH_SZ - 1))
450
451  extern __inline__ void hash_pid(struct task_struct *p)
452  {
453          struct task_struct **htable = &pidhash[pid_hashfn(p->pid)];
454
455          if((p->pidhash_next = *htable) != NULL)
456                  (*htable)->pidhash_pprev = &p->pidhash_next;
457          *htable = p;
458          p->pidhash_pprev = htable;
459  }
460
461  extern __inline__ void unhash_pid(struct task_struct *p)
462  {
463          if(p->pidhash_next)
464                  p->pidhash_next->pidhash_pprev = p->pidhash_pprev;
465          *p->pidhash_pprev = p->pidhash_next;
466  }
467
468  extern __inline__ struct task_struct *find_task_by_pid(int pid)
469  {
470          struct task_struct *p, **htable = &pidhash[pid_hashfn(pid)];
471
472          for(p = *htable; p && p->pid != pid; p = p->pidhash_next)
```

```
473                    ;
474
475         return p;
476 }
477
478 /* per-UID process charging. */
479 extern int alloc_uid(struct task_struct *);
480 void free_uid(struct task_struct *);
481
482 #include <asm/current.h>
483
484 extern unsigned long volatile jiffies;
485 extern unsigned long itimer_ticks;
486 extern unsigned long itimer_next;
487 extern struct timeval xtime;
488 extern void do_timer(struct pt_regs *);
489
490 extern unsigned int * prof_buffer;
491 extern unsigned long prof_len;
492 extern unsigned long prof_shift;
493
494 #define CURRENT_TIME (xtime.tv_sec)
495
496 extern void FASTCALL(__wake_up(wait_queue_head_t *q, unsigned int mode));
497 extern void FASTCALL(__wake_up_sync(wait_queue_head_t *q, unsigned int mode));
498 extern void FASTCALL(sleep_on(wait_queue_head_t *q));
499 extern long FASTCALL(sleep_on_timeout(wait_queue_head_t *q,
500                                       signed long timeout));
501 extern void FASTCALL(interruptible_sleep_on(wait_queue_head_t *q));
502 extern long FASTCALL(interruptible_sleep_on_timeout(wait_queue_head_t *q,
503                                                     signed long timeout));
504 extern void FASTCALL(wake_up_process(struct task_struct * tsk));
505
506 #define wake_up(x)                      __wake_up((x),TASK_UNINTERRUPTIBLE |
                                            TASK_INTERRUPTIBLE | TASK_EXCLUSIVE)
507 #define wake_up_all(x)                  __wake_up((x),TASK_UNINTERRUPTIBLE |
                                            TASK_INTERRUPTIBLE)
508 #define wake_up_sync(x)                 __wake_up_sync((x),TASK_UNINTERRUPTIBLE
                                            | TASK_INTERRUPTIBLE | TASK_EXCLUSIVE)
509 #define wake_up_interruptible(x)        __wake_up((x),TASK_INTERRUPTIBLE |
                                            TASK_EXCLUSIVE)
510 #define wake_up_interruptible_all(x)    __wake_up((x),TASK_INTERRUPTIBLE)
511 #define wake_up_interruptible_sync(x)   __wake_up_sync((x),TASK_INTERRUPTIBLE |
                                            TASK_EXCLUSIVE)
512
513 extern int in_group_p(gid_t);
514 extern int in_egroup_p(gid_t);
515
516 extern void flush_signals(struct task_struct *);
517 extern void flush_signal_handlers(struct task_struct *);
518 extern int dequeue_signal(sigset_t *, siginfo_t *);
519 extern int send_sig_info(int, struct siginfo *, struct task_struct *);
520 extern int force_sig_info(int, struct siginfo *, struct task_struct *);
521 extern int kill_pg_info(int, struct siginfo *, pid_t);
```

```
522 extern int kill_si_info(int, struct siginfo *, pid_t);
523 extern int kill_proc_info(int, struct siginfo *, pid_t);
524 extern int kill_something_info(int, struct siginfo *, int);
525 extern void notify_parent(struct task_struct *, int);
526 extern void force_sig(int, struct task_struct *);
527 extern int send_sig(int, struct task_struct *, int);
528 extern int kill_pg(pid_t, int, int);
529 extern int kill_sl(pid_t, int, int);
530 extern int kill_proc(pid_t, int, int);
531 extern int do_sigaction(int, const struct k_sigaction *, struct k_sigaction *);
532 extern int do_sigaltstack(const stack_t *, stack_t *, unsigned long);
533
534 extern inline int signal_pending(struct task_struct *p)
535 {
536         return (p->sigpending != 0);
537 }
538
539 /* Reevaluate whether the task has signals pending delivery.
540    This is required every time the blocked sigset_t changes.
541    All callers should have t->sigmask_lock.   */
542
543 static inline void recalc_sigpending(struct task_struct *t)
544 {
545         unsigned long ready;
546         long i;
547
548         switch (_NSIG_WORDS) {
549         default:
550                 for (i = _NSIG_WORDS, ready = 0; --i >= 0 ;)
551                         ready |= t->signal.sig[i] &~ t->blocked.sig[i];
552                 break;
553
554         case 4: ready  = t->signal.sig[3] &~ t->blocked.sig[3];
555                 ready |= t->signal.sig[2] &~ t->blocked.sig[2];
556                 ready |= t->signal.sig[1] &~ t->blocked.sig[1];
557                 ready |= t->signal.sig[0] &~ t->blocked.sig[0];
558                 break;
559
560         case 2: ready  = t->signal.sig[1] &~ t->blocked.sig[1];
561                 ready |= t->signal.sig[0] &~ t->blocked.sig[0];
562                 break;
563
564         case 1: ready  = t->signal.sig[0] &~ t->blocked.sig[0];
565         }
566
567         t->sigpending = (ready != 0);
568 }
569
570 /* True if we are on the alternate signal stack.   */
571
572 static inline int on_sig_stack(unsigned long sp)
573 {
574         return (sp - current->sas_ss_sp < current->sas_ss_size);
575 }
```

```
576
577 static inline int sas_ss_flags(unsigned long sp)
578 {
579          return (current->sas_ss_size == 0 ? SS_DISABLE
580                  : on_sig_stack(sp) ? SS_ONSTACK : 0);
581 }
582
583 extern int request_irq(unsigned int,
584                        void (*handler)(int, void *, struct pt_regs *),
585                        unsigned long, const char *, void *);
586 extern void free_irq(unsigned int, void *);
587
588 /*
589  * This has now become a routine instead of a macro, it sets a flag if
590  * it returns true (to do BSD-style accounting where the process is flagged
591  * if it uses root privs). The implication of this is that you should do
592  * normal permissions checks first, and check suser() last.
593  *
594  * [Dec 1997 -- Chris Evans]
595  * For correctness, the above considerations need to be extended to
596  * fsuser(). This is done, along with moving fsuser() checks to be
597  * last.
598  *
599  * These will be removed, but in the mean time, when the SECURE_NOROOT
600  * flag is set, uids don't grant privilege.
601  */
602 extern inline int suser(void)
603 {
604          if (!issecure(SECURE_NOROOT) && current->euid == 0) {
605                  current->flags |= PF_SUPERPRIV;
606                  return 1;
607          }
608          return 0;
609 }
610
611 extern inline int fsuser(void)
612 {
613          if (!issecure(SECURE_NOROOT) && current->fsuid == 0) {
614                  current->flags |= PF_SUPERPRIV;
615                  return 1;
616          }
617          return 0;
618 }
619
620 /*
621  * capable() checks for a particular capability.
622  * New privilege checks should use this interface, rather than suser() or
623  * fsuser(). See include/linux/capability.h for defined capabilities.
624  */
625
626 extern inline int capable(int cap)
627 {
628 #if 1 /* ok now */
629          if (cap_raised(current->cap_effective, cap))
```

```
630 #else
631          if (cap_is_fs_cap(cap) ? current->fsuid == 0 : current->euid == 0)
632 #endif
633          {
634                  current->flags |= PF_SUPERPRIV;
635                  return 1;
636          }
637          return 0;
638 }
639
640 /*
641  * Routines for handling mm_structs
642  */
643 extern struct mm_struct * mm_alloc(void);
644
645 extern struct mm_struct * start_lazy_tlb(void);
646 extern void end_lazy_tlb(struct mm_struct *mm);
647
648 /* mmdrop drops the mm and the page tables */
649 extern inline void FASTCALL(__mmdrop(struct mm_struct *));
650 static inline void mmdrop(struct mm_struct * mm)
651 {
652          if (atomic_dec_and_test(&mm->mm_count))
653                  __mmdrop(mm);
654 }
655
656 /* mmput gets rid of the mappings and all user-space */
657 extern void mmput(struct mm_struct *);
658 /* Remove the current tasks stale references to the old mm_struct */
659 extern void mm_release(void);
660
661 /*
662  * Routines for handling the fd arrays
663  */
664 extern struct file ** alloc_fd_array(int);
665 extern int expand_fd_array(struct files_struct *, int nr);
666 extern void free_fd_array(struct file **, int);
667
668 extern fd_set *alloc_fdset(int);
669 extern int expand_fdset(struct files_struct *, int nr);
670 extern void free_fdset(fd_set *, int);
671
672 /* Expand files.  Return <0 on error; 0 nothing done; 1 files expanded,
673  * we may have blocked.
674  *
675  * Should be called with the files->file_lock spinlock held for write.
676  */
677 static inline int expand_files(struct files_struct *files, int nr)
678 {
679          int err, expand = 0;
680 #ifdef FDSET_DEBUG
681          printk (KERN_ERR __FUNCTION__ " %d: nr = %d\n", current->pid, nr);
682 #endif
683
```

```
684          if (nr >= files->max_fdset) {
685                  expand = 1;
686                  if ((err = expand_fdset(files, nr)))
687                          goto out;
688          }
689          if (nr >= files->max_fds) {
690                  expand = 1;
691                  if ((err = expand_fd_array(files, nr)))
692                          goto out;
693          }
694          err = expand;
695  out:
696  #ifdef FDSET_DEBUG
697          if (err)
698                  printk (KERN_ERR __FUNCTION__ " %d: return %d\n", current->pid,
                             err);
699  #endif
700          return err;
701  }
702
703  extern int  copy_thread(int, unsigned long, unsigned long, struct task_struct *,
     struct pt_regs *);
704  extern void flush_thread(void);
705  extern void exit_thread(void);
706
707  extern void exit_mm(struct task_struct *);
708  extern void exit_fs(struct task_struct *);
709  extern void exit_files(struct task_struct *);
710  extern void exit_sighand(struct task_struct *);
711
712  extern void daemonize(void);
713
714  extern int do_execve(char *, char **, char **, struct pt_regs *);
715  extern int do_fork(unsigned long, unsigned long, struct pt_regs *);
716
717  extern inline void add_wait_queue(wait_queue_head_t *q, wait_queue_t * wait)
718  {
719          unsigned long flags;
720
721          wq_write_lock_irqsave(&q->lock, flags);
722          __add_wait_queue(q, wait);
723          wq_write_unlock_irqrestore(&q->lock, flags);
724  }
725
726  extern inline void add_wait_queue_exclusive(wait_queue_head_t *q,
727                                                      wait_queue_t * wait)
728  {
729          unsigned long flags;
730
731          wq_write_lock_irqsave(&q->lock, flags);
732          __add_wait_queue_tail(q, wait);
733          wq_write_unlock_irqrestore(&q->lock, flags);
734  }
735
```

```
736 extern inline void remove_wait_queue(wait_queue_head_t *q, wait_queue_t * wait)
737 {
738         unsigned long flags;
739
740         wq_write_lock_irqsave(&q->lock, flags);
741         __remove_wait_queue(q, wait);
742         wq_write_unlock_irqrestore(&q->lock, flags);
743 }
744
745 #define __wait_event(wq, condition)                                         \
746 do {                                                                        \
747         wait_queue_t __wait;                                                \
748         init_waitqueue_entry(&__wait, current);                             \
749                                                                             \
750         add_wait_queue(&wq, &__wait);                                       \
751         for (;;) {                                                          \
752                 set_current_state(TASK_UNINTERRUPTIBLE);                    \
753                 if (condition)                                              \
754                         break;                                              \
755                 schedule();                                                 \
756         }                                                                   \
757         current->state = TASK_RUNNING;                                      \
758         remove_wait_queue(&wq, &__wait);                                    \
759 } while (0)
760
761 #define wait_event(wq, condition)                                           \
762 do {                                                                        \
763         if (condition)                                                      \
764                 break;                                                      \
765         __wait_event(wq, condition);                                        \
766 } while (0)
767
768 #define __wait_event_interruptible(wq, condition, ret)                      \
769 do {                                                                        \
770         wait_queue_t __wait;                                                \
771         init_waitqueue_entry(&__wait, current);                             \
772                                                                             \
773         add_wait_queue(&wq, &__wait);                                       \
774         for (;;) {                                                          \
775                 set_current_state(TASK_INTERRUPTIBLE);                      \
776                 if (condition)                                              \
777                         break;                                              \
778                 if (!signal_pending(current)) {                             \
779                         schedule();                                         \
780                         continue;                                           \
781                 }                                                           \
782                 ret = -ERESTARTSYS;                                         \
783                 break;                                                      \
784         }                                                                   \
785         current->state = TASK_RUNNING;                                      \
786         remove_wait_queue(&wq, &__wait);                                    \
787 } while (0)
788
789 #define wait_event_interruptible(wq, condition)                             \
```

```
790 ({                                                                  \
791         int __ret = 0;                                              \
792         if (!(condition))                                           \
793                 __wait_event_interruptible(wq, condition, __ret);   \
794         __ret;                                                      \
795 })
796
797 #define REMOVE_LINKS(p) do { \
798         (p)->next_task->prev_task = (p)->prev_task; \
799         (p)->prev_task->next_task = (p)->next_task; \
800         if ((p)->p_osptr) \
801                 (p)->p_osptr->p_ysptr = (p)->p_ysptr; \
802         if ((p)->p_ysptr) \
803                 (p)->p_ysptr->p_osptr = (p)->p_osptr; \
804         else \
805                 (p)->p_pptr->p_cptr = (p)->p_osptr; \
806         } while (0)
807
808 #define SET_LINKS(p) do { \
809         (p)->next_task = &init_task; \
810         (p)->prev_task = init_task.prev_task; \
811         init_task.prev_task->next_task = (p); \
812         init_task.prev_task = (p); \
813         (p)->p_ysptr = NULL; \
814         if (((p)->p_osptr = (p)->p_pptr->p_cptr) != NULL) \
815                 (p)->p_osptr->p_ysptr = p; \
816         (p)->p_pptr->p_cptr = p; \
817         } while (0)
818
819 #define for_each_task(p) \
820         for (p = &init_task ; (p = p->next_task) != &init_task ; )
821
822
823 static inline void del_from_runqueue(struct task_struct * p)
824 {
825         nr_running--;
826         list_del(&p->run_list);
827         p->run_list.next = NULL;
828 }
829
830 extern inline int task_on_runqueue(struct task_struct *p)
831 {
832         return (p->run_list.next != NULL);
833 }
834
835 extern inline void unhash_process(struct task_struct *p)
836 {
837         if (task_on_runqueue(p)) BUG();
838         write_lock_irq(&tasklist_lock);
839         nr_threads--;
840         unhash_pid(p);
841         REMOVE_LINKS(p);
842         write_unlock_irq(&tasklist_lock);
843 }
```

```
844
845 static inline int task_lock(struct task_struct *p)
846 {
847         down(&p->exit_sem);
848         if (p->p_pptr)
849                 return 1;
850         /* He's dead, Jim. You take his wallet, I'll take the tricorder... */
851         up(&p->exit_sem);
852         return 0;
853 }
854
855 static inline void task_unlock(struct task_struct *p)
856 {
857         up(&p->exit_sem);
858 }
859
860 #endif /* __KERNEL__ */
861
862 #endif
```

The Linux
VM Manager

Memory is a primary resource in a Linux system; it must be carefully managed. Obviously, every programmer would like infinite memory. Unfortunately this is not yet possible, and so early computer architects implemented a memory hierarchy, with a small amount of very fast, expensive, volatile cache; dozens or hundreds of megabytes of medium-speed, medium-price, volatile RAM; and hundreds and then thousands of megabytes—and upward—of nonvolatile, cheap disk storage. It is up to the operating system to coordinate how these memories are used.

To do this, the Linux memory manager manages a number of tables that list existing pages of virtual memory, their status, their age, and other useful information. The memory manager also makes use of the hardware functionality of the CPU to translate virtual memory address-es into RAM addresses. The CPU itself has a table, called translation look-aside buffer (TLB) to speed up the translation process.

Because the virtual memory subsystem has huge impact on the per-formance of user programs (the kernel itself is not pageable in Linux as it is, for instance, in AIX), special care was given to the C source code comprising the functionality of the memory manager.

This chapter first examines the general aspects of the virtual memory manager and its functions, and then addresses the peculiarities of its implementation in the 2.4 kernel. Because VM is among the least under-stood concepts of OS theory, we will spend more time explaining the workings of VM than we have for other subsystems in other chapters of this book. We will see which tables are maintained by the kernel and which algorithms interact with them. Finally we will see, using the example of a new page replacement algorithm, how a kernel hacker would change things.

VM Concepts

Each user process sees a single, private contiguous VM address space and each such space can contain several types of memory objects. Objects such as program text and program data are effectively a single memory-mapped file (the binary file being run), but program code is read-only, while program data is copy-on-write. Arbitrary files can be memory-mapped into the address space as well, which is how the shared library mechanism works. Such mappings can require modifications to remain private to the process creating them.

Furthermore, the memory manager must be able to handle system calls like `fork()` or `__clone()`. When a process forks, the result is two processes—each with its own private address space, including any modifications made by the original process prior to the call to `fork()`. It would be a waste of precious CPU cycles if the VM system were to make a complete copy of the data at the time of the `fork()`, because quite possibly at least one of the two processes will only need to read from that page from then on, thus allowing the original page to continue to be used. What was a private page is now made copy-on-write again, because each process (parent and child) expects its own personal post-fork modifications to remain private to itself and not affect the other. A virtual memory page with the program's binary text is one example: each program binary contains a previously (at compile time) initialized data section that is initially mapped directly from the program file.

When a program is loaded into a process's virtual address space, this area is initially memory-mapped and backed by the program binary itself, allowing the VM system to free or reuse the page and later load it back in from the binary. The moment a process modifies this data, however, the VM system must make a private copy of the page for that process. Because the private copy has been modified, the VM system may no longer free it, because there is no longer any way to restore it later on.

Swapping

Private data pages are initially either copy-on-write or zero-fill pages. When a change, and therefore a copy, is made, the original backing object (usually a file) can no longer be used to save a copy of the page when the VM system needs to reuse it for other purposes. This is where swapping comes in. Swapping is obviously only necessary for written pages (dirty pages). Indeed, there's no reason to ever write pure code pages into swap space, because you can just page them from the original image. Only writeable pages should ever swap out; if an executable page's page frame is reclaimed, then the page should be unmapped and forgotten, to be reread from the image when faulted in. You can never get to a state in which the disk containing the image could be unmounted while the image is running, because it will always be busy.

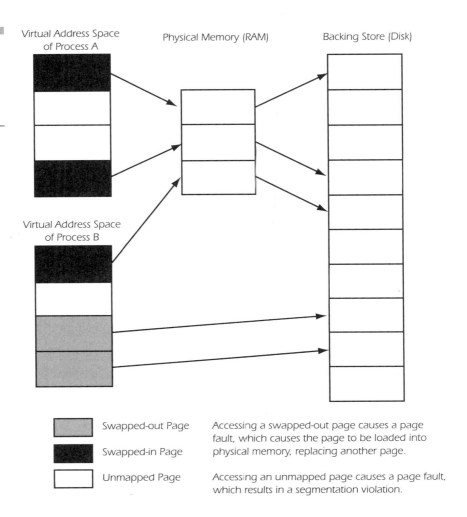

Figure 5.1
Relation between virtual memory, physical memory, and auxiliary swap space on disk.

Virtual Address Space of Process A

Physical Memory (RAM)

Backing Store (Disk)

Virtual Address Space of Process B

Swapped-out Page — Accessing a swapped-out page causes a page fault, which causes the page to be loaded into physical memory, replacing another page.

Swapped-in Page

Unmapped Page — Accessing an unmapped page causes a page fault, which results in a segmentation violation.

Page Replacement

When a page fault occurs, the VM manager has to choose a page to remove from memory to make room for the page that has to be brought in. If the page to be removed has been modified while in memory, it must be rewritten to the disk to bring the disk copy up to date. If, however, the page has not been changed, no refresh is needed. The page to be read in overwrites the page being evicted.

Replacing pages at random might actually be a practical implementation of a page replacement algorithm. However, it might be much more worthwhile to implement an algorithm that selects a page that is not heavily used. In the 2.4 kernels, Linux uses the least recently used (LRU) algorithm. As the name implies, this algorithm is on the lookout for pages not referenced in a long time, on the assumption that they will continue to be unreferenced for longer, probably even never again. LRU is not cheap, in terms of overhead. Linux has to maintain a linked list of all pages in memory, with the most recently used page at the front and the least recently used page at the end. The difficulty is that the list must be updated on every memory reference. Finding a page in the list, deleting it, and then moving it to the front is a very time-consuming operation.

The Linux 2.4 Implementation

In this section we explore the Linux VM implementation and the algorithms and data structures involved. It is important to remember that this book is based on the IA32 (Intel x86) architecture. The VM of any operating system is one of the most platform-dependent areas in the kernel. The kernel of a multi-architecture OS like Linux, needs, nonetheless, to be able to support a generalized approach.

Address Translation

For the translation of logical addresses to physical addresses and vice versa, the kernel makes use of the hardware facilities available within the CPU, called the Memory Management Unit (MMU).

The MMU has been present in CPUs for almost 30 years, and was introduced in its present modern form on the General Electric 645 computer, designed to run the legendary Multics[1] project. Multics was the first modern OS to have a virtual memory concept with demand paging. (The Atlas computer had demand paging, back in 1962. IBM's MFP (multiple fixed partitions) operating system[2] had swapping of whole partitions a few years earlier. It did not, however, feature demand paging. The developers of UNIX directly took over the VM paradigm from the Multics project and applied it to the DEC PDP architecture, which had an optional MMU in certain models.)

---

1 More information about the ground-breaking Multics project can be found at **www.best.com/~thvv/~thvv/~thvv/multics.html**.

2 *IBM Systems Journal* Vol 5. 1966, "The Functional Structure of OS/360."

The MMU and the kernel work together to translate addresses. The kernel asks the MMU which virtual pages to map onto physical pages for each user address space. The MMU then carries out the translation for the kernel. The MMU has the capability to send out a signal, an interrupt, whenever an error occurs during translation. The most common error condition is that the physical page is not available in RAM. When this *page fault* occurs, the kernel has to retrieve the required page from the swapping device or swapping file.

Another possibility for an error condition is when a user-space program is trying to address a virtual address that lies within another user's address space. Or it might try to access the kernel's protected memory. Another possibility is trying to write to a read-only area of a user's own address space. All these errors are signaled by the MMU to the kernel so that the kernel can take appropriate measures.

The Linux VM manager has a three-tier notion of address translation tables. The IA32 has a hard-wired two-tier approach to address translation. This, as we shall shortly see, is not an impediment. Other processors might have different architectures, but the kernel knows how to deal with them through its generalized approach to address translation. The diagram in Figure 5.2 shows the process to translate an address. Whenever a user-space program needs to have access to a virtual memory address, the MMU breaks that address down into three components:

1. A page directory entry (PGD) or level-1.
2. A page table entry (PTE), (sometimes also called page frame number, [PFN]) or level-2.
3. An offset or level-3.

The page directory is an array of pointers to page tables. Each page is an array of pointers to pages. Therefore, translating addresses means traversing the whole chain of pointers to get to the address within the physical page. A page table directory points, therefore, to a page table. This in turn points to a page. The offset, finally, points to an address within that page.

Linux runs on a great variety of architectures, and architecture-dependent code has to be kept to a minimum. Therefore, the kernel designers decided to adopt a three-tier view of the MMU. To make this three-tier view work with the two-tier (or two-level) paradigm present in IA32, the size of the page middle directory was set to 1. The page middle directory has therefore, for all intents and purposes, the same behavior as the page directory.

In the IA32, of the total 32-bit virtual address, 10 bits are reserved for the page directory entry (PGD), 10 bits are for the page table entry (PTE) and the remaining 12 bits are for the offset. This is why you have 4,096 offsets within a page ($4K = 2^{12}$).

Figure 5.2
The Linux three-tier address resolution process.

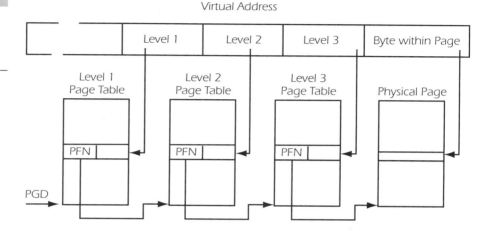

The TLB in Linux

To speed up the process of address translation, the kernel uses the TLB. There is actually not much for the kernel to do to manage the TLB; the CPU does it all by itself. The only intervention required of the kernel happens when the scheduler is switching to another user's address space for execution and the TLB has to be reloaded with the cache entries for the new address space. To do this, all the kernel needs to do is load a value into the TLB, which forces the CPU to think it is invalidated and flush it. Through the normal address translation work, the CPU repopulates the TLB with new entries.

This flushing is done by calling the __flush_tlb assembler macro. All it does is save the CR3 value to the temporary variable tmpreg and then copy tmpreg back into CR3. That's enough to invalidate the TLB. The code for this is in inlude/asm-i386/pgtable.h.

```
#define __flush_tlb()                                    \
    do {                                                 \
        unsigned int tmpreg;                             \
                                                         \
        __asm__ __volatile__(                            \
            "movl %%cr3, %0;  # flush TLB \n"            \
```

```
            "movl %0, %%cr3;                    \n"      \
            : "=r" (tmpreg)                              \
            :: "memory");                                \
    } while (0)
```

Page Allocation and Deallocation

The page allocator in kernel 2.4 is zone based. The physical memory is split into zones. The allocator tries to coalesce free memory in big chunks of physical contiguous memory. The chunks are naturally aligned in the physical memory. Order is 0 for allocating or freeing a single page. Order is 1 for allocating two contiguous physical pages (for example the `taskstruct` + `kernelstack` is allocated with order 1, because it's 8,192 bytes in size). For hashtables, the order grows much more—up to allocating 2Mbytes of contiguous physical memory.

The mechanisms and data structures used for page allocation and deallocation are perhaps the most critical in maintaining the efficiency of the virtual memory subsystem. All the physical pages in the system are described by the `mem_map` data structure, which is a linked list of `mem_map_t` . Each `mem_map_t` describes a single physical page in the system. Important fields (so far as memory management is concerned) are:

- `count`—This is a count of the number of users of this page. The count is greater than one when the page is shared between many processes.
- `age`—This field describes the age of the page and is used to decide if the page is a good candidate for discarding or swapping.
- `map_nr`—This is the physical PFN that the `mem_map_t` describes.

The `free_area` structure is used by the page allocation code to find and free pages. The whole buffer management scheme is supported by this mechanism and, so far as the code is concerned, the size of the page and physical paging mechanisms used by the CPU are irrelevant.

Each element of `free_area` contains information about blocks of pages. The first element in the array describes single pages, the next, blocks of two pages, and so on upwards in powers of two. The `list` element is used as a queue head and has pointers to the page structures in the `mem_map` array. Free blocks of pages are queued here. `map` is a pointer to a bitmap, which keeps track of allocated groups of pages of this size. Bit N of the bitmap is set if the Nth block of pages is free.

Figure 5.3 shows the `free_area` structure. Element 0 has one free page (PFN 0) and element 2 has two free blocks of four pages, the first starting at PFN 4 and the second at PFN 56.

Figure 5.3
The free_area
structure.

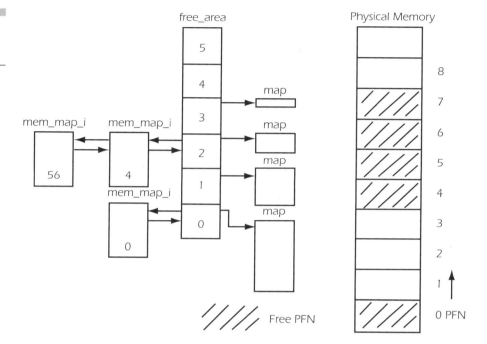

Page Deallocation

Allocating blocks of pages tends to fragment memory, with larger blocks of free pages broken down into smaller ones. The page deallocation code recombines free pages into larger blocks whenever it can. The page block size is important; it allows for an easy combination of blocks into larger blocks. Whenever a block of pages is freed, the adjacent block of the same size is checked to see if it is free. If it is, then it is combined with the newly freed block of pages to form a new free block of pages for the next size block of pages. Each time two blocks of pages are recombined into a bigger block of free pages, the page deallocation code attempts to recombine that block into a yet larger one. In this way the blocks of free pages are as large as memory usage will allow.

For example, in Figure 5.3, if PFN 1 were to be freed, then that would be combined with the already free PFN 0 and queued onto element 1 of the `free_area` as a free block of two pages in size.

The Least Recently Used (LRU) Algorithm

Linux uses the LRU algorithm to decide which pages are to be selected for page out. The LRU implementation in Linux is pretty much based on common knowledge in OS theory. There is a variable, `lru_page`, that points to the head of the LRU. Each time a page gets added to any kind of freeable cache (so that `shrink_mmap` may later need to shrink when the memory gets low) the page is queued at one end of the LRU list. At the other end, `shrink_mmap` tries to release the pages. A reference bit of aging is involved in this process, to avoid the cost of rolling the list at each cache hit. All the LRU handling is SMP threaded and allows the VM to shrink the cache even while another CPU is querying on the page cache.

Swapping and Discarding Pages

When memory becomes scarce, the Linux memory management subsystem attempts to free physical pages. This function is performed by the kernel swap daemon (`kswapd`). The name *swap daemon* is a bit of a misnomer, because the daemon does more than just swap modified pages out to the swap file. Its task is to keep the memory management system operating efficiently. `kswapd` is started by the kernel `init` process at startup time, and sits waiting for the kernel swap timer to periodically expire. Awakened by the VM manager every time the timer expires, `kswapd` looks to see if the number of free pages in the system is getting too low.

The main function of `kswapd` is to provide free memory for atomic allocations. These happen inside interrupt context and can't sleep, because they need to be fast in order not to hurt IRQ or soft IRQ latency. The `kswapd` daemon is an autonomous kernel thread whose only task is to infinitely run the `kswapd()` function in `mm/vmscan.c`. The `kswapd` daemon typically sleeps on the `kswapd_wait` wait queue. It is awakenead by the zone allocator if memory pressure within a given zone (or globally) goes above a given threshold; `kswapd()` then tries to free pages so that memory pressure returns to the proper low state. That's all it does.

Freeing pages is a complex task that involves five steps:

1. Try to free "clean" pages (page cache, buffer cache).

   2. Shrink the `dentry` cache.
   3. Shrink the `inode` cache.
   4. Try to swap shared memory out.
   5. Try to free "dirty" pages.

   The VM manager tries not to have too many pages written to the swap file at the same time, so it uses `nr_async_pages` to keep count of the number of pages currently being written to the swap file. The `free_pages_low` and `free_pages_high` parameters are set at system startup time and are related to the number of physical pages in the system. If there are enough free pages, the `swap` daemon sleeps until its timer expires; otherwise the `swap` daemon tries three ways to reduce the number of physical pages used by the system:

   1. Reduce the size of the buffer and page caches.
   2. Swap out shared pages.
   3. Swap out or discarding pages.

   By default, the `swap` daemon tries to free up four pages each time it runs. The above methods are each tried in turn until enough pages have been freed. The `swap` daemon then sleeps again until its timer expires.

Swapping Pages Out

The `swap` daemon looks at each process in the system in turn to see if it is a good candidate for swapping. Good candidates are processes that can be swapped (some cannot) and that have one or more pages that can be swapped or discarded from memory. Pages are swapped only if the data in them cannot be retrieved another way. A lot of the contents of an executable image come from the image's file and can easily be reread from that file. For example, the executable instructions of an image will never be modified by the image and so will never be written to the swap file. These pages can simply be discarded; when they are again referenced by the process, they will be brought back into memory from the executable image.

   Once the process to swap has been located, the `swap` daemon looks through all of its virtual memory regions looking for areas that are not shared or locked. Linux does not swap out all the swappable pages of the process that it has selected; instead it removes only a small number of pages. Pages cannot be swapped or discarded if they:

- Are locked in memory
- Are shared.

There is a separate, explicit mechanism for swapping out these pages.
The swap algorithm uses *page aging*. Each page has a counter (held
in the `mem_map_t` data structure) that gives the kernel `swap` daemon
some idea whether or not a page is worth swapping. Pages age when
they are unused, and rejuvenate on access; the `swap` daemon only swaps
out old pages. The default action, when a page is first allocated, is to
give it an initial age of 3. Each time it is touched by the memory management subsystem, its age is increased by 3 to a maximum of 20. Each
time the kernel `swap` daemon runs, it ages pages, decrementing their
age by 1. These default actions can be changed and for this reason they
(and other swap-related information) are stored in `swap_control`.

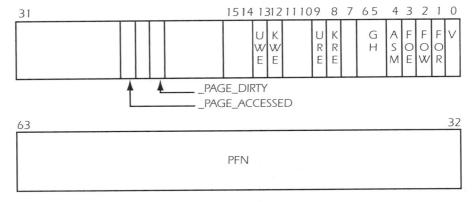

Figure 5.4
Alpha AXP page table
entry.

If the page is old, the `swap` daemon processes it further. *Dirty* pages
are pages which can be swapped out. Linux uses an architecture-specific
bit in the PTE to describe pages this way. However, not all dirty pages
are necessarily written to the swap file. Every virtual memory region of
a process may have its own swap method and, in this case, that method
is used. Otherwise, the `swap` daemon will allocate a page in the swap file
and write the page out to the swap file device. If the swap file is used,
the page's page table entry (PTE) is replaced by one which is marked as
invalid but contains information about where the page is in the swap
file. Whatever the swap method used, the original physical page is made
free by putting it back into the `free_area`. Clean (or rather, not dirty)
pages can be discarded and put back into the `free_area` for re-use. The
PTEs for these pages are made invalid. These pages will be re-read from

the executable image running when the process attempts to access them.

Because the process's PTEs have been changed, the CPU's Translation Lookaside Buffers (TLBs), which contain cached, internal, CPU-readable copies of PTEs, must be updated. This update mechanism is architecture specific. If enough of the swappable process's pages have been swapped out or discarded, the swap daemon will again sleep. The next time it wakes it will consider the next process in the system. In this way, the swap daemon nibbles away at each process's physical pages until the system is again in balance. This is much fairer than swapping out whole processes.

Linux is quite sophisticated in the swap-out stage because it keeps a *swap cache*. This is like the page cache for the file system. The swap cache, for example, avoids our having to write to disk two times if we are going to swap out for a second time a page that is still up to date upon swap. It also avoids our having to swap in from disk if we swapped out the page and we fault into it again soon after (it becomes a minor fault instead of a major fault). Another function of the swap cache is to avoid a task having to fork a child, which then does major faults (swap-ins) of the swapped-out pages in the parent VM. (Because 2.0.x does not have the swap cache, often you see constant swap-in each time Apache forks a child. I discovered the cause of this problem in mid-2.1.x; the problem was fixed properly in 2.2.x, which makes better use of the swap cache.)

The swap-out goes through these steps:

1. Search out, in round-robin fashion, across all the page tables of the task, an anonymous page with the PTE marked "old."
2. Add such a page to the swap cache marked as "locked."
3. Write such a page to disk in async mode (per-page locked bit gets released by the IO-completion interrupt).
4. Set the PTE with the swap-entry information and mark the PTE as "page-not-present."

There are three watermarks in 2.4:

```
high = min*3
low  = min*2
min
```

The kswapd daemon wakes up as soon as somebody needs memory, once the number of free pages is under the low watermark. If the number of free pages goes under the min watermark, then the task block halts and kswapd frees memory itself, if it can. After a wakeup, kswapd continues to run until the number of free pages returns over the high watermark. In other words, its job is to move from low to high.

kswapd is therefore useful to free pages in the background, and to free pages for allocations (as is done inside bottom-half handlers or IRQ handlers that can't free memory themselves because they can't block).

Reducing the Size of the Page and Buffer Caches

Each time the kernel swap daemon tries to shrink page and buffer caches, it examines a number of pages in the mem_map page vector to see if any can be discarded from physical memory. The number of pages examined is defined by the priority at which the code is called. The blocks of pages are examined in a cyclical manner; a different block of pages is examined each time an attempt is made to shrink the memory map.

Each page being examined is checked to see if it is cached in either the page cache or the buffer cache. Shared pages are not considered for discarding at this time, and a page cannot be in both caches at the same time. If the page is not in either cache, then the next page in the mem_map page vector is examined.

Pages are cached in the buffer cache (or rather the buffers within the pages are cached) to make buffer allocation and deallocation more efficient. The memory map that is shrinking code tries to free the buffers that are contained within the page being examined. If the all the buffers are freed, then the pages that contain them are also freed. Pages are queued in the page cache to speed up access to images and data on disk. If the examined page is in this cache, it is removed from the page cache and freed.

When enough pages have been freed on this attempt, then the kernel swap daemon waits until the next time it is awakened. Because none of the freed pages were part of any process's virtual memory (they were cached pages), no page tables need updating. If there were not enough cached pages discarded, then the swap daemon will try to swap out some shared pages.

Swapping Out Shared Pages

Physical pages that have been shared between processes are swapped out separately from ordinary pages. When the `swap` daemon attempts to swap out shared pages, it uses `shm_segs`, a vector of pointers to `shmid_ds` data structures, to look through the shared pages for good candidates for swapping. For each `shmid_ds`, there is a list of `vm_area_struct` structures, each of which describes how the virtual memory of a particular process is related to this shared memory area. Just like nonshared memory, the page table entries must be modified to show that the page is in the swap file. However, the page tables of all the sharing processes must be modified before the page is written to the swap file and freed. The page table entries for each process are found by following the `vm_mm` pointer in each `vm_area_struct` structure. Each `vm_mm` pointer points at the level 1 page table for the process.

Swapping Pages In (Demand Paging)

Whatever architecture Linux is running on, its page fault handler is called. The relevant page table entry (PTE) is examined, and if it is an invalid entry, there are three possible ways of dealing with it: *page in swap*, *shared page in swap*, and *executable image page*.

Page in Swap

If the PTE is marked as page in swap, then the page must be read from the swap file and the `swap_cache` and PTE updated.

Shared Page in Swap

Shared pages in the swap file are handled separately from nonshared pages.

A physical page is allocated and the page is read into it from the swap file using the swap file information in the PTE and the information held in the `swap_info_struct` tree for the swap file. Because the page is a shared page, the page tables for all the processes sharing that virtual memory must be updated to show that the page again exists in physical memory.

Executable Image Page

If the PTE is not marked as being in swap, the appropriate page from the executable image is brought into memory and the PTE is updated to reflect the newly allocated and filled physical page. However the page is brought into memory, a new PTE is created for that page and the TLB is updated to reflect the page table changes that have been made.

Addressing Beyond 4GB on an Intel x86

Recently, kernel hacker Andrea Arcangeli proposed a way to address more than 4GB of RAM on the IA32 architecture. The design that allows IA32 to break the old memory limit in 2.3.x, (and in 2.2.x with an additional patch) works like this:

1. Basically you have 4GB of physical RAM and 4GB of virtual RAM:

```
-------------------------------------------------------------
|  userspace virtual 0-3g            |  kernelvirtual 3-4g |
-------------------------------------------------------------
```

2. To access physical memory, we must first set up proper virtual-to-physical mapping. The kernel maps the 3GB to 4GB range to the 0 to 1GB physical range:

```
-------------------------------------------------------------
|  kernel-physical 0-1GB | unused-physical-memory 1(3?)-4GB  |
-------------------------------------------------------------
```

and the user space _virtual_ addresses (0 to 3GB area) maps with 4kbyte (`PAGE_SIZE`) granularity all over the physical memory that the kernel can address, all depending on user page tables setting.

The limitation of the old 2.2.x design, which is removed with this new design, is that the kernel isn't able to deal with memory that couldn't be accessed via identity mapping, the 3 to 4GB virtual area (where the kernel runs) which points to the 0 to 1GB physical memory).

In other words, the kernel was always doing:

```
*(virtual_address) = 0;
```

to write to the physical memory at address `virtual_address - 3GB`:

```
-------------------------------------------------------------
|                   VIRTUAL SPACE       | kernel virt 3-4g |
-------------------------------------------------------------
                              | virtual write here
--------------------------------------
            |
          \ | / physical write happens here
-------------------------------------------------------------
|   kernel phys  |   PHYSICAL SPACE                          |
-------------------------------------------------------------
```

As you can see, the last address that the kernel could access while writing to the ident mapping happens to be a 4GB-1 and it points to the physical address 1GB-1. Then the virtual addresses wrap around because of the 32-bit virtual address limitation that hobbles the IA32 family of CPUs.

NOTE

We can't use the user space's virtual space to write beyond the 1GB address in physical RAM. This is because the user-space page tables belong to the process memory layout, and we can't change them without clobbering the user space mappings and without flushing away user TLB.

The new design's main achievement is to allow the kernel to access the physical memory above the kernel-physical area, beyond 1GB. To do this cleanly, a pool of virtual pages at the end of the virtual memory was reserved (around address 4GB), and the page tables were put there to map them to the physical space just above the 2GB range.

This exactly how the 2.4 kernel supports more than 1GB of RAM on IA32. The following diagram shows this novelty (as of kernel 2.3.41):

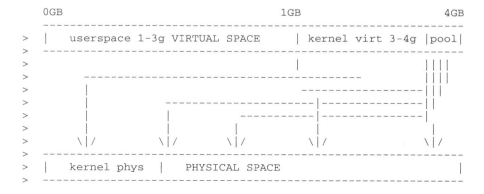

As you can see, with the pool of virtual pages placed near virtual address 4GB, we can now address all the physical space available from the kernel. In the diagram, the physical space is as large as the virtual space (4GB). With the new Physical Address Extension (PAE) support, the code works in exactly the same way, with the difference that with the three-level page tables of the PAE mode, the physical space is larger than 4GB—it's a whopping 64GB. So, the diagram should be changed, moving the end of the physical space to address 64GB and not 4GB. That's the only difference between PAE mode and non-PAE mode.

The user space continues to point all over the physical space. But now the physical space that the user space can address via its page tables is no longer limited to 0 to 1GB of physical RAM; rather, it can address all the physical memory, exactly as our pool of virtual kernel pages can. This because the kernel is now able to deal with the physical range after 1GB, and can allow user space to use it, too.

Of course, as you can see from the diagram, there's a performance penalty in accessing memory beyond 1GB, because we have to set up a virtual-to-physical mapping and flush away old TLB entries. However, it's very reasonable to incur such a performance penalty for the sake of handling more memory. Together with Andrea Arcangeli, I measured the performance hit in the worst case (with maximal page-faults rate) at only 2 percent. In daily operations, such a hit is imperceptible.

To map and unmap the reserved virtual pages to access the memory, Andrea created two helper functions called `kmap()` and `kunmap()` that deal automatically with the virtual-to-physical mapping.

The 2.3.x code that uses the reserved pool to access the memory over 1GB looks like this:

```
page = get_page();
virtual_address = kmap(page);
*(virtual_address) = 0;
kunmap(page);
```

This is another fine example of superb engineering, showing that things hitherto thought impossible can actually be done with creativity and persistence.

Improving the VM

Once more we try to improve the kernel with new functionality. Obviously, the practicality and real need for these improvements can be argued. The point is rather the learning aspect, which is much higher if the student tries to enhance the object of his or her study.

Implementing Page Coloring

Page coloring is a performance optimization designed to ensure that accesses to contiguous pages in virtual memory make the best use of the processor cache. In ancient times (i.e., 10 or more years ago) processor caches tended to map virtual memory rather than physical memory. This led to a huge number of problems, including having to clear the cache on every context switch in some cases, and problems with data aliasing in the cache.

Modern processor caches map physical memory in a manner designed to solve precisely these problems. This means that two side-by-side pages in a process's address space do not necessarily correspond to two side-by-side pages in the cache. In fact, if you aren't careful, side-by-side pages in virtual memory could wind up using the same page in the processor cache—leading to cacheable data being thrown away prematurely and reducing CPU performance. This is true even with multi-way set-associative caches (though the effect is mitigated somewhat).

A per-task tracker of virtual memory page cache allocations is the best way to implement dynamic page coloring; checking page tables looks quite slow to me. Perfect static coloring (when possible) may well be the worst thing to do for an unlucky application.

There were some preliminary implementations using this technique being developed as this book was written, but none were yet ready to be included here.

Data Structures—include/linux/sched.h

```
#ifndef _LINUX_SCHED_H
#define _LINUX_SCHED_H

#include <asm/param.h>  /* for HZ */

extern unsigned long event;

#include <linux/binfmts.h>
#include <linux/personality.h>
#include <linux/threads.h>
#include <linux/kernel.h>
#include <linux/types.h>
```

```
#include <linux/times.h>
#include <linux/timex.h>

#include <asm/system.h>
#include <asm/semaphore.h>
#include <asm/page.h>
#include <asm/ptrace.h>

#include <linux/smp.h>
#include <linux/tty.h>
#include <linux/sem.h>
#include <linux/signal.h>
#include <linux/securebits.h>

/*
 * cloning flags:
 */
#define CSIGNAL         0x000000ff    /* signal mask to be sent at exit */
#define CLONE_VM        0x00000100    /* set if VM shared between processes */
#define CLONE_FS        0x00000200    /* set if fs info shared between processes */
#define CLONE_FILES     0x00000400    /* set if open files shared between processes */
#define CLONE_SIGHAND   0x00000800    /* set if signal handlers shared */
#define CLONE_PID       0x00001000    /* set if pid shared */
#define CLONE_PTRACE    0x00002000    /* set if we want to let tracing continue on the
                                         child too */
#define CLONE_VFORK     0x00004000    /* set if the parent wants the child to wake it
                                         up on mm_release */
#define CLONE_PARENT    0x00008000    /* set if we want to have the same parent as the
                                         cloner */

/*
 * These are the constant used to fake the fixed-point load-average
 * counting. Some notes:
 *  - 11 bit fractions expand to 22 bits by the multiplies: this gives
 *    a load-average precision of 10 bits integer + 11 bits fractional
 *  - if you want to count load-averages more often, you need more
 *    precision, or rounding will get you. With 2-second counting freq,
 *    the EXP_n values would be 1981, 2034 and 2043 if still using only
 *    11 bit fractions.
 */
extern unsigned long avenrun[];         /* Load averages */

#define FSHIFT       11                 /* nr of bits of precision */
#define FIXED_1      (1<<FSHIFT)         /* 1.0 as fixed-point */
#define LOAD_FREQ    (5*HZ)             /* 5 sec intervals */
#define EXP_1        1884               /* 1/exp(5sec/1min) as fixed-point */
#define EXP_5        2014               /* 1/exp(5sec/5min) */
#define EXP_15       2037               /* 1/exp(5sec/15min) */

#define CALC_LOAD(load,exp,n) \
    load *= exp; \
    load += n*(FIXED_1-exp); \
    load >>= FSHIFT;
```

```
#define CT_TO_SECS(x)    ((x) / HZ)
#define CT_TO_USECS(x)   (((x) % HZ) * 1000000/HZ)

extern int nr_running, nr_threads;
extern int last_pid;

#include <linux/fs.h>
#include <linux/time.h>
#include <linux/param.h>
#include <linux/resource.h>
#include <linux/timer.h>

#include <asm/processor.h>

#define TASK_RUNNING            0
#define TASK_INTERRUPTIBLE      1
#define TASK_UNINTERRUPTIBLE    2
#define TASK_ZOMBIE             4
#define TASK_STOPPED            8
#define TASK_EXCLUSIVE          32

#define __set_task_state(tsk, state_value)          \
    do { (tsk)->state = (state_value); } while (0)
#ifdef __SMP__
#define set_task_state(tsk, state_value)            \
    set_mb((tsk)->state, (state_value))
#else
#define set_task_state(tsk, state_value)            \
    __set_task_state((tsk), (state_value))
#endif

#define __set_current_state(state_value)                \
    do { current->state = (state_value); } while (0)
#ifdef __SMP__
#define set_current_state(state_value)              \
    set_mb(current->state, (state_value))
#else
#define set_current_state(state_value)              \
    __set_current_state(state_value)
#endif

/*
 * Scheduling policies
 */
#define SCHED_OTHER             0
#define SCHED_FIFO      1
#define SCHED_RR        2

/*
 * This is an additional bit set when we want to
 * yield the CPU for one re-schedule..
 */
#define SCHED_YIELD             0x10
```

```
struct sched_param {
    int sched_priority;
};

#ifdef __KERNEL__

#include <linux/spinlock.h>

/*
 * This serializes "schedule()" and also protects
 * the run-queue from deletions/modifications (but
 * _adding_ to the beginning of the run-queue has
 * a separate lock).
 */
extern rwlock_t tasklist_lock;
extern spinlock_t runqueue_lock;

extern void sched_init(void);
extern void init_idle(void);
extern void show_state(void);
extern void cpu_init (void);
extern void trap_init(void);
extern void update_one_process( struct task_struct *p,
    unsigned long ticks, unsigned long user, unsigned long system, int cpu);

#define  MAX_SCHEDULE_TIMEOUT    LONG_MAX
extern signed long FASTCALL(sche dule_timeout(signed long timeout));
asmlinkage void schedule(void);

/*
 * The default fd array needs to be at least BITS_PER_LONG,
 * as this is the granularity returned by copy_fdset().
 */
#define NR_OPEN_DEFAULT BITS_PER_LONG

/*
 * Open file table structure
 */
struct files_struct {
    atomic_t count;
    rwlock_t file_lock;
    int max_fds;
    int max_fdset;
    int next_fd;
    struct file ** fd; /* current fd array */
    fd_set *close_on_exec;
    fd_set *open_fds;
    fd_set close_on_exec_init;
    fd_set open_fds_init;
    struct file * fd_array[NR_OPEN_DEFAULT];
};

#define INIT_FILES { \
    ATOMIC_INIT(1), \
```

```
        RW_LOCK_UNLOCKED, \
        NR_OPEN_DEFAULT, \
        __FD_SETSIZE, \
        0, \
        &init_files.fd_array[0], \
        &init_files.close_on_exec_init, \
        &init_files.open_fds_init, \
        { { 0, } }, \
        { { 0, } }, \
        { NULL, } \
}

struct fs_struct {
        atomic_t count;
        int umask;
        struct dentry * root, * pwd;
};

#define INIT_FS { \
        ATOMIC_INIT(1), \
        0022, \
        NULL, NULL \
}

/* Maximum number of active map areas.. This is a random (large) number */
#define MAX_MAP_COUNT   (65536)

/* Number of map areas at which the AVL tree is activated. This is arbitrary. */
#define AVL_MIN_MAP_COUNT   32

struct mm_struct {
        struct vm_area_struct * mmap;         /* list of VMAs */
        struct vm_area_struct * mmap_avl;     /* tree of VMAs */
        struct vm_area_struct * mmap_cache;   /* last find_vma result */
        pgd_t * pgd;
        atomic_t mm_users;   /* How many users with user space? */
        atomic_t mm_count;   /* How many references to "struct mm_struct" (users count
                                as 1) */
        int map_count;       /* number of VMAs */
        struct semaphore mmap_sem;
        spinlock_t page_table_lock;
        unsigned long context;
        unsigned long start_code, end_code, start_data, end_data;
        unsigned long start_brk, brk, start_stack;
        unsigned long arg_start, arg_end, env_start, env_end;
        unsigned long rss, total_vm, locked_vm;
        unsigned long def_flags;
        unsigned long cpu_vm_mask;
        unsigned long swap_cnt; /* number of pages to swap on next pass */
        unsigned long swap_address;
        /*
         * This is an architecture-specific pointer: the portable
         * part of Linux does not know about any segments.
         */
```

```
        void * segments;
};

#define INIT_MM(name) {                         \
        &init_mmap, NULL, NULL,                 \
        swapper_pg_dir,                         \
        ATOMIC_INIT(2), ATOMIC_INIT(1), 1,      \
        __MUTEX_INITIALIZER(name.mmap_sem),     \
        SPIN_LOCK_UNLOCKED,                     \
        0,                                      \
        0, 0, 0, 0,                             \
        0, 0, 0,                                \
        0, 0, 0, 0,                             \
        0, 0, 0,                                \
        0, 0, 0, 0, NULL }

struct signal_struct {
    atomic_t        count;
    struct k_sigaction action[_NSIG];
    spinlock_t          siglock;
};


#define INIT_SIGNALS { \
        ATOMIC_INIT(1), \
        { {{0,}}, }, \
        SPIN_LOCK_UNLOCKED }

/*
 * Some day this will be a full-fledged user tracking system..
 * Right now it is only used to track how many processes a
 * user has, but it has the potential to track memory usage etc.
 */
struct user_struct;

struct task_struct {
/* these are hardcoded - don't touch */
    volatile long state;    /* -1 unrunnable, 0 runnable, >0 stopped */
    unsigned long flags;    /* per process flags, defined below */
    int sigpending;
    mm_segment_t addr_limit;    /* thread address space:
                                0-0xBFFFFFFF for user-thead
                                0-0xFFFFFFFF for kernel-thread
                            */
    struct exec_domain *exec_domain;
    volatile long need_resched;

    cycles_t avg_slice;
    int lock_depth;             /* Lock depth. We can context switch in and out of
                                holding a syscall kernel lock... */
/* begin intel cache line */
    long counter;
    long priority;
    unsigned long policy;
```

```
/* memory management info */
    struct mm_struct *mm, *active_mm;
    int has_cpu;
    int processor;
    struct list_head run_list;
    struct task_struct *next_task, *prev_task;
    int last_processor;

/* task state */
    struct linux_binfmt *binfmt;
    int exit_code, exit_signal;
    int pdeath_signal;  /*  The signal sent when the parent dies  */
    /* ??? */
    unsigned long personality;
    int dumpable:1;
    int did_exec:1;
    pid_t pid;
    pid_t pgrp;
    pid_t tty_old_pgrp;
    pid_t session;
    /* boolean value for session group leader */
    int leader;
    /*
     * pointers to (original) parent process, youngest child, younger sibling,
     * older sibling, respectively.  (p->father can be repla ced with
     * p->p_pptr->pid)
     */
    struct task_struct *p_opptr, *p_pptr, *p_cptr, *p_ysptr, *p_osptr;

    /* PID hash table linkage. */
    struct task_struct *pidhash_next;
    struct task_struct **pidhash_pprev;

    wait_queue_head_t wait_chldexit; /* for wait4() */
    struct semaphore *vfork_sem;     /* for vfork() */
    unsigned long rt_priority;
    unsigned long it_real_value, it_prof_value, it_virt_value;
    unsigned long it_real_incr, it_prof_incr, it_virt_incr;
    struct timer_list real_timer;
    struct tms times;
    unsigned long start_time;
    long per_cpu_utime[NR_CPUS], per_cpu_stime[NR_CPUS];
/* mm fault and swap info: this can arguably be seen as either mm-specific or
   thread-specific */
    unsigned long min_flt, maj_flt, nswap, cmin_flt, cmaj_flt, cnswap;
    int swappable:1;
/* process credentials */
    uid_t uid,euid,suid,fsuid;
    gid_t gid,egid,sgid,fsgid;
    int ngroups;
    gid_t    groups[NGROUPS];
    kernel_cap_t  cap_effective, cap_inheritable, cap_permitted;
    struct user_struct *user;
/* limits */
```

```
        struct rlimit rlim[RLIM_NLIMITS];
        unsigned short used_math;
        char comm[16];
/* file system info */
        int link_count;
        struct tty_struct *tty; /* NULL if no tty */
/* ipc stuff */
        struct sem_undo *semundo;
        struct sem_queue *semsleeping;
/* CPU-specific state of this task */
        struct thread_struct thread;
/* filesystem information */
        struct fs_struct *fs;
/* open file information */
        struct files_struct *files;
/* signal handlers */
        spinlock_t sigmask_lock;        /* Protects signal and blocked */
        struct signal_struct *sig;
        sigset_t signal, blocked;
        struct signal_queue *sigqueue, **sigqueue_tail;
        unsigned long sas_ss_sp;
        size_t sas_ss_size;

/* Thread group tracking */
        u32 parent_exec_id;
        u32 self_exec_id;
/* Protection of fields allocatio/deallocation */
        struct semaphore exit_sem;
};

/*
 * Per process flags
 */
#define PF_ALIGNWARN    0x00000001      /* Print alignment warning msgs */
                                        /* Not implemented yet, only for 486*/
#define PF_STARTING     0x00000002      /* being created */
#define PF_EXITING      0x00000004      /* getting shut down */
#define PF_PTRACED      0x00000010      /* set if ptrace (0) has been called */
#define PF_TRACESYS     0x00000020      /* tracing system calls */
#define PF_FORKNOEXEC   0x00000040      /* forked but didn't exec */
#define PF_SUPERPRIV    0x00000100      /* used super-user privileges */
#define PF_DUMPCORE     0x00000200      /* dumped core */
#define PF_SIGNALED     0x00000400      /* killed by a signal */
#define PF_MEMALLOC     0x00000800      /* Allocating memory */
#define PF_VFORK        0x00001000      /* Wake up parent in mm_release */

#define PF_USEDFPU      0x00100000      /* task used FPU this quantum (SMP) */
#define PF_DTRACE       0x00200000      /* delayed trace (used on m68k, i386) */

/*
 * Limit the stack by to some sane default: root can always
 * increase this limit if needed.. 8MB seems reasonable.
 */
#define _STK_LIM    (8*1024*1024)
```

```
#define DEF_PRIORITY    (20*HZ/100)    /* 200 ms time slices */

/*
 *  INIT_TASK is used to set up the first task table, touch at
 * your own risk!. Base=0, limit=0x1fffff (=2MB)
 */
#define INIT_TASK(tsk) \
{                                                     \
    state:          0,                        \
    flags:          0,                        \
    sigpending:         0,                         \
    addr_limit:         KERNEL_DS,                     \
    exec_domain:    &default_exec_domain,              \
    lock_depth:         -1,                    \
    counter:        DEF_PRIORITY,                  \
    priority:       DEF_PRIORITY,                  \
    policy:         SCHED_OTHER,                   \
    mm:             NULL,                  \
    active_mm:      &init_mm,               \
    run_list:       LIST_HEAD_INIT(tsk.run_list),         \
    next_task:      &tsk,                   \
    prev_task:      &tsk,                   \
    p_opptr:        &tsk,                   \
    p_pptr:         &tsk,                   \
    wait_chldexit: __WAIT_QUEUE_HEAD_INITIALIZER(tsk.wait_chldexit),\
    real_timer:         {                  \
     function:      it_real_fn              \
     },                                     \
    cap_effective: CAP_INIT_EFF_SET,             \
    cap_inheritable:    CAP_INIT_INH_SET,              \
    cap_permitted: CAP_FULL_SET,                 \
    rlim:       INIT_RLIMITS,                \
    comm:       "swapper",                   \
    thread:         INIT_THREAD,                   \
    fs:             &init_fs,               \
    files:          &init_files,                   \
    sigmask_lock:   SPIN_LOCK_UNLOCKED,                  \
    sig:        &init_signals,               \
    signal:         {{0}},                         \
    blocked:        {{0}},                         \
    sigqueue:       NULL,                  \
sigqueue_tail:&tsk.sigqueue,                 \
    exit_sem:       __MUTEX_INITIALIZER(tsk.exit_sem)            \
}


#ifndef INIT_TASK_SIZE
# define INIT_TASK_SIZE 2048*sizeof(long)
#endif

union task_union {
    struct task_struct task;
    unsigned long stack[INIT_TASK_SIZE/sizeof(long)];
```

```
};

extern union task_union init_task_union;

extern struct    mm_struct init_mm;
extern struct task_struct *init_tasks[NR_CPUS];

/* PID hashing. (shouldnt this be dynamic?) */
#define PIDHASH_SZ (4096 >> 2)
extern struct task_struct *pidhash[PIDHASH_SZ];

#define pid_hashfn(x)   ((((x) >> 8) ^ (x)) & (PIDHASH_SZ - 1))

extern __inline__ void hash_pid(struct task_struct *p)
{
    struct task_struct **htable = &pidhash[pid_hashfn(p->pid)];

    if((p->pidhash_next = *htable) != NULL)
        (*htable)->pidhash_pprev = &p->pidhash_next;
    *htable = p;
    p->pidhash_pprev = htable;
}

extern __inline__ void unhash_pid(struct task_struct *p)
{
    if(p->pidhash_next)
        p->pidhash_next->pidhash_pprev = p->pidhash_pprev;
    *p->pidhash_pprev = p->pidhash_next;
}

extern __inline__ struct task_struct *find_task_by_pid(int pid)
{
    struct task_struct *p, **htable = &pidhash[pid_hashfn(pid)];

    for(p = *htable; p && p->pid != pid; p = p->pidhash_next)
        ;

    return p;
}

/* per-UID process charging. */
extern int alloc_uid(struct task_struct *);
void free_uid(struct task_struct *);

#include <asm/current.h>

extern unsigned long volatile jiffies;
extern unsigned long itimer_ticks;
extern unsigned long itimer_next;
extern struct timeval xtime;
extern void do_timer(struct pt_regs *);

extern unsigned int * prof_buffer;
extern unsigned long prof_len;
```

```
extern unsigned long prof_shift;

#define CURRENT_TIME (xtime.tv_sec)

extern void FASTCALL(__wake_up(wait_queue_head_t *q, unsigned int mode));
extern void FASTCALL(__wake_up_sync(wait_queue_head_t *q, unsigned int mode));
extern void FASTCALL(sleep_on(wait_queue_head_t *q));
extern long FASTCALL(sleep_on_timeout(wait_queue_head_t *q,
                     signed long timeout));
extern void FASTCALL(interruptible_sleep_on(wait_queue_head_t *q));
extern long FASTCALL(interruptible_sleep_on_timeout(wait_queue_head_t *q,
                          signed long timeout));
extern void FASTCALL(wake_up_process(struct task_struct * tsk));

#define wake_up(x)          __wake_up((x),TASK_UNINTERRUPTIBLE | TASK_INTERRUPTIBLE |
                            TASK_EXCLUSIVE)
#define wake_up_all(x)      __wake_up((x),TASK_UNINTERRUPTIBLE | TASK_INTERRUPTIBLE)
#define wake_up_sync(x)     __wake_up_sync((x),TASK_UNINTERRUPTIBLE |
                            TASK_INTERRUPTIBLE | TASK_EXCLUSIVE)
#define wake_up_interruptible(x)  __wake_up((x),TASK_INTERRUPTIBLE | TASK_EXCLUSIVE)
#define wake_up_interruptible_all(x)  __wake_up((x),TASK_INTERRUPTIBLE)
#define wake_up_interruptible_sync(x)  __wake_up_sync((x),TASK_INTERRUPTIBLE |
                                   TASK_EXCLUSIVE)

extern int in_group_p(gid_t);
extern int in_egroup_p(gid_t);

extern void flush_signals(struct task_struct *);
extern void flush_signal_handlers(struct task_struct *);
extern int dequeue_signal(sigset_t *, siginfo_t *);
extern int send_sig_info(int, struct siginfo *, struct task_struct *);
extern int force_sig_info(int, struct siginfo *, struct task_struct *);
extern int kill_pg_info(int, struct siginfo *, pid_t);
extern int kill_sl_info(int, struct siginfo *, pid_t);
extern int kill_proc_info(int, struct siginfo *, pid_t);
extern int kill_something_info(int, struct siginfo *, int);
extern void notify_parent(struct task_struct *, int);
extern void force_sig(int, struct task_struct *);
extern int send_sig(int, struct task_struct *, int);
extern int kill_pg(pid_t, int, int);
extern int kill_sl(pid_t, int, int);
extern int kill_proc(pid_t, int, int);
extern int do_sigaction(int, const struct k_sigaction *, struct k_sigaction *);
extern int do_sigaltstack(const stack_t *, stack_t *, unsigned long);

extern inline int signal_pending(struct task_struct *p)
{
    return (p->sigpending != 0);
}

/* Reevaluate whether the task has signals pending delivery.
   This is required every time the blocked sigset_t changes.
   All callers should have t->sigmask_lock.   */
```

```
static inline void recalc_sigpending(struct task_struct *t)
{
    unsigned long read y;
    long i;

    switch (_NSIG_WORDS) {
    default:
        for (i = _NSIG_WORDS, ready = 0; --i >= 0 ;)
            ready |= t->signal.sig[i] &~ t->blocked.sig[i];
        break;

    case 4: ready  = t->signal.sig[3] &~ t->blocked.sig[3];
        ready |= t->signal.sig[2] &~ t->blocked.sig[2];
        ready |= t->signal.sig[1] &~ t->blocked.sig[1];
        ready |= t->signal.sig[0] &~ t->blocked.sig[0];
        break;

    case 2: ready  = t->signal.sig[1] &~ t->blocked.sig[1];
        ready |= t->signal.sig[0] &~ t->blocked.sig[0];
        break;

    case 1: ready  = t->signal.sig[0] &~ t->blocked.sig[0];
    }

    t->sigpending = (ready != 0);
}

/* True if we are on the alternate signal stack.   */

static inline int on_sig_stack(unsigned long sp)
{
    return (sp - current->sas_ss_sp < current->sas_ss_size);
}

static inline int sas_ss_flags(unsigned long sp)
{
    return (current->sas_ss_size == 0 ? SS_DISABLE
        : on_sig_stack(sp) ? SS_ONSTACK : 0);
}

extern int request_irq(unsigned int,
                void (*handler)(int, void *, struct pt_regs *),
                unsigned long, const char *, void *);
extern void free_irq(unsigned int, void *);

/*
 * This has now become a routine instead of a macro, it sets a flag if
 * it returns true (to do BSD-style accounting where the process is flagged
 * if it uses root privs). The implication of this is that you should do
 * normal permissions checks first, and check suser() last.
 *
 * [Dec 1997 -- Chris Evans]
 * For correctness, the above considerations need to be extended to
 * fsuser(). This is done, along with moving fsuser() checks to be
```

```
 * last.
 *
 * These will be removed, but in the mean time, when the SECURE_NOROOT
 * flag is set, uids don't grant privilege.
 */
extern inline int suser(void)
{
    if (!issecure(SECURE_NOROOT) && current->euid == 0) {
        current->flags |= PF_SUPERPRIV;
        return 1;
    }
    return 0;
}

extern inline int fsuser(void)
{
    if (!issecure(SECURE_NOROOT) && current->fsuid == 0) {
        current->flags |= PF_SUPERPRIV;
        return 1;
    }
    return 0;
}

/*
 * capable() checks for a particular capability.
 * New privilege checks should use this interface, rather than suser() or
 * fsuser(). See include/linux/capability.h for defined capabilities.
 */

extern inline int capable(int cap)
{
#if 1 /* ok now */
    if (cap_raised(current->cap_effective, cap))
#else
    if (cap_is_fs_cap(cap) ? current->fsuid == 0 : current->euid == 0)
#endif
    {
        current->flags |= PF_SUPERPRIV;
        return 1;
    }
    return 0;
}

/*
 * Routines for handling mm_structs
 */
extern struct mm_struct * mm_alloc(void);

extern struct mm_struct * start_lazy_tlb(void);
extern void end_lazy_tlb(struct mm_struct *mm);

/* mmdrop drops the mm and the page tables */
extern inline void FASTCALL(__mmdrop(struct mm_struct *));
static inline void mmdrop(struct mm_struct * mm)
```

```
{
    if (atomic_dec_and_test(&mm->mm_count))
        __mmdrop(mm);
}

/* mmput gets rid of the mappings and all user-space */
extern void mmput(struct mm_struct *);
/* Remove the current tasks stale references to the old mm_struct */
extern void mm_release(void);

/*
 * Routines for handling the fd arrays
 */
extern struct file ** alloc_fd_array(int);
extern int expand_fd_array(struct files_struct *, int nr);
extern void free_fd_array(struct file **, int);

extern fd_set *alloc_fdset(int);
extern int expand_fdset(struct files_struct *, int nr);
extern void free_fdset(fd_set *, int);

/* Expand files.  Return <0 on error; 0 nothing done; 1 files expanded,
 * we may have blocked.
 *
 * Should be called with the files->file_lock spinlock held for write.
 */
static inline int expand_files(struct files_struct *files, int nr)
{
    int err, expand = 0;
#ifdef FDSET_DEBUG
    printk (KERN_ERR __FUNCTION__ " %d: nr = %d\n", current->pid, nr);
#endif

    if (nr >= files->max_fdset) {
        expand = 1;
        if ((err = expand_fdset(files, nr)))
            goto out;
    }
    if (nr >= files->max_fds) {
        expand = 1;
        if ((err = expand_fd_array(files, nr)))
            goto out;
    }
    err = expand;
 out:
#ifdef FDSET_DEBUG
    if (err)
        printk (KERN_ERR __FUNCTION__ " %d: return %d\n", current->pid, err);
#endif
    return err;
}

extern int  copy_thread(int , unsigned long, unsigned long, struct task_struct *,
struct pt_regs *);
```

```
extern void flush_thread(void);
extern void exit_thread(void);

extern void exit_mm(struct task_struct *);
extern void exit_fs(struct task_struct *);
extern void exit_files(struct task_struct *);
extern void exit_sighand(struct task_struct *);

extern void daemonize(void);

extern int do_execve(char *, char **, char **, struct pt_regs *);
extern int do_fork(unsigned long, unsigned long, struct pt_regs *);

extern inline void add_wait_queue(wait_queue_head_t *q, wait_queue_t * wait)
{
    unsigned long flags;

    wq_write_lock_irqsave(&q->lock, flags);
    __add_wait_queue(q, wait);
    wq_write_unlock_irqrestore(&q->lock, flags);
}

extern inline void add_wait_queue_exclusive(wait_queue_head_t *q,
                                wait_queue_t * wait)
{
    unsigned long flags;

    wq_write_lock_irqsave(&q->lock, flags);
    __add_wait_queue_tail(q, wait);
    wq_write_unlock_irqrestore(&q->lock, flags);
}

extern inline void remove_wait_queue(wait_queue_head_t *q, wait_queue_t * wait)
{
    unsigned long flags;

    wq_write_lock_irqsave(&q->lock, flags);
    __remove_wait_queue(q, wait);
    wq_write_unlock_irqrestore(&q->lock, flags);
}

#define __wait_event(wq, condition)                            \
do {                                                    \
    wait_queue_t __wait;                                   \
    init_waitqueue_entry(&__wait, current);                       \
                                                   \
    add_wait_queue(&wq, &__wait);                            \
    for (;;) {                                        \
        set_current_state(TASK_UNINTERRUPTIBLE);           \
        if (condition)                              \
            break;                                 \
        schedule();                                 \
    }                                             \
    current->state = TASK_RUNNING;                               \
```

```
        remove_wait_queue(&wq, &__wait);                        \
} while (0)

#define wait_event(wq, condition)                               \
do {                                                    \
    if (condition)                                      \
        break;                                          \
    __wait_event(wq, condition);                            \
} while (0)

#define __wait_event_interruptible(wq, condition, ret)          \
do {                                                \
    wait_queue_t __wait;                                \
    init_waitqueue_entry(&__wait, current);                 \
                                            \
    add_wait_queue(&wq, &__wait);                       \
    for (;;) {                                      \
        set_current_state(TASK_INTERRUPTIBLE);              \
        if (condition)                              \
            break;                                  \
        if (!signal_pending(current)) {                     \
            schedule();                             \
            continue;                           \
        }                                   \
        ret = -ERESTARTSYS;                         \
        break;                                  \
    }                                       \
    current->state = TASK_RUNNING;                      \
    remove_wait_queue(&wq, &__wait);                    \
} while (0)

#define wait_event_interruptible(wq, condition)                 \
({                                          \
    int __ret = 0;                                  \
    if (!(condition))                               \
        __wait_event_interruptible(wq, condition, __ret);    \
    __ret;                                      \
})

#define REMOVE_LINKS(p) do { \
    (p)->next_task->prev_task = (p)->prev_task; \
    (p)->prev_task->next_task = (p)->next_task; \
    if ((p)->p_osptr) \
        (p)->p_osptr->p_ysptr = (p)->p_ysptr; \
    if ((p)->p_ysptr) \
        (p)->p_ysptr->p_osptr = (p)->p_osptr; \
    else \
        (p)->p_pptr->p_cptr = (p)->p_osptr; \
    } while (0)

#define SET_LINKS(p) do { \
    (p)->next_task = &init_task; \
    (p)->prev_task = init_task.prev_task; \
    init_task.prev_task->next_task = (p); \
```

```
        init_task.prev_task = (p); \
        (p)->p_ysptr = NULL; \
        if (((p)->p_osptr = (p)->p_pptr->p_cptr) != NULL) \
            (p)->p_osptr->p_ysptr = p; \
        (p)->p_pptr->p_cptr = p; \
        } while (0)

#define for_each_task(p) \
        for (p = &init_task ; (p = p->next_task) != &init_task ; )


static inline void del_from_runqueue(struct task_struct * p)
{
        nr_running--;
        list_del(&p->run_list);
        p->run_list.next = NULL;
}

extern inline int task_on_runqueue(struct task_struct *p)
{
        return (p->run_list.next != NULL);
}

extern inline void unhash_process(struct task_struct *p)
{
        if (task_on_runqueue(p)) BUG();
        write_lock_irq(&tasklist_lock);
        nr_threads--;
        unhash_pid(p);
        REMOVE_LINKS(p);
        write_unlock_irq(&tasklist_lock);
}

static inline int task_lock(struct task_struct *p)
{
        down(&p->exit_sem);
        if (p->p_pptr)
            return 1;
        /* He's dead, Jim. You take his wallet, I'll take the tricorder... */
        up(&p->exit_sem);
        return 0;
}

static inline void task_unlock(struct task_struct *p)
{
        up(&p->exit_sem);
}

#endif /* __KERNEL__ */

#endif
```

Data Structures—linux/include/mm.h

```
#ifndef _LINUX_MM_H
#define _LINUX_MM_H

#include <linux/sched.h>
#include <linux/errno.h>

#ifdef __KERNEL__

#include <linux/config.h>
#include <linux/string.h>
#include <linux/list.h>
#include <linux/mmzone.h>

extern unsigned long max_mapnr;
extern unsigned long num_physpages;
extern void * high_memory;
extern int page_cluster;

#include <asm/page.h>
#include <asm/pgtable.h>
#include <asm/atomic.h>

/*
 * Linux kernel virtual memory manager primitives.
 * The idea being to have a "virtual" mm in the same way
 * we have a virtual fs - giving a cleaner interface to the
 * mm details, and allowing different kinds of memory mappings
 * (from shared memory to executable loading to arbitrary
 * mmap() functions).
 */

/*
 * This struct defines a memory VMM memory area. There is one of these
 * per VM-area/task.  A VM area is any part of the process virtual memory
 * space that has a special rule for the page-fault handlers (ie a shared
 * library, the executable area etc).
 */
struct vm_area_struct {
    struct mm_struct * vm_mm;    /* VM area parameters */
    unsigned long vm_start;
    unsigned long vm_end;

    /* linked list of VM areas per task, sorted by address */
    struct vm_area_struct *vm_next;

    pgprot_t vm_page_prot;
    unsigned long vm_flags;

    /* AVL tree of VM areas per task, sorted by address */
    short vm_avl_height;
    struct vm_area_struct * vm_avl_left;
```

```
        struct vm_area_struct * vm_avl_right;

        /* For areas with inode, the list inode->i_mmap, for shm areas,
         * the list of attaches, otherwise unused.
         */
        struct vm_area_struct *vm_next_share;
        struct vm_area_struct **vm_pprev_share;

        struct vm_operations_struct * vm_ops;
        unsigned long vm_pgoff;    /* offset in PAGE_SIZE units, *not* PAGE_CACHE_SIZE */
        struct file * vm_file;
        void * vm_private_data;    /* was vm_pte (shared mem) */
};

/*
 * vm_flags..
 */
#define VM_READ         0x00000001      /* currently active flags */
#define VM_WRITE        0x00000002
#define VM_EXEC         0x00000004
#define VM_SHARED       0x00000008

#define VM_MAYREAD      0x00000010      /* limits for mprotect() etc */
#define VM_MAYWRITE     0x00000020
#define VM_MAYEXEC      0x00000040
#define VM_MAYSHARE     0x00000080

#define VM_GROWSDOWN    0x00000100      /* general info on the segment */
#define VM_GROWSUP      0x00000200
#define VM_SHM          0x00000400      /* shared memory area, don't swap out */
#define VM_DENYWRITE    0x00000800      /* ETXTBSY on write attempts.. */

#define VM_EXECUTABLE   0x00001000
#define VM_LOCKED       0x00002000
#define VM_IO           0x00004000      /* Memory mapped I/O or similar */

#define VM_STACK_FLAGS 0x00000177

/*
 * mapping from the currently active vm_flags protection bits (the
 * low four bits) to a page protection mask..
 */
extern pgprot_t protection_map[16];


/*
 * These are the virtual MM functions - opening of an area, closing and
 * unmapping it (needed to keep files on disk up-to-date etc), pointer
 * to the functions called when a no-page or a wp-page exception occurs.
 */
struct vm_operations_struct {
        void (*open)(struct vm_area_struct * area);
        void (*close)(struct vm_area_struct * area);
        void (*unmap)(struct vm_area_struct *area, unsigned long, size_t);
```

```
        void (*protect)(struct vm_area_struct *area, unsigned long, size_t, unsigned int
            newprot);
        int (*sync)(struct vm_area_struct *area, unsigned long, size_t, unsigned int
            flags);
        void (*advise)(struct vm_area_struct *area, unsigned long, size_t, unsigned int
            advise);
        struct page * (*nopage)(struct vm_area_struct * area, unsigned long address, int
            write_access);
        struct page * (*wppage)(struct vm_area_struct * area, unsigned long address,
            struct page * page);
        int (*swapout)(struct page *, struct file *);
};

/*
 * A swap entry has to fit into a "unsigned long", as
 * the entry is hidden in the "index" field of the
 * swapper address space.
 */
typedef struct {
    unsigned long val;
} swp_entry_t;

/*
 * Try to keep the most commonly accessed fields in single cache lines
 * here (16 bytes or greater).  This ordering should be particularly
 * beneficial on 32-bit processors.
 *
 * The first line is data used in page cache lookup, the second line
 * is used for linear searches (eg. clock algorithm scans).
 */
typedef struct page {
    struct list_head list;
    struct address_space *mapping;
    unsigned long index;
    struct page *next_hash;
    atomic_t count;
    unsigned long flags;    /* atomic flags, some possibly updated asynchronously */
    struct list_head lru;
    wait_queue_head_t wait;
    struct page **pprev_hash;
    struct buffer_head * buffers;
    unsigned long virtual; /* nonzero if kmapped */
    struct zone_struct *zone;
} mem_map_t;

#define get_page(p)             atomic_inc(&(p)->count)
#define put_page(p)             __free_page(p)
#define put_page_testzero(p)    atomic_dec_and_test(&(p)->count)
#define page_count(p)           atomic_read(&(p)->count)
#define set_page_count(p,v)     atomic_set(&(p)->count, v)

/* Page flag bit values */
#define PG_locked        0
#define PG_error         1
```

```
#define PG_referenced           2
#define PG_uptodate             3
#define PG__unused_00           4
#define PG_decr_after           5
#define PG_unused_01            6
#define PG__unused_02           7
#define PG_slab                 8
#define PG_swap_cache           9
#define PG_skip                 10
#define PG_swap_entry           11
#define PG_highmem              12
                                /* bits 21-30 unused */
#define PG_reserved             31


/* Make it prettier to test the above... */
#define Page_Uptodate(page)     test_bit(PG_uptodate, &(page)->flags)
#define SetPageUptodate(page)   set_bit(PG_uptodate, &(page)->flags)
#define ClearPageUptodate(page) clear_bit(PG_uptodate, &(page)->flags)
#define PageLocked(page)        test_bit(PG_locked, &(page)->flags)
#define LockPage(page)          set_bit(PG_locked, &(page)->flags)
#define TryLockPage(page)       test_and_set_bit(PG_locked, &(page)->flags)
#define UnlockPage(page)        do { \
                                    clear_bit(PG_locked, &(page)->flags); \
                                    wake_up(&page->wait); \
                                } while (0)
#define PageError(page)         test_bit(PG_error, &(page)->flags)
#define SetPageError(page)      test_and_set_bit(PG_error, &(page)->flags)
#define ClearPageError(page)    clear_bit(PG_error, &(page)->flags)
#define PageReferenced(page)    test_bit(PG_referenced, &(page)->flags)
#define PageDecrAfter(page)     test_bit(PG_decr_after, &(page)->flags)
#define PageSlab(page)          test_bit(PG_slab, &(page)->flags)
#define PageSwapCache(page)     test_bit(PG_swap_cache, &(page)->flags)
#define PageReserved(page)      test_bit(PG_reserved, &(page)->flags)

#define PageSetSlab(page)       set_bit(PG_slab, &(page)->flags)
#define PageSetSwapCache(page)  set_bit(PG_swap_cache, &(page)->flags)

#define PageTestandSetSwapCache(page) test_and_set_bit(PG_swap_cache, &(page)->flags)

#define PageClearSlab(page)     clear_bit(PG_slab, &(page)->flags)
#define PageClearSwapCache(page) clear_bit(PG_swap_cache, &(page)->flags)

#define PageTestandClearSwapCache(page)    test_and_clear_bit(PG_swap_cache,
                                           &(page)->flags)

#ifdef CONFIG_HIGHMEM
#define PageHighMem(page)       test_bit(PG_highmem, &(page)->flags)
#else
#define PageHighMem(page)       0 /* needed to optimize away at compile time */
#endif

#define SetPageReserved(page)       set_bit(PG_reserved, &(page)->flags)
#define ClearPageReserved(page)     clear_bit(PG_reserved, &(page)->flags)
```

```
/*
 * Error return values for the *_nopage functions
 */
#define NOPAGE_SIGBUS   (NULL)
#define NOPAGE_OOM ((struct page *) (-1))


/*
 * Various page->flags bits:
 *
 * PG_reserved is set for a page which must never be accessed (which
 * may not even be present).
 *
 * PG_DMA has been removed, page->zone now tells exactly wether the
 * page is suited to do DMAing into.
 *
 * Multiple processes may "see" the same page. E.g. for untouched
 * mappings of /dev/null, all processes see the same page full of
 * zeroes, and text pages of executables and shared libraries have
 * only one copy in memory, at most, normally.
 *
 * For the non-reserved pages, page->count denotes a reference count.
 *    page->count == 0 means the page is free.
 *    page->count == 1 means the page is used for exactly one purpose
 *    (e.g. a private data page of one process).
 *
 * A page may be used for kmalloc() or anyone else who does a
 * __get_free_page(). In this case the page->count is at least 1, and
 * all other fields are unused but should be 0 or NULL. The
 * management of this page is the responsibility of the one who uses
 * it.
 *
 * The other pages (we may call them "process pages") are completely
 * managed by the Linux memory manager: I/O, buffers, swapping etc.
 * The following discussion applies only to them.
 *
 * A page may belong to an inode's memory mapping. In this case,
 * page->inode is the pointer to the inode, and page->offset is the
 * file offset of the page (not necessarily a multiple of PAGE_SIZE).
 *
 * A page may have buffers allocated to it. In this case,
 * page->buffers is a circular list of these buffer heads. Else,
 * page->buffers == NULL.
 *
 * For pages belonging to inodes, the page->count is the number of
 * attaches, plus 1 if buffers are allocated to the page.
 *
 * All pages belonging to an inode make up a doubly linked list
 * inode->i_pages, using the fields page->next and page->prev. (These
 * fields are also used for freelist management when page->count==0.)
 * There is also a hash table mapping (inode,offset) to the page
 * in memory if present. The lists for this hash table use the fields
 * page->next_hash and page->pprev_hash.
```

```
 *
 * All process pages can do I/O:
 * - inode pages may need to be read from disk,
 * - inode pages which have been modified and are MAP_SHARED may need
 *   to be written to disk,
 * - private pages which have been modified may need to be swapped out
 *   to swap space and (later) to be read back into memory.
 * During disk I/O, PG_locked is used. This bit is set before I/O
 * and reset when I/O completes. page->wait is a wait queue of all
 * tasks waiting for the I/O on this page to complete.
 * PG_uptodate tells whether the page's contents is valid.
 * When a read completes, the page becomes uptodate, unless a disk I/O
 * error happened.
 *
 * For choosing which pages to swap out, inode pages carry a
 * PG_referenced bit, which is set any time the system accesses
 * that page through the (inode,offset) hash table.
 *
 * PG_skip is used on sparc/sparc64 architectures to "skip" certain
 * parts of the address space.
 *
 * PG_error is set to indicate that an I/O error occurred on this page.
 */

extern mem_map_t * mem_map;

/*
 * There is only one page-allocator function, and two main namespaces to
 * it. The alloc_page*() variants return 'struct page *' and as such
 * can allocate highmem pages, the *get*page*() variants return
 * virtual kernel addresses to the allocated page(s).
 */
extern struct page * FASTCALL(__alloc_pages(zonelist_t *zonelist, unsigned long
order));
extern struct page * alloc_pages_node(int nid, int gfp_mask, unsigned long order);

#ifndef CONFIG_DISCONTIGMEM
extern inline struct page * alloc_pages(int gfp_mask, unsigned long order)
{
    /*  temporary check. */
    if (contig_page_data.node_zonelists[gfp_mask].gfp_mask != (gfp_mask))
        BUG();
    /*
     * Gets optimized away by the compiler.
     */
    if (order >= MAX_ORDER)
        return NULL;
    return __alloc_pages(contig_page_data.node_zonelists+(gfp_mask), order);
}
#else /* !CONFIG_DISCONTIGMEM */
extern struct page * alloc_pages(int gfp_mask, unsigned long order);
#endif /* !CONFIG_DISCONTIGMEM */

#define alloc_page(gfp_mask) \
```

```
        alloc_pages(gfp_mask, 0)

extern inline unsigned long __get_free_pages (int gfp_mask, unsigned long order)
{
    struct page * page;

    page = alloc_pages(gfp_mask, order);
    if (!page)
        return 0;
    return page_address(page);
}

#define __get_free_page(gfp_mask) \
        __get_free_pages((gfp_mask),0)

#define __get_dma_pages(gfp_mask, order) \
        __get_free_pages((gfp_mask) | GFP_DMA,(order))

extern inline unsigned long get_zeroed_page(int gfp_mask)
{
    unsigned long page;

    page = __get_free_page(gfp_mask);
    if (page)
        clear_page((void *)page);
    return page;
}

/*
 * The old interface name will be removed in 2.5:
 */
#define get_free_page get_zeroed_page

/*
 * There is only one 'core' page-freeing function.
 */
extern void FASTCALL(__free_pages_ok(struct page * page, unsigned long order));

extern inline void __free_pages(struct page *page, unsigned long order)
{
    if (!put_page_testzero(page))
        return;
    __free_pages_ok(page, order);
}

#define __free_page(page) __free_pages(page, 0)

extern inline void free_pages(unsigned long addr, unsigned long order)
{
    unsigned long map_nr;

#ifdef CONFIG_DISCONTIGMEM
    if (addr == 0) return;
#endif
```

```
        map_nr = MAP_NR(addr);
        if (map_nr < max_mapnr)
            __free_pages(mem_map + map_nr, order);
}


#define free_page(addr) free_pages((addr),0)

extern void show_free_areas(void);
extern void show_free_areas_node(int nid);

extern void clear_page_tables(struct mm_struct *, unsigned long, int);

extern int map_zero_setup(struct vm_area_struct *);

extern void zap_page_range(struct mm_struct *mm, unsigned long address, unsigned
long size);
extern int copy_page_range(struct mm_struct *dst, struct mm_struct *src, struct
vm_area_struct *vma);
extern int remap_page_range(unsigned long from, unsigned long to, unsigned long
size, pgprot_t prot);
extern int zeromap_page_range(unsigned long from, unsigned long size, pgprot_t
prot);

extern void vmtruncate(struct inode * inode, loff_t offset);
extern int handle_mm_fault(struct task_struct *tsk,struct vm_area_struct *vma,
unsigned long address, int write_access);
extern int make_pages_present(unsigned long addr, unsigned long end);
extern int access_process_vm(struct task_struct *tsk, unsigned long addr, void *buf,
int len, int write);
extern int ptrace_readdata(struct task_struct *tsk, unsigned long src, char *dst,
int len);
extern int ptrace_writedata(struct task_struct *tsk, char * src, unsigned long dst,
int len);

extern int pgt_cache_water[2];
extern int check_pgt_cache(void);

extern void free_area_init(unsigned long * zones_size);
extern void free_area_init_node(int nid, pg_data_t *pgdat,
        unsigned long * zones_size, unsigned long zone_start_paddr);
extern void mem_init(void);
extern void show_mem(void);
extern void si_meminfo(struct sysinfo * val);
extern void swapin_readahead(swp_entry_t);

/* mmap.c */
extern void vma_init(void);
extern void merge_segments(struct mm_struct *, unsigned long, unsigned long);
extern void insert_vm_struct(struct mm_struct *, struct vm_area_struct *);
extern void build_mmap_avl(struct mm_struct *);
extern void exit_mmap(struct mm_struct *);
extern unsigned long get_unmapped_area(unsigned long, unsigned long);

extern unsigned long do_mmap_pgoff(struct file *file, unsigned long addr,
```

```
        unsigned long len, unsigned long prot,
        unsigned long flag, unsigned long pgoff);

extern inline unsigned long do_mmap(struct file *file, unsigned long addr,
        unsigned long len, unsigned long prot,
        unsigned long flag, unsigned long offset)
{
        unsigned long ret = -EINVAL;
        if ((offset + PAGE_ALIGN(len)) < offset)
            goto out;
        if (!(offset & ~PAGE_MASK))
            ret = do_mmap_pgoff(file, addr, len, prot, flag, offset >> PAGE_SHIFT);
out:
        return ret;
}

extern int do_munmap(unsigned long, size_t);
extern unsigned long do_brk(unsigned long, unsigned long);

struct zone_t;
/* filemap.c */
extern void remove_inode_page(struct page *);
extern unsigned long page_unuse(struct page *);
extern int shrink_mmap(int, int, zone_t *);
extern void truncate_inode_pages(struct address_space *, loff_t);

/* generic vm_area_ops exported for stackable file systems */
extern int filemap_swapout(struct page * page, struct file *file);
extern pte_t filemap_swapin(struct vm_area_struct * vma,
                unsigned long offset, unsigned long entry);
extern int filemap_sync(struct vm_area_struct * vma, unsigned long address,
                size_t size, unsigned int flags);
extern struct page *filemap_nopage(struct vm_area_struct * area,
                unsigned long address, int no_share);

/*
 * GFP bitmasks..
 */
#define __GFP_WAIT 0x01
#define __GFP_HIGH 0x02
#define __GFP_IO   0x04
#define __GFP_DMA  0x08
#ifdef CONFIG_HIGHMEM
#define __GFP_HIGHMEM   0x10
#else
#define __GFP_HIGHMEM   0x0 /* noop */
#endif


#define GFP_BUFFER (__GFP_HIGH | __GFP_WAIT)
#define GFP_ATOMIC (__GFP_HIGH)
#define GFP_USER   (__GFP_WAIT | __GFP_IO)
#define GFP_HIGHUSER    (GFP_USER | __GFP_HIGHMEM)
#define GFP_KERNEL (__GFP_HIGH | __GFP_WAIT | __GFP_IO)
```

```
#define GFP_NFS          (__GFP_HIGH | __GFP_WAIT | __GFP_IO)
#define GFP_KSWAPD (__GFP_IO)

/* Flag - indicates that the buffer will be suitable for DMA.  Ignored on some
   platforms, used as appropriate on others */

#define GFP_DMA          __GFP_DMA

/* Flag - indicates that the buffer can be taken from high memory which is not
   permanently mapped by the kernel */

#define GFP_HIGHMEM      __GFP_HIGHMEM

/* vma is the first one with  address < vma->vm_end,
 * and even  address < vma->vm_start. Have to extend vma. */
static inline int expand_stack(struct vm_area_struct * vma, unsigned long address)
{
    unsigned long grow;

    address &= PAGE_MASK;
    grow = (vma->vm_start - address) >> PAGE_SHIFT;
    if (vma->vm_end - address > current->rlim[RLIMIT_STACK].rlim_cur ||
        ((vma->vm_mm->total_vm + grow) << PAGE_SHIFT) > current-
>rlim[RLIMIT_AS].rlim_cur)
            return -ENOMEM;
    vma->vm_start = address;
    vma->vm_pgoff -= grow;
    vma->vm_mm->total_vm += grow;
    if (vma->vm_flags & VM_LOCKED)
        vma->vm_mm->locked_vm += grow;
    return 0;
}

/* Look up the first VMA which satisfies  addr < vm_end,  NULL if none. */
extern struct vm_area_struct * find_vma(struct mm_struct * mm, unsigned long addr);
extern struct vm_area_struct * find_vma_prev(struct mm_struct * mm, unsigned long
      addr,
                        struct vm_area_struct **pprev);

/* Look up the first VMA which intersects the interval start_addr..end_addr-1,
   NULL if none.  Assume start_addr < end_addr. */
static inline struct vm_area_struct * find_vma_intersection(struct mm_struct * mm,
      unsigned long start_addr, unsigned long end_addr)
{
    struct vm_area_struct * vma = find_vma(mm,start_addr);

    if (vma && end_addr <= vma->vm_start)
        vma = NULL;
    return vma;
}

extern struct vm_area_struct *find_extend_vma(struct task_struct *tsk, unsigned long
      addr);
```

```
#define buffer_under_min()  (atomic_read(&buffermem_pages) * 100 < \
                  buffer_mem.min_percent * num_physpages)
#define pgcache_under_min() (atomic_read(&page_cache_size) * 100 < \
                  page_cache.min_percent * num_physpages)

#define vmlist_access_lock(mm)         spin_lock(&mm->page_table_lock)
#define vmlist_access_unlock(mm) spin_unlock(&mm->page_table_lock)
#define vmlist_modify_lock(mm)         vmlist_access_lock(mm)
#define vmlist_modify_unlock(mm) vmlist_access_unlock(mm)

#endif /* __KERNEL__ */

#endif
```

The Linux Scheduler

Operating system components, such as demand paging and signals handling, either work correctly or they don't. The individual implementation is not that important. The implementation choices for these components are transparent to the user-space programs. They are simply services that accomplish a required function. Quite the contrary, however, is true for another important component of an OS: the scheduler. More than any other component, the scheduler influences the perceived behavior of a system as a whole, especially on multiple-CPU systems.

A scheduler is responsible for the coordination of the running of processes to manage their access to the system resources such that each candidate process gets a fair share of the available process time, with the utilization of the CPU being maximized. The scheduler (dispatcher) must ensure that a process gains access to the CPU for a time relative to its designated priority and process class and that no process is starved of access to the CPU, even if it is the lowest priority task available.

A process may choose to voluntarily give up its use of the microprocessor when it must wait, usually for some system resource or for synchronization with another process. Alternatively, the scheduler may preemptively remove the thread or process from the CPU at the expiry of its allocated time quantum. The scheduler chooses which is the most appropriate process to run next.

Scheduling is an operation of the kernel, which defines the following process states:

- Running. The process is the current system process and is on the CPU carrying out its execution.
- Running: Ready to Run. The process is in a run queue ready to use the CPU when available.
- Waiting: Interruptible. The process is waiting for a resource or event, but signals are not blocked and it may be interrupted.
- Waiting: Uninterruptible. The process is waiting for a resource or event but has disable signals such that it cannot be interrupted.
- Stopped: The process has been stopped, usually by a SIGSTOP signal, such as when performing debugging.
- Zombie. The process has completed and is ready to die; the scheduler has not yet detected this so its task_struct structure is still present.

The scheduling of tasks on different operating systems is similar, but each OS solves the problem in its own way. In Linux 2.4, tasks have a priority, which ranges from a setting of -20 to $+20$. The default priority of a task is 0, with -20 being the highest. Only the administrator can reset a process's priority to be less than 0, but normal users can adjust priorities in the positive range. This is done using the `renice` command, although internally Linux uses a time quantum counter (in jiffies) to record this in the `task_struct`.

New processes inherit the priority of their parent. Real-time processes are supported. Any real-time process will have higher priority than all non-real–time processes. Threads that have already received some CPU time will have lower priority than others of the same priority which have not.

The data consistency and race condition problems may be addressed by the implementation of *mutual exclusion* and *synchronization* rules between processes, whereas starvation is a function of the scheduler.

There are a number of synchronisation primitives, as shown in Table 6.1.

TABLE 6.1 *Synchronization Primitives*		
Events	A thread may wait for events such as the setting of a flag, integer, signal, or presence of an object. Until that event occurs the thread will be blocked and will be removed from the run queue.
Critical Sections	These are areas of code that can only be accessed by a single thread at any one time.
Mutual Exclusions	Mutexes are objects that ensure that only a single thread has access to a protected variable or code at any one time.
Semaphores	These are similar to mutual exclusions but may include counters allowing only a specified number of threads access to a protected variable or code at any one time.
Atomic operations	This mechanism ensures that a nondecomposable transaction is completed by a thread before access to the same atomic operation is granted to another thread. The thread may have noninterruptible access to the CPU until the operation is completed.

`Deadlock` is a permanent blocking of a set of processes that either compete for system resources or communicate with each other. Deadlock may be addressed by *mutual exclusion* or by *deadlock avoidance*. Mutual exclusion prevents two threads accessing the same resource simultaneously. Deadlock avoidance can include initiation denial or allocation denial, both of which serve to eliminate the state required for deadlock before it arises. Linux implements multiprocessor mutual exclusion mechanisms called spin locks, which effectively stall the processor until a lock is achieved for a critical section.

The Linux scheduler has undergone considerable changes (for the better) since version 1.0. The algorithms for the scheduling of tasks have steadily improved and are now smart enough to be able to predict (well, mostly) the requirements of processes and act accordingly.

In this chapter we will first review the relationships between the main building blocks of scheduling units, tasks, threads, and processes. Then, we will explore a peculiarity of the Linux scheduler, *scheduling heuristics*. The preemption strategies will be discussed, as well as some more general aspects of scheduling as done in Linux. Finally, we will close with two examples of how to improve the functionality provided by the Linux scheduler.

Scheduling Classes

As the scheduler improves, user-space programs experience better throughput and overall shorter latencies for vital kernel tasks. In Linux 2.2.x there are three classes of processes, as can be seen from the data definition for the scheduler. You can find them in `linux/include/linux/sched.h`:

```
/*
 * Scheduling policies
 */
#define SCHED_OTHER       0
#define SCHED_FIFO        1
#define SCHED_R           2
```

- `SCHED_OTHER` tasks are the normal user tasks (default).
- Tasks running in `SCHED_FIFO` will never be preempted. They will leave the CPU only for waiting sync kernel events or if an explicit sleep or reschedule has been requested from user space.
- Tasks running in `SCHED_RR` are real-time too, but they will leave the CPU if there is another real-time task in the run queue. The CPU power will be distributed among all `SCHED_RR` tasks.

If at least one real-time task is running, no `SCHED_OTHER` task will be allowed to run in any CPU.

Each real-time (RT) task has an `rt_priority`, so the `SCHED_RR` class is allowed to custom-distribute CPU power among all the `SCHED_RR` tasks. The `rt_priority` of the `SCHED_RR` class works exactly like the normal priority field for the `SCHED_OTHER` (default) class. Only the root user can change the class of the current task to RT (more precisely, the task must hold the `CAP_SYS_NICE` capability) via the `sched_setscheduler` system call.

One of the tasks of a kernel is to make sure the system remains firmly under its control, even in situations of misbehaving programs. One such misbehaving program might, for instance, fork() too many processes too quickly and the kernel become so busy with itself that it cannot tend to its other responsibilities. Linux has no limit to how fast user-land programs can spawn children. Many commercial UNIX systems have a limit of one fork() per processor tick (jiffy). I wrote the following patch for my kernel, to allow it a maximum of one fork() per jiffie (usually 1/100 sec):

```
--- 2.3.26/kernel/fork.c      Thu Oct 28 22:30:51 1999
+++ /tmp/fork.c     Tue Nov  9 01:34:36 1999
@@ -591,6 +591,14 @@
     int retval = -ENOMEM;
     struct task_struct *p;
     DECLARE_MUTEX_LOCKED(sem);
+    static long last_fork;
+
+    while (time_after(last_fork+1, jiffies))
+    {
+         __set_current_state(TASK_INTERRUPTIBLE);
+         schedule_timeout(1);
+    }
+    last_fork = jiffies;

     if (clone_flags & CLONE_PID) {
          /* This is only allowed from the boot up thread */
```

Threads

Threads, as we saw earlier, are necessary to endow processes with the capability to make use of multiple CPUs. To reiterate, Linux doesn't really make any distinction between a process and a thread from a memory management and scheduling point of view. Some operating systems, like Solaris, make thread management happen within the user process. Inside their threads library, the scheduling of the user-space threads is handled autonomously. The kernel in those operating systems only sees the process and doesn't know which thread—if any—is executing at any given moment inside the user process. This saves the kernel from having to manage lists with thousands of entries for each thread, for each process. As such, this approach is well suited to workloads with relatively few processes, when each process has many hundreds or thousands of threads.

In the Linux implementation of threads, the kernel sees every thread in every process and has to maintain kernel resources (e.g. scheduling lists) for them all. Still, the standard Linux threads model does not preclude the same approach taken by OSs such as Solaris. All that needs to be done is to create an appropriate thread library. The kernel continues to see and schedule the task as a single process.

One shortcoming of the Solaris approach is that threads emulated on the top of one single user process won't be allowed to run concurrently on an SMP system; the user-space approach won't scale in SMP and as such is not very useful. Threading is strictly necessary only when all the threads are CPU-bound. If all the threads are CPU-bound, then you definitely want to scale SMP.

Using threads only to wait for events is overkill; having threads sleep on schedule is a waste of resources and of performance. Almost all kernel subsystems offer asynchronous event registration. It is preferable to manage each asynchronous event via the SIGIO signal, which is a kind of IRQ-driven handling, as opposed to the polled handling as done using threads.

With the user-space approach, you'll at least avoid the translation look-aside buffer (TLB) flushing, as all the threads share the same memory view.

The advantage of having threads managed in user space through the threads library is that this gives the time which would be spent in kernel CPU scheduling over instead to user-space processes. It is true that in user space you may choose to implement a very fast and unfair round-robin scheduler that may cut down the scheduling cost, compared to the clever (but more expensive) kernel scheduler. Still, it is not really worthwhile to adopt the user-space approach, because SMP spin locking is a big hindrance. If the number of running threads is very high, there are kernel patches that make the Linux scheduler a modified scheduler.

Speaking of SMP: as of 2.3.99, pre-2 there is no possibility to declare the processor affinity of any given userspace process. A solution to implement this functionality is presented at the end of this chapter in the section "Improving the Kernel: CPU Affinity."

The 2.2.x kernel scheduler has a bug that makes it, in SMP, sometimes less efficient than the UP (uniprocessor) scheduler. Andrea Arcangeli of Italy fixed all such bugs and rewrote the heuristics from scratch, and his new SMP scheduler gives an impressive SMP improvement under load.

You can get the patch at **ftp://ftp.suse.com/pub/people/andrea/ kernel-patches/my-2.2.12/SMP-scheduler-2_2_11-E**.

This patch can be applied to kernels 2.2.11 and 2.2.12 to speed up both kernels on SMP systems.

The patch was merged into 2.3.15, but not yet into 2.2.x because it's a performance issue only. Some, however, believe it deserves to be integrated into 2.2.x, because it speeds up operation so much on SMP machines. The patch has proven remarkably stable.

SMP Scheduler Heuristics

The 2.4 kernel scheduler for multi-CPU systems implements a modern, heuristic approach. In other words, based on past experience with a task and its behavior, the scheduler will try to predict its future resource requirements and devise and appropriate scheduling policy. The SMP scheduler heuristic works as a function of (in random order):

- The idle CPUs.
- The last CPU where the awakened task ran.
- The MM of the task (for kernel–threads reschedule).
- The *goodness* (a composite assessment, loosely, of importance or priority, explained below) of the tasks running on the busy CPUs.
- The time necessary to invalidate the L2 cache on the running CPU (`cacheflush_time`).
- The average timeslice (`avg_slice`) of the awakened task (how much time the task is allotted to run before returning to sleep).

The algorithm collects the above data and chooses the best CPU on which to reschedule the awakened task.

There are two paths involved in the Linux scheduler behavior:

- `Schedule()`—The running or current task is a SCHED_OTHER task that expired its timeslice, so the kernel runs a `schedule()` while returning from the timer IRQ handler for switching to the next running task.
- `Reschedule_idle()`—A task was awakened (usually from an IRQ) and we try to reschedule such awakened tasks on the best CPU by invoking a `schedule()` on it; it's a kind of controlled `schedule()`.

Both the above share the `goodness()` function. The `goodness()` function can be considered the core of the SMP scheduler. It calculates the goodness of a task as a function of:

- The task currently running
- The task that wants to run
- The current CPU

The goodness function described below can be found in `linux/kernel/sched.c`:

```
/*
 * This is the function that decides how desirable a process is..
 * You can weigh different processes against each other depending
 * on what CPU they've run on lately etc to try to handle cache
 * and TLB miss penalties.
 *
 * Return values:
 *    -1000: never select this
 *        0: out of time, recalculate counters (but it might still be
 *        selected)
 *      +ve: "goodness" value (the larger, the better)
 *    +1000: realtime process, select this.
 */

static inline int goodness(struct task_struct * p, int this_cpu, struct mm_struct
*this_mm)
{
    int weight;

    /*
     * Realtime process, select the first one on the
     * runqueue (taking priorities within processes
     * into account).
     */
    if (p->policy != SCHED_OTHER) {
        weight = 1000 + p->rt_priority;
        goto out;
    }

    /*
     * Give the process a first-approximation goodness value
     * according to the number of clock-ticks it has left.
     *
     * Don't do any other calculations if the time slice is
     * over..
     */
    weight = p->counter;
    if (!weight)
        goto out;

#ifdef __SMP__
    /* Give a largish advantage to the same processor...   */
    /* (this is equivalent to penalizing other processors) */
    if (p->processor == this_cpu)
        weight += PROC_CHANGE_PENALTY;
```

```
#endif

    /* .. and a slight advantage to the current MM */
    if (p->mm == this_mm)
        weight += 1;
    weight += p->priority;

out:
    return weight;
}
------- cut and paste from linux/kernel/sched.c ---------
```

In the new 2.4 kernel, when all CPUs are busy the kernel tries to reschedule only the preferred CPU, while the old 2.2.x code tried to reschedule all busy CPUs, thereby always moving the tasks onto the wrong CPUs. One very subtle bug, which is fixed in 2.4, was that if both the current task and the running task (the running task is the one we are trying to reschedule) are mutexing the kernel, it may not be true that there will be a lock contention if we do the reschedule. This is because the big kernel lock is a schedule-aware per-task lock that gets released and reacquired automatically inside scheduler. A plain schedule() only works based on goodness(). As you can see, a plain schedule() is SMP-aware. Notice that the goodness of the potential next task increases if its last CPU is the current CPU.

Nevertheless reschedule_idle() is far more critical for CPU affinity and scheduler latencies; for example, if you comment out reschedule_idle() the scheduler latency becomes infinity. Reschedule_idle() also takes care of the cache flush time and of the task average timeslice; it is the interesting part of the SMP scheduler. In UP, reschedule_idle is negligible.

This is the reschedule_idle() implementation taken from 2.3.26:

```
------- cut and paste from linux/kernel/sched.c ---------
static void reschedule_idle(struct task_struct * p)
{
#ifdef __SMP__
    int this_cpu = smp_processor_id(), target_cpu;
    struct task_struct *tsk, *target_tsk;
    int cpu, best_cpu, i;
    unsigned long flags;

    spin_lock_irqsave(&runqueue_lock, flags);

    /*
     * shortcut if the woken up task's last CPU is
     * idle now.
     */
```

```
            best_cpu = p->processor;
            target_tsk = idle_task(best_cpu);
            if (cpu_curr(best_cpu) == target_tsk)
                  goto send_now;

            target_tsk = NULL;
            for (i = 0; i < smp_num_cpus; i++) {
                  cpu = cpu_logical_map(i);
                  tsk = cpu_curr(cpu);
                  if (tsk == idle_task(cpu))
                        target_tsk = tsk;
            }

            if (target_tsk && p->avg_slice > cacheflush_time)
                  goto send_now;

            tsk = cpu_curr(best_cpu);
            if (preemption_goodness(tsk, p, best_cpu) > 0)
                  target_tsk = tsk;

            /*
             * found any suitable CPU?
             */
            if (!target_tsk)
                  goto out_no_target;

send_now:
      target_cpu = target_tsk->processor;
      target_tsk->need_resched = 1;
      spin_unlock_irqrestore(&runqueue_lock, flags);
      /*
       * the APIC stuff can go outside of the lock because
       * it uses no task information, only CPU#.
       */
      if (target_cpu != this_cpu)
            smp_send_reschedule(target_cpu);
      return;
out_no_target:
      spin_unlock_irqrestore(&runqueue_lock, flags);
      return;
#else /* UP */
      int this_cpu = smp_processor_id();
      struct task_struct *tsk;

      tsk = cpu_curr(this_cpu);
      if (preemption_goodness(tsk, p, this_cpu) > 0)
            tsk->need_resched = 1;
#endif
}
------- cut and paste from linux/kernel/sched.c ---------
```

The only final goal of `reschedule_idle` is to call a `schedule()` on a CPU to reschedule the awakened task on it. We use goodness in reschedule_idle() because we want to predict the effect of the future schedule() that we'll send to such a CPU. By predicting the effect of the future schedule() we can choose the best CPU to reschedule at wakeup time. If the CPU to reschedule is not the current one, we send a reschedule event via inter-CPU message passing (SMP-IPI interrupt on x86). goodness() is the core of the Linux scheduler, and it is SMP aware. But reschedule_idle() is the real core of the clever SMP heuristics.

Kernel Preemption and User Preemption

Linux can do only user preemption. Linus Torvalds doesn't believe in kernel preemption. That's not a problem; all is fine for semaphores. Critical sections protected by semaphores can be preempted at any time, as every contention will end in a schedule and there can't be any deadlock. Here is how it works (Figure 6.1).

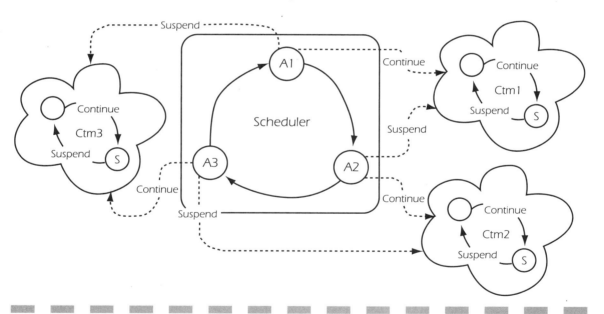

Figure 6.1 The flow of scheduling in the kernel.

Assume that every task, represented by the connected timing machines Ctm1, Ctm2, and Ctm3 in Figure 6.1, has the property that every state, s, has an auxiliary state to which it can be triggered by a suspend signal, and to which it can be restored by a continue signal.

Then the scheduler may "preempt" any task by sending it a suspend signal. Likewise, at its whim, the scheduler may signal a task to resume with a continue signal. Thus, when A1 times out, it suspends Ctm3 and signals Ctm1 to resume; and then, when A2 times out, it suspends Ctm1, and continues Ctm2, and so on. The diagram in Figure 6.1 is an extremely simple rendition of *preemptive multitasking*, which, in a real system, may involve prioritization; synchronization; changing timeouts; interrupt handlers, and ready, running, and waiting states.

Critical sections protected by fast spinlocks or by hand locks can't be preempted unless we block the timer IRQ. All the spinlocks should be IRQ-safe spinlocks, and IRQs should be clear before each critical section, then increase in IRQ latency by an order of magnitude. And all this is to save one check for current need_resched:

```
if (current->need_resched)
    schedule();
```

in a strategic place.

Avoiding kernel preemption makes the kernel simpler and more robust.

Implications of the Linux Approach

Linux, due to its GPL nature, allows us to do things faster than other operating systems do. For example, some popular very-closed binary-only operating system, in order to allow the same binary-only driver to work "fine" on both SMP and UP kernels, can't inline much material. In such an operating system, a spin_lock() or spin_unlock() for example must be called through a function pointer and can't be inlined. This because the same binary-only driver must work fine on both SMP and UP kernels. A spin_unlock is one locked ASM instruction:

```
#define spin_unlock_string \
    "lock ; btrl $0,%0"
```

and calling such a clear-bit instruction through a function pointer is complete overkill. Such silly binary-only constraints aren't in Linux, and we can run at the full CPU speed.

Another plus of the Linux system is that it scales very well in SMP and has nice garbage collection for cache pages. Last but not least, the

SMP scheduler in Linux is very clever. Having a clever SMP scheduler is critical for performance. If the scheduler is not aware of SMP, then the performance on an SMP machine can be even worse than on a UP machine (which occurs is in 2.2.x without the new heuristics).

Improving the Scheduler

We will now examine a few examples of how we might add our own functionality to the kernel. The beauty of having source available for the kernel is exactly this: if a kernel hacker feels particularly bold about the improvement, bug fix, or added feature, he or she can send same to Linus Torvalds or to his Number-Two man, Alan Cox, and hope it will be included in a future version. In my experience, however, it is extremely difficult to have a patch accepted by Linus Torvalds into a future version. For one thing, most ideas have already been discussed in the past at some point or another, and there are usually very good reasons for not including a concept, functionality, or change. Also, it takes formidable knowledge of the functioning of a whole Linux system, together with user-space programs and subsystems, to understand the full implications of a small change in the kernel. Only very few people actually have this overview, and accordingly it is up to them to decide on any changes. Still, participation is not only appreciated but actively encouraged.

Let's now look at a good example of an improvement in the kernel.

Varying CPUs Offline and Online

At present (kernel 2.4.x), it is not possible to take a CPU offline during execution, but it's not very hard to implement that maneuver either. Basically, the function `cpu_idle()` must check whether the current CPU should be shut down before calling the ASM instruction `halt` (an *unsigned long* word could provide such info). If it should be shut down, we can simply enter a loop; the hardware would remove the power to the CPU, thus allowing its removal from the slot or socket (the function to stop the CPU is `stop_this_cpu()`—it basically enters an infinite loop). The last thing that we must do is to let the scheduler know that a shutdown CPU must execute the idle task ASAP (or that we'll be able to shut down CPUs only if the system is not heavily CPU loaded).

CPU Affinity

Many UNIX systems (Solaris, for instance) offer the system administrator the possibility to bind a process to one desired CPU only. This binding to a selected CPU is more commonly known as *CPU affinity*. The rationale behind it is that the CPU primary and secondary cache lines most likely contain the entries particular to the process in question and thus benefit the process's performance overall. This can result in greatly reduced memory access by that CPU, and thus much faster execution. However, faster execution is not necessary when all the process is doing is, for example, spinning on a `spin_lock()` and faster execution is less important than earlier execution when the process has been asleep holding a `wait_lock()` that another process may need.

Thus, great care must be used when playing with affinity, because there is a high chance of seriously disturbing the delicate load balance of the system. CPU affinity probably makes most sense when a process is bound to a certain CPU and no other process can execute on that CPU. This, however, only makes sense if there is a very great number of CPUs available. On a Sun E10000 with 64 CPUs it might make sense to dedicate one CPU to a certain process. On a dual-CPU system, affinity is certainly too expensive.

For the sake of the example here, let's assume there are enough CPUs and let's further assume the workload warrants CPU affinity for a certain process. In that case the following patch might help:

```
--- 2.3.38-pset/include/linux/sched.h.~1~       Tue Jan 11 14:46:45 2000
+++ 2.3.38-pset/include/linux/sched.h   Tue Jan 11 17:58:52 2000
@@ -363,6 +363,7 @@
        u32 self_exec_id;
 /* Protection of fields allocatio/deallocation */
        struct semaphore exit_sem;
+       int bind_cpu;
 };

 /*
@@ -430,6 +431,7 @@
 /* signals */  SPIN_LOCK_UNLOCKED, &init_signals, {{0}}, {{0}}, NULL, \
                &init_task.sigqueue, 0, 0, \
 /* exec cts */ 0,0, \
 /* exit_sem */ __MUTEX_INITIALIZER(name.exit_sem),      \
+NO_PROC_ID,
 }

 #ifndef INIT_TASK_SIZE
--- 2.3.38-pset/kernel/sched.c.~1~        Sun Jan  9 20:45:31 2000
```

```
+++ 2.3.38-pset/kernel/sched.c   Tue Jan 11 18:16:45 2000
@@ -72,11 +72,13 @@
        struct schedule_data {
                struct task_struct * curr;
                cycles_t last_schedule;
+               int bind;
        } schedule_data;
        char __pad [SMP_CACHE_BYTES];
 } aligned_data [NR_CPUS] __cacheline_aligned = { {{&init_task,0}}};

 #define cpu_curr(cpu) aligned_data[(cpu)].schedule_data.curr
+#define cpu_bind(cpu) (aligned_data[(cpu)].bind)

 struct kernel_stat kstat = { 0 };

@@ -94,6 +96,25 @@

 void scheduling_functions_start_here(void) { }

+static int not_deadlocking(void)
+{
+       int i;
+
+       for (i = 0; i < smp_num_cpus; i++) {
+               int cpu;
+
+               cpu = cpu_logical_map(i);
+               if (!cpu_bind(cpu))
+                       return 1;
+       }
   return 0;
+}
+
+void set_bind_cpu(int cpu, int set)
+{
+       cpu_bind(cpu_logical_map(cpu)) = set;
+}
+
 /*
  * This is the function that decides how desirable a process is..
  * You can weigh different processes against each other depending
@@ -111,6 +132,9 @@
 static inline int goodness(struct task_struct * p, int this_cpu, struct mm_struct
                *this_mm)
 {
        int weight;
+
+       if (not_deadlocking() && cpu_bind(this_cpu) && p->bind_cpu != this_cpu)
+               return 0;

        /*
         * Realtime process, select the first one on the
--- 2.3.38-pset/kernel/sys.c.~1~      Tue Nov  2 12:06:25 1999
+++ 2.3.38-pset/kernel/sys.c    Tue Jan 11 18:18:34 2000
```

```
@@ -1027,6 +1027,19 @@
                        }
                        current->dumpable = arg2;
                        break;
+               case PR_SET_CPU:
+                       {
+                               extern void set_bind_cpu(int, int);
+
+                               error = -EINVAL;
+                               if (arg2 >= smp_num_cpus || arg2 < 0)
+                                       break;
+
+                               error = 0;
+                               current->bind_cpu = cpu_logical_map(arg2);
+                               set_bind_cpu(arg3, 1);
+                               break;
+                       }
                default:
                        error = -EINVAL;
                        break;
```

Hint-Based Scheduling

Some OS researchers say that the scheduler can best do its work when it is given hints by the programmer of user-space applications. These hints would ideally tell the scheduler which resources the program is likely to consume and how heavily. How would one implement hint-based scheduling with the 2.4. kernel?

Let's assume you are a userland program executing a critical code section (say, a mutex on a shared memory part) and you want to give a hint to the scheduler not to preempt you right now, because it will actually prevent other tasks from doing anything because another task has the mutex. How do we address this problem?

Actually it's the other task that must go to sleep immediately in the slow fail-path. When the other task notices the lock is busy, it should call sched_yield(), and it must not loop in user space.

Giving a hint to the kernel will be a win in most cases, because you should give the hint in the fast path—you should enter the kernel before acquiring the mutex. It's worth the risk of messing with the fairness of the scheduler.

Entering the kernel is always expensive, so it is better to let the fast path be very fast, and to make the lock fine grained to reduce contentions. Better to make the slow path even slower than to harm the fast path. If the critical section is very large, then a signal-driven wakeup/sleep signal probably is better than using a spinlock that tries to reacquire the lock inside a loop. Implementing the hint can be done easily via the prctl system call. It would be possible to call:

```
prctl(PR_RESET_TIMESLICE);
```

Andrea Arcangeli wrote an implementation (that doesn't care about the scheduler fairness) against kernel 2.2.13:

```
--- 2.2.13/kernel/sys.c Sun Oct 31 23:31:39 1999
+++ /tmp/sys.c Sun Nov 28 18:00:13 1999
@@ -995,6 +995,9 @@
                }
                current->pdeath_signal = sig;
                break;
+       case PR_RESET_TIMESLICE:
+               current->counter += current->priority >> 1;
+               break;
        default:
                error = -EINVAL;
                break;
--- 2.2.13/include/linux/prctl.h      Sun Oct 31 23:31:38 1999
+++ /tmp/prctl.h    Sun Nov 28 18:01:01 1999
@@ -4,6 +4,7 @@
 /*  Values to pass as first argument to prctl()  */

 #define PR_SET_PDEATHSIG  1  /*  Second arg is a signal  */
+#define PR_RESET_TIMESLICE  2  /*  Second arg is a signal  */


 #endif /* _LINUX_PRCTL_H */
```

In his patch, Andrea Arcangeli gives a new half-timeslice to the process calling the `prctl(PR_RESET_TIMESLICE)` syscall. The patch is obviously not secure, because everybody could run his task all the time by calling `prctl` all the time, but a real implementation should take care of all the security details. My implementation should work just fine if used in a trusted environment, and you can take it as an example.

Data Structures—linux/sched.h

```
ifndef _LINUX_SCHED_H
2 #define _LINUX_SCHED_H
3
4 #include <asm/param.h>  /* for HZ */
5
6 extern unsigned long event;
7
```

```
8  #include <linux/binfmts.h>
9  #include <linux/personality.h>
10 #include <linux/threads.h>
11 #include <linux/kernel.h>
12 #include <linux/types.h>
13 #include <linux/times.h>
14 #include <linux/timex.h>
15
16 #include <asm/system.h>
17 #include <asm/semaphore.h>
18 #include <asm/page.h>
19 #include <asm/ptrace.h>
20
21 #include <linux/smp.h>
22 #include <linux/tty.h>
23 #include <linux/sem.h>
24 #include <linux/signal.h>
25 #include <linux/securebits.h>
26
27 /*
28  * cloning flags:
29  */
30 #define CSIGNAL         0x000000ff      /* signal mask to be sent at exit */
31 #define CLONE_VM        0x00000100      /* set if VM shared between processes */
32 #define CLONE_FS        0x00000200      /* set if fs info shared between
                                              processes */
33 #define CLONE_FILES     0x00000400      /* set if open files shared between
                                              processes */
34 #define CLONE_SIGHAND   0x00000800      /* set if signal handlers shared */
35 #define CLONE_PID       0x00001000      /* set if pid shared */
36 #define CLONE_PTRACE    0x00002000      /* set if we want to let tracing continue
                                              on the child too */
37 #define CLONE_VFORK     0x00004000      /* set if the parent wants the child to
                                              wake it up on mm_release */
38 #define CLONE_PARENT    0x00008000      /* set if we want to have the same parent
                                              as the cloner */
39
40 /*
41  * These are the constant used to fake the fixed-point load-average
42  * counting. Some notes:
43  *  - 11 bit fractions expand to 22 bits by the multiplies: this gives
44  *    a load-average precision of 10 bits integer + 11 bits fractional
45  *  - if you want to count load-averages more often, you need more
46  *    precision, or rounding will get you. With 2-second counting freq,
47  *    the EXP_n values would be 1981, 2034 and 2043 if still using only
48  *    11 bit fractions.
49  */
50 extern unsigned long avenrun[];         /* Load averages */
51
52 #define FSHIFT       11                 /* nr of bits of precision */
53 #define FIXED_1      (1<<FSHIFT)         /* 1.0 as fixed-point */
54 #define LOAD_FREQ    (5*HZ)             /* 5 sec intervals */
55 #define EXP_1        1884              /* 1/exp(5sec/1min) as fixed-point */
56 #define EXP_5        2014              /* 1/exp(5sec/5min) */
```

```
57  #define EXP_15              2037           /* 1/exp(5sec/15min) */
58
59  #define CALC_LOAD(load,exp,n) \
60          load *= exp; \
61          load += n*(FIXED_1-exp); \
62          load >>= FSHIFT;
63
64  #define CT_TO_SECS(x)   ((x) / HZ)
65  #define CT_TO_USECS(x)  (((x) % HZ) * 1000000/HZ)
66
67  extern int nr_running, nr_threads;
68  extern int last_pid;
69
70  #include <linux/fs.h>
71  #include <linux/time.h>
72  #include <linux/param.h>
73  #include <linux/resource.h>
74  #include <linux/timer.h>
75
76  #include <asm/processor.h>
77
78  #define TASK_RUNNING            0
79  #define TASK_INTERRUPTIBLE      1
80  #define TASK_UNINTERRUPTIBLE    2
81  #define TASK_ZOMBIE             4
82  #define TASK_STOPPED            8
83  #define TASK_EXCLUSIVE          32
84
85  #define __set_task_state(tsk, state_value)              \
86          do { (tsk)->state = (state_value); } while (0)
87  #ifdef __SMP__
88  #define set_task_state(tsk, state_value)                \
89          set_mb((tsk)->state, (state_value))
90  #else
91  #define set_task_state(tsk, state_value)                \
92          __set_task_state((tsk), (state_value))
93  #endif
94
95  #define __set_current_state(state_value)                        \
96          do { current->state = (state_value); } while (0)
97  #ifdef __SMP__
98  #define set_current_state(state_value)          \
99          set_mb(current->state, (state_value))
100 #else
101 #define set_current_state(state_value)          \
102         __set_current_state(state_value)
103 #endif
104
105 /*
106  * Scheduling policies
107  */
108 #define SCHED_OTHER             0
109 #define SCHED_FIFO              1
110 #define SCHED_RR                2
```

```
111
112 /*
113  * This is an additional bit set when we want to
114  * yield the CPU for one re-schedule.
115  */
116 #define SCHED_YIELD              0x10
117
118 struct sched_param {
119          int sched_priority;
120 };
121
122 #ifdef __KERNEL__
123
124 #include <linux/spinlock.h>
125
126 /*
127  * This serializes "schedule()" and also protects
128  * the run-queue from deletions/modifications (but
129  * _adding_ to the beginning of the run-queue has
130  * a separate lock).
131  */
132 extern rwlock_t tasklist_lock;
133 extern spinlock_t runqueue_lock;
134
135 extern void sched_init(void);
136 extern void init_idle(void);
137 extern void show_state(void);
138 extern void cpu_init (void);
139 extern void trap_init(void);
140 extern void update_one_process( struct task_struct *p,
141          unsigned long ticks, unsigned long user, unsigned long system, int cpu);
142
143 #define MAX_SCHEDULE_TIMEOUT     LONG_MAX
144 extern signed long FASTCALL(schedule_timeout(signed long timeout));
145 asmlinkage void schedule(void);
146
147 /*
148  * The default fd array needs to be at least BITS_PER_LONG,
149  * as this is the granularity returned by copy_fdset().
150  */
151 #define NR_OPEN_DEFAULT BITS_PER_LONG
152
153 /*
154  * Open file table structure
155  */
156 struct files_struct {
157          atomic_t count;
158          rwlock_t file_lock;
159          int max_fds;
160          int max_fdset;
161          int next_fd;
162          struct file ** fd;         /* current fd array */
163          fd_set *close_on_exec;
164          fd_set *open_fds;
```

```
165          fd_set close_on_exec_init;
166          fd_set open_fds_init;
167          struct file * fd_array[NR_OPEN_DEFAULT];
168 };
169
170 #define INIT_FILES { \
171          ATOMIC_INIT(1), \
172          RW_LOCK_UNLOCKED, \
173          NR_OPEN_DEFAULT, \
174          __FD_SETSIZE, \
175          0, \
176          &init_files.fd_array[0], \
177          &init_files.close_on_exec_init, \
178          &init_files.open_fds_init, \
179          { { 0, } }, \
180          { { 0, } }, \
181          { NULL, } \
182 }
183
184 struct fs_struct {
185          atomic_t count;
186          int umask;
187          struct dentry * root, * pwd;
188 };
189
190 #define INIT_FS { \
191          ATOMIC_INIT(1), \
192          0022, \
193          NULL, NULL \
194 }
195
196 /* Maximum number of active map areas.. This is a random (large) number */
197 #define MAX_MAP_COUNT   (65536)
198
199 /* Number of map areas at which the AVL tree is activated. This is arbitrary. */
200 #define AVL_MIN_MAP_COUNT        32
201
202 struct mm_struct {
203          struct vm_area_struct * mmap;          /* list of VMAs */
204          struct vm_area_struct * mmap_avl;      /* tree of VMAs */
205          struct vm_area_struct * mmap_cache;    /* last find_vma result */
206          pgd_t * pgd;
207          atomic_t mm_users;                     /* How many users with user
                                                        space? */
208          atomic_t mm_count;                     /* How many references to
                                                        "struct mm_struct" (users
                                                        count as 1) */
209          int map_count;                         /* number of VMAs */
210          struct semaphore mmap_sem;
211          spinlock_t page_table_lock;
212          unsigned long context;
213          unsigned long start_code, end_code, start_data, end_data;
214          unsigned long start_brk, brk, start_stack;
215          unsigned long arg_start, arg_end, env_start, env_end;
```

```
216          unsigned long rss, total_vm, locked_vm;
217          unsigned long def_flags;
218          unsigned long cpu_vm_mask;
219          unsigned long swap_cnt; /* number of pages to swap on next pass */
220          unsigned long swap_address;
221          /*
222           * This is an architecture-specific pointer: the portable
223           * part of Linux does not know about any segments.
224           */
225          void * segments;
226 };
227
228 #define INIT_MM(name) {                                             \
229                 &init_mmap, NULL, NULL,                             \
230                 swapper_pg_dir,                                     \
231                 ATOMIC_INIT(2), ATOMIC_INIT(1), 1,                  \
232                 __MUTEX_INITIALIZER(name.mmap_sem),                 \
233                 SPIN_LOCK_UNLOCKED,                                 \
234                 0,                                                  \
235                 0, 0, 0, 0,                                         \
236                 0, 0, 0,                                            \
237                 0, 0, 0, 0,                                         \
238                 0, 0, 0,                                            \
239                 0, 0, 0, 0, NULL }
240
241 struct signal_struct {
242          atomic_t                count;
243          struct k_sigaction      action[_NSIG];
244          spinlock_t              siglock;
245 };
246
247
248 #define INIT_SIGNALS { \
249                 ATOMIC_INIT(1), \
250                 { {{0,}}, }, \
251                 SPIN_LOCK_UNLOCKED }
252
253 /*
254  * Some day this will be a full-fledged user tracking system.
255  * Right now it is only used to track how many processes a
256  * user has, but it has the potential to track memory usage etc.
257  */
258 struct user_struct;
259
260 struct task_struct {
261 /* these are hardcoded - don't touch */
262          volatile long state;    /* -1 unrunnable, 0 runnable, >0 stopped */
263          unsigned long flags;    /* per process flags, defined below */
264          int sigpending;
265          mm_segment_t addr_limit;        /* thread address space:
266                                                  0-0xBFFFFFFF for user-thead
267                                                  0-0xFFFFFFFF for kernel-thread
268                                          */
269          struct exec_domain *exec_domain;
```

```
270          volatile long need_resched;
271
272          cycles_t avg_slice;
273          int lock_depth;           /* Lock depth. We can context switch in and out
                                          of holding a syscall kernel lock... */
274 /* begin intel cache line */
275          long counter;
276          long priority;
277          unsigned long policy;
278 /* memory management info */
279          struct mm_struct *mm, *active_mm;
280          int has_cpu;
281          int processor;
282          struct list_head run_list;
283          struct task_struct *next_task, *prev_task;
284          int last_processor;
285
286 /* task state */
287          struct linux_binfmt *binfmt;
288          int exit_code, exit_signal;
289          int pdeath_signal;   /* The signal sent when the parent dies  */
290          /* ??? */
291          unsigned long personality;
292          int dumpable:1;
293          int did_exec:1;
294          pid_t pid;
295          pid_t pgrp;
296          pid_t tty_old_pgrp;
297          pid_t session;
298          /* boolean value for session group leader */
299          int leader;
300          /*
301           * pointers to (original) parent process, youngest child, younger sibling,
302           * older sibling, respectively.  (p->father can be replaced with
303           * p->p_pptr->pid)
304           */
305          struct task_struct *p_opptr, *p_pptr, *p_cptr, *p_ysptr, *p_osptr;
306
307          /* PID hash table linkage. */
308          struct task_struct *pidhash_next;
309          struct task_struct **pidhash_pprev;
310
311          wait_queue_head_t wait_chldexit;        /* for wait4() */
312          struct semaphore *vfork_sem;            /* for vfork() */
313          unsigned long rt_priority;
314          unsigned long it_real_value, it_prof_value, it_virt_value;
315          unsigned long it_real_incr, it_prof_incr, it_virt_incr;
316          struct timer_list real_timer;
317          struct tms times;
318          unsigned long start_time;
319          long per_cpu_utime[NR_CPUS], per_cpu_stime[NR_CPUS];
320 /* mm fault and swap info: this can arguably be seen as either mm-specific or
        thread-specific */
321          unsigned long min_flt, maj_flt, nswap, cmin_flt, cmaj_flt, cnswap;
```

```
322          int swappable:1;
323 /* process credentials */
324          uid_t uid,euid,suid,fsuid;
325          gid_t gid,egid,sgid,fsgid;
326          int ngroups;
327          gid_t   groups[NGROUPS];
328          kernel_cap_t  cap_effective, cap_inheritable, cap_permitted;
329          struct user_struct *user;
330 /* limits */
331          struct rlimit rlim[RLIM_NLIMITS];
332          unsigned short used_math;
333          char comm[16];
334 /* file system info */
335          int link_count;
336          struct tty_struct *tty; /* NULL if no tty */
337 /* ipc stuff */
338          struct sem_undo *semundo;
339          struct sem_queue *semsleeping;
340 /* CPU-specific state of this task */
341          struct thread_struct thread;
342 /* filesystem information */
343          struct fs_struct *fs;
344 /* open file information */
345          struct files_struct *files;
346 /* signal handlers */
347          spinlock_t sigmask_lock;          /* Protects signal and blocked */
348          struct signal_struct *sig;
349          sigset_t signal, blocked;
350          struct signal_queue *sigqueue, **sigqueue_tail;
351          unsigned long sas_ss_sp;
352          size_t sas_ss_size;
353
354 /* Thread group tracking */
355          u32 parent_exec_id;
356          u32 self_exec_id;
357 /* Protection of fields allocatio/deallocation */
358          struct semaphore exit_sem;
359 };
360
361 /*
362  * Per process flags
363  */
364 #define PF_ALIGNWARN      0x00000001      /* Print alignment warning msgs */
365                                          /* Not implemented yet, only for 486*/
366 #define PF_STARTING       0x00000002      /* being created */
367 #define PF_EXITING        0x00000004      /* getting shut down */
368 #define PF_PTRACED        0x00000010      /* set if ptrace (0) has been called */
369 #define PF_TRACESYS       0x00000020      /* tracing system calls */
370 #define PF_FORKNOEXEC     0x00000040      /* forked but didn't exec */
371 #define PF_SUPERPRIV      0x00000100      /* used super-user privileges */
372 #define PF_DUMPCORE       0x00000200      /* dumped core */
373 #define PF_SIGNALED       0x00000400      /* killed by a signal */
374 #define PF_MEMALLOC       0x00000800      /* Allocating memory */
375 #define PF_VFORK          0x00001000      /* Wake up parent in mm_release */
```

```
376
377 #define PF_USEDFPU      0x00100000      /* task used FPU this quantum (SMP) */
378 #define PF_DTRACE       0x00200000      /* delayed trace (used on m68k, i386) */
379
380 /*
381  * Limit the stack by to some sane default: root can always
382  * increase this limit if needed.  8MB seems reasonable.
383  */
384 #define _STK_LIM        (8*1024*1024)
385
386 #define DEF_PRIORITY    (20*HZ/100)      /* 200 ms time slices */
387
388 /*
389  *  INIT_TASK is used to set up the first task table, touch at
390  * your own risk!. Base=0, limit=0x1fffff (=2MB)
391  */
392 #define INIT_TASK(name) \
393 /* state etc */ { 0,0,0,KERNEL_DS,&default_exec_domain,0, \
394 /* avg_slice */ 0, -1, \
395 /* counter */   DEF_PRIORITY,DEF_PRIORITY,SCHED_OTHER, \
396 /* mm */        NULL, &init_mm, \
397 /* has_cpu */   0,0, \
398 /* run_list */  LIST_HEAD_INIT(init_task.run_list), \
399 /* next_task */ &init_task,&init_task, \
400 /* last_proc */ 0, \
401 /* binfmt */    NULL, \
402 /* ec,brk... */ 0,0,0,0,0,0, \
403 /* pid etc.. */ 0,0,0,0,0, \
404 /* proc links*/ &init_task,&init_task,NULL,NULL,NULL, \
405 /* pidhash */   NULL, NULL, \
406 /* chld wait */ __WAIT_QUEUE_HEAD_INITIALIZER(name.wait_chldexit), NULL, \
407 /* timeout */   0,0,0,0,0,0,0, \
408 /* timer */     { NULL, NULL, 0, 0, it_real_fn }, \
409 /* utime */     {0,0,0,0},0, \
410 /* per CPU times */ {0, }, {0, }, \
411 /* flt */       0,0,0,0,0,0, \
412 /* swp */       0, \
413 /* process credentials */                           \
414 /* uid etc */   0,0,0,0,0,0,0,0,                     \
415 /* suppl grps*/ 0, {0,},                             \
416 /* caps */      CAP_INIT_EFF_SET,CAP_INIT_INH_SET,CAP_FULL_SET, \
417 /* user */      NULL,                               \
418 /* rlimits */   INIT_RLIMITS, \
419 /* math */      0, \
420 /* comm */      "swapper", \
421 /* fs info */   0,NULL, \
422 /* ipc */       NULL, NULL, \
423 /* thread */    INIT_THREAD, \
424 /* fs */        &init_fs, \
425 /* files */     &init_files, \
426 /* signals */   SPIN_LOCK_UNLOCKED, &init_signals, {{0}}, {{0}}, NULL,
                    &init_task.sigqueue, 0, 0, \
427 /* exec cts */  0,0, \
428 /* exit_sem */  __MUTEX_INITIALIZER(name.exit_sem),      \
```

```
429 }
430
431 #ifndef INIT_TASK_SIZE
432 # define INIT_TASK_SIZE 2048*sizeof(long)
433 #endif
434
435 union task_union {
436         struct task_struct task;
437         unsigned long stack[INIT_TASK_SIZE/sizeof(long)];
438 };
439
440 extern union task_union init_task_union;
441
442 extern struct   mm_struct init_mm;
443 extern struct task_struct *init_tasks[NR_CPUS];
444
445 /* PID hashing. (shouldnt this be dynamic?) */
446 #define PIDHASH_SZ (4096 >> 2)
447 extern struct task_struct *pidhash[PIDHASH_SZ];
448
449 #define pid_hashfn(x)   ((((x) >> 8) ^ (x)) & (FIDHASH_SZ - 1))
450
451 extern __inline__ void hash_pid(struct task_struct *p)
452 {
453         struct task_struct **htable = &pidhash[pid_hashfn(p->pid)];
454
455         if((p->pidhash_next = *htable) != NULL)
456                 (*htable)->pidhash_pprev = &p->pidhash_next;
457         *htable = p;
458         p->pidhash_pprev = htable;
459 }
460
461 extern __inline__ void unhash_pid(struct task_struct *p)
462 {
463         if(p->pidhash_next)
464                 p->pidhash_next->pidhash_pprev = p->pidhash_pprev;
465         *p->pidhash_pprev = p->pidhash_next;
466 }
467
468 extern __inline__ struct task_struct *find_task_by_pid(int pid)
469 {
470         struct task_struct *p, **htable = &pidhash[pid_hashfn(pid)];
471
472         for(p = *htable; p && p->pid != pid; p = p->pidhash_next)
473                 ;
474
475         return p;
476 }
477
478 /* per-UID process charging. */
479 extern int alloc_uid(struct task_struct *);
480 void free_uid(struct task_struct *);
481
482 #include <asm/current.h>
```

```
483
484 extern unsigned long volatile jiffies;
485 extern unsigned long itimer_ticks;
486 extern unsigned long itimer_next;
487 extern struct timeval xtime;
488 extern void do_timer(struct pt_regs *);
489
490 extern unsigned int * prof_buffer;
491 extern unsigned long prof_len;
492 extern unsigned long prof_shift;
493
494 #define CURRENT_TIME (xtime.tv_sec)
495
496 extern void FASTCALL(__wake_up(wait_queue_head_t *q, unsigned int mode));
497 extern void FASTCALL(__wake_up_sync(wait_queue_head_t *q, unsigned int mode));
498 extern void FASTCALL(sleep_on(wait_queue_head_t *q));
499 extern long FASTCALL(sleep_on_timeout(wait_queue_head_t *q,
500                                       signed long timeout));
501 extern void FASTCALL(interruptible_sleep_on(wait_queue_head_t *q));
502 extern long FASTCALL(interruptible_sleep_on_timeout(wait_queue_head_t *q,
503                                                     signed long timeout));
504 extern void FASTCALL(wake_up_process(struct task_struct * tsk));
505
506 #define wake_up(x)                    __wake_up((x),TASK_UNINTERRUPTIBLE |
                                          TASK_INTERRUPTIBLE | TASK_EXCLUSIVE)
507 #define wake_up_all(x)                __wake_up((x),TASK_UNINTERRUPTIBLE |
                                          TASK_INTERRUPTIBLE)
508 #define wake_up_sync(x)               __wake_up_sync((x),TASK_UNINTERRUPTIBLE
                                          | TASK_INTERRUPTIBLE | TASK_EXCLUSIVE)
509 #define wake_up_interruptible(x)      __wake_up((x),TASK_INTERRUPTIBLE |
                                          TASK_EXCLUSIVE)
510 #define wake_up_interruptible_all(x)  __wake_up((x),TASK_INTERRUPTIBLE)
511 #define wake_up_interruptible_sync(x) __wake_up_sync((x),TASK_INTERRUPTIBLE |
                                          TASK_EXCLUSIVE)
512
513 extern int in_group_p(gid_t);
514 extern int in_egroup_p(gid_t);
515
516 extern void flush_signals(struct task_struct *);
517 extern void flush_signal_handlers(struct task_struct *);
518 extern int dequeue_signal(sigset_t *, siginfo_t *);
519 extern int send_sig_info(int, struct siginfo *, struct task_struct *);
520 extern int force_sig_info(int, struct siginfo *, struct task_struct *);
521 extern int kill_pg_info(int, struct siginfo *, pid_t);
522 extern int kill_sl_info(int, struct siginfo *, pid_t);
523 extern int kill_proc_info(int, struct siginfo *, pid_t);
524 extern int kill_something_info(int, struct siginfo *, int);
525 extern void notify_parent(struct task_struct *, int);
526 extern void force_sig(int, struct task_struct *);
527 extern int send_sig(int, struct task_struct *, int);
528 extern int kill_pg(pid_t, int, int);
529 extern int kill_sl(pid_t, int, int);
530 extern int kill_proc(pid_t, int, int);
531 extern int do_sigaction(int, const struct k_sigaction *, struct k_sigaction *);
```

```
532 extern int do_sigaltstack(const stack_t *, stack_t *, unsigned long);
533
534 extern inline int signal_pending(struct task_struct *p)
535 {
536         return (p->sigpending != 0);
537 }
538
539 /* Reevaluate whether the task has signals pending delivery.
540    This is required every time the blocked sigset_t changes.
541    All callers should have t->sigmask_lock.   */
542
543 static inline void recalc_sigpending(struct task_struct *t)
544 {
545         unsigned long ready;
546         long i;
547
548         switch (_NSIG_WORDS) {
549         default:
550                 for (i = _NSIG_WORDS, ready = 0; --i >= 0 ;)
551                         ready |= t->signal.sig[i] &~ t->blocked.sig[i];
552                 break;
553
554         case 4: ready  = t->signal.sig[3] &~ t->blocked.sig[3];
555                 ready |= t->signal.sig[2] &~ t->blocked.sig[2];
556                 ready |= t->signal.sig[1] &~ t->blocked.sig[1];
557                 ready |= t->signal.sig[0] &~ t->blocked.sig[0];
558                 break;
559
560         case 2: ready  = t->signal.sig[1] &~ t->blocked.sig[1];
561                 ready |= t->signal.sig[0] &~ t->blocked.sig[0];
562                 break;
563
564         case 1: ready  = t->signal.sig[0] &~ t->blocked.sig[0];
565         }
566
567         t->sigpending = (ready != 0);
568 }
569
570 /* True if we are on the alternate signal stack.   */
571
572 static inline int on_sig_stack(unsigned long sp)
573 {
574         return (sp - current->sas_ss_sp < current->sas_ss_size);
575 }
576
577 static inline int sas_ss_flags(unsigned long sp)
578 {
579         return (current->sas_ss_size == 0 ? SS_DISABLE
580                 : on_sig_stack(sp) ? SS_ONSTACK : 0);
581 }
582
583 extern int request_irq(unsigned int,
584                        void (*handler)(int, void *, struct pt_regs *),
585                        unsigned long, const char *, void *);
```

```
586 extern void free_irq(unsigned int, void *);
587
588 /*
589  * This has now become a routine instead of a macro, it sets a flag if
590  * it returns true (to do BSD-style accounting where the process is flagged
591  * if it uses root privs). The implication of this is that you should do
592  * normal permissions checks first, and check suser() last.
593  *
594  * [Dec 1997 -- Chris Evans]
595  * For correctness, the above considerations need to be extended to
596  * fsuser(). This is done, along with moving fsuser() checks to be
597  * last.
598  *
599  * These will be removed, but in the mean time, when the SECURE_NOROOT
600  * flag is set, uids don't grant privilege.
601  */
602 extern inline int suser(void)
603 {
604         if (!issecure(SECURE_NOROOT) && current->euid == 0) {
605                 current->flags |= PF_SUPERPRIV;
606                 return 1;
607         }
608         return 0;
609 }
610
611 extern inline int fsuser(void)
612 {
613         if (!issecure(SECURE_NOROOT) && current->fsuid == 0) {
614                 current->flags |= PF_SUPERPRIV;
615                 return 1;
616         }
617         return 0;
618 }
619
620 /*
621  * capable() checks for a particular capability.
622  * New privilege checks should use this interface, rather than suser() or
623  * fsuser(). See include/linux/capability.h for defined capabilities.
624  */
625
626 extern inline int capable(int cap)
627 {
628 #if 1 /* ok now */
629         if (cap_raised(current->cap_effective, cap))
630 #else
631         if (cap_is_fs_cap(cap) ? current->fsuid == 0 : current->euid == 0)
632 #endif
633         {
634                 current->flags |= PF_SUPERPRIV;
635                 return 1;
636         }
637         return 0;
638 }
639
```

```
640 /*
641  * Routines for handling mm_structs
642  */
643 extern struct mm_struct * mm_alloc(void);
644
645 extern struct mm_struct * start_lazy_tlb(void);
646 extern void end_lazy_tlb(struct mm_struct *mm);
647
648 /* mmdrop drops the mm and the page tables */
649 extern inline void FASTCALL(__mmdrop(struct mm_struct *));
650 static inline void mmdrop(struct mm_struct * mm)
651 {
652         if (atomic_dec_and_test(&mm->mm_count))
653                 __mmdrop(mm);
654 }
655
656 /* mmput gets rid of the mappings and all user-space */
657 extern void mmput(struct mm_struct *);
658 /* Remove the current tasks stale references to the old mm_struct */
659 extern void mm_release(void);
660
661 /*
662  * Routines for handling the fd arrays
663  */
664 extern struct file ** alloc_fd_array(int);
665 extern int expand_fd_array(struct files_struct *, int nr);
666 extern void free_fd_array(struct file **, int);
667
668 extern fd_set *alloc_fdset(int);
669 extern int expand_fdset(struct files_struct *, int nr);
670 extern void free_fdset(fd_set *, int);
671
672 /* Expand files.  Return <0 on error; 0 nothing done; 1 files expanded,
673  * we may have blocked.
674  *
675  * Should be called with the files->file_lock spinlock held for write.
676  */
677 static inline int expand_files(struct files_struct *files, int nr)
678 {
679         int err, expand = 0;
680 #ifdef FDSET_DEBUG
681         printk (KERN_ERR __FUNCTION__ " %d: nr = %d\n", current->pid, nr);
682 #endif
683
684         if (nr >= files->max_fdset) {
685                 expand = 1;
686                 if ((err = expand_fdset(files, nr)))
687                         goto out;
688         }
689         if (nr >= files->max_fds) {
690                 expand = 1;
691                 if ((err = expand_fd_array(files, nr)))
692                         goto out;
693         }
```

```
694         err = expand;
695  out:
696  #ifdef FDSET_DEBUG
697         if (err)
698                 printk (KERN_ERR __FUNCTION__ " %d: return %d\n", current->pid,
err);
699  #endif
700         return err;
701  }
702
703  extern int  copy_thread(int, unsigned long, unsigned long, struct task_struct *,
struct pt_regs *);
704  extern void flush_thread(void);
705  extern void exit_thread(void);
706
707  extern void exit_mm(struct task_struct *);
708  extern void exit_fs(struct task_struct *);
709  extern void exit_files(struct task_struct *);
710  extern void exit_sighand(struct task_struct *);
711
712  extern void daemonize(void);
713
714  extern int do_execve(char *, char **, char **, struct pt_regs *);
715  extern int do_fork(unsigned long, unsigned long, struct pt_regs *);
716
717  extern inline void add_wait_queue(wait_queue_head_t *q, wait_queue_t * wait)
718  {
719         unsigned long flags;
720
721         wq_write_lock_irqsave(&q->lock, flags);
722         __add_wait_queue(q, wait);
723         wq_write_unlock_irqrestore(&q->lock, flags);
724  }
725
726  extern inline void add_wait_queue_exclusive(wait_queue_head_t *q,
727                                                  wait_queue_t * wait)
728  {
729         unsigned long flags;
730
731         wq_write_lock_irqsave(&q->lock, flags);
732         __add_wait_queue_tail(q, wait);
733         wq_write_unlock_irqrestore(&q->lock, flags);
734  }
735
736  extern inline void remove_wait_queue(wait_queue_head_t *q, wait_queue_t * wait)
737  {
738         unsigned long flags;
739
740         wq_write_lock_irqsave(&q->lock, flags);
741         __remove_wait_queue(q, wait);
742         wq_write_unlock_irqrestore(&q->lock, flags);
743  }
744
745  #define __wait_event(wq, condition)                                    \
```

```
746 do {                                                                      \
747         wait_queue_t __wait;                                              \
748         init_waitqueue_entry(&__wait, current);                          \
749                                                                           \
750         add_wait_queue(&wq, &__wait);                                    \
751         for (;;) {                                                        \
752                 set_current_state(TASK_UNINTERRUPTIBLE);                  \
753                 if (condition)                                            \
754                         break;                                            \
755                 schedule();                                               \
756         }                                                                 \
757         current->state = TASK_RUNNING;                                    \
758         remove_wait_queue(&wq, &__wait);                                 \
759 } while (0)
760
761 #define wait_event(wq, condition)                                        \
762 do {                                                                      \
763         if (condition)                                                    \
764                 break;                                                    \
765         __wait_event(wq, condition);                                     \
766 } while (0)
767
768 #define __wait_event_interruptible(wq, condition, ret)                   \
769 do {                                                                      \
770         wait_queue_t __wait;                                              \
771         init_waitqueue_entry(&__wait, current);                          \
772                                                                           \
773         add_wait_queue(&wq, &__wait);                                    \
774         for (;;) {                                                        \
775                 set_current_state(TASK_INTERRUPTIBLE);                    \
776                 if (condition)                                            \
777                         break;                                            \
778                 if (!signal_pending(current)) {                           \
779                         schedule();                                       \
780                         continue;                                         \
781                 }                                                         \
782                 ret = -ERESTARTSYS;                                       \
783                 break;                                                    \
784         }                                                                 \
785         current->state = TASK_RUNNING;                                    \
786         remove_wait_queue(&wq, &__wait);                                 \
787 } while (0)
788
789 #define wait_event_interruptible(wq, condition)                          \
790 ({                                                                        \
791         int __ret = 0;                                                    \
792         if (!(condition))                                                 \
793                 __wait_event_interruptible(wq, condition, __ret);        \
794         __ret;                                                            \
795 })
796
797 #define REMOVE_LINKS(p) do { \
798         (p)->next_task->prev_task = (p)->prev_task; \
799         (p)->prev_task->next_task = (p)->next_task; \
```

```
800            if ((p)->p_osptr) \
801                    (p)->p_osptr->p_ysptr = (p)->p_ysptr; \
802            if ((p)->p_ysptr) \
803                    (p)->p_ysptr->p_osptr = (p)->p_osptr; \
804            else \
805                    (p)->p_pptr->p_cptr = (p)->p_osptr; \
806            } while (0)
807
808 #define SET_LINKS(p) do { \
809            (p)->next_task = &init_task; \
810            (p)->prev_task = init_task.prev_task; \
811            init_task.prev_task->next_task = (p); \
812            init_task.prev_task = (p); \
813            (p)->p_ysptr = NULL; \
814            if (((p)->p_osptr = (p)->p_pptr->p_cptr) != NULL) \
815                    (p)->p_osptr->p_ysptr = p; \
816            (p)->p_pptr->p_cptr = p; \
817            } while (0)
818
819 #define for_each_task(p) \
820            for (p = &init_task ; (p = p->next_task) != &init_task ; )
821
822
823 static inline void del_from_runqueue(struct task_struct * p)
824 {
825            nr_running--;
826            list_del(&p->run_list);
827            p->run_list.next = NULL;
828 }
829
830 extern inline int task_on_runqueue(struct task_struct *p)
831 {
832            return (p->run_list.next != NULL);
833 }
834
835 extern inline void unhash_process(struct task_struct *p)
836 {
837            if (task_on_runqueue(p)) BUG();
838            write_lock_irq(&tasklist_lock);
839            nr_threads--;
840            unhash_pid(p);
841            REMOVE_LINKS(p);
842            write_unlock_irq(&tasklist_lock);
843 }
844
845 static inline int task_lock(struct task_struct *p)
846 {
847            down(&p->exit_sem);
848            if (p->p_pptr)
849                    return 1;
850            /* He's dead, Jim. You take his wallet, I'll take the tricorder... */
851            up(&p->exit_sem);
852            return 0;
853 }
```

```
854
855 static inline void task_unlock(struct task_struct *p)
856 {
857          up(&p->exit_sem);
858 }
859
860 #endif /* __KERNEL__ */
861
862 #endif
```

Signals
Handling

Signals are used to notify a process or thread of a particular event. This chapter describes how the Linux 2.4 kernel handles these signals. As in all other chapters, the data structures referred to in the chapter can be found at the end.

Processes operate within their own virtual address space and are protected by the operating system from interference by other processes. By default a user process cannot communicate with another process unless it makes use of secure, kernel-managed mechanisms. There are many times when processes need to share common resources or synchronize their actions. One possibility is to use threads, which by definition can share memory within a process. This option is not always possible (or wise) due to the many disadvantages that can be experienced with threads. Methods of passing messages or data between processes are therefore required.

Many computer science researchers compare signals with hardware interrupts, which occur when a hardware subsystem such as a disk I/O interface (an SCSI host adapter, for example) generates an interrupt to a processor as a result of a completed I/O. This event in turn causes the processor to enter an interrupt handler, so subsequent processing can be done in the operating system based on the source and cause of the interrupt.

One could therefore aptly describe signals as software interrupts. When a signal is sent to a process or thread, a signal handler may be entered (depending on the current disposition of the signal), which is similar to the system's entering an interrupt handler as the result of receiving an interrupt.

The early implementations of signals in UNIX were deemed unreliable. The unreliability stemmed from the fact that in the old days the kernel would reset the signal handler to its default if a process caught a signal and invoked its own handler, and the reset occurred before the handler was invoked. Attempts to address this issue in user code by having the signal handler first reinstall itself did not always solve the problem, because successive occurrences of the same signal resulted in race conditions, where the default action was invoked before the user-defined handler was reinstalled. For signals that had a default action of terminating the process, this created severe problems. This problem (and some others) were addressed in 4.3BSD UNIX and SVR3 in the mid-'80s.

The implementation of correct and reliable signals has been in place for many years now, where an installed signal handler remains persistent and is not reset by the kernel. The POSIX standards provided a fairly well-defined set of interfaces for using signals in code, and today the Linux implementation of signals is fully POSIX compliant. It should be noted that reliable signals require the use of the newer `sigaction(2)` interface, as opposed to the traditional `signal(3C)` call.

The occurrence of a signal may be synchronous or asynchronous to the process or thread, depending on the source of the signal and the underlying reason or cause. Synchronous signals occur as a direct result of the executing instruction stream, where an unrecoverable error (such as an illegal instruction or illegal address reference) requires an immediate termination of the process. Such signals are directed to the thread whose execution stream caused the error. Because an error of this type causes a trap in a kernel trap handler, synchronous signals are sometimes referred to as *traps*.

Asynchronous signals are external to (and in some cases unrelated to) the current execution context. One obvious example would be the sending of a signal to a process from another process or thread, via a `kill(2)`, `_lwp_kill(2)`, or `sigsend(2)` system call, or a `thr_kill(3T)`, `pthread_kill(3T)`, or `sigqueue(3R)` library invocation. Asynchronous signals are also aptly referred to as *interrupts*.

Every signal has a unique signal name, an abbreviation that begins with `SIG` (`SIGINT` for interrupt signal, for example) and a corresponding signal number. Additionally, for all possible signals, the OS defines a default disposition, or action to take when a signal occurs. There are four possible default dispositions:

- **Exit**—Forces the process to exit.
- **Core**—Forces the process to exit and create a core file.
- **Stop**—Stops the process.
- **Ignore**—Ignores the signal; no action taken.

A signal's disposition within a process's context designates what action the system will take on behalf of the process when a signal is delivered. All threads within a process share the signal disposition, which is processwide and cannot be unique among tasks or threads within the same process.

Table 7.1 provides a complete list of signals, along with a description and default action.

TABLE 7.1

Signal list and default actions

Name	Number	Default action	Description
SIGHUP	1	Exit	Hangup (ref termio(7I)).
SIGINT	2	Exit	Interrupt (ref termio(7I)).
SIGQUIT	3	Core	Quit (ref termio(7I))
SIGILL	4	Core	Illegal instruction
SIGTRAP	5	Core	Trace or breakpoint trap
SIGABRT	6	Core	Abort
SIGEMT	7	Core	Emulation trap
SIGFPE	8	Core	Arithmetic exception
SIGKILL	9	Exit	Kill
SIGBUS	10	Core	Bus error—actually a misaligned address error
SIGSEGV	11	Core	Segmentation fault—an address reference boundary error
SIGSYS	12	Core	Bad system call
SIGPIPE	13	Exit	Broken pipe
SIGALRM	14	Exit	Alarm clock
SIGTERM	15	Exit	Terminated
SIGUSR1	16	Exit	User-defined signal 1
SIGUSR2	17	Exit	User-defined signal 2
SIGCHLD	18	Ignore	Child process status changed
SIGPWR	19	Ignore	Power fail or restart
SIGWINCH	20	Ignore	Window size change
SIGURG	21	Ignore	Urgent socket condition
SIGPOLL	22	Exit	Pollable event (ref streamio(7I))
SIGSTOP	23	Stop	Stop (cannot be caught or ignored)
SIGTSTP	24	Stop	Stop (job control, e.g., ^z))
SIGCONT	25	Ignore	Continued
SIGTTIN	26	Stop	Stopped—tty input (ref termio(7I))

continued on next page

TABLE 7.1

continued

Name	Number	Default action	Description
SIGTTOU	27	Stop	Stopped—tty output (ref termio(7I))
SIGVTALRM	28	Exit	Virtual timer expired
SIGPROF	29	Exit	Profiling timer expired
SIGXCPU	30	Core	CPU time limit exceeded (ref getrlimit(2)
SIGXFSZ	31	Core	File size limit exceeded (ref getrlimit(2))
SIGWAITING	32	Ignore	Concurrency signal used by threads library
SIGLWP	33	Ignore	Inter-LWP signal used by threads library
SIGFREEZE	34	Ignore	Checkpoint suspend
SIGTHAW	35	Ignore	Checkpoint resume
SIGCANCEL	36	Ignore	Cancellation signal used by threads library
SIGLOST	37	Ignore	Resource lost
SIGRTMIN	38	Exit	Highest priority real-time signal
SIGRTMAX	45	Exit	Lowest priority real-time signal

The data structures in the kernel to support signals in Linux are to be found in the task structure we discussed in Chapter 4 on Linux Processes.

Here are the most common elements of the task structure pertaining to signals:

- `current->sig` are the signal handlers.
- `sigmask_lock` is a per-thread spinlock,which protects the signal queue and atomicity of other signal operations.
- `current->signal` and `current->blocked` are a (currently 64-bit long but freely expandable) bitmask of pending and permanently blocked signals.
- `sigqueue` and `sigqueue_tail` are double-linked lists of pending signals. Linux has RT signals that can get queued as well. "Traditional" signals are internally mapped to RT signals.

Signal Description and Default Action

The disposition of a signal can be changed from its default, and a process can arrange to catch a signal and invoke a signal handling routine of its own, or ignore a signal that may not have a default disposition of Ignore, as we said before. The only exceptions are SIGKILL and SIGSTOP, whose default dispositions cannot be changed. The interfaces for defining and changing signal disposition are the signal(3C) and sigset(3C) libraries, and the sigaction(2) system call. Signals can also be blocked, which means the process has temporarily prevented delivery of a signal. The generation of a signal that has been blocked results in the signal's remaining pending to the process, until it is explicitly unblocked or the disposition is changed to Ignore.

We saw earlier that a signal may originate from several different places, for a variety of different reasons. The first three signals listed in the table above—SIGHUP, SIGINT, and SIGQUIT—are generated by a keyboard entry from the controlling terminal (SIGINT and SIGHUP), or they are generated if the control terminal becomes disconnected (SIGHUP—use of the nohup(1) command makes processes "immune" from hangups by setting the disposition of SIGHUP to Ignore).

Other terminal I/O-related signals include SIGSTOP, SIGTTIN, SIGTTOU, and SIGTSTP. For those signals that originate from a keyboard command, the actual key sequence that generates the signals, usually ^C (Ctrl-C), is defined within the parameters of the terminal session, typically via stty(1), which results in a SIGINT being sent to a process; it has a default disposition of Exit.

Signals generated as a direct result of an error encountered during instruction execution start with a hardware trap on the system. Different processor architectures define various traps that result in an immediate vectored transfer of control to a kernel trap-handling function. The Linux kernel builds a trap table and inserts trap-handling routines in the appropriate locations based on the architecture specification of the Linux-supported processors. In Intel x86 parlance they're called *interrupt descriptor tables* or IDTs.

The kernel-installed trap handler ultimately generates a signal to the thread that caused the trap. The signals that result from hardware traps are SIGILL, SIGFPE, SIGSEGV, SIGTRAP, SIGBUS, and SIGEMT.

In addition to terminal I/O and error trap conditions, signals can originate from sources, such as an explicit signal, sent programmatically via kill(2) or thr_kill(3T), or from a shell issuing a kill(1) command. Parent processes are notified of status change in a child process via SIGCHLD.

Applications can create user-defined signals as a somewhat crude form of interprocess communication by defining handlers for SIGUSR1 and/or SIGUSR2 and then sending those signals between processes. The kernel sends SIGXCPU if a process exceeds its processor time resource limit, or SIGXFSZ if a file write exceeds the file size resource limit. A SIGABRT is sent as a result of an invocation of the abort(3C) library. If a process is writing to a pipe and the reader has terminated, SIGPIPE is generated.

These examples of signals generated as a result of events beyond hard errors and terminal I/O do not represent the complete list, but rather provide a well-rounded set of examples of the process-induced and external events that can generate signals.

In terms of actual implementation, a signal is represented as a bit in a data structure (several data structures, as we'll see shortly). More succinctly, the posting of a signal by the kernel results in a bit getting set in a structure member at either the process or thread level. Because each signal has a unique signal number, a structure member of sufficient width is used, to allow every signal to be represented by setting the bit that corresponds to the signal number of the signal we wish to post (for example, setting the 17th bit to post signal 17, SIGUSR1).

When you consider that a signal is represented by the setting of a bit in a data structure, intuition indicates that a periodic check must be made for set bits (pending signals) by the kernel. This is, in fact, precisely how delivery is made. A check is made for posted signals at several points during the typical execution flow of a process:

1. Returning from a system call.
2. Returning from a trap.
3. Waking up from a sleep.

In essence, the determination of the existence of a signal is a polling process in which the signal fields in the process are examined frequently for the presence of a set bit. Once the check is made, and it's determined that there is a signal posted, the appropriate action can be taken based on the signal's current disposition in the context of the process that received it.

This is why you can't kill zombie processes. (As any horror-movie fan knows, you can't kill a zombie.) A process must be executing in order to take delivery of a signal. A zombie process is, by definition, a process that has terminated. It exists only as a process table entry; all of its execution resources (i.e. allocated memory, constants, and variables storage) have been freed by the kernel.

Much of the up-front work in `sigtoproc()` deals with job control and the terminal I/O signals. In compliance with the POSIX specifications, this behavior is documented in the `signal(5)` manual page, which I'll summarize here: any pending `SIGCONT` signals are discarded upon receipt of a `SIGSTOP`, `SIGTSTP`, `SIGTTIN`, or `SIGTTOU` signal, regardless of the disposition. The inverse is also true; if any of those four signals are pending when a `SIGCONT` is received, they're discarded (again, regardless of the disposition). In both cases, the posted signal is delivered following the flow described in the section entitled "Asynchronous Signals," below.

Synchronous Signals

Synchronous, or trap, *signals* originate from within the kernel trap handler. When an executing instruction stream causes a trap event, the hardware detects it and execution is redirected to a kernel trap handler. The trap handler code populates a `siginfo` structure with the appropriate information about the trap, then invokes the `trap_cleanup()` function. The entry point into the kernel signal subsystem is via the `trapsig()` function, which is executed next. In `trapsig()`, if the signal is masked, or the disposition has been set to Ignore, `trapsig()` unmasks the signal and sets the disposition to default. The `siginfo` structure is placed on the `kthread`'s `t_sigqueue` list, and `sigtoproc()` is called to post the signal.

User tasks in Linux, created via explicit calls to either `thr_create(3T)` or `pthread_create(3T)`, all have their own signal masks. Linux threads call `clone()` with `CLONE_SIGHAND`; this shares all signal handlers between threads via sharing the `current->sig` pointer. Delivered signals are unique to a thread.

In some operating systems, like Solaris 7, signals generated as a result of a trap (`SIGFPE`, `SIGILL`, etc.) are sent to the thread that caused the trap. Asynchronous signals are delivered to the first thread that is found not blocking the signal. In Linux it is almost exactly the same. Synchronous signals occurring in the context of a given thread are delivered to that thread. Asynchronous in-kernel signals (e.g. asynchronous network I/O) are delivered to the thread that generated the asynchronous I/O. Explicit user-generated signals get delivered to the right thread as well.

However, if `CLONE_PID` is used, all places that use the PID to deliver a signal will behave in a weird way. The signal gets randomly delivered to the first thread in the `pidhash`. Linux threads don't use `CLONE_PID` so there is no such problem if you are using the `pthreads.h` thread API.

When a signal is sent to a user task, for example when a user-space program accesses an illegal page, the following happens:

1. `page_fault` (`entry.S`)—Low-level pagefault handler.
2. `do_page_fault()` (`fault.c`)—Fetches i386-specific parameters of the fault and does basic validation of the memory range involved.
3. `handle_mm_fault()` (`memory.c`)—Generic MM code (i386-independent), gets called. The MM reads the page table entry and uses the VMA to find out whether the memory access is legal.

The following case details an illegal access—a write was attempted to a read-only mapping. `handle_mm_fault()` returns 0 to `do_page_fault()` in this case:

```
{
        int fault = handle_mm_fault(tsk, vma, address, write);
        if (fault < 0)
                goto out_of_memory;
        if (!fault)
                goto do_sigbus;
}

...

do_sigbus:
        up(&mm->mmap_sem);

        /*
         * Send a sigbus, regardless of whether we were in kernel
         * or user mode.
         */
        tsk->thread.cr2 = address;
        tsk->thread.error_code = error_code;
        tsk->thread.trap_no = 14;
        force_sig(SIGBUS, tsk);
```

As you can see, locking of the MM is very fine grained (and it better be!), the `mm->mmap_sem` is per-MM semaphore used (which typically varies from process to process).

`force_sig(SIGBUS, current)` is used to "force" the `SIGBUS` signal on the faulting task. `force_sig()` delivers the signal even if the process has attempted to ignore `SIGBUS`.

`force_sig` fills out the signal event structure and queues it into the process's signal queue (`current->sigqueue` and `current->sigqueue_tail`)

The signal queue holds an indefinite number of queued signals. The semantics of *classic* signals are that follow-up signals are ignored—this is emulated in the signal code `kernel/signal.c`. *Generic* (or RT) signals can be queued arbitrarily—there are, however, reasonable limits to the length of the signal queue.

The signal is queued, and `current->signal` updated. Now comes the tricky part: the kernel returns to user-space. Return to user-space happens from `do_page_fault` => `page_fault` (entry.S), then the low-level exit code in `entry.S` is executed in the order detailed here:

```
page_fault => (called do_page_fault) => error_code =>
ret_from_exception => (checks if return to userspace) =>
ret_with_reschedule => (sees that current->signal is nonzero) =>
calls do_signal().
```

Next, `do_signal()` unqueues the signal to be executed. In this case it's SIGBUS. It then calls `handle_signal()` with the "unqueued" signal (which can potentially hold extra event information in case of real time signals or messages).

It then calls `setup_frame`, where all user-space registers are saved and the kernel stack frame return address is modified to point to the handler of the installed signal handler. A small sequence of jump code is put on the user stack (obviously, first the code makes sure the user stack is valid), which will return us to kernel space once the signal handler has finished:

```
{
    err |= __put_user(frame->retcode, &frame->pretcode);
    /* This is popl %eax ; movl $,%eax ; int $0x80 */
    err |= __put_user(0xb858, (short *)(frame->retcode+0));
    err |= __put_user(__NR_sigreturn, (int *)(frame->retcode+2));
    err |= __put_user(0x80cd, (short *)(frame->retcode+6));
}
```

NOTE

This area is one of the least understood pieces of the Linux kernel. And for a good reason—it is really tough code to read and follow.

The `popl %eax ; movl $,%eax ; int $0x80` x86 assembly sequence calls `sys_sigret()`, which will, later on, restore the kernel stack frame return address to a point to the original (faulting) user-address.

What is all this magic good for? Well, first, the kernel has to guarantee that signal handlers get called properly and that the original state is restored. The kernel also has to deal with binary compatibility issues.

Linux guarantees that on the IA32 (Intel x86) architecture we can run any iBC86-compliant binary code. Finally, speed is an issue, too.

Finally we return into `entry.S`, but `current->signal` is already cleared, so we do not execute `do_signal`, but jump to `restore_all`:

```
restore_all:
        RESTORE_ALL

#define RESTORE_ALL        \
        popl %ebx;         \
        popl %ecx;         \
        popl %edx;         \
        popl %esi;         \
        popl %edi;         \
        popl %ebp;         \
        popl %eax;         \
1:      popl %ds;          \
2:      popl %es;          \
        addl $4,%esp;      \
3:      iret;              \
```

which executes the `iret` that brings us into user-space; suddenly we are magically executing the signal handler.

Did you get lost yet? No? Here is some more magic: Once the signal handler finishes (it does an assembly ret like all well-behaved functions), it executes the small jump function we have set up on the user-stack. We again return into the kernel, but now we execute the `sys_sigreturn` system call, which lives in `arch/i386/kernel/signal.c` as well. It essentially executes the following code section:

```
if (restore_sigcontext(regs, &frame->sc, &eax))
        goto badframe;
return eax;
```

The above code restores the exact user-register contents into the kernel stack frame (including the return address and flags register), and executes a normal `ret_from_syscall`, which brings us back to the original faulting code. Hopefully the SIGBUS handler has fixed the problem of why we were faulting.

Now, while reading the above description, you might think that all this is awfully complex and slow. Well, it actually isn't, `lmbench` reveals that Linux has the fastest signal handler installation and execution performance by far of any UNIX-type system running:

```
moon:~/l> ./lat_sig install
Signal handler installation: 1.688 microseconds
```

```
moon:~/l> ./lat_sig catch
Signal handler overhead: 3.186 microseconds
```

Best of all, it scales linearly on SMP:

```
moon:~/l> ./lat_sig catch & ./lat_sig catch &
Signal handler overhead: 3.264 microseconds
Signal handler overhead: 3.248 microseconds

moon:~/l> ./lat_sig install & ./lat_sig install &
Signal handler installation: 1.721 microseconds
Signal handler installation: 1.689 microseconds
```

Signals and Interrupts, a Perfect Couple

Signals can be sent from system calls, interrupts, and bottom-half handlers alike; there is no difference. In other words, the Linux signal queue is interrupt safe, as strange and recursive as it sounds. So it's pretty flexible.

An interesting signal-delivery case, however, is on SMP: imagine a thread is executing on one processor, and it gets an asynchronous event (e.g. synchronous socket I/O signal) from an IRQ handler (or another process) on another CPU. In that case we send a cross-CPU message to that running process, so there is no latency in signal delivery. The speed of cross-CPU delivery is about 5 microseconds on a 350MHz Pentium II.

Data Structure—include/linux/signal.h

```
1 #ifndef _LINUX_SIGNAL_H
2 #define _LINUX_SIGNAL_H
3
4 #include <asm/signal.h>
5 #include <asm/siginfo.h>
6
7 #ifdef __KERNEL__
8 /*
9  * Real Time signals may be queued.
10  */
11
12 struct signal_queue
13 {
14         struct signal_queue *next;
15         siginfo_t info;
16 };
17
```

```
18 /*
19  * Define some primitives to manipulate sigset_t.
20  */
21
22 #ifndef __HAVE_ARCH_SIG_BITOPS
23 #include <asm/bitops.h>
24
25 /* We don't use <asm/bitops.h> for these because there is no need to
26    be atomic.   */
27 extern inline void sigaddset(sigset_t *set, int _sig)
28 {
29         unsigned long sig = _sig - 1;
30         if (_NSIG_WORDS == 1)
31                 set->sig[0] |= 1UL << sig;
32         else
33                 set->sig[sig / _NSIG_BPW] |= 1UL << (sig % _NSIG_BPW);
34 }
35
36 extern inline void sigdelset(sigset_t *set, int _sig)
37 {
38         unsigned long sig = _sig - 1;
39         if (_NSIG_WORDS == 1)
40                 set->sig[0] &= ~(1UL << sig);
41         else
42                 set->sig[sig / _NSIG_BPW] &= ~(1UL << (sig % _NSIG_BPW));
43 }
44
45 extern inline int sigismember(sigset_t *set, int _sig)
46 {
47         unsigned long sig = _sig - 1;
48         if (_NSIG_WORDS == 1)
49                 return 1 & (set->sig[0] >> sig);
50         else
51                 return 1 & (set->sig[sig / _NSIG_BPW] >> (sig % _NSIG_BPW));
52 }
53
54 extern inline int sigfindinword(unsigned long word)
55 {
56         return ffz(~word);
57 }
58
59 #define sigmask(sig)    (1UL << ((sig) - 1))
60
61 #endif /* __HAVE_ARCH_SIG_BITOPS */
62
63 #ifndef __HAVE_ARCH_SIG_SETOPS
64 #include <linux/string.h>
65
66 #define _SIG_SET_BINOP(name, op)                                        \
67 extern inline void name(sigset_t *r, const sigset_t *a, const sigset_t *b) \
68 {                                                                       \
69         unsigned long a0, a1, a2, a3, b0, b1, b2, b3;                   \
70         unsigned long i;                                                \
71                                                                         \
```

```
72          for (i = 0; i < _NSIG_WORDS/4; ++i) {                         \
73                  a0 = a->sig[4*i+0]; a1 = a->sig[4*i+1];               \
74                  a2 = a->sig[4*i+2]; a3 = a->sig[4*i+3];               \
75                  b0 = b->sig[4*i+0]; b1 = b->sig[4*i+1];               \
76                  b2 = b->sig[4*i+2]; b3 = b->sig[4*i+3];               \
77                  r->sig[4*i+0] = op(a0, b0);                           \
78                  r->sig[4*i+1] = op(a1, b1);                           \
79                  r->sig[4*i+2] = op(a2, b2);                           \
80                  r->sig[4*i+3] = op(a3, b3);                           \
81          }                                                            \
82          switch (_NSIG_WORDS % 4) {                                    \
83              case 3:                                                   \
84                  a0 = a->sig[4*i+0]; a1 = a->sig[4*i+1]; a2 = a->sig[4*i+2]; \
85                  b0 = b->sig[4*i+0]; b1 = b->sig[4*i+1]; b2 = b->sig[4*i+2]; \
86                  r->sig[4*i+0] = op(a0, b0);                           \
87                  r->sig[4*i+1] = op(a1, b1);                           \
88                  r->sig[4*i+2] = op(a2, b2);                           \
89                  break;                                                \
90              case 2:                                                   \
91                  a0 = a->sig[4*i+0]; a1 = a->sig[4*i+1];               \
92                  b0 = b->sig[4*i+0]; b1 = b->sig[4*i+1];               \
93                  r->sig[4*i+0] = op(a0, b0);                           \
94                  r->sig[4*i+1] = op(a1, b1);                           \
95                  break;                                                \
96              case 1:                                                   \
97                  a0 = a->sig[4*i+0]; b0 = b->sig[4*i+0];               \
98                  r->sig[4*i+0] = op(a0, b0);                           \
99                  break;                                                \
100         }                                                            \
101 }

102
103 #define _sig_or(x,y)    ((x) | (y))
104 _SIG_SET_BINOP(sigorsets, _sig_or)
105
106 #define _sig_and(x,y)   ((x) & (y))
107 _SIG_SET_BINOP(sigandsets, _sig_and)
108
109 #define _sig_nand(x,y)  ((x) & ~(y))
110 _SIG_SET_BINOP(signandsets, _sig_nand)
111
112 #undef _SIG_SET_BINOP
113 #undef _sig_or
114 #undef _sig_and
115 #undef _sig_nand
116
117 #define _SIG_SET_OP(name, op)                                         \
118 extern inline void name(sigset_t *set)                                \
119 {                                                                    \
120         unsigned long i;                                             \
121                                                                      \
122         for (i = 0; i < _NSIG_WORDS/4; ++i) {                        \
123                 set->sig[4*i+0] = op(set->sig[4*i+0]);               \
124                 set->sig[4*i+1] = op(set->sig[4*i+1]);               \
125                 set->sig[4*i+2] = op(set->sig[4*i+2]);               \
```

```
126                        set->sig[4*i+3] = op(set->sig[4*i+3]);         \
127             }                                                          \
128          switch (_NSIG_WORDS % 4) {                                    \
129             case 3: set->sig[4*i+2] = op(set->sig[4*i+2]);            \
130             case 2: set->sig[4*i+1] = op(set->sig[4*i+1]);            \
131             case 1: set->sig[4*i+0] = op(set->sig[4*i+0]);            \
132          }                                                             \
133 }
134
135 #define _sig_not(x)      (~(x))
136 _SIG_SET_OP(signotset, _sig_not)
137
138 #undef _SIG_SET_OP
139 #undef _sig_not
140
141 extern inline void sigemptyset(sigset_t *set)
142 {
143          switch (_NSIG_WORDS) {
144          default:
145                  memset(set, 0, sizeof(sigset_t));
146                  break;
147          case 2: set->sig[1] = 0;
148          case 1: set->sig[0] = 0;
149                  break;
150          }
151 }
152
153 extern inline void sigfillset(sigset_t *set)
154 {
155          switch (_NSIG_WORDS) {
156          default:
157                  memset(set, -1, sizeof(sigset_t));
158                  break;
159          case 2: set->sig[1] = -1;
160          case 1: set->sig[0] = -1;
161                  break;
162          }
163 }
164
165 extern char * render_sigset_t(sigset_t *set, char *buffer);
166
167 /* Some extensions for manipulating the low 32 signals in particular.  */
168
169 extern inline void sigaddsetmask(sigset_t *set, unsigned long mask)
170 {
171          set->sig[0] |= mask;
172 }
173
174 extern inline void sigdelsetmask(sigset_t *set, unsigned long mask)
175 {
176          set->sig[0] &= ~mask;
177 }
178
179 extern inline int sigtestsetmask(sigset_t *set, unsigned long mask)
```

```
180 {
181         return (set->sig[0] & mask) != 0;
182 }
183
184 extern inline void siginitset(sigset_t *set, unsigned long mask)
185 {
186         set->sig[0] = mask;
187         switch (_NSIG_WORDS) {
188         default:
189                 memset(&set->sig[1], 0, sizeof(long)*(_NSIG_WORDS-1));
190                 break;
191         case 2: set->sig[1] = 0;
192         case 1:
193             }
194 }
195
196 extern inline void siginitsetinv(sigset_t *set, unsigned long mask)
197 {
198         set->sig[0] = ~mask;
199         switch (_NSIG_WORDS) {
200         default:
201                 memset(&set->sig[1], -1, sizeof(long)*(_NSIG_WORDS-1));
202                 break;
203         case 2: set->sig[1] = -1;
204         case 1:
205             }
206 }
207
208 #endif /* __HAVE_ARCH_SIG_SETOPS */
209
210 #endif /* __KERNEL__ */
211
212 #endif /* _LINUX_SIGNAL_H */
213
```

Data Structure—include/linux/kernel.h

```
1 #ifndef _LINUX_KERNEL_H
2 #define _LINUX_KERNEL_H
3
4 /*
5  * 'kernel.h' contains some often-used function prototypes etc
6  */
7
8 #ifdef __KERNEL__
9
10 #include <stdarg.h>
11 #include <linux/linkage.h>
12
13 /* Optimization barrier */
```

```
14 /* The "volatile" is due to gcc bugs */
15 #define barrier() __asm__ __volatile__("": : :"memory")
16
17 #define INT_MAX           ((int)(~0U>>1))
18 #define UINT_MAX          (~0U)
19 #define LONG_MAX          ((long)(~0UL>>1))
20 #define ULONG_MAX         (~0UL)
21
22 #define STACK_MAGIC       0xdeadbeef
23
24 #define ARRAY_SIZE(x) (sizeof(x) / sizeof((x)[0]))
25
26 #define KERN_EMERG        "<0>"   /* system is unusable               */
27 #define KERN_ALERT        "<1>"   /* action must be taken immediately */
28 #define KERN_CRIT         "<2>"   /* critical conditions              */
29 #define KERN_ERR          "<3>"   /* error conditions                 */
30 #define KERN_WARNING      "<4>"   /* warning conditions               */
31 #define KERN_NOTICE       "<5>"   /* normal but significant condition */
32 #define KERN_INFO         "<6>"   /* informational                    */
33 #define KERN_DEBUG        "<7>"   /* debug-level messages             */
34
35 # define NORET_TYPE       /**/
36 # define ATTRIB_NORET     __attribute__((noreturn))
37 # define NORET_AND        noreturn,
38
39 #ifdef __i386__
40 #define FASTCALL(x)       x __attribute__((regparm(3)))
41 #else
42 #define FASTCALL(x)       x
43 #endif
44
45 extern void math_error(void);
46 extern struct notifier_block *panic_notifier_list;
47 NORET_TYPE void panic(const char * fmt, ...)
48         __attribute__ ((NORET_AND format (printf, 1, 2)));
49 NORET_TYPE void do_exit(long error_code)
50         ATTRIB_NORET;
51 extern unsigned long simple_strtoul(const char *,char **,unsigned int);
52 extern long simple_strtol(const char *,char **,unsigned int);
53 extern int sprintf(char * buf, const char * fmt, ...);
54 extern int vsprintf(char *buf, const char *, va_list);
55 extern int get_option(char **str, int *pint);
56 extern char *get_options(char *str, int nints, int *ints);
57
58 extern int session_of_pgrp(int pgrp);
59
60 asmlinkage int printk(const char * fmt, ...)
61         __attribute__ ((format (printf, 1, 2)));
62
63 #if DEBUG
64 #define pr_debug(fmt,arg...) \
65         printk(KERN_DEBUG fmt,##arg)
66 #else
67 #define pr_debug(fmt,arg...) \
```

```
 68          do { } while (0)
 69 #endif
 70
 71 #define pr_info(fmt,arg...) \
 72          printk(KERN_INFO fmt,##arg)
 73
 74 /*
 75  *      Display an IP address in readable format.
 76  */
 77
 78 #define NIPQUAD(addr) \
 79          ((unsigned char *)&addr)[0], \
 80          ((unsigned char *)&addr)[1], \
 81          ((unsigned char *)&addr)[2], \
 82          ((unsigned char *)&addr)[3]
 83
 84 #endif /* __KERNEL__ */
 85
 86 #define SI_LOAD_SHIFT    16
 87 struct sysinfo {
 88          long uptime;                    /* Seconds since boot */
 89          unsigned long loads[3];         /* 1, 5, and 15 minute load averages */
 90          unsigned long totalram;         /* Total usable main memory size */
 91          unsigned long freeram;          /* Available memory size */
 92          unsigned long sharedram;        /* Amount of shared memory */
 93          unsigned long bufferram;        /* Memory used by buffers */
 94          unsigned long totalswap;        /* Total swap space size */
 95          unsigned long freeswap;         /* swap space still available */
 96          unsigned short procs;           /* Number of current processes */
 97          unsigned long totalhigh;        /* Total high memory size */
 98          unsigned long freehigh;         /* Available high memory size */
 99          unsigned int mem_unit;          /* Memory unit size in bytes */
100           char _f[20-2*sizeof(long)-sizeof(int)]; /* Padding: libc5 uses this.. */
101 };
102
103 #endif
104
```

## CHAPTER 8

kHTTPd

kHTTPd, an HTTP-daemon, is a Web server for Linux. kHTTPd is different from other Web servers in that it runs from within the Linux kernel as a module (device driver).

kHTTPd handles only *static* (file-based) Web pages, and passes all requests for nonstatic information to a regular user-space Web server, such as Apache or Zeus. Static Web pages, although not a very complex thing to serve, are nevertheless very important. This is because virtually all images are static, as are a large portion of HTML pages. A "regular" Web server has little added value for static pages; it is simply a "copy-file-to-network" operation. The Linux kernel is very good at this—for example, the network file system (NFS) daemon also runs in the kernel.

Accelerating the simple case of serving static pages within the kernel leaves user-space daemons free to do what they are very good at: generating user-specific, dynamic content. A user-space Web server such as Apache is typically loaded with features and has lots of execution paths, so it can't be as fast as kHTTPd. There are, however, a few Web servers that are as simple as kHTTPd, but implemented in user space, which are not expensive consumers of processor cycles even compared to kHTTPd.

kHTTPd is very simple; it doesn't handle dynamic content. So it proxies all requests for those directories that you configure via the `sysctl` called `dynamic` to a fully functional user-space Web server such as Apache.

For this reason, kHTTPd is faster only for static pages. Dynamic pages incur a bit more latency under a kHTTPd Web server, because they need to be forwarded to another Web server like Apache. It's a global win, though, because most of the transfers of a common Web server are images, which are definitely static.

kHTTPd is actually a bird not much different from a normal HTTP daemon in principle. The main difference is that it bypasses the system call layer. Normally you have code like this:

```
socket(..)
bind(..)
listen(..)
accept(..)
```

and each call has to enter the kernel, look up kernel structures as function(s) of the parameter(s) passed, return information to user space, and so forth.

kHTTPd directly runs the internals of such system calls, because being a kernel daemon itself, it interfaces directly with the internal kernel structures involved and avoids the user–kernel interaction completely. Also because it's a kernel daemon, it avoids `switch_mm` and TLB flushes. And, last but not least, it avoids all enterancd and exit kernel overhead.

There are not many data structures for kHTTPd. They are found in `net/kHTTPd/structure.h`. The first is a per-connection structure. The second is a per-kHTTPd-thread structure through which many `http_request`s can be queued:

```
struct http_request
{
    /* Linked list */
    struct http_request *Next;

    /* Network and File data */
    struct socket *sock;
    struct file   *filp;

    /* Raw data about the file */

    int     FileLength;      /* File length in bytes */
    int     Time;            /* mtime of the file, unix format */
    int     BytesSent;       /* The number of bytes already sent */
    int     IsForUser space; /* 1 means let User space handle this one */

    /* Wait queue */

    wait_queue_t sleep;      /* For putting in the socket's waitqueue */

    /* HTTP request information */
    char    FileName[256];   /* The requested filename */
    int     FileNameLength;  /* The length of the string representing the filename */
    char    Agent[128];      /* The agent-string of the remote browser */
    char    IMS[128];        /* If-modified-since time, rfc string format */
    char    Host[128];       /* Value given by the Host: header */
    int     HTTPVER;         /* HTTP-version; 9 for 0.9, 10 for 1.0 and above */


    /* Derived date from the above fields */
    int     IMS_Time;        /* if-modified-since time, unix format */
    char    TimeS[64];       /* File mtime, rfc string representation */
    char    LengthS[14];     /* File length, string representation */
    char    *MimeType;       /* Pointer to a string with the mime-type
                                based on the filename */
    __kernel_size_t  MimeLength;   /* The length of this string */

};


/*
```

```
struct khttpd_threadinfo represents the four queues that 1 thread has to deal with.
It is padded to occupy 1 (Intel) cache-line, to avoid "cacheline-pingpong".

*/
struct khttpd_threadinfo
{
    struct http_request* WaitForHeaderQueue;
    struct http_request* DataSendingQueue;
    struct http_request* LoggingQueue;
    struct http_request* User spaceQueue;
    char  dummy[16];   /* Padding for cache-lines */
};
```

kHTTPd can be compiled as a loadable module, or it can be linked statically into the kernel. Linking statically into the kernel provides better performance, because it will be allocated in a more efficient and TLB-persistent page table mapping.

Controlling kHTTPd

The kHTTPd daemon is controlled via system controls (sysctls) in /proc/sys/net/khttpd. These are the system controls, with a description for each (from documentation):

serverport	8080	The port khttpd listens to.
clientport	80	The port of the user space HTTP daemon.
threads	2	The number of server threads. Should be one per CPU for small web sites, two per CPU for big (the active files do not fit in the RAM) web sites.
documentroot/var/www		The directory holding document files.
start	0	Set to 1 to start kHTTPd. (This also resets "stop" to 0.)
stop	0	Set to 1 to stop kHTTPd. (This also resets "start" to 0.)
unload	0	Set to 1 to prepare kHTTPd to be unloaded.
sloppymime	0	If set to 1, unknown MIME types are set to text/html. If set to 0, files with unknown MIME types are handled by the user space daemon.
perm_required	S_IROTH	Minimum permissions required; for values see man 2 stat.
perm_forbid	dir+sticky+ execute	Permission mask with forbidden permissions. (For values see man 2 stat.)

continued on next page

| dynamic | cgi-bin .. | Strings that, if they are a subset of the URL, indicate dynamic content. |
| maxconnect | 1000 | Maximum number of concurrent connections. |

Data Structure—linux/net/structure.h

```
#ifndef _INCLUDE_GUARD_STRUCTURE_H_
#define _INCLUDE_GUARD_STRUCTURE_H_

#include <linux/time.h>
#include <linux/wait.h>


struct http_request;

struct http_request
{
    /* Linked list */
    struct http_request *Next;

    /* Network and File data */
    struct socket *sock;
    struct file   *filp;

    /* Raw data about the file */

    int   FileLength;        /* File length in bytes */
    int   Time;              /* mtime of the file, unix format */
    int   BytesSent;         /* The number of bytes already sent */
    int   IsForUser space;   /* 1 means let User space handle this one */

    /* Wait queue */

    wait_queue_t sleep;      /* For putting in the socket's waitqueue */

    /* HTTP request information */
    char  FileName[256];     /* The requested filename */
    int   FileNameLength;    /* The length of the string representing the filename */
    char  Agent[128];        /* The agent-string of the remote browser */
    char  IMS[128];          /* If-modified-since time, rfc string format */
    char  Host[128];         /* Value given by the Host: header */
    int   HTTPVER;           /* HTTP-version; 9 for 0.9, 10 for 1.0 and above */


    /* Derived date from the above fields */
    int    IMS_Time;         /* if-modified-since time, unix format */
    char   TimeS[64];        /* File mtime, rfc string representation */
    char   LengthS[14];      /* File length, string representation */
    char   *MimeType;        /* Pointer to a string with the mime-type
                                based on the filename */
```

```
        __kernel_size_t    MimeLength;    /* The length of this string */

};



/*

struct khttpd_threadinfo represents the four queues that 1 thread has to deal with.
It is padded to occupy 1 (Intel) cache-line, to avoid "cacheline-pingpong".

*/
struct khttpd_threadinfo
{
    struct http_request* WaitForHeaderQueue;
    struct http_request* DataSendingQueue;
    struct http_request* LoggingQueue;
    struct http_request* User spaceQueue;
    char  dummy[16];  /* Padding for cache-lines */
};



#endif
```

CHAPTER **9**

Linux
System Calls

This chapter will give you an understanding of the dynamics of system calls in Linux. Wherever code sections are mentioned, unless otherwise specified, I refer to the 2.3.52 (soon to be 2.4) series of kernels.

To review a few broad terms:

- A *kernel* is the operating system software, running in protected mode and having access to the hardware's privileged registers.
- Some operating systems employ a *microkernel architecture*, wherein device drivers and other code are loaded and executed on demand, and are not necessarily always present in memory.
- By contrast, a *monolithic architecture* is more common among UNIX implementations. It is employed by classic designs such as BSD.

The Linux kernel is a mostly monolithic kernel: all device drivers are part of the kernel proper. Unlike BSD, a Linux kernel's device drivers can be loadable, that is, they can be loaded and unloaded from memory through user commands. The kernel is not a separate process running on the system. It is the guts of the operating system, which controls the scheduling of processes to achieve multitasking and provides a set of routines, constantly in memory, to which every user space process has access.

The kernel also contains the routines that implement the interface between user programs and hardware devices, paging in and out of virtual memory, file management, and many other aspects of the system. To achieve all this, kernel routines can be called from user-space code in a number of ways. One direct method to utilize the kernel is for a process to execute a system call. There are 116 system calls; documentation for these can be found in the man(2) pages.

System Calls and Event Classes on the IA32

A system call, then, is a request by a running task to the kernel to provide some sort of service on its behalf. In general, the kernel services invoked by system calls comprise an abstraction layer between hardware and user-space programs, allowing a programmer to implement an operating environment without having to tailor his program(s) too specifically to one single brand or precise specific combination of system hardware components. System calls also serve this generalization function across programming languages; for example the `read` system call will read data from a file descriptor. To the programmer, this looks like another C function, but in actuality the code for `read` is contained within the kernel. The IA32 CPU recognizes two classes of events needing special processor attention: *interrupts* and *exceptions*. Both cause a forced context switch to a new procedure or task.

Interrupts

For a detailed treatise on interrupts, please check Chapter 3, "Kernel Base Functions." Interrupts can occur at unexpected times during the execution of a program, and they are used to signal the need for processor attention from hardware. When a hardware device issues an interrupt, the interrupt handler is found within the kernel. Two sources of interrupts are recognized by the IA32: *maskable interrupts*, the vectors for which are determined by the hardware; and *nonmaskable interrupts* (NMIs).

Exceptions

Exceptions are either processor detected, or else issued (*thrown*) from software: When a procedure or method encounters an abnormal condition (an *exception condition*) that it can't handle itself, it may throw an exception. Exceptions of either type are *caught* by handler routines (*exception handlers*) positioned along the thread's procedure or method invocation stack—the calling procedure or method or, if that doesn't include code to handle the exception condition, then its calling procedure or method, and so on up. If one of the threads of your program throws an exception that isn't caught by any procedure (or method), then that thread will expire.

An exception indicates to a calling procedure that an abnormal (although not necessarily rare) condition has occurred; for example, when a method is invoked with an invalid argument. When you throw an exception, you are performing a kind of structured "go to" from the place in your program where an abnormal condition was detected to a place where it can be handled. Exception handlers should be stationed at program-module levels in accordance with how general a range of errors each is capable of handling, so that as few exception handlers as possible will cover as wide a variety of exceptions as may be encountered in field application of your programs.

An Example of Exceptions as Objects from Java

In Java, exceptions are objects; in addition to throwing objects whose class is declared in `java.lang`, you can throw objects of your own design. To create your own class of throwable objects, you need only declare it as a subclass of some member of the Throwable family. In general, however, the throwable classes you define should extend class Exception—they should be "exceptions." Usually, the class of the exception object itself indicates the type of abnormal condition that was encountered. For example, if a thrown exception object has class `illegalArgumentException`, that indicates someone passed an illegal argument to a method.

When you throw an exception, you instantiate and throw an object whose class, declared in `java.lang`, descends from Throwable. Throwable has two direct subclasses, Exception and Error. Errors (members of the Error family) are usually thrown for more serious problems, such as `OutOfMemoryError`, which may not be so easy to handle. Errors are usually thrown by the methods of the Java API, or by the Java Virtual Machine itself. In general, code you write should throw only exceptions, not errors.

The Java Virtual Machine uses the class of the exception object you throw to decide which `catch` clause, if any, should be allowed to handle the exception. The `catch` clause can also get information about the abnormal condition by querying the exception object directly for information you embedded in it during instantiation before throwing it. The Exception class allows you to specify a String detail message that can be retrieved by invoking `getMessage()` on the exception object.

Vectors

Each interrupt or exception has a number, which is referred to by the IA32 literature as its *vector*. The NMI interrupt and the processor-detected exceptions have been assigned vectors in the range 0 through 31, inclusive. The vectors for maskable interrupts are determined by the hardware. External interrupt controllers put the vector on the bus during the interrupt–acknowledge cycle. Any vector in the range of 32 through 255, inclusive, can be used for maskable interrupts or programmed exceptions.

The `startup_32()` code found in `/usr/src/linux/boot/head.S` starts everything off at boot time by calling `setup_idt()`. This routine sets up an Interrupt Descriptor Table (IDT) with 256 entries, each 4 bytes long, with a total of 1,024 bytes and offsets 0 to 255. It should be noted that the IDT contains vectors to both interrupt handlers and exception handlers, and so IDT is somewhat of a misnomer, but that's the way it is.

No interrupt entry points are actually loaded by `startup_32()`, because that is done only after paging has been enabled and the kernel has been relocated to `0xC000000`. At times, mostly during boot, the kernel has to be loaded into certain addresses because the underlying BIOS architecture demands it.

After control is passed to the kernel exclusively, the Linux kernel can put itself wherever it wants. Usually this is very high up in memory, but below the 2GB limit.

When `start_kernel()` (found in `/usr /src/linux/init/main.c`) is called, it invokes `trap_init()` (found in `/usr/src/linux/kernel/traps.c`). `trap_init()` sets up the IDT via the macro `set_trap_gate()` (found in `/usr/include/asm/system.h`). `trap_init()` initializes the interrupt descriptor table as shown in Table 9.1

TABLE 9.1

Interrupt Descriptor
Table

OFFSET	DESCRIPTION
0	Divide error exception
1	Debug exception
2	NMI (nonmaskable interrupt)
3	Breakpoint exception
4	INTO-detected overflow exception
5	BOUND range exceeded exception
6	Invalid opcode exception
7	Coprocessor not available exception
8	Double fault exception (whatever the devil that is)
9	Coprocessor segment overrun exception
10	Invalid task state segment exception

continued on next page

TABLE 9.1

continued

OFFSET	DESCRIPTION
11	Segment not present exception
12	Stack fault exception
13	General protection fault exception
14	Page fault exception
15	Reserved
16	Coprocessor error exception
17	Alignment check exception
18-48	Reserved

At this point, the interrupt vector for the system calls is not set up. It is initialized by `sched_init()` (found in `/usr/src/linux/kernel/sched.c`). A call to `set_system_gate(0x80, &system_call)` sets interrupt `0x80` to be a vector to the `system_call()` entry point.

At what point are the offsets 32 to 255 set up as the maskable interrupts? Well, they are never set up during the module loading. They are set up at boot, once and for all. Then a device driver can request an interrupt line and the kernel unmasks the interrupt. Then, when and only when the interrupt occurs, the processor jumps to execute this previously initialized vector.

But when are these table entries filled? In 2.3.99-pre3 (this is 2.4; kernels 2.2.x are completely equivalent in the design but a few names of files may have unintentionally changed).

The table is the interrupt descriptor table `idt_table`. It's allocated in `arch/i386/kernel/traps.c`. It gets initialized in `arch/i386/kernel/i8259.c` in `init_IRQ()` using the `set_intr_gate` macro and passing to the macro the vector:

```
/*
 * Cover the whole vector space, no vector can escape
 * us. (some of these will be overridden and become
 * 'special' SMP interrupts)
 */
for (i = 0; i < NR_IRQS; i++) {
    int vector = FIRST_EXTERNAL_VECTOR + i;
    if (vector != SYSCALL_VECTOR)
        set_intr_gate(vector, interrupt[i]);
}
```

FIRST_EXTERNAL_VECTOR is indeed 32; the entry points below 32 are used for the CPU exceptions.

As you will undoubtedly notice, the kernel avoids overwriting the vector 0x80 that corresponds to the system call entry point (int 0x80), but allocates all the entry points so that it can also trap and report spurious interrupts.

The exceptions (lower than 0x20) and system-call entry points are initialized in trap_init() in arch/i386/kernel/traps.c. Vectors never change at runtime. All is done at kernel boot time. During runtime, the priority of simultaneously seen interrupts and exceptions is as follows:

- Highest
  - Faults except debug faults
  - Trap instructions INTO, INT n, INT 3
  - Debug traps for this instruction
  - Debug traps for next instruction
  - NMI interrupt
- Lowest
  - INTR interrupt

The Linux System Call Interface

The Linux system call interface is vectored through a stub in libc (often glibc), and is exclusively register-parametered—the stack is not used for parameter passing. Each call within the libc library is generally a syscallX() macro, where X is the number of parameters used by the actual routine. Under Linux, the execution of a system call is invoked by a maskable interrupt or exception class transfer (e.g. throwing an exception object), caused by the instruction int 0x80. We use vector 0x80 to transfer control to the kernel. This interrupt vector is initialized during system startup, along with other important vectors like the system clock vector. On the assembly level (in user space), it goes like this:

```
ae531:   b8 15 00 00 00        movl    $0x15,%eax
ae536:   53                    pushl   %ebx
ae537:   89 c3                 movl    %eax,%ebx
ae539:   b8 75 00 00 00        movl    $0x75,%eax
ae53e:   cd 80                 int     $0x80
ae540:   5b                    popl    %ebx
ae541:   89 c6                 movl    %eax,%esi
ae543:   81 fe 00 f0 ff ff     cmpl    $0xfffff000,%esi
```

Nowadays, this code is contained in the `glibc2.1` library. `0x80` is hardcoded both into Linux and `glibc`, to be the system call number that transfers control to the kernel. At bootup the kernel has set up the interrupt descriptor table (IDT) vector `0x80` to be a *call gate*—see `arch/i386/kernel/traps.c:trap_init()`:

```
set_system_gate(SYSCALL_VECTOR,&system_call)
```

The vector layout is defined in `include/asm-i386/hw_irq.h`.

Not until the `int $0x80` is executed does the call transfer to the kernel entry point `_system_call()`. This entry point is the same for all system calls. It is responsible for saving all registers, checking to make sure a valid system call was invoked, and then ultimately transferring control to the actual system-call code via the offsets in the `_sys_call_table`. It is also responsible for calling `_ret_from_sys_call()` when the system call has been completed, but before returning to user space.

Actual code for the `system_call` entry point can be found in `/usr/src/linux/kernel/sys_call.S` and the code for many of the system calls can be found in `/usr/src/linux/kernel/sys.c`. Code for the rest is distributed all over the source files. Some system calls, like `fork()`, have their own source file (e.g. `kernel/fork.c`) devoted to them.

The next instruction the CPU executes after the `int $0x80` is the `pushl %eax` in `entry.S:system_call()`. There, we first save all user-space registers, then we range-check `%eax` and call into `sys_call_table[%eax]`, which is the actual system call.

Because the Linux system call interface is exclusively register-parametered and the stack is not used for parameter passing, at most six parameters can be used with a single system call. `%eax` is the syscall number; `%ebx`, `%ecx`, `%edx`, `%esi`, `%edi`, and `%ebp` are the six generic registers used as parameters 0 to 5; and `%esp` cannot be used because it's overwritten by the kernel on `ring0-entry`.

In case more parameters are needed, a structure, placed wherever you want within your address space, is pointed to from a register (neither the instruction pointer, nor the stack pointer; the kernel space functions use the stack for parameters and local variables). This case is extremely rare though; most system calls are 0- or 1-parameter only.

Once the system call returns, we check one or more status flags in the process structure; the exact number depends on the system call. A `creat()` might leave a dozen flags (existing, created, locked, etc.) whereas a `sync()` might return only one. If no work is pending, then we restore user space registers and return to user space via `iret`. The next instruction after the `iret` is the user space `popl %ebx` instruction in the above example.

More-Complex System Calls

Some system calls are more complex than others because of variable length argument lists. Examples of a complex system call include `open()` and `ioctl()`. However, even these complex system calls must use the same entry point; they just have more parameter setup overhead. Each system-call macro expands to an assembly routine which sets up the calling stack frame and calls `_system_call()` through an interrupt, via the instruction `int $0x80`.

For example, the `setuid` system call is coded as:

```
_syscall1(int,setuid,uid_t,uid);
```

which expands to:

```
_setuid:
subl $4,%exp
pushl %ebx
movzwl 12(%esp),%eax
movl %eax,4(%esp)
movl $23,%eax
movl 4(%esp),%ebx
int $0x80
movl %eax,%edx
testl %edx,%edx
jge L2
negl %edx
movl %edx,_errno
movl $-1,%eax
popl %ebx
addl $4,%esp

ret

L2:

movl %edx,%eax
popl %ebx
addl $4,%esp
ret
```

The User-Space System-Call Code Library

The user-space call code library can be found in /usr/src/libc/syscall. The hardcoding of the parameter layout and actual system-call numbers is not a problem, because system calls are never really changed; they are only "introduced" and "obsoleted." An "obsoleted" system call is marked with the old_ prefix in entry.S's system call table. Reference to it is removed from the next glibc, and once no application uses the system call anymore, its slot is marked unused and is potentially reusable for a newly introduced system call.

Tracing System Calls

If a user wishes to trace a program, it is equally important to know what happens during system calls, so the trace of a program usually includes a trace through the system calls as well. This is done through SIGSTOP and SIGCHLD ping-ponging between parent (tracing process) and child (traced process). When a traced process is executed, then every system call is preceded by a sys_ptrace() call.

This makes the traced process send a SIGCHILD to the tracing process every time a system call is made. At once, the traced process enters TASK_STOPPED (a flag is set in the task_struct structure of the task) state. The tracing process then examines the entire address space of the traced process, through the use of _ptrace, which is a multi-purpose system call; the tracing process then sends a SIGSTOP to allow execution to begin again.

How to Add Your Own System Calls

Adding your own system calls is actually quite easy if you use following simple steps. Remember that if you do not make these system calls available on other machines where your program may run, the result is nonportable code.

1. Create a directory under the /usr/src/linux/ directory to hold your code.
2. Put any include files in /usr/include/sys/ and /usr/include/linux/.

3. Add the relocatable module produced by the link of your new kernel code to the ARCHIVES and the subdirectory to the SUBDIRS lines of the top level Makefile. (See fs/Makefile, target fs.o for an example.)

4. Add a #define __NR_xx to unistd.h to assign a call number for your system call, where *xx*, the index, is something descriptive relating to your system call. It will be used to set up the vector through sys_call_table to invoke your code.

5. Add an entry point for your system call to the sys_call_table in sys.h. It should match the index (*xx*) that you assigned in the previous step.

6. The NR_syscalls variable will be recalculated automatically.

7. Modify any kernel code in kernel/fs/mm/ or elsewhere to take into account the environment needed to support your new code.

8. Run make from the top source code directory level to produce the new kernel incorporating your new code.

At this point, you will have to either add a system call to your libraries, or use the proper _syscalln() macro in your user program for your programs to access the new system call. The *386DX Microprocessor Programmer's Reference Manual* is a helpful reference, as is James Turley's *Advanced 80386 Programming Techniques*.

List of Linux/IA32 Kernel System Calls

These are not libc user space system calls, but real kernel system calls provided by Linux kernel. The sources of information is the Gnu libc project **www.gnu.org**. Check with the proper source code files and the include files for comprehensive reference.

00 sys_setup [sys_ni_syscall]	07 sys_waitpid	14 sys_mknod
01 sys_exit	08 sys_creat	15 sys_chmod
02 sys_fork	09 sys_link	16 sys_lchown
03 sys_read	10 sys_unlink	17 sys_break [sys_ni_syscall]
04 sys_write	11 sys_execve	18 sys_oldstat [sys_stat]
05 sys_open	12 sys_chdir	19 sys_lseek
06 sys_close	13 sys_time	20 sys_getpid

21 sys_mount

22 sys_umount [sys_oldumount]

23 sys_setuid

24 sys_getuid

25 sys_stime

26 sys_ptrace

27 sys_alarm

28 sys_oldfstat [sys_fstat]

29 sys_pause

30 sys_utime

31 sys_stty [sys_ni_syscall]

32 sys_gtty [sys_ni_syscall]

33 sys_access

34 sys_nice

35 sys_ftime [sys_ni_syscall]

36 sys_sync

37 sys_kill

38 sys_rename

39 sys_mkdir

40 sys_rmdir

41 sys_dup

42 sys_pipe

43 sys_times

44 sys_prof [sys_ni_syscall]

45 sys_brk

46 sys_setgid

47 sys_getgid

48 sys_signal

49 sys_geteuid

50 sys_getegid

51 sys_acct

52 sys_umount2 [sys_umount] (+2.2)

53 sys_lock [sys_ni_syscall]

54 sys_ioctl

55 sys_fcntl

56 sys_mpx [sys_ni_syscall]

57 sys_setpgid

58 sys_ulimit [sys_ni_syscall]

59 sys_oldolduname

60 sys_umask

61 sys_chroot

62 sys_ustat

63 sys_dup2

64 sys_getppid

65 sys_getpgrp

66 sys_setsid

67 sys_sigaction

68 sys_sgetmask

69 sys_ssetmask

70 sys_setreuid

71 sys_setregid

72 sys_sigsuspend

73 sys_sigpending

74 sys_sethostname

75 sys_setrlimit

76 sys_getrlimit

77 sys_getrusage

78 sys_gettimeofday

79 sys_settimeofday

80 sys_getgroups

81 sys_setgroups

82 sys_select [old_select]

83 sys_symlink

84 sys_oldlstat [sys_lstat]

85 sys_readlink

86 sys_uselib

87 sys_swapon

88 sys_reboot

89 sys_readdir [old_readdir]

90 sys_mmap [old_mmap]

91 sys_munmap

92 sys_truncate

93 sys_ftruncate

94 sys_fchmod

95 sys_fchown

96 sys_getpriority

97 sys_setpriority

98 sys_profil [sys_ni_syscall]

99 sys_statfs

100 sys_fstatfs

101 sys_ioperm

102 sys_socketcall

103 sys_syslog

104 sys_setitimer

105 sys_getitimer

106 sys_stat [sys_newstat]

107 sys_lstat [sys_newlstat]

108 sys_fstat [sys_newfstat]

109 sys_olduname [sys_uname]

110 sys_iopl

111 sys_vhangup

112 sys_idle

113 sys_vm86old

114 sys_wait4

115 sys_swapoff

116 sys_sysinfo

117 sys_ipc

118 sys_fsync

119 sys_sigreturn

120 sys_clone

121 sys_setdomainname

122 sys_uname [sys_newuname]

123 sys_modify_ldt

124 sys_adjtimex

125 sys_mprotect

126 sys_sigprocmask

127 sys_create_module

128 sys_init_module

129 sys_delete_module

130 sys_get_kernel_syms

131 sys_quotactl

132 sys_getpgid

133 sys_fchdir

134 sys_bdflush

135 sys_sysfs

136 sys_personality

137 sys_afs_syscall [sys_ni_syscall]

138 sys_setfsuid

139 sys_setfsgid

140 sys__llseek [sys_lseek]

141 sys_getdents

142 sys__newselect [sys_select]

143 sys_flock

144 sys_msync

145 sys_readv

146 sys_writev

147 sys_getsid

148 sys_fdatasync

149 sys__sysctl [sys_sysctl]

150 sys_mlock

151 sys_munlock

152 sys_mlockall

153 sys_munlockall

154 sys_sched_setparam

155 sys_sched_getparam

156 sys_sched_setscheduler

157 sys_sched_getscheduler

158 sys_sched_yield

159 sys_sched_get_priority_max

160 sys_sched_get_priority_min

161 sys_sched_rr_get_interval

162 sys_nanosleep

163 sys_mremap

164 sys_setresuid (+2.2)

165 sys_getresuid (+2.2)

166 sys_vm86

167 sys_query_module (+2.2)

168 sys_poll (+2.2)

169 sys_nfsservctl (+2.2)

170 sys_setresgid (+2.2)

171 sys_getresgid (+2.2)

172 sys_prctl (+2.2)

173 sys_rt_sigreturn (+2.2)

174 sys_rt_sigaction (+2.2)

175 sys_rt_sigprocmask (+2.2)

176 sys_rt_sigpending (+2.2)

177 sys_rt_sigtimedwait (+2.2)

178 sys_rt_sigqueueinfo (+2.2)

179 sys_rt_sigsuspend (+2.2)

180 sys_pread (+2.2)

181 sys_pwrite (+2.2)

182 sys_chown (+2.2)

183 sys_getcwd (+2.2)

184 sys_capget (+2.2)

185 sys_capset (+2.2)

186 sys_sigaltstack (+2.2)

187 sys_sendfile (+2.2)

188 sys_getpmsg [sys_ni_syscall]

189 sys_putpmsg [sys_ni_syscall]

190 sys_vfork (+2.2)

Data Structures—include/linux/sys.h

```
1 #ifndef _LINUX_SYS_H
2 #define _LINUX_SYS_H
3
4 /*
5  * system call entry points ... but not all are defined
6  */
7 #define NR_syscalls 256
8
9 /*
10  * These are system calls that will be removed at some time
11  * due to newer versions existing..
12  * (please be careful - ibcs2 may need some of these).
13  */
14 #ifdef notdef
15 #define _sys_waitpid     _sys_old_syscall          /* _sys_wait4 */
16 #define _sys_olduname    _sys_old_syscall          /* _sys_newuname */
17 #define _sys_uname       _sys_old_syscall          /* _sys_newuname */
18 #define _sys_stat        _sys_old_syscall          /* _sys_newstat */
19 #define _sys_fstat       _sys_old_syscall          /* _sys_newfstat */
20 #define _sys_lstat       _sys_old_syscall          /* _sys_newlstat */
21 #define _sys_signal      _sys_old_syscall          /* _sys_sigaction */
22 #define _sys_sgetmask    _sys_old_syscall          /* _sys_sigprocmask */
23 #define _sys_ssetmask    _sys_old_syscall          /* _sys_sigprocmask */
24 #endif
25
26 /*
27  * These are system calls that haven't been implemented yet
28  * but have an entry in the table for future expansion..
29  */
30 #endif
31
```

Data Structures—include/asm-i386/hw_irq.h

```
1 #ifndef _ASM_HW_IRQ_H
2 #define _ASM_HW_IRQ_H
3
4 /*
5  *        linux/include/asm/hw_irq.h
6  *
7  *        (C) 1992, 1993 Linus Torvalds, (C) 1997 Ingo Molnar
8  *
9  *        moved some of the old arch/i386/kernel/irq.h to here. VY
10  *
11  *        IRQ/IPI changes taken from work by Thomas Radke
12  *        <tomsoft@informatik.tu-chemnitz.de>
13  */
14
```

```
15 #include <asm/irq.h>
16
17 /*
18  * IDT vectors usable for external interrupt sources start
19  * at 0x20:
20  */
21 #define FIRST_EXTERNAL_VECTOR    0x20
22
23 #define SYSCALL_VECTOR           0x80
24
25 /*
26  * Vectors 0x20-0x2f are used for ISA interrupts.
27  */
28
29 /*
30  * Special IRQ vectors used by the SMP architecture, 0x30-0x4f
31  *
32  *  some of the following vectors are 'rare', they are merged
33  *  into a single vector (CALL_FUNCTION_VECTOR) to save vector space.
34  *  TLB, reschedule and local APIC vectors are performance-critical.
35  */
36 #define INVALIDATE_TLB_VECTOR    0x30
37 #define LOCAL_TIMER_VECTOR       0x31
38 #define RESCHEDULE_VECTOR        0x40
39
40 /* 'rare' vectors: */
41 #define CALL_FUNCTION_VECTOR     0x41
42
43 /*
44  * These IRQs should never really happen on perfect hardware running
45  * a perfect kernel, but we nevertheless print a message to catch the
46  * rest ;) Subtle, the APIC architecture mandates the spurious vector
47  * to have bits 0-3 set to 1. Note that these vectors do not occur
48  * normally, so we violate the 'only 2 vectors per priority level'
49  * rule here.
50  */
51 #define SPURIOUS_APIC_VECTOR     0x3f
52 #define ERROR_APIC_VECTOR        0x43
53
54 /*
55  * First APIC vector available to drivers: (vectors 0x51-0xfe)
56  * we start at 0x51 to spread out vectors between priority levels
57  * evenly. (note that 0x80 is the syscall vector)
58  */
59 #define IRQ0_TRAP_VECTOR         0x51
60
61 extern int irq_vector[NR_IRQS];
62 #define IO_APIC_VECTOR(irq)      irq_vector[irq]
63
64 /*
65  * Various low-level irq details needed by irq.c, process.c,
66  * time.c, io_apic.c and smp.c
67  *
68  * Interrupt entry/exit code at both C and assembly level
```

```
69   */
70
71   extern void no_action(int cpl, void *dev_id, struct pt_regs *regs);
72   extern void mask_irq(unsigned int irq);
73   extern void unmask_irq(unsigned int irq);
74   extern void disable_8259A_irq(unsigned int irq);
75   extern void enable_8259A_irq(unsigned int irq);
76   extern int i8259A_irq_pending(unsigned int irq);
77   extern void make_8259A_irq(unsigned int irq);
78   extern void init_8259A(int aeoi);
79   extern void FASTCALL(send_IPI_self(int vector));
80   extern void init_VISWS_APIC_irqs(void);
81   extern void  setup_IO_APIC(void);
82   extern void disable_IO_APIC(void);
83   extern void print_IO_APIC(void);
84   extern int IO_APIC_get_PCI_irq_vector(int bus, int slot, int fn);
85   extern void send_IPI(int dest, int vector);
86
87   extern unsigned long io_apic_irqs;
88   extern volatile unsigned long irq_err_count;
89
90   extern char _stext, _etext;
91
92   #define IO_APIC_IRQ(x) (((x) >= 16) || ((1<<(x)) & io_apic_irqs))
93
94   #define __STR(x) #x
95   #define STR(x) __STR(x)
96
97   #define SAVE_ALL \
98           "cld\n\t" \
99           "pushl %es\n\t" \
100          "pushl %ds\n\t" \
101          "pushl %eax\n\t" \
102          "pushl %ebp\n\t" \
103          "pushl %edi\n\t" \
104          "pushl %esi\n\t" \
105          "pushl %edx\n\t" \
106          "pushl %ecx\n\t" \
107          "pushl %ebx\n\t" \
108          "movl $" STR( __KERNEL_DS) ",%edx\n\t" \
109          "movl %edx,%ds\n\t" \
110          "movl %edx,%es\n\t"
111
112  #define IRQ_NAME2(nr) nr##_interrupt(void)
113  #define IRQ_NAME(nr) IRQ_NAME2(IRQ##nr)
114
115  #define  GET_CURRENT \
116          "movl %esp, %ebx\n\t" \
117          "andl $-8192, %ebx\n\t"
118
119  /*
120   *        SMP has a few special interrupts for IPI messages
121   */
122
```

```
123          /* there is a second layer of macro just to get the symbolic
124             name for the vector evaluated. This change is for RTLinux */
125 #define BUILD_SMP_INTERRUPT(x,v) XBUILD_SMP_INTERRUPT(x,v)
126 #define XBUILD_SMP_INTERRUPT(x,v)\
127 asmlinkage void x(void); \
128 asmlinkage void call_##x(void); \
129 __asm__( \
130 "\n"__ALIGN_STR"\n" \
131 SYMBOL_NAME_STR(x) ":\n\t" \
132         "pushl $"#v"\n\t" \
133         SAVE_ALL \
134         SYMBOL_NAME_STR(call_##x)":\n\t" \
135         "call "SYMBOL_NAME_STR(smp_##x)"\n\t" \
136         "jmp ret_from_intr\n");
137
138 #define BUILD_SMP_TIMER_INTERRUPT(x,v) XBUILD_SMP_TIMER_INTERRUPT(x,v)
139 #define XBUILD_SMP_TIMER_INTERRUPT(x,v) \
140 asmlinkage void x(struct pt_regs * regs); \
141 asmlinkage void call_##x(void); \
142 __asm__( \
143 "\n"__ALIGN_STR"\n" \
144 SYMBOL_NAME_STR(x) ":\n\t" \
145         "pushl $"#v"\n\t" \
146         SAVE_ALL \
147         "movl %esp,%eax\n\t" \
148         "pushl %eax\n\t" \
149         SYMBOL_NAME_STR(call_##x)":\n\t" \
150         "call "SYMBOL_NAME_STR(smp_##x)"\n\t" \
151         "addl $4,%esp\n\t" \
152         "jmp ret_from_intr\n");
153
154 #define BUILD_COMMON_IRQ() \
155 asmlinkage void call_do_IRQ(void); \
156 __asm__( \
157         "\n" __ALIGN_STR"\n" \
158         "common_interrupt:\n\t" \
159         SAVE_ALL \
160         "pushl $ret_from_intr\n\t" \
161         SYMBOL_NAME_STR(call_do_IRQ)":\n\t" \
162         "jmp "SYMBOL_NAME_STR(do_IRQ));
163
164 /*
165  * subtle. orig_eax is used by the signal code to distinct between
166  * system calls and interrupted 'random user-space'. Thus we have
167  * to put a negative value into orig_eax here. (the problem is that
168  * both system calls and IRQs want to have small integer numbers in
169  * orig_eax, and the syscall code has won the optimization conflict ;)
170  *
171  * Subtle as a pigs ear. VY
172  */
173
174 #define BUILD_IRQ(nr) \
175 asmlinkage void IRQ_NAME(nr); \
176 __asm__( \
```

```
177 "\n"__ALIGN_STR"\n" \
178 SYMBOL_NAME_STR(IRQ) #nr "_interrupt:\n\t" \
179         "pushl $"#nr"-256\n\t" \
180         "jmp common_interrupt");
181
182 /*
183  * x86 profiling function, SMP safe. We might want to do this in
184  * assembly totally?
185  */
186 static inline void x86_do_profile (unsigned long eip)
187 {
188         if (prof_buffer && current->pid) {
189                 eip -= (unsigned long) &_stext;
190                 eip >>= prof_shift;
191                 /*
192                  * Don't ignore out-of-bounds EIP values silently,
193                  * put them into the last histogram slot, so if
194                  * present, they will show up as a sharp peak.
195                  */
196                 if (eip > prof_len-1)
197                         eip = prof_len-1;
198                 atomic_inc((atomic_t *)&prof_buffer[eip]);
199         }
200 }
201
202 #ifdef __SMP__  /*more of this file should probably be ifdefed SMP */
203 static inline void hw_resend_irq(struct hw_interrupt_type *h, unsigned int i) {
204         if (IO_APIC_IRQ(i))
205                 send_IPI_self( IO_APIC_VECTOR(i));
206 }
207 #else
208 static inline void hw_resend_irq(struct hw_interrupt_type *h, unsigned int i) {}
209 #endif
210
211 #endif /* _ASM_HW_IRQ_H */
212
```

File Systems

In this chapter we quickly explore the various components of the file system interface and touch on peculiarities of the file system implementation of Linux 2.4, with emphasis on one particular implementation of a logging file system: the IBM Journaling File System (JFS).

A file system is an indispensable component, providing the superblock- and file-operation system calls required by the Linux Virtual File System (VFS) layer, so that the OS can provide itself and applications with such basic storage management capabilities as:

- Create and delete files (i.e. allocate and deallocate space on the storage medium).
- Open files for reading and writing.
- Seek within a file (*Note*: Linux does not provide kernel-level support for the notion of file records).
- Close files.
- Create directories to hold groups of files.
- List the contents of a directory.
- Remove files from a directory.

These functions have evolved until what we now commonly know as the modern UNIX environment offers complex file manipulation capabilities and provides an extensive set of data management interfaces.

Logical Volume Manager (LVM)

One huge area of improvement for Linux has been the inclusion of the Logical Volume Manager (LVM) subsystem, as of kernel 2.3.48. The LVM in Linux very much resembles the HP-UX LVM, with which many system administrators have had very good experiences. LVM completely rethinks the way file systems and volumes are managed. It allows drives to span disks, be resized, and be managed in a more flexible way than can be done using the current partition table schemes.

The Logical Volume Manager adds an additional layer, a new logical layer, of *logical volumes* (LVs) between the physical peripherals and the I/O interface in the kernel. This allows the concatenation of several disks (*physical volumes* or PVs) to form a storage pool (volume group or VG) with allocation units called *physical extents* (called PEs). These physical extents are mapped to offsets and blocks on the disk(s) in the volume group. Parts out of the volume group then can be allocated in the form of logical volumes in units called *logical extents* (LEs). Each logical extent is mapped to a corresponding physical extent of equal size. The logical volumes can then be used through device special files similar to `/dev/sd[a-z]*` or `/dev/hd[a-z]*` named `/dev/VolumeGroupName/LogicalVolumeName`.

The configuration information for each physical volume, the volume group, and the logical volume(s) is stored on each physical volume in an area called the *volume group descriptor area* or VGDA. At the time of this writing the VGDA is physically located immediately after the superblock, but this may change in the very next release. The configuration information is also stored in automatically created backup files, which are stored in the `/etc/lvmtab.d` directory.

An LVM driver holds mapping tables between the logical extents of logical volumes and the physical extents of physical volumes. These tables are created, updated or deleted by superuser LVM commands. The main mapping function of the driver is called for a logical block in a logical volume from functions `ll_rw_block()` and `ll_rw_swap_file()` in the file `/usr/src/linux/drivers/block/ll_rw_blk.c`. The mapping function looks up the corresponding physical block/disk pair in a table. Then it returns this pair to the calling `ll_rw_*()` function thus causing a physical I/O request to the disk block(s) to be queued.

The main data structures to implement LVM are:

```
pv_disk_t
vg_disk_t
lv_disk_t
```

and

```
disk_pe_t
```

As of this writing, these are in `/usr/src/linux/include/linux/lvm.h` (`pv_disk_t` is stored at offset 0), but this will drastically change in the next version. `pv_disk_t` describes a physical volume's characteristics, that is, to which volume group the physical volume belongs, its internal number in the volume group, its size, and more. `vg_disk_t` holds the name of the volume group, its internal number, the maximum number of logical volumes in this volume group, the physical extent's size, and more. The member `vg_on_disk` of the `pv_disk_t` structure describes where the `vg_disk_t` information is stored on disk.

An array of `lv_disk_t` structures is stored on disk to hold information about each of the logical volumes that exist in the volume group. This array is stored at the disk location shown by the `lv_on_disk` member of the `pv_disk_t` structure. Each `lv_disk_t` structure holds information about a logical volume, for example, its name, its access state (read/write), its internal number, its size, and more.

The `disk_pe_t` array holds on disk the mapping information of logical extents to logical volumes and physical extents to physical volumes. It can be found starting from the location that the `pe_on_disk` member of `pv_disk_t` holds. Each slot in the `disk_pe_t` array corresponds to a physical extent on this physical volume—slot 0 corresponds to physical extent 0, slot 1 to physical extent 1, and so on.

The mapping information in the `disk_pe_t` array tells that a physical extent is used, and to which logical extent in which logical volume it is mapped.

How does LVM interact with the kernel's block devices tables and with the IRQ handlers? It only remaps a logical `rdev/rsector` pair in the `buffer_head` of an I/O request to a physical pair. This takes place in `drivers/block/ll_rw_blk.c` in function `ll_rw_block()`. Afterwards, the request gets queued like any other request in Linux.

The correct configuration and maintenance of LVM necessitates learning a host of new commands. In Appendix C, the official LVM Abstract is reprinted for an introduction to configuration and maintenance.

How does LVM fit into the existing 2.3.x kernel? It's very simple, because the abstractions in the kernel are so powerful. A block device in Linux is simply a driver that can take `buffer_heads` and either fill them with data from some storage device, or else write their data to a storage device. How that read or write works is irrelevant. In particular, it is perfectly legal for a device driver to fulfill the I/O request by performing another I/O to a different device, or even, indeed, to several devices. Both LVM and the software RAID drivers take advantage of that, implementing I/O to the virtual device by performing one or more I/Os to one or more disks that belong to the logical volume or RAID set.

There is a special optimization used when a single I/O to the LVM or RAID driver results in just a single I/O to an underlying disk. In that case, we don't actually have to create a new I/O operation to send to the underlying device; rather, the logical device just adds a marker to the `buffer_head` that is being read or written, to say that the I/O should actually be performed to a different physical device than the logical volume—namely, the block device driver to which the given physical device was mounted at boot time.

The Linux Kernel's Relation to the File System

Because the number of files on a UNIX system may easily range into the hundreds of thousands or more, the task of organizing the file system control structures is insulated from applications and yet is, strictly speaking, not a kernel either. The Linux kernel's file subsystem has an unusually abstract view of a file system. There is no knowledge whatsoever in the Linux kernel of Linux's own native `ext2`, nor `procfs`, nor `reiserfs`, nor any other file system; all file systems are treated equally. The kernel provides only very basic hooks into which each file system mounted at boot time can attach itself and provide (to both the kernel and to applications) the actual functionality, via the creation and management of intermediate control structures. This high level of abstraction is the key to allowing all file handling to be implemented as kernel system calls acting on instantiated control structure objects, rather than as user space file system handling code. This in turn allows control structures for open files to be allocated and deallocated dynamically both systemwide and per process.

An application uses the file as an abstraction to address a linear range of bytes stored on some form of I/O medium, typically a storage device such as an SCSI disk. To access a file, the OS provides file manipulation interfaces to open, close, read, and write the data within each file.

Kernel Data Structure Objects for File System Control Operations

Listed below are those common data structure objects instantiated by the kernel to control file system operations in Version 2.4. The abstractions as represented in these data structures are very generic. In the 2.3 kernel the developers finally managed to make them scale extremely well on SMP, while still remaining general-purpose enough to be able to describe `procfs`, `devfs`, and other virtual file systems, NFS, Novell, and Microsoft clients, and other network file systems, as well as various disk file systems.

There are three main changes in 2.4. First, 2.4 scales much better on SMP. The new data structures are all organized so that we don't need to hold any SMP locks while copying data between the caches and user space.

Second, the kernel now allows the buffer cache and the page cache to share the same memory. The buffer cache has always been used to cache data being written to disk, because the write-back code relies on having the physical locations of the data available; the buffer cache is the only cache is suitable for physically tagged blocks. In older kernels, that task (the tagging of buffered blocks to physical addresses) required us to copy page-cache data into separate memory when writing it to disk, but that inefficiency is eliminated in 2.4.

Third, at long last, we have support for large (>2GB) files, by virtue of defining all the offsets into our caches in units of file system blocks rather than by byte offsets.

The Common Data Structure Objects Instantiated by the Kernel

- struct super_block—Represents an entire file system mounted at a certain mount point in the directory tree.
- struct inode—Represents a single object (file, directory, etc.) within that file system.
- struct file—Represents a particular opening of a file. A new struct file is created every time you open a file, so you can have many struct files attached to a single inode. A closed file won't have any struct files, although inodes representing it may still exist in the kernel's object cache.
- struct dentry—Represents the result of a directory lookup, that is, looking up a certain name in a certain directory.
- struct address_space—The primary data cache in Linux is the page cache, and all pages are indexed in the page cache by offsets within an address_space. Every file inode has its own address space assigned within the page cache to identify cached data as belonging to that inode.
- struct page—The main page descriptor for the virtual memory system; struct pages are used extensively by cache and I/O management functions.
- struct buffer_head—Describes a buffer in the buffer cache. The buffer cache is used to cache certain metadata on a file system, which doesn't correspond to a real file. Buffers represent cached contents of a physical disk, not cached contents of files (files are virtual objects). For example, the buffer cache is used when we cache bitmaps or inode tables under most disk file systems. It is never used for network file systems—only when there is a disk involved.

▥ struct request—Describes an outstanding I/O request to a disk.

Buffers, Caches, and Memory Garbage Collection

Buffers represent not the cached contents of files, but rather cached contents of a physical disk. In contrast, caches actually cache file contents. Linux's exploitation of buffers and caches is heavily dependent on VM functionality and performance, which is discussed in Chapter 5, "The Linux VM Manager."

How does the kernel allocate buffers from the main memory, and how does it manages caches? As far as each file system is concerned, caching and buffer allocation are both very simple. The file system asks for a new page for the page cache or a new buffer the buffer cache, and the cache just takes a page off the kernel's free page list to satisfy that request. Of course, at some point we will run out of memory if that's all we do. So, there is an entirely separate mechanism, which makes sure that we don't run low on free pages.

That mechanism comprises a twofold reclamation regimen. First, if a kernel process requests a free page and the request isn't urgent (e.g. we're not in the middle of trying to find space for an incoming network packet), then the call to the memory allocator in turn calls the memory-reclaim functions to find something to evict from memory.

Second, even if there are no memory allocation calls happening, a background daemon—kswapd—regularly checks the free memory situation and starts reclaiming memory if we get too low.

In either case, the reclamation process is the same. The kernel cycles through various data structures, including the page tables that processes use to map files into virtual memory, and the page and buffer caches. It looks for pages that have not been accessed since the last time we passed over that page, and when it finds them, it removes those pages from use and returns them to the free list.

Linux's Use of Inodes

During startup, the kernel initializes the table, which holds general information about the accessibility of files, by calling a routine (in the kernel's memory allocator code) that creates a cache for kernel objects.

The kernel does not actually create the first object, which is a file control structure, until a file is opened.

The distinct kernel objects, which are stored in said cache, are called *inodes*. An inode is a distinct object, within the kernel, which is managed by a file system, a network redirector, or some other storage management system. Linux implements inodes in plain C, but the design is very abstract and very object oriented. An inode can itself represent another object, like a file or a directory. There is an inode for each file; a file is uniquely identified by the file system on which it resides and its inode number on the file system.

Every inode contains pointers to various methods, which can operate on itself or on the object it represents. These methods can read or write data, seek to a specific offset in the file, do directory operations such as creating new files or renaming existing ones, and so on. Not all operations or methods will be valid on all inodes. For example, you can't rename on a regular file, because in UNIX a rename is an operation on the parent directory, not on the file itself. As another example, you can't seek on a pipe.

Each inode contains a count of the number of data blocks that it contains. The number of actual data blocks is the sum of the allocated data blocks and the indirect blocks. `fsck` computes the actual number of data blocks and compares that block count against the actual number of blocks the inode claims. If an inode contains an incorrect count, `fsck` prompts the operator to fix it.

Each inode contains a 64-bit size field. The size is the number of data bytes in the file associated with the inode. The accuracy of the size field is roughly checked by computing from the size field the maximum number of blocks that should be associated with the inode, and comparing that expected block count against the actual number of blocks the inode claims.

Each inode contains the following information:

- The device where the node resides
- Mode of file
- Type of file
- Locking information
- File length (the number of bytes in the file)
- Link count (the number of links to the file)
- The owner's user and group IDs
- Access privileges
- Time of last access to the file
- Time the inode itself was last modified

- Time of last modification of the file
- The addresses of the file's blocks on the disk (pointers to the extents that contain the file's data)

In an ext2fs file system, an inode occupies 128 bytes.[1] There are eight Inodes in a standard ext2fs block of 1,024 bytes. The inode structure is padded. In reality it could be smaller than 100 bytes, but things are easier if file system structures align nicely with block boundaries. The number of inodes on a file system is decided when mkfs is run. There is one 128-byte inode allocated for each 4,096 bytes of disk space in a standard ext2fs file system, resulting in one block of inodes for each 32 blocks of data. This is an initial overhead of 3.12 percent.

Disk space for the inodes is allocated when mkfs is run. In standard ext2fs, a bitmap and an inode allocation map are allocated for each block group. These allocation maps cannot span block boundaries in ext2fs.

Linux keeps a cache of active and recently used inodes. There are two paths by which these inodes can be accessed. The first is through the dcache. Each dentry in the dcache refers to an inode, and thereby keeps that inode in the cache. The second path is through the inode *hash table*. Each inode is hashed to an 8-bit number based on the address of the file system's super-block and the inode number. Inodes with the same hash value are chained together in a doubly linked list.

Access through the hash table is achieved using the iget function, which is only called by a file system when looking up an inode which wasn't found in the dcache, and by nfsd. Basing the hash on the inode number is a bit restrictive, because it assumes that every file system can uniquely identify a file in 32 bits. This is a problem at least of the NFS file system, which prefers to use the 256-bit file handle as the unique identifier in the hash. The nfsd usage might be better served by having the file system provide a file handle-to-inode mapping function that interprets the file handle in the most appropriate manner.

Performance Issues and Optimization Strategies

File system performance is a major component of overall system performance and is heavily dependent on the nature of the application gen-

---

1 In a Veritas file system, the default size is 256 bytes.

erating the load. To achieve optimal performance, the underlying file system configuration must be balanced to match application characteristics. If you're a developer, you might already have a good idea of how your application is reading or writing through the file system. If you're an administrator of an application, however, you might need to spend some time analyzing the application to understand the type of I/O profile being presented to the file system. Once we have a good understanding of the application, we can optimize the file system configuration to make the most efficient use of the underlying storage device(s).

Our objectives are to:

1. Reduce the number of I/Os to the underlying device(s) where possible.
2. Group smaller I/Os together into larger I/Os wherever possible.
3. Optimize the seek pattern to reduce the amount of time spent waiting for disk seeks.
4. Cache as much as data as we realistically can, to reduce physical I/Os.

And to make transactions faster, one must consider what can be done to each of a transaction's different parts to increase speed.

A transaction consists of:

1. Logging the start of a transaction.
2. Logging data, which will be subject to change, before changes are done.
3. Accessing database records from storage.
4. Performing different operations with the data.
5. Logging data, which have been subject to change, after the changes are done.
6. Logging end of transaction.

One can easily see that quite an amount of I/O is needed, because the database as well as the log file must be kept on nonvolatile storage.

Raw I/O

One recent feature in Linux is the implementation of a *raw* I/O device, one whose accesses are not handled through the caching layer, but go instead straight to the low-level device itself. A raw device could be used in cases where a sophisticated application wants complete control over how it performs data caching, and the overhead of the usual cache is not justified. A raw device could also be used in data-critical situations, where we want to ensure that the data gets written to the disk immediately so that, in the event of a system failure, no data are lost.

Previous proposals for raw I/O device support were not deemed fit for inclusion, as they required literally doubling the number of device nodes, to give every block device a raw device node. Regrettably, this is the implementation that many commercial UNIX systems use.

The 2.4 Linux implementation uses a pool of device nodes, which can be associated with any arbitrary block device. To facilitate this, 2.4 includes a new object called a *kiobuf*. A kiobuf is just an abstract description of an arbitrary bunch of kernel pages, set up during boot time by the code in `init.c`, as empty pages in kernel space to be used as buffers. Kiobufs can be used to describe any sort of buffer at all.

Raw I/O works by creating a kiobuf and populating it with the physical pages, which contain the data buffer that a process is using for I/O. Once the correct physical pages of memory have been located for the data, the kiobuf is then passed to the I/O layers for reading or writing. The I/O layers don't have to know that the pages concerned happen to belong to a user process: kiobufs hide all that detail from them. All the I/O layers see is a set of physical pages and an I/O request into those pages.

Process Resource Limits

Within the context of processes, limits exist for several system resources that are used by processes when they execute; the system establishes default values and maximum values for each of the resources controlled by these resource limits. These resource limits are practically the only limitation. For each of the six resource limits defined, there is a `rlim_cur` (current resource limit), which is the default value, and a `rlim_max` (maximum resource limit), which is the system-imposed maximum value for the resource. In Linux 2.4, the default limit value set by the system for open files, per process, is 1,024.

Each process can only have open, at any given moment, up to `rlim_fd_cur` files. Remember that, for any process, the total number of open files always contains three additional ones, because every process has three open files as soon as it comes into existence: `stdin`, `stdout`, and `stderr` (standard input, output, and error). These represent the input, output, and error output files for the process.

You can display `rlim_fd_cur` by using the `ulimit(1)` or `limit(1)` command, depending on which shell you're using. Use the `ulimit(1)` command if you're using `sh` or `bash`. Use `limit(1)` if you're using the C shell (/bin/csh).

```
[root@hatta /root]# ulimit -a
core file size    (blocks)    1000000
data seg size     (kbytes)    unlimited
file size         (blocks)    unlimited
max memory size   (kbytes)    unlimited
stack size        (kbytes)    8192
cpu time          (seconds)   unlimited
max user processes            2048
pipe size         (512 bytes) 8
open files                    1024
virtual memory    (kbytes)    2105343
```

`rlim_fd_cur` is displayed as "open files," seen here at its default value (in most distributions) of 1,024 open files per process.

As root, you can bypass the resource limit check and set the open process limit to, theoretically, 3 billion (signed int data type max value). Obviously, you would never get anywhere near that amount, because you would run out of process virtual address space for the per-process file structure (`uf_entry`) that you need for every file you open. Fortunately, we never encounter situations that need that many files opened. However, we do see more and more installations where per-process open files go into the thousands, and even tens of thousands.

Keep in mind, also, that the same file can have multiple file control data structures associated with it. If different processes executing on the same system open the same file, each process will have a unique representation of the file, through that file's file descriptor, to a file control data structure specific to that process. Thus, each process, as it reads and writes the file, changes the `f_offset` member of its file control data structure.

Moreover, the behavior differs with file descriptors inherited via the `fork()` or `__clone()` system calls, or when a process issues the `dup()` system call for duplicating file descriptors. In these scenarios, both the file structure and the `f_offset` field are shared; thus, a read or write by the parent process to a file changes that file's `f_offset` as seen by the child process in the case of a `fork(2)`, or changes references to the file descriptors returned by `dup(2)` and `dup2(2)`.

Extent-based Allocation (General)

Extent-based allocation file systems, such as Veritas' VxFS and IBM's JFS, allocate disk blocks in *extents*; an extent is a contiguous sequence of multiple blocks allocated as a unit. Extents are described by a triple consisting of logical offset/length/physical, beginning when the file is first created. The addressing structure is a B+-tree[2] populated with extent descriptors (the triples), rooted in the inode, and keyed by logical offset within the file. Note that file system metadata is written when the file is first created, which differs from block-based allocation. Because initial allocation is sequential, subsequent reads, writes, and seeks are forced to be sequential; within the first allocated extent of blocks they do not require additional metadata writes until the next extent is allocated. This optimizes the disk seek pattern. The grouping of block writes into clusters allows the file system to issue larger physical disk writes to the storage device, saving the overhead of many small SCSI transfers. See Figure 10.1.

Under block-based allocation, a block address number is required for every logical block in an allocated file, resulting in a lot of metadata for each file. In extent-based allocation, only the start block number and length are required for each contiguous extent of data blocks. Such a file, with only a few very large extents, requires only a small amount of metadata.

Extent-based file systems provide good performance for sequential file access, because of the sequential allocation policy and block clustering into larger writes. For example, if we want to read sequentially through an extent-based file, we only need to read the start block number and its length. Then, we can continue to read all of the data blocks in that extent. Very little metadata read overhead is incurred in reading sequentially.

---

2 A B-tree is a special kind of balanced m-ary tree that allows us to test for, retrieve, insert, and delete records (leaves), which contain either physical address data or indexing pointer data. B+-trees have their data pointed to only by leaf nodes, use virtual keys, and can have a search key value appear more than once. A B+-tree, usually, is built up in such a way that its node size is defined by the page size. Only when the search path follows an edge is paging required. Also, data are only stored in the leafs and not in the nodes. In the nodes are kept only reference keys, or "road maps." Therefore, the B+-tree, with more branches possible and a flatter branch structure, is favored. The B+-tree is the best structure for an efficient search for keys. But the real problems arise with the three different tasks one performs: lookup, insert, delete. In the case of a concurrent deletion and lookup, there is a 50 percent chance that it might work out or lead to a deadlock. Therefore, parallelism is not a good strategy for optimizing performance in an extent-based allocation file system.

Figure10.1
Block allocation
versus extent
allocation.

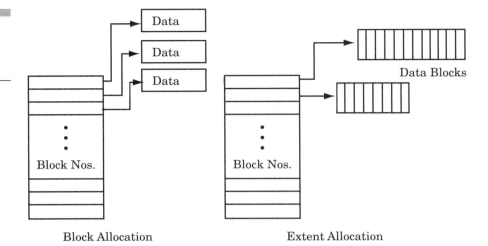

Block Allocation

Extent Allocation

However, extent-based file systems don't provide so much advantage when the file system is used for random I/O. If we read a file in a random manner, we need to look up the block address for the desired block for every data block read, similar to what we would do with a block-based file system.

Table 10.1 shows the various file systems and their allocation formats.

TABLE 10.1

File System
Allocation Formats

File System	Allocation Format
Ext2	Block-based; allocator tries to allocate sequential blocks
reiserfs	Extent-based
JFS	Extent-based

Block-based Allocation (General)

The block-based allocation strategy is used by a traditional UNIX file system. When a file is extended, the policy is to allocate to the file, on the fly, a minimal number of blocks (as defined by the file system). Blocks are allocated from a free block map.

Although this policy attempts to conserve storage space, blocks are sometimes allocated in random order. This can cause excessive disk seeking, and later reads from the file system will result in the disk mechanism seeking to all of the random block locations that were allocated during the extension of the file. Random block allocation can be avoided by optimizing the block allocation policy so that it attempts to allocate a contiguous (sequential) series of blocks. If large sequential allocations can be achieved by using a smarter block allocation policy, disk seeking will be greatly reduced. However, contiguous file system block allocation will eventually end up with file blocks fragmented across the file system, and file system access will eventually revert to a random nature.

Also, the block allocation scheme must write information about where each new block is allocated every time the file is extended. If the file is extended one block at a time, a lot of extra disk I/O required to write the file system block control structure information. (File system block control structure information is known as *metadata*.)

In the ext2 file system, metadata is written asynchronously to the storage device, so that operations that change the size of a file do not need to wait for each metadata operation to complete. This greatly improves speed of updates to files, but increases the risk of inconsistent data if a system crash occurs after changing the file's contents, but before the metadata was actually written.

The Transaction-Processing or Database Issue of Safety

For managing synchronized access to the same file from multiple processes or threads, file locking interfaces are provided (discussed in my forthcoming book on Linux file systems to be published by McGraw-Hill). Linux, or any UNIX-type OS, does not provide kernel-level support for the notion of file records. In this section, we shall look at the differences between *static*, *journaling*, and *logging* file systems.

All database files must reside on a file system. The native file system of Linux, ext2fs, fared well for Linux three or four years ago. It is, however, not well poised to handle the challenges of the Linux market today. For one thing, ext2fs is *static*: it does not keep track of changes to make sure all updates on the disk are done safely. Furthermore, ext2fs is one of the few file systems on any OS to write metadata asynchronously. Although this considerably accelerates file operations, it also means that the information about the file, such as creation and change dates, ownership, permissions, etc., is written in a deferred fashion relative to the file contents. If power goes off after writing the updates to the file, but before actually writing the file header, we have a problem.

These shortcomings of ext2fs are a major hindrance to a more widespread employment of Linux on database servers. Oracle8i for Linux, for instance, does not support raw I/O devices (although there has been raw I/O support since the 2.2.x kernel). For some time now, there has been a quest among Linux hackers to come up with a journaling and/or logging file system, to counter the deficiencies of ext2fs.

Advantages of Journaling over Nonjournaling

The journaling file system (JFS) which will be considered here is a key technology for Internet file servers, because it provides fast file system restart times in the event of a system crash. Using database journaling techniques, JFS can restore a file system to a consistent state in a matter of seconds or minutes. In nonjournaling file systems, file recovery can take hours or days. Most file server customers cannot tolerate the downtime associated with nonjournaling file systems. Only by a technology shift to journaling could these file systems avoid the time-consuming process of examining all of a file system's metadata to verify and restore the file system to a consistent state.

In a static file system such as ext2fs, there is a map of inode locations. These inodes point to directory blocks, which contain lists of other inodes and each one's associated filename, and to data blocks. A Linux directory, like any UNIX directory, is an association between the file leafnames and inode numbers. A file's inode number can be found using the -i switch to ls.

An inode contains ownership and permission information, along with a pointer to where on the disk the data blocks for a file reside. What happens when we change the contents of file test.file? Let's assume that the inode for test.file lists four data blocks.

The data for test.file reside at disk locations 3110, 3111, 3506, and 3507. The gaps are there because, during the initial allocation of disk blocks, those between 3111 and 3506 were already allocated to some other file(s). We therefore notice that this file is fragmented. The hard drive must seek to the 3110 area on the disk surface, read two blocks, then seek over to the 3506 area and read two blocks to read the entire file.

Let's say you modify the third block. The file system reads the third block, makes your changes, and rewrites the third block, still located at 3506. If you append to the file, you could have blocks allocated anywhere.

There is danger if the power fails. Imagine being in the midst of updating a directory. You've just modified 23 file entries in the fifth block of some giant directory. Just as the disk is in the middle of writing this block, there is a power outage; the block is incomplete and therefore corrupted.

During reboot, Linux (like all UNIX systems) runs a program called fsck (file system check) that steps through the entire file system, validating all entries and making sure that blocks are allocated and referenced correctly. It will find this corrupted directory entry and attempt to repair it. However, there is no certainty that fsck will actually manage to repair the damage. Quite often, it does not. Sometimes, in such a situation all the directory entries are lost.

For large file systems, fsck can take a very long time. On a machine with many gigabytes of files, fsck can run for up to 10 or more hours. During this time, the system is not available, and this represents for some installations an unacceptable amount of downtime.

Journaling or logging file systems solve the problem...but introduce new ones. Let's see why and how.

How a Journaling File System Works

A journaling file system uses techniques originally developed for databases to log information about operations performed on the file system metadata as atomic transactions. In the event of a system failure, a file system is restored to a consistent state by replaying the log and applying log records for the appropriate transactions. The recovery time associated with this log-based approach is much faster, because the replay utility need only examine the log records produced by recent file system activity rather than examine all file system metadata.

A journaling file system such as JFS provides improved structural consistency and recoverability, and much faster restart times (JFS can restore a file system to a consistent state in a matter of seconds or minutes), than nonjournaling file systems such as HPFS, ext2fs, and traditional UNIX file systems. These other file systems are subject to corruption in the event of system failure, because a logical write-file operation often takes multiple media I/Os to accomplish and may not be totally reflected on the media at any given time. These file systems rely on restart-time utilities (which in Linux usually means `fsck`), which examine all of the file system's metadata (such as directories and disk addressing structures) to detect and repair structural integrity problems. This is a time-consuming and error-prone process, which, in the worst case, can lose or misplace data.

Journaling file systems keep track only of inode changes, but not changes to the contents of a file; whereas logging file systems keep track of changes made to both data and inodes. All changes, all appends, and all deletes would be logged to a growing part of the file system known as the *log*.

In our first example with the `test.file` file, rather than modifying the data in the 3506 block, a logging file system would store a copy of the inodes of both `test.file` and the third block in new locations on the disk.

The in-memory list of inodes would be changed to point `test.file` to the new inode as well. Every once in a while, the file system will checkpoint and update the on-disk list of inodes, as well as freeing the unused parts of files (e.g. the original third block of `test.file`).

A logging file system has a dramatically improved write speed because it's only appending to the same area of the disk and never really needs to seek around looking for blocks on the disk.

The writing speed is therefore improved as is the recovery time (actually, there is no recovery time at all because of its structure).

Logging file systems, when compared to static file systems, have nearly identical read speed because their file data blocks are still easily seekable. The inode map has the lists of blocks, and those can be read quickly because they are usually memory mapped. Thus, logging file systems represent the best of both worlds. The read time is comparable to that of the static file system—well, possibly a bit slower due to more fragmentation: The major problem with logging file systems is that they can get fragmented easily.

Metadata Logging

When a file system makes changes to its on-disk structure, it uses several disconnected, synchronous writes to make those changes. If an outage occurs halfway through an operation, the state of the file system is unknown, and the whole file system must be checked for consistency.

If one block, say, is appended to the end of a file, the on-disk map that tells the file system where each block for the file is located needs to be read, modified, and rewritten to the disk before the data block is written.

When a failure occurs, the file system must be checked before it is mounted at boot; the file system manager doesn't know if the block map is correct, and it also doesn't know which file was being modified during the crash. This results in a full file system scan.

A metadata logging file system has a wrap-around, append-only log area on the disk, which it uses to record the state of each disk transaction. Before any on-disk structures are changed, an intent-to-commit record is written to the log. The directory structure is then updated and the log entry is marked complete. Because every change to the file system structure is in the log, file system consistency can be checked by looking in the log without the need for a full file system scan. At mount time, if an intent-to-commit entry is found but not marked complete, then the file structure for that block is checked and, if necessary, fixed.

Figure 10.2 shows a file's data block (gray) and its inode information (modification times, pointers to data blocks, etc.) in a regular (static) file system, like ext2fs, and what happens when you change the data in that file.

Figure 10.2
Static file system data processing. (Courtesy DEC Spain.)

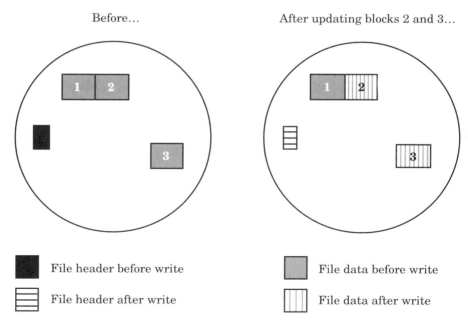

Before...

After updating blocks 2 and 3...

■ File header before write   ▦ File data before write

▤ File header after write   ▥ File data after write

Figure 10.3 shows a similar file in a logging file system, and what happens when it is being modified.

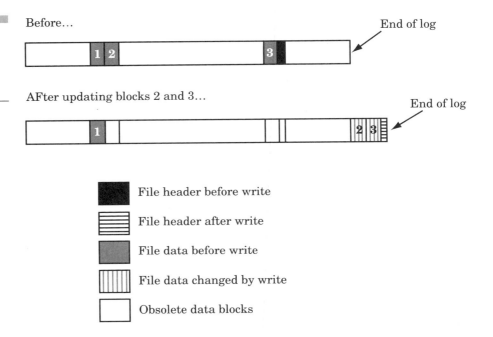

Figure 10.3
Logging file system data processing. (Courtesty DEC Spain.)

Notice how everything that is changed is appended at the end of the log.

This speeds up things, because the disk doesn't need to seek all over the disk to write to parts of a file. Also it's much safer, because the original data blocks of the file aren't "lost" until the log has successfully written the "new" data blocks. This leads to very stable file systems with nearly no `fsck` time required after a crash. Such file systems come back online after a crash almost immediately, because only the file system updates after the last checkpoint must be checked.

All the changes in the log can be reapplied quickly. The corrupted part of the disk is always the last change added to the log, and it can be thrown away as invalid. The only data lost will be the single change that was lost at power-off. Metadata logging file systems of 20GB and more typically take 4 or 5 seconds to `fsck` and repair after a crash. Thus, a metadata logging file system can make the difference between mounting a heavily populated file system in a few seconds or in 10 or more hours without a log.

It should, however, be noted that logging doesn't come free, and there is a significant performance overhead. Logging requires more slow synchronous writes, and the most popular implementation of logging, metadata logging, requires at least three writes per file update, which is significantly more than would be required without logging. As a result, we should pay attention to our requirements: do we want the file system to be fast, or do we need maximum reliability?

Some logging file systems provide an option to put file data into the log together with the metadata, thus avoiding a second seek and write. The data is first written to the log, and then replayed into the file system. This achieves two things: it ensures data integrity up to but not including the last block written and it helps performance for small synchronous writes, as in email and news servers, which would otherwise require two or more writes to different parts of the disk for every application write (one for the data and one for the log write).

Available Journaling File Systems

Journaling file systems have been around for quite some time. Solaris's native file system, the UFS file system, has always had the same reliability problem (namely delayed metadata writes) as ext2fs. Veritas (see **www.veritas.com**) has been offering a journaling file system and logical volume manager (LVM) for Solaris for many years now; most Solaris shops use Veritas's product, VxFS. On January 19, 2000, Veritas announced the forthcoming porting of VxFS to Linux. No specific date was divulged, though.

Sun has its own improved file system, available with its Solstice Disk Suite.

SGI (formerly Silicon Graphics Inc.) as of this writing is committed to making its excellent xfs journaling file system available for Linux under Open Source. The xfs file system is rock solid and very fast. xfs also has several other benefits to offer the Linux community. xfs is a 64-bit file system, which means that it can support large files (9 million terabytes), and even larger file systems (18 million terabytes). The storage space addressable by xfs will therefore put a stop to complaints of this type for a few years. xfs delivers all this capacity and reliability with amazing speed. xfs is also compatible with other popular services including various backup solutions, and file sharing via NFS or Samba.

Linux 2.4 includes all of the file systems present in Linux 2.2, including FAT12 and FAT16 (for floppy drives and hard disks for the assorted DOS versions), NTFS (for Windows NT), VFAT and FAT32 (for Windows 9x), HFS (for MacOS), HPFS (for OS/2), UFS, and many more. However, in this chapter we have only treated the ever-present ext2 file system, as well as the new IBM journaling file system, JFS. It is clearly impossible to cover in a single chapter all, or even a significant part of, file systems available for Linux. For a detailed study on Linux 2.4 file systems, see my upcoming book *Linux File Systems*, to be published by McGraw-Hill.[3]

IBM's JFS

JFS provides the superblock- and file-operation system calls required by the Linux Virtual File system layer. JFS, a log-based, byte-level file system, is both robust and scalable; although tailored primarily for the high throughput and reliability requirements of transaction-oriented, high-performance servers (from single processor systems to advanced multi-processor and clustered systems), JFS is also applicable to client configurations where performance and reliability are desired. In February 2000 IBM announced that JFS will be made available to the public. See **http://www-4.ibm.com/software/developer/library/jfs.html**.

Main JFS Data Structures and Algorithms

Superblocks: Primary Aggregate Superblock and Secondary Aggregate Superblock

The superblocks contain aggregate-wide information such as the size of the aggregate, size of allocation groups, aggregate block size, etc. The secondary aggregate superblock is a direct copy of the primary aggre-

---

3 In December 1999, I first proposed to IBM the idea of releasing the excellent JFS (Journaled File System) under the GPL license. In February 2000 IBM announced that JFS will be made available to the public. Other logging file systems have been announced, such as ext3fs, Veritas VxFS (port announced January 19, 2000, no availability date specified), and SGI's xfs. Very talented and bright Linux hacker Hans Reiser has also written his own journaling file system, reiserfs. As of this writing, the only readily available options are reiserfs and IBM's JFS; reiserfs is not yet available for the 2.4 kernel.

Although JFS is only in its 0.4 version, it is already quite a capable competitor to ext3fs and reiserfs, against which it shows improved reliability.

gate superblock. The secondary superblock is used if the primary aggregate superblock is corrupted. These superblocks are at fixed locations. This allows JFS to always be able to find these without depending on any other information. The superblock structure is defined in `linux\include\linux\JFS\JFS_superblock.h`, struct JFS_superblock.

Inodes

A JFS on-disk inode is 512 bytes. It contains four basic sets of information. The first set describes the POSIX attributes of the JFS object. The second set describes additional attributes for JFS object; these attributes include information necessary for the VFS support, information specific to the OS environment, and the header for the B+-tree. The third set either contains the extent allocation descriptors of the root of the B+-tree, or in-line data. The fourth set contains extended attributes, more in-line data, or additional extent allocation descriptors.

The definition of the on-disk inode structure is found in `linux\include\JFS\JFS_dinode.h`, struct dinode.

Standard Administrative Utilities

JFS provides standard administration utilities for creating and maintaining the file system.

The *create a file system* utility provides the JFS-specific portion of the `mkfs` command, initializing a JFS file system on a specified drive. This utility operates at a low level and assumes that any creation/initialization of the volume on which the file system is to reside is handled outside of this utility at a higher level. The user can provide information like block size during `mkfs`, which will change the characteristics of the file system.

The *check/recover a file system* utility provides the JFS-specific portion of the `fsck` command. It checks the file system for consistency and repairs problems discovered. It replays the log and applies committed changes to the file system metadata. If the file system is declared clean as a result of the log replay, no further action is taken. If the file system is not deemed clean, indicating that the log was not replayed completely and correctly for some reason, or that the file system could not be restored to a consistent state simply by replaying the log, then a full pass of the file system is performed.

In performing a full integrity check, the check/repair utility's primary goal is to achieve a reliable file system state to prevent future file system corruption or failures, with a secondary goal of preserving data in the face of corruption. This means the utility may throw away data in the interest of achieving file system consistency. Specifically, data is discarded when the utility does not have the information needed to restore a structurally inconsistent file or directory to a consistent state without making assumptions. In the case of an inconsistent file or directory, the entire file or directory is discarded with no attempt to save any portion. Any file or subdirectories orphaned by the deletion of a corrupted directory are placed in the lost+found directory located at the root of the file system.

An important consideration for a file system check/repair utility is the amount of virtual memory it requires. Traditionally, the amount of virtual memory required by these utilities is dependent on file system size, because the bulk of the required virtual memory is used to track the allocation state of the individual blocks in the file system. As file systems grow larger, the number of blocks increases and so does the amount of virtual memory needed to track these blocks.

The design of the JFS check/repair utility differs from the ordinary Linux fsck in that its virtual memory requirements are dictated by the number of files and directories within the file system, rather than by the file system's number of blocks. The virtual memory requirements for the JFS check/repair utility are on the order of 32 bytes per file or directory, or approximately 32 Mbytes for a file system that contains 1 million files and directories, regardless of the file system size. Like all other file systems, the JFS utility needs to track block allocation states—but avoids using virtual memory to do so by using a small reserved work area located within the actual file system.

How JFS is Set Up at Boot Time

At boot time the file system create utility, mkfs, creates an aggregate that is wholly contained within each logical volume (partition) mounted. An *aggregate* is an array of disk blocks allocated according to a specific format. The aggregate includes:

- A superblock, which identifies the partition as a JFS aggregate.
- An allocation map, which describes the allocation state of each data block within the aggregate.

Block Allocation Map

The block allocation map is used to track the allocated or freed disk blocks for an entire aggregate. Because all of the filesets[4] within an aggregate share the same pool of disk blocks, this allocation map is used by all of the filesets within an aggregate when allocating or freeing disk blocks.

The Block Allocation Map is itself a file, which is described by aggregate inode 2. When the aggregate is initially created, the data blocks for the map to cover the aggregate space are allocated. The map may grow or shrink dynamically as the aggregate is expanded or shrunk. Each page of the map is 4K in length. The map contains three types of pages: the *bmap control page*, the *dmap control pages*, and the *dmap pages*.

Each dmap contains a single bit to represent each aggregate block. The nth bit represents the allocation status of the nth logical aggregate block. This is defined by `struct dmap_t`, in `linux\include\linux\JFS\ JFS_dmap.h` file. Each dmap page covers 8K of aggregate blocks.

Because the block allocation map may have many dmap pages, they are managed through the dmap control pages. These pages improve the performance of finding large extents of free blocks. The size of the aggregate determines how many of these pages and how many levels are needed. If not all of the levels are needed, then the block map inode will be a sparse file with holes for the first page of each of the unused levels.

JFS employs a commit strategy to ensure that the control data is reliably updated. "Reliable update" means that a consistent JFS structure and resource allocation state is maintained in the face of system failures. To ensure that the block allocation map is in a consistent state, JFS maintains two maps in the dmap structure, the *working map* and the *persistent map*. The working map records the current allocation state. The persistent map records the committed allocation state, consisting of the allocation state as found on disk or described by records within the JFS log or committed JFS transactions.

When an aggregate block is freed, the permanent map is updated first; when an aggregate block is allocated, the working map is updated first. A bit of 0 represents a free resource and a value of 1 an allocated resource.

---

4 The fileset(s) are mountable entity or entities, analogous to an ext2fs file system. A fileset manages files and directories. Files and directories are represented persistently by inodes; each inode describes the attributes of the file or directory and serves as the starting point for finding the file or directory's data on disk. JFS also uses inodes to represent other file system objects, such as the map that describes the allocation state and location on disk of each inode in the fileset.

The dmap control pages of the block allocation map contain a tree similar to the tree in a dmap structure, except that the leaf level contains 1024 elements. The dmap control page is defined by `struct dmapctl_t` which is found in the `linux\include\linux\JFS\JFS_dmap.h`.

At the top of the block allocation map there is a map control structure, `struct dbmap_t`. This structure contains summary information that speeds up the finding of AGs which have more-than-average free space. This structure is found in the `linux\include\linux\JFS\JFS_dmap.h`.

The block allocation map is not journaled: it can be repaired during recovery time by `logredo`, or reconstructed by `fsck`.

Inode Allocation Map

The inode allocation map solves the forward lookup problem. The aggregate and each fileset maintain an inode allocation map, which is a dynamic array of *inode allocation groups* (IAGs). The IAG is the data for the inode allocation map. For the aggregate, the inodes mapped by the inode allocation map are also known as the *aggregate inode table*. For a fileset, the inodes mapped by the inode allocation map are also known as the *file inode table*.

Each IAG is 4K in size and describes 128 physical inode extents on the disk. Because each inode extent contains 32 inodes, each IAG describes 4,096 inodes. An IAG can exist anywhere in the aggregate. All of the inode extents for an IAG exist in one allocation group. The IAG is tied to that aggregate group (AG) until all of its inode extents are freed. At that point an inode extent could be allocated for it in any AG, and then the IAG would be tied to that AG. The IAG is defined by the `iag_t` structure, which is found in the file `linux\include\linux\JFS\JFS_imap.h`.

The first 4K page of the inode allocation map is a control page. This page contains summary information for the inode allocation map. The definition for the `dinomap_t` structure is found in the `linux\include\linux\JFS\JFS_imap.h` file.

Abstractly, the inode allocation map is a dynamically extensible array of the IAG structures: `struct iag inode_allocation_map [ 1..N ]`. Physically, the inode allocation map is itself a file within the aggregate. The aggregate inode allocation map is described by the aggregate self-node.

The fileset inode allocation map is described by `Fileset_Inode`. Its pages are allocated and freed as necessary under standard B+-tree indexing. The key for the B+-tree is the byte offset of the IAG page.

AG Free Inode List

The AG free inode list solves the reverse lookup problem. To reduce the overhead of extending or truncating the aggregate, JFS sets a maximum number of AGs allowed per aggregate. Therefore, there will be a fixed number of AG free inode list headers. The header for the list is in the control page of the inode allocation map. The nth entry is the header for a doubly linked list of all inode allocation map entries (IAGs) with free inodes contained in the nth AG.

The IAG number is used as the index in the list. A -1 indicates the end of the list. Each IAG control section contains forward and backward pointers for the list. The definition for describing the AG Free list is in `struct dinomap_t`, in the `linux\include\linux\JFS\JFS_imap.h` file.

IAG Free List

The IAG free list solves the problem of the free inode number lookup. It allows JFS to find the IAG without any corresponding allocated inode extents. The definition for describing the IAG free list is in `struct inomap_t`, in the `linux\include\linux\JFS\JFS_dinode.h` file.

Fileset Allocation Map Inodes

The fileset allocation map inodes in the aggregate inode table are a special type of inode. Because they represent the fileset, they are the "super-inode" for the fileset. They contain some fileset-specific information in the top half of the inode, instead of the normal inode data. They also track the location of the fileset inode allocation map in its B+-tree. The structure is defined by `struct dinode_t` in the `linux\include\linux\JFS\JFS_dinode.h` file.

Every JFS object is represented by an inode. Inodes contain the object-specific information such as time stamps and file type (regular vs. directory, etc.). They also contain a B+-tree to record the allocation of the extents.

Note specifically that all JFS metadata structures (except for the superblock) are represented as "files." By using the inode structure for data, the data format (on-disk layout) becomes inherently extensible. Directories map user-specified names to the inodes allocated for files and (sub)directories and form the traditional name hierarchy. Files contain user data, and there are no restrictions or formats implied in the data. That is, user data is treated, by JFS, as an uninterpreted byte stream. Extent-based addressing structures rooted in the inode are used for mapping file data to disk blocks. A "file" is allocated in sequences of extents.

Together, the aggregate's superblock and disk allocation map, file descriptor and inode map, inodes, directories, and addressing structures comprise the JFS control structures—its metadata.

Design Features of JFS versus Other File Systems

JFS was designed with fully integrated journaling rather than adding journaling to an existing file system. A number of features in JFS distinguish it from other file systems.

- **Internal JFS (potential) limits**—JFS is a full 64-bit file system. All of the appropriate file system structure fields are 64 bits in size thus allowing JFS to support both large files and large partitions.
- **Removable media**—JFS does not support diskettes as an underlying file system device.
- **File system size**—The minimum file system (fileset) size supported by JFS is 16 Mbytes. The maximum file system size is a function of the file system block size and the maximum number of blocks supported by the file system metadata structures. JFS supports a maximum file system size of 512 terabytes (with block size of 512 bytes) to 4 petabytes (with block size of 4 Kbytes).
- **File size**—The maximum file size is the largest file size that virtual file system framework supports. For example, if the framework only supports 32bits, then this limits the file size.

JFS extensively uses B+-trees as extent-based addressing structures.

In the allocation of extents, a file is represented by an inode containing the root of the B+-tree, which describes the extent containing user data. An extent is a variable-length sequence of contiguous aggregate blocks allocated to a JFS object as a unit. Each extent is wholly contained within a single aggregate.

There are two values needed to define an extent, its length and its address. The length is measured in units of aggregate block size. JFS uses a 24-bit value to represent the length of an extent, so an extent can range in size from 1 to $(2^{24}-1)$ aggregate blocks. The address is the address of the first block of the extent, in units of the aggregate blocks (it is the block offset from the beginning of the aggregate). An extent may span multiple allocation groups (AGs). These extents are indexed in a B+-tree for optimum performance of inserting new extents, locating particular extents, etc.

With a 512-byte aggregate block size (the smallest allowable), the maximum extent is $512 \times (2^{24}-1)$ bytes long (slightly under 8G). With a 4,096-byte aggregate block size (the largest allowable), the maximum extent is $4,096 \times (2^{24}-1$ bytes long (slightly under 64G). These limits only apply to a single extent; in no way do they have any limiting effects on overall file size.

An extent-based file system combined with a user-specified aggregate block size does not allow JFS to have separate support for internal fragmentation. The user can configure the aggregate with a small aggregate block size (e.g., 512 bytes) to minimize internal fragmentation for aggregates with large number of small size files.

In general, the allocation policy for JFS tries to maximize contiguous allocation by allocating a minimum number of extents, with each extent as large and contiguous as possible. This allows for large I/O transfers and results in improved performance. To improve performance of locating a specific directory entry, a B+-tree, sorted by name, is used.

JFS uses extent-based addressing structures, along with aggressive block allocation policies, to produce compact, efficient, and scalable structures for mapping logical offsets within files to physical addresses on disk. An extent, as mentioned earlier, is a sequence of contiguous blocks allocated to a file as a unit and is described by a triple, consisting of logical offset/length/physical. The addressing structure is a B+-tree, populated with extent descriptors (the triples above), rooted in the inode and keyed by logical offset within the file.

JFS's Further Extensive Use of B+-Trees

This section describes the B+-tree data structure used for file layout. B+-trees were selected to increase the performance of reading and writing extents, the most common operations JFS. B+-trees provide a fast search for reading a particular extent of a file. They also provide an efficient append or insert of an extent in a file. Less commonly, JFS may traverse an entire B+-tree when removing a file, to ensure that JFS removes the blocks used for the B+-tree as well as the file data. The B+-tree is also efficient for traversal.

An extent allocation descriptor (xad structure) describes the extent and adds two more fields that are needed for representing files: an *offset*, describing the logical byte address the extent represents, and a *flags field*. The extent allocation descriptor structure is defined in linux\include\JFS\JFS_xtree.h, struct xad.

There is one generic B+-tree index structure for all index objects in JFS, except directories. The data being indexed depend on the object. The B+-tree is keyed by offset of xad of data being described by the tree. The entries are sorted by the offsets of the xad structures. A xad structure is an entry in a node of a B+-tree.

Once the eight xad structures in the inode are filled, an attempt is made to use the last quadrant of the inode for more xad structures. If the INLINEEA bit is set in the di_mode field of the inode, then the last quadrant of the inode is available. The bottom of the second section of a disk inode contains a data descriptor, which tells what is stored in the second half of the inode. The second half may contain in-line data for the file, if they are small enough.

If the file data won't fit in the in-line data space for the inode, they are contained in extents, and the inode will contain the root node of the B+-tree. The header indicates how many xads are in use and how many are available.

Generally, the inode will contain eight xad structures for the root of the B+-tree. If there are eight or fewer extents for the file, then these eight xad structures are also a leaf node of the B+-tree. They describe the extents.

Otherwise the eight xad structures in the inode point either to the leaves or internal nodes of the B+-tree. Once the eight xad structures in the inode are filled, an attempt is made to use the last quadrant of the inode for more xad structures. If the INLINEEA bit is set in the di_mode field of the inode, then the last quadrant of the inode is available. Once all of the available xad structures in the inodes are used, the B+-tree must be split.

Leaf Nodes

JFS allocates 4K of disk space for a *leaf node* of the B+-tree. A leaf node is a logical array of xad entries with a header. The header points to the first free xad entry in the node; all xad entries following that are also not allocated. The eight xad entries are copied from the inode to the leaf node; the header is initialized to point to the ninth entry as the first free entry. JFS updates the root of the B+-tree into the inode's first xad structure; this xad structure points to the newly allocated leaf node.

The offset for this new xad structure is the offset of the first entry in the leaf node. The header in the inode is updated to indicate that now only one xad is being used for the B+-tree. The header in the inode also must be updated to indicate that the inode now contains the pure root of the B+-tree.

As new extents are added to the file, they continue to be added to this same leaf node in the necessary order. This continues until this node is filled. Once the node is filled, a new 4K of disk space is allocated for another leaf node of the B+-tree. The second xad structure from the inode is set to point to this newly allocated node. This continues until all eight xad structures in the inode are filled, at which time another split of the B+-tree occurs. This split creates internal nodes of the B+-tree, which are used purely to route the searches of the tree.

Internal Nodes

JFS allocates 4K of disk space for an *internal node* of the B+-tree. An internal node looks the same as a leaf node. The eight xad entries are copied from the inode to the internal node; the header is initialized to point to the ninth entry as the first free entry. JFS updates the root of the B+-tree by making the inode's first xad structure point to the newly allocated internal inode.

The header in the inode is updated to indicate that only one xad is being used for the B+-tree. The file linux\include\linux\JFS\JFS_xtree.h describes the header for the root of the B+-tree in struct xtpage_t. The file linux\include\linux\JFS\JFS_btree.h is the header for an internal node or a leaf node in struct btpage_t.

Variable Block Size

JFS supports block sizes of 512, 1,024, 2,048, and 4,096 bytes on a per-file system basis, allowing users to optimize space utilization based on their application environment. Smaller block sizes reduce the amount of internal fragmentation within files and directories and are more space efficient.

However, small blocks can increase path length, because block allocation activities may occur more often than when a large block size is used. The default block size is 4,096 bytes because performance, rather than space utilization, is generally the primary consideration for server systems.

JFS dynamically allocates space for disk inodes as required, freeing the space when it is no longer required. This support avoids the traditional approach of reserving a fixed amount of space for disk inodes at file system creation time, and thus eliminating the need for users to estimate the maximum number of files and directories that a file system will contain. Additionally, this support decouples disk inodes from fixed disk locations.

Directory Organization

Two different directory organizations are provided in JFS. The first organization is used for small directories and stores the directory contents within the directory's inode. This eliminates the need for separate directory block I/O as well as the need to allocate separate storage. Up to eight entries may be stored in-line within the inode, excluding the self(.) and parent(..) directory entries, which are stored in separate areas of the inode.

The second organization is used for larger directories and represents each directory as a B+-tree keyed on name. A Linux directory, like any UNIX directory, is an association between the file leafnames and inodes numbers. A file's inode number can be found using the -i switch to ls.

It provides faster directory lookup, insertion, and deletion capabilities when compared to traditional unsorted directory organizations.

JFS's Support for Sparse and Dense Files

JFS supports both sparse and dense files, on a per-file system basis. *Sparse files* allow data to be written to random locations within a file without instantiating previously unwritten intervening file blocks. The file size reported is the highest byte that has been written to, but the actual allocation of any given block in the file does not occur until a write operation is performed on that block. For example, suppose a new file is created in a file system designated for sparse files. An application writes a block of data to block 100 in the file. JFS reports the size of this file as 100 blocks, although only one block of disk space has been allocated to it. If the application next reads block 50 of the file, JFS returns a block of zero-filled bytes. Suppose the application then writes a block of data to block 50 of the file. JFS still reports the size of this file as 100 blocks, and now two blocks of disk space have been allocated to it. Sparse files are of interest to applications that require a large logical space but only use a (small) subset of this space.

For *dense files*, disk resources are allocated to cover the file size. In the above example, the first write (a block of data to block 100 in the file) would cause 100 blocks of disk space to be allocated to the file. A read operation on any block that has been implicitly written to will return a block of zero-filled bytes, just as in the case of the sparse file.

Aggregates and Filesets

In JFS, a *file* is represented by an inode containing the root of a B+-tree, which describes the extents containing user data. The B+-tree is indexed by the offset of the extents. A directory is a journaled metadata file.

A Linux directory, like any UNIX directory, is an association between the file leafnames and inode numbers. A file's inode number can be found using the -i switch to ls.

A directory is composed of entries, which indicate the objects contained within the directory. A directory entry links a name to an inode number. The specified inode describes the object with the specified name. To improve performance in locating a specific directory entry, a B+-tree, sorted by name, is used.

The directory inodes' di_size field represents just the leaf pages of the directory B+-tree. When the leaf node of the directory is contained within the inode, the di_size field's value is 256. A directory does not contain specific entries for self (.) and parent (..). Instead, these are represented in the inode itself. Self is the directory's own inode number. Parent is a special field in the inode, idotdot, struct dtroot_t, in the linux\include\linux\JFS\JFS_dtree.h file.

The directory inode contains the root of its B+-tree in a manner similar to that of a normal file. A Linux directory, like any UNIX directory, is an association between the file leafnames and inode numbers. However, this B+-tree is keyed by name. The leaf nodes of a directory B+-tree contain the directory entry and are keyed from the complete name of the entry.

The directory B+-tree uses suffix compression for the last internal nodes of the B+-tree. The rest of the internal nodes use the same compressed suffix. Suffix compression truncates the name to just enough characters to distinguish the current entry from the previous entry.

As we explained before, directories map user-specified names to the inodes allocated for files and (sub)directories. This forms the traditional name hierarchy. Files contain user data, without restrictions or formats implied in the data. JFS treats user data as an uninterpreted byte stream. Extent-based addressing structures rooted in the inode are used to map file data to disk blocks. The aggregate's superblock and disk allocation map, file descriptor and inode map, inodes, directories, and addressing structures comprise the JFS control structures, or metadata.

Logs

JFS logs are maintained in each aggregate and used to record information about operations on metadata. The log has a format that also is set by the file system creation utility. A single log may be used simultaneously by multiple mounted filesets within the aggregate. Several aspects of log-based recovery are of interest. First, JFS only logs operations on metadata, so replaying the log only restores the consistency of structural relationships and resource allocation states within the file system. It does not log file data or recover this data to consistent state. Consequently, some file data may be lost or stale after recovery, and customers with a critical need for data consistency should use synchronous I/O.

Logging is not particularly effective in the face of media errors. Specifically, an I/O error during the write-to-disk of the log or metadata means that a time-consuming and potentially intrusive full integrity check is required after a system crash to restore the file system to a consistent state. This implies that bad block relocation is a key feature of any storage manager or device residing below JFS.

JFS logging semantics are such that, when a file system operation that involves changes to metadata (e.g., `unlink()`) returns a successful return code, the effects of the operation have been committed to the file system and will be seen even if the system crashes. For example, once a file has been successfully removed, it remains removed and will not reappear if the system crashes and is restarted.

This logging style introduces a synchronous write to the log disk into each inode or virtual file system (VFS) operation that modifies metadata. (For database mavens, this is a redo-only, physical after-image, write-ahead logging protocol using a no-steal buffer policy.) In terms of performance, this compares well with many nonjournaling file systems that rely upon multiple careful synchronous metadata writes for consistency. However, it is a performance disadvantage when compared to other journaling file systems, such as Veritas VxFS and Transarc Episode, which use different logging styles and lazily write log data to disk. In the server environment, where multiple concurrent operations are performed, this performance cost is reduced by *group commit*, which combines multiple synchronous write operations into a single write operation. The logging style of JFS has been improved over time and now provides asynchronous logging, which increases performance of the file system.

Obviously there is much more to say about JFS, but as JFS is enhanced further, and new functionality and features will creep in, a complete discussion of JFS cannot be given here.

Logical Volume Manager Abstract

The goal of the Logical Volume Manager abstract is to implement a very flexible virtual disk subsystem to handle disk storage, online allocation and relocation of storage, and online extension and reduction of storage.

The Logical Volume Manager (LVM) adds an additional layer between the physical peripherals and the I/O interface in the kernel, which allows us a logical view of disks. This also permits the concatenation of several disks (physical volumes or PVs) to form a storage pool (Volume Group or VG) with allocation units called physical extents (PEs).

Parts of this VG then can be allocated in the form of Logical Volumes (LVs) in units called logical extents (LEs). Each logical extent is mapped to a corresponding physical extent of equal size. These physical extents are mapped to offsets and blocks on the disk(s).

The LVs can then be used through device special files similar to `/dev/sd[a-z]*` or `/dev/hd[a-z]*` named `/dev/VolumeGroupName/LogicalVolumeName`.

Going beyond this, you are able to extend or reduce VGs AND LVs at runtime.

Configuration Concept

The configuration information for the physical volume, volume group, and logical volume(s) is stored on each physical volume and in automatically created backup files, which are stored in the /etc/lvmtab.d directory.

The config area on the disk(s) is called *volume group descriptor area* or VGDA.

An LVM driver holds mapping tables between the LEs of LVs and the PEs of PVs. These tables are created/updated/deleted by super-user LVM commands.

The main mapping function of the driver is called with a logical block in an LV from functions in /usr/src/linux/drivers/block/ll_rw_blk.c (in functions ll_rw_block() and ll_rw_swap_file()) and looks up the corresponding physical block/disk pair in a table. Then it returns this pair to the calling ll_rw_*() function, causing a physical I/O request to the disk block(s) to be queued.

Example

If the capacity of an LV gets too small and your VG containing this LV is full, you could add another PV to that VG and simply extend the LV afterwards. If you reduce or delete an LV you can use the freed capacity for different LVs of the same VG. This scenario is represented in Figure 10.4.

Figure 10.4
Extending a logical
volume (LV).

```
/-----------------------------------------------\
|  /--------\        VG 1      /--------\        |
|  |        |                  |        |        |
|  | PV 1   |     ......       | PV n   |        |
|  |    /----------------------------\  |        |
|  |    \-------LV 1-----------/      |  |        |
|  \--------/                  \--------/        |
\-----------------------------------------------/
```

In the illustgration let PV 1 be /dev/sdc1; PV n be /dev/sde1; VG 1 be vg00; and LV 1 be /dev/test_vg/test_lv.

The configuration steps for getting the above scenario are:

1. After installing LVM do an insmod lvm or set up kerneld/kmod to load it automatically (see INSTALL).
2. Set up partitions (#1) on both disks with partition type 0x8e (I used this type to avoid using Linux primary partitions.)

3. Do a `pvcreate /dev/sd[ce]1`. For testing purposes, you can use more than one primary and/or extended partition on a disk. Don't do that for normal LVM operation for performance reasons; if you must, don't stripe logical volumes over physical volumes associated to partitions on the same disk.

4. Do a `vgcreate test_vg /dev/sd[ce]1`. (`vgcreate` activates the volume group, too).

5. Do a `lvcreate -L100 -ntest_lv test_vg` to get a 100-MB linear LV or a `lvcreate -i2 -I4 -l100 -nanother_test_lv test_vg` to get a 100-LE large logical volume with two stripes and a stripe size of 4 KB.

6. Use created LVs as you like; for example, generate a file system in one with `mke2fs /dev/test_vg/test_lv` and mount it.

Overview and Concept of Commands

I grouped and named LVM commands so that the commands for physical volume handling all start with `pv`, those for volume group handling start with `vg`; and those for logical volumes start with `lv`. Table 10.2 list the LVM commands.

TABLE 10.2 Logical Volume Manager Commands	`e2fsadm`	Administration wrapper for logical volume including file system resizing for `lvextend`, `lvreduce`, `e2fsck`, and `resize2fs`.
	`lvchange`	Change attributes of a logical volume.
	`lvcreate`	Create a logical volume.
	`lvdisplay`	Display logical volume config data.
	`lvextend`	Extend a logical volume in size.
	`lvreduce`	Reduce a logical volume in size.
	`lvremove`	Remove a logical volume.
	`lvrename`	Rename an inactive logical volume.
	`lvscan`	Find all existing logical volumes.
	`lvmchange`	Emergency program to change attributes of the LVM.
	`lvmdiskscan`	Scan all disks/partitions and multiple devices and list them.
	`lvmsadc`	Statistic data collector.
	`lvmsar`	Statistic data reporter.
	`pvchange`	Change attributes of physical volumes.

continued on next page

TABLE 10.2	`pvcreate`	Create a physical volume.
continued	`pvdata`	Debug list physical volume group descriptor area.
	`pvdisplay`	Display physical volume config information.
	`pvmove`	Move logical extents to a different physical volume.
	`pvscan`	Find all existing physical volumes.
	`vgcfgbackup`	Back up all volume group descriptor areas.
	`vgcfgrestore`	Restore volume group descriptor area(s) to disk(s).
	`vgchange`	Activate/deactivate volume group(s).
	`vgck`	Check volume group descriptor area for consistency.
	`vgcreate`	Create a volume group from physical volume(s).
	`vgdisplay`	Display volume group config information.
	`vgexport`	Export volume group (make it unknown to the system).
	`vgextend`	Extend a volume group by one or more physical volumes.
	`vgimport`	Import a volume group (make it known to the/another system).
	`vgmerge`	Merge two volume groups into one.
	`vgmknodes`	Create volume group directory with all logical volume specials.
	`vgreduce`	Reduce a volume group by one or more empty physical volume(s).
	`vgremove`	Remove an empty volume group.
	`vgrename`	Rename an inactive volume group.
	`vgscan`	Scan for volume groups.
	`vgsplit`	Split one volume group into two.

Sample LVM Session Output

```
# create physical volumes on 9 SCSI disk primary partition 1
pvcreate /dev/sd[b-eg-k]1
pvcreate -- /dev/sdb1 has an invalid physical volume identifier
pvcreate -- physical volume on /dev/sdb1 successfully created
pvcreate -- reinitializing physical volume
pvcreate -- physical volume on /dev/sdc1 successfully created
pvcreate -- reinitializing physical volume
pvcreate -- physical volume on /dev/sdd1 successfully created
pvcreate -- reinitializing physical volume
pvcreate -- physical volume on /dev/sde1 successfully created
pvcreate -- reinitializing physical volume
```

```
pvcreate -- physical volume on /dev/sdg1 successfully created
pvcreate -- reinitializing physical volume
pvcreate -- physical volume on /dev/sdh1 successfully created
pvcreate -- reinitializing physical volume
pvcreate -- physical volume on /dev/sdi1 successfully created
pvcreate -- reinitializing physical volume
pvcreate -- physical volume on /dev/sdj1 successfully created
pvcreate -- reinitializing physical volume
pvcreate -- physical volume on /dev/sdk1 successfully created


# create a volume group with default physical extent size
# from these physical volumes
vgcreate my_first_vg /dev/sd[b-eg-k]1
vgcreate -- INFO: using default physical extent size 4096 KB
vgcreate -- INFO: maximum logical volume size is 256 GB
vgcreate -- doing automatic backup of vg05
vgcreate -- volume group my_first_vg successfully created


# Oops ;-)
# Don't like the limitations caused by default physical extent
size
# --> deactivate and delete volume
vgchange -an my_first_vg
vgchange -- my_first_vg successfully deactivated

vgremove my_first_vg
vgremove -- volume group my_first_vg successfully removed



# create a volume group with physical extent size of 8192 KB
# from these physical volumes
vgcreate -s 8192 my_first_vg /dev/sd[b-eg-k]1
vgcreate -- INFO: maximum logical volume size is 512 GB
vgcreate -- doing automatic backup of my_first_vg
vgcreate -- volume group my_first_vg successfully created



# display volume group config
vgdisplay my_first_vg
--- Volume group ---
VG Name             my_first_vg
VG Write Access     read/write
VG Status           available
VG #                1
MAX LV              31
Cur LV              0
Open LV             0
MAX LV Size         512 GB
Max PV              256
```

```
Cur PV                 9
Act PV                 9
VG Size                12636 MB
PE Size                8192 KB
Total PE               1579
Alloc PE / Size        0 / 0 KB
Free  PE / Size        1579 / 12632 MB


# do it again Sam but verbose
vgdisplay -v my_first_vg
--- Volume group ---
VG Name                my_first_vg
VG Write Access        read/write
VG Status              available
VG #                   1
MAX LV                 31
Cur LV                 0
Open LV                0
MAX LV Size            512 GB
Max PV                 256
Cur PV                 9
Act PV                 9
VG Size                12636 MB
PE Size                8192 KB
Total PE               1579
Alloc PE / Size        0 / 0 KB
Free  PE / Size        1579 / 12636 MB


--- No logical volumes defined in my_first_vg ---


--- Physical volumes ---
PV Name (#)            /dev/sdb1 (1)
PV Status              available / allocatable
Total PE / Free PE     131 / 131

PV Name (#)            /dev/sdc1 (2)
PV Status              available / allocatable
Total PE / Free PE     131 / 131

PV Name (#)            /dev/sdd1 (3)
PV Status              available / allocatable
Total PE / Free PE     131 / 131

PV Name (#)            /dev/sde1 (4)
PV Status              available / allocatable
Total PE / Free PE     131 / 131

PV Name (#)            /dev/sdg1 (5)
PV Status              available / allocatable
Total PE / Free PE     131 / 131

PV Name (#)            /dev/sdh1 (6)
```

```
PV Status              available / allocatable
Total PE / Free PE     131 / 131

PV Name (#)            /dev/sdi1 (7)
PV Status              available / allocatable
Total PE / Free PE     131 / 131

PV Name (#)            /dev/sdj1 (8)
PV Status              available / allocatable
Total PE / Free PE     125 / 125

PV Name (#)            /dev/sdk1 (9)
PV Status              available / allocatable
Total PE / Free PE     537 / 537
```

```
# create a linear physical volume with all space of the volume
group
lvcreate -l1579 my_first_vg
lvcreate -- doing automatic backup of my_first_vg
lvcreate -- logical volume /dev/my_first_vg/lvol1 successfully
created
```

```
# create an ext2fs on newly created logical volume
mke2fs /dev/my_first_vg/lvol1
mke2fs 1.10, 24-Apr-97 for EXT2 FS 0.5b, 95/08/09
Linux ext2 file system format
File system label=
3235840 inodes, 12939264 blocks
646963 blocks (5.00%) reserved for the super user
First data block=1
Block size=1024 (log=0)
Fragment size=1024 (log=0)
1580 block groups
8192 blocks per group, 8192 fragments per group
2048 inodes per group
Superblock backups stored on blocks:
     8193, 16385, 24577, 32769, 40961, 49153, 57345, 65537, 73729,
     81921, 90113, 98305, 106497, 114689, 122881, 131073, 139265,
147457,

Writing superblocks and file system accounting information: done
0.66user 26.55system 3:06.62elapsed 14%CPU (0avgtext+0avgdata
0maxresident)k
0inputs+0outputs (97major+522minor)pagefaults 0swaps
```

```
# and mount it (not very exiting :-) )
mount /dev/my_first_vg/lvol1 /mnt
```

Data Structures—include/llinux/fsh

```
1 #ifndef _LINUX_FS_H
2 #define _LINUX_FS_H
3
4 /*
5  * This file has definitions for some important file table
6  * structures etc.
7  */
8
9 #include <linux/config.h>
10 #include <linux/linkage.h>
11 #include <linux/limits.h>
12 #include <linux/wait.h>
13 #include <linux/types.h>
14 #include <linux/vfs.h>
15 #include <linux/net.h>
16 #include <linux/kdev_t.h>
17 #include <linux/ioctl.h>
18 #include <linux/list.h>
19 #include <linux/dcache.h>
20 #include <linux/stat.h>
21 #include <linux/cache.h>
22 #include <linux/stddef.h>
23 #include <linux/string.h>
24
25 #include <asm/atomic.h>
26 #include <asm/bitops.h>
27
28 struct poll_table_struct;
29
30
31 /*
32  * It's silly to have NR_OPEN bigger than NR_FILE, but you can change
33  * the file limit at runtime and only root can increase the per-process
34  * nr_file rlimit, so it's safe to set up a ridiculously high absolute
35  * upper limit on files-per-process.
36  *
37  * Some programs (notably those using select()) may have to be
38  * recompiled to take full advantage of the new limits..
39  */
40
41 /* Fixed constants first: */
42 #undef NR_OPEN
43 #define NR_OPEN (1024*1024)        /* Absolute upper limit on fd num */
44 #define INR_OPEN 1024              /* Initial setting for nfile rlimits */
45
46 #define BLOCK_SIZE_BITS 10
47 #define BLOCK_SIZE (1<<BLOCK_SIZE_BITS)
48
49 /* And dynamically-tunable limits and defaults: */
50 extern int max_files, nr_files, nr_free_files;
51 extern int max_super_blocks, nr_super_blocks;
```

```
52
53 #define NR_FILE  8192     /* this can well be larger on a larger system */
54 #define NR_RESERVED_FILES 10 /* reserved for root */
55 #define NR_SUPER 256
56
57 #define MAY_EXEC 1
58 #define MAY_WRITE 2
59 #define MAY_READ 4
60
61 #define FMODE_READ 1
62 #define FMODE_WRITE 2
63
64 #define READ 0
65 #define WRITE 1
66 #define READA 2            /* read-ahead  - don't block if no resources */
67 #define SPECIAL 4          /* For non-blockdevice requests in request queue */
68
69 #define WRITERAW 5         /* raw write - don't play with buffer lists */
70
71 #define NIL_FILP           ((struct file *)0)
72 #define SEL_IN             1
73 #define SEL_OUT            2
74 #define SEL_EX             4
75
76 /* public flags for file_system_type */
77 #define FS_REQUIRES_DEV 1
78 #define FS_NO_DCACHE       2 /* Only dcache the necessary things. */
79 #define FS_NO_PRELIM       4 /* prevent preloading of dentries, even if
80                                * FS_NO_DCACHE is not set.
81                                */
82
83 /*
84  * These are the fs-independent mount-flags: up to 16 flags are supported
85  */
86 #define MS_RDONLY          1     /* Mount read-only */
87 #define MS_NOSUID          2     /* Ignore suid and sgid bits */
88 #define MS_NODEV           4     /* Disallow access to device special files */
89 #define MS_NOEXEC          8     /* Disallow program execution */
90 #define MS_SYNCHRONOUS     16    /* Writes are synced at once */
91 #define MS_REMOUNT         32    /* Alter flags of a mounted FS */
92 #define MS_MANDLOCK        64    /* Allow mandatory locks on an FS */
93 #define S_QUOTA            128   /* Quota initialized for file/directory/symlink */
94 #define S_APPEND           256   /* Append-only file */
95 #define S_IMMUTABLE        512   /* Immutable file */
96 #define MS_NOATIME         1024  /* Do not update access times. */
97 #define MS_NODIRATIME      2048   /* Do not update directory access times */
98
99 #define MS_ODD_RENAME      32768   /* Temporary stuff; will go away as soon
100                                     * as nfs_rename() will be cleaned up
101                                     */
102
103 /*
104  * Flags that can be altered by MS_REMOUNT
105  */
```

```
106 #define MS_RMT_MASK       (MS_RDONLY|MS_NOSUID|MS_NODEV|MS_NOEXEC|\
107                           MS_SYNCHRONOUS|MS_MANDLOCK|MS_NOATIME|MS_NODIRATIME)
108
109 /*
110  * Magic mount flag number. Has to be or-ed to the flag values.
111  */
112 #define MS_MGC_VAL 0xC0ED0000    /* magic flag number to indicate "new" flags */
113 #define MS_MGC_MSK 0xffff0000    /* magic flag number mask */
114
115 /*
116  * Note that nosuid etc flags are inode-specific: setting some file-system
117  * flags just means all the inodes inherit those flags by default. It might be
118  * possible to override it selectively if you really wanted to with some
119  * ioctl() that is not currently implemented.
120  *
121  * Exception: MS_RDONLY is always applied to the entire file system.
122  *
123  * Unfortunately, it is possible to change a filesystems flags with it mounted
124  * with files in use. This means that all of the inodes will not have their
125  * i_flags updated. Hence, i_flags no longer inherit the superblock mount
126  * flags, so these have to be checked separately. -- rmk@arm.uk.linux.org
127  */
128 #define __IS_FLG(inode,flg) (((inode)->i_sb && (inode)->i_sb->s_flags & (flg)) \
129                                 || (inode)->i_flags & (flg))
130
131 #define IS_RDONLY(inode) (((inode)->i_sb) && ((inode)->i_sb->s_flags & MS_RDON-
LY))
132 #define IS_NOSUID(inode)        __IS_FLG(inode, MS_NOSUID)
133 #define IS_NODEV(inode)         __IS_FLG(inode, MS_NODEV)
134 #define IS_NOEXEC(inode)        __IS_FLG(inode, MS_NOEXEC)
135 #define IS_SYNC(inode)          __IS_FLG(inode, MS_SYNCHRONOUS)
136 #define IS_MANDLOCK(inode)      __IS_FLG(inode, MS_MANDLOCK)
137
138 #define IS_QUOTAINIT(inode)     ((inode)->i_flags & S_QUOTA)
139 #define IS_APPEND(inode)        ((inode)->i_flags & S_APPEND)
140 #define IS_IMMUTABLE(inode)     ((inode)->i_flags & S_IMMUTABLE)
141 #define IS_NOATIME(inode)       __IS_FLG(inode, MS_NOATIME)
142 #define IS_NODIRATIME(inode)    __IS_FLG(inode, MS_NODIRATIME)
143
144
145 /* the read-only stuff doesn't really belong here, but any other place is
146     probably as bad and I don't want to create yet another include file. */
147
148 #define BLKROSET    _IO(0x12,93)  /* set device read-only (0 = read-write) */
149 #define BLKROGET    _IO(0x12,94)  /* get read-only status (0 = read_write) */
150 #define BLKRRPART   _IO(0x12,95)  /* re-read partition table */
151 #define BLKGETSIZE  _IO(0x12,96)  /* return device size */
152 #define BLKFLSBUF   _IO(0x12,97)  /* flush buffer cache */
153 #define BLKRASET    _IO(0x12,98)  /* Set read ahead for block device */
154 #define BLKRAGET    _IO(0x12,99)  /* get current read ahead setting */
155 #define BLKFRASET   _IO(0x12,100)/* set filesystem (mm/filemap.c) read-ahead */
156 #define BLKFRAGET   _IO(0x12,101)/* get filesystem (mm/filemap.c) read-ahead */
157 #define BLKSECTSET  _IO(0x12,102)/* set max sectors per request (ll_rw_blk.c) */
158 #define BLKSECTGET  _IO(0x12,103)/* get max sectors per request (ll_rw_blk.c) */
```

```
159 #define BLKSSZGET    _IO(0x12,104)/* get block device sector size */
160 #if 0
161 #define BLKPG        _IO(0x12,105)/* See blkpg.h */
162 #define BLKELVGET    _IO(0x12,106)/* elevator get */
163 #define BLKELVSET    _IO(0x12,107)/* elevator set */
164 /* This was here just to show that the number is taken -
165    probably all these _IO(0x12,*) ioctls should be moved to blkpg.h. */
166 #endif
167
168
169 #define BMAP_IOCTL 1              /* obsolete - kept for compatibility */
170 #define FIBMAP      _IO(0x00,1)   /* bmap access */
171 #define FIGETBSZ    _IO(0x00,2)   /* get the block size used for bmap */
172
173 #ifdef __KERNEL__
174
175 #include <asm/semaphore.h>
176 #include <asm/byteorder.h>
177
178 extern void update_atime (struct inode *);
179 #define UPDATE_ATIME(inode) update_atime (inode)
180
181 extern void buffer_init(unsigned long);
182 extern void inode_init(void);
183 extern void file_table_init(void);
184 extern void dcache_init(void);
185
186 /* bh state bits */
187 #define BH_Uptodate    0    /* 1 if the buffer contains valid data */
188 #define BH_Dirty       1    /* 1 if the buffer is dirty */
189 #define BH_Lock        2    /* 1 if the buffer is locked */
190 #define BH_Req         3    /* 0 if the buffer has been invalidated */
191 #define BH_Mapped      4    /* 1 if the buffer has a disk mapping */
192 #define BH_New         5    /* 1 if the buffer is new and not yet written out */
193 #define BH_Protected   6    /* 1 if the buffer is protected */
194
195 /*
196  * Try to keep the most commonly used fields in single cache lines (16
197  * bytes) to improve performance. This ordering should be
198  * particularly beneficial on 32-bit processors.
199  *
200  * We use the first 16 bytes for the data which is used in searches
201  * over the block hash lists (ie. getblk() and friends).
202  *
203  * The second 16 bytes we use for lru buffer scans, as used by
204  * sync_buffers() and refill_freelist(). -- sct
205  */
206 struct buffer_head {
207 /* First cache line: */
208 struct buffer_head *b_next;    /* Hash queue list */
209 unsigned long b_blocknr;       /* block number */
210 unsigned short b_size;         /* block size */
211 unsigned short b_list;         /* List that this buffer appears */
212 kdev_t b_dev;                  /* device (B_FREE = free) */
```

```
213
214 atomic_t b_count;              /* users using this block */
215 kdev_t b_rdev;                 /* Real device */
216 unsigned long b_state;         /* buffer state bitmap (see above) */
217 unsigned long b_flushtime;     /* Time when (dirty) buffer should be written */
218
219 struct buffer_head *b_next_free;/* lru/free list linkage */
220 struct buffer_head *b_prev_free;/* doubly linked list of buffers */
221 struct buffer_head *b_this_page;/* circular list of buffers in one page */
222 struct buffer_head *b_reqnext;  /* request queue */
223
224 struct buffer_head **b_pprev;   /* doubly linked list of hash-queue */
225 char * b_data;                  /* pointer to data block (512 byte) */
226 struct page *b_page;            /* the page this bh is mapped to */
227 void (*b_end_io)(struct buffer_head *bh, int uptodate); /* I/O completion */
228 void *b_dev_id;
229
230 unsigned long b_rsector;        /* Real buffer location on disk */
231 wait_queue_head_t b_wait;
232 struct kiobuf * b_kiobuf;       /* kiobuf which owns this IO */
233 };
234
235 typedef void (bh_end_io_t)(struct buffer_head *bh, int uptodate);
236 void init_buffer(struct buffer_head *, bh_end_io_t *, void *);
237
238 #define __buffer_state(bh, state)   (((bh)->b_state & (1UL << BH_##state)) != 0)
239
240 #define buffer_uptodate(bh)        __buffer_state(bh,Uptodate)
241 #define buffer_dirty(bh)           __buffer_state(bh,Dirty)
242 #define buffer_locked(bh)          __buffer_state(bh,Lock)
243 #define buffer_req(bh)             __buffer_state(bh,Req)
244 #define buffer_mapped(bh)          __buffer_state(bh,Mapped)
245 #define buffer_new(bh)             __buffer_state(bh,New)
246 #define buffer_protected(bh)       __buffer_state(bh,Protected)
247
248 #define bh_offset(bh)              ((unsigned long)(bh)->b_data & ~PAGE_MASK)
249
250 extern void set_bh_page(struct buffer_head *bh, struct page *page, unsigned long
          offset);
251
252 #define touch_buffer(bh)           set_bit(PG_referenced, &bh->b_page->flags)
253
254
255 #include <linux/pipe_fs_i.h>
256 #include <linux/minix_fs_i.h>
257 #include <linux/ext2_fs_i.h>
258 #include <linux/hpfs_fs_i.h>
259 #include <linux/ntfs_fs_i.h>
260 #include <linux/msdos_fs_i.h>
261 #include <linux/umsdos_fs_i.h>
262 #include <linux/iso_fs_i.h>
263 #include <linux/nfs_fs_i.h>
264 #include <linux/sysv_fs_i.h>
265 #include <linux/affs_fs_i.h>
```

```
266 #include <linux/ufs_fs_i.h>
267 #include <linux/efs_fs_i.h>
268 #include <linux/coda_fs_i.h>
269 #include <linux/romfs_fs_i.h>
270 #include <linux/smb_fs_i.h>
271 #include <linux/hfs_fs_i.h>
272 #include <linux/adfs_fs_i.h>
273 #include <linux/qnx4_fs_i.h>
274 #include <linux/bfs_fs_i.h>
275 #include <linux/udf_fs_i.h>
276 #include <linux/ncp_fs_i.h>
277 #include <linux/proc_fs_i.h>
278 #include <linux/usbdev_fs_i.h>
279
280 /*
281  * Attribute flags. These should be or-ed together to figure out what
282  * has been changed!
283  */
284 #define ATTR_MODE       1
285 #define ATTR_UID        2
286 #define ATTR_GID        4
287 #define ATTR_SIZE       8
288 #define ATTR_ATIME      16
289 #define ATTR_MTIME      32
290 #define ATTR_CTIME      64
291 #define ATTR_ATIME_SET  128
292 #define ATTR_MTIME_SET  256
293 #define ATTR_FORCE      512       /* Not a change, but a change it */
294 #define ATTR_ATTR_FLAG  1024
295
296 /*
297  * This is the Inode Attributes structure, used for notify_change(). It
298  * uses the above definitions as flags, to know which values have changed.
299  * Also, in this manner, a Filesystem can look at only the values it cares
300  * about. Basically, these are the attributes that the VFS layer can
301  * request to change from the FS layer.
302  *
303  * Derek Atkins <warlord@MIT.EDU> 94-10-20
304  */
305 struct iattr {
306         unsigned int    ia_valid;
307         umode_t         ia_mode;
308         uid_t           ia_uid;
309         gid_t           ia_gid;
310         loff_t          ia_size;
311         time_t          ia_atime;
312         time_t          ia_mtime;
313         time_t          ia_ctime;
314         unsigned int    ia_attr_flags;
315 };
316
317 /*
318  * This is the inode attributes flag definitions
319  */
```

```
320 #define ATTR_FLAG_SYNCRONOUS     1       /* Syncronous write */
321 #define ATTR_FLAG_NOATIME        2       /* Don't update atime */
322 #define ATTR_FLAG_APPEND         4       /* Append-only file */
323 #define ATTR_FLAG_IMMUTABLE      8       /* Immutable file */
324 #define ATTR_FLAG_NODIRATIME     16      /* Don't update atime for directory */
325
326 /*
327  * Includes for diskquotas and mount structures.
328  */
329 #include <linux/quota.h>
330 #include <linux/mount.h>
331
332 /*
333  * oh the beauties of C type declarations.
334  */
335 struct page;
336 struct address_space;
337
338 struct address_space_operations {
339         int (*writepage) (struct dentry *, struct page *);
340         int (*readpage)(struct dentry *, struct page *);
341         int (*prepare_write)(struct file *, struct page *, unsigned, unsigned);
342         int (*commit_write)(struct file *, struct page *, unsigned, unsigned);
343         /* Unfortunately this kludge is needed for FIBMAP. Don't use it */
344         int (*bmap)(struct address_space *, long);
345 };
346
347 struct address_space {
348         struct list_head          pages;         /* list of pages */
349         unsigned long             nrpages;       /* number of pages */
350         struct address_space_operations *a_ops; /* methods */
351         void                      *host;         /* owner: inode, block_device */
352         struct vm_area_struct     *i_mmap;       /* list of mappings */
353         spinlock_t                i_shared_lock; /* and spinlock protecting it */
354 };
355
356 struct block_device {
357         struct list_head          bd_hash;
358         atomic_t                  bd_count;
359 /*      struct address_space      bd_data; */
360         dev_t                     bd_dev; /* not a kdev_t - it's a search key */
361         atomic_t                  bd_openers;
362         const struct block_device_operations *bd_op;
363         struct semaphore          bd_sem; /* open/close mutex */
364 };
365
366 struct inode {
367         struct list_head          i_hash;
368         struct list_head          i_list;
369         struct list_head          i_dentry;
370
371         unsigned long             i_ino;
372         unsigned int              i_count;
373         kdev_t                    i_dev;
```

```
374        umode_t                 i_mode;
375        nlink_t                 i_nlink;
376        uid_t                   i_uid;
377        gid_t                   i_gid;
378        kdev_t                  i_rdev;
379        loff_t                  i_size;
380        time_t                  i_atime;
381        time_t                  i_mtime;
382        time_t                  i_ctime;
383        unsigned long           i_blksize;
384        unsigned long           i_blocks;
385        unsigned long           i_version;
386        struct semaphore        i_sem;
387        struct semaphore        i_zombie;
388        struct inode_operations *i_op;
389        struct file_operations  *i_fop; /* former ->i_op->default_file_ops */
390        struct super_block      *i_sb;
391        wait_queue_head_t       i_wait;
392        struct file_lock        *i_flock;
393        struct address_space    *i_mapping;
394        struct address_space    i_data;
395        struct dquot            *i_dquot[MAXQUOTAS];
396        struct pipe_inode_info  *i_pipe;
397        struct block_device     *i_bdev;
398
399        unsigned long           i_state;
400
401        unsigned int            i_flags;
402        unsigned char           i_sock;
403
404        atomic_t                i_writecount;
405        unsigned int            i_attr_flags;
406        __u32                   i_generation;
407        union {
408                struct minix_inode_info         minix_i;
409                struct ext2_inode_info          ext2_i;
410                struct hpfs_inode_info          hpfs_i;
411                struct ntfs_inode_info          ntfs_i;
412                struct msdos_inode_info         msdos_i;
413                struct umsdos_inode_info        umsdos_i;
414                struct iso_inode_info           isofs_i;
415                struct nfs_inode_info           nfs_i;
416                struct sysv_inode_info          sysv_i;
417                struct affs_inode_info          affs_i;
418                struct ufs_inode_info           ufs_i;
419                struct efs_inode_info           efs_i;
420                struct romfs_inode_info         romfs_i;
421                struct coda_inode_info          coda_i;
422                struct smb_inode_info           smbfs_i;
423                struct hfs_inode_info           hfs_i;
424                struct adfs_inode_info          adfs_i;
425                struct qnx4_inode_info          qnx4_i;
426                struct bfs_inode_info           bfs_i;
427                struct udf_inode_info           udf_i;
```

```
428                 struct ncp_inode_info            ncpfs_i;
429                 struct proc_inode_info           proc_i;
430                 struct socket                    socket_i;
431                 struct usbdev_inode_info         usbdev_i;
432                 void                             *generic_ip;
433         } u;
434 };
435
436 /* Inode state bits.. */
437 #define I_DIRTY           1
438 #define I_LOCK            2
439 #define I_FREEING         4
440 #define I_CLEAR           8
441
442 extern void __mark_inode_dirty(struct inode *);
443 static inline void mark_inode_dirty(struct inode *inode)
444 {
445         if (!(inode->i_state & I_DIRTY))
446                 __mark_inode_dirty(inode);
447 }
448
449 struct fown_struct {
450         int pid;                 /* pid or -pgrp where SIGIO should be sent */
451         uid_t uid, euid;         /* uid/euid of process setting the owner */
452         int signum;              /* posix.1b rt signal to be delivered on IO */
453 };
454
455 struct file {
456         struct list_head         f_list;
457         struct dentry            *f_dentry;
458         struct vfsmount          *f_vfsmnt;
459         struct file_operations   *f_op;
460         atomic_t                 f_count;
461         unsigned int             f_flags;
462         mode_t                   f_mode;
463         loff_t                   f_pos;
464         unsigned long            f_reada, f_ramax, f_raend, f_ralen, f_rawin;
465         struct fown_struct       f_owner;
466         unsigned int             f_uid, f_gid;
467         int                      f_error;
468
469         unsigned long            f_version;
470
471         /* needed for tty driver, and maybe others */
472         void                     *private_data;
473 };
474 extern spinlock_t files_lock;
475 #define file_list_lock() spin_lock(&files_lock);
476 #define file_list_unlock() spin_unlock(&files_lock);
477
478 #define get_file(x)      atomic_inc(&(x)->f_count)
479 #define file_count(x)    atomic_read(&(x)->f_count)
480
481 extern int init_private_file(struct file *, struct dentry *, int);
```

```
482
483 #define FL_POSIX        1
484 #define FL_FLOCK        2
485 #define FL_BROKEN       4       /* broken flock() emulation */
486 #define FL_ACCESS       8       /* for processes suspended by mandatory locking */
487 #define FL_LOCKD        16      /* lock held by rpc.lockd */
488
489 /*
490  * The POSIX file lock owner is determined by
491  * the "struct files_struct" in the thread group
492  * (or NULL for no owner - BSD locks).
493  *
494  * Lockd stuffs a "host" pointer into this.
495  */
496 typedef struct files_struct *fl_owner_t;
497
498 struct file_lock {
499         struct file_lock *fl_next;      /* singly linked list for this inode  */
500         struct file_lock *fl_nextlink;  /* doubly linked list of all locks */
501         struct file_lock *fl_prevlink;  /* used to simplify lock removal */
502         struct file_lock *fl_nextblock; /* circular list of blocked processes */
503         struct file_lock *fl_prevblock;
504         fl_owner_t fl_owner;
505         unsigned int fl_pid;
506         wait_queue_head_t fl_wait;
507         struct file *fl_file;
508         unsigned char fl_flags;
509         unsigned char fl_type;
510         loff_t fl_start;
511         loff_t fl_end;
512
513         void (*fl_notify)(struct file_lock *);  /* unblock callback */
514         void (*fl_insert)(struct file_lock *);  /* lock insertion callback */
515         void (*fl_remove)(struct file_lock *);  /* lock removal callback */
516
517         union {
518                 struct nfs_lock_info    nfs_fl;
519         } fl_u;
520 };
521
522 /* The following constant reflects the upper bound of the file/locking space */
523 #ifndef OFFSET_MAX
524 #define INT_LIMIT(x)    (~((x)1 << (sizeof(x)*8 - 1)))
525 #define OFFSET_MAX      INT_LIMIT(loff_t)
526 #endif
527
528 extern struct file_lock                 *file_lock_table;
529
530 #include <linux/fcntl.h>
531
532 extern int fcntl_getlk(unsigned int, struct flock *);
533 extern int fcntl_setlk(unsigned int, unsigned int, struct flock *);
534
535 /* fs/locks.c */
```

```
536 extern void locks_remove_posix(struct file *, fl_owner_t);
537 extern void locks_remove_flock(struct file *);
538 extern struct file_lock *posix_test_lock(struct file *, struct file_lock *);
539 extern int posix_lock_file(struct file *, struct file_lock *, unsigned int);
540 extern void posix_block_lock(struct file_lock *, struct file_lock *);
541 extern void posix_unblock_lock(struct file_lock *);
542
543 struct fasync_struct {
544         int     magic;
545         int     fa_fd;
546         struct  fasync_struct   *fa_next; /* singly linked list */
547         struct  file            *fa_file;
548 };
549
550 struct nameidata {
551         struct dentry *dentry;
552         struct vfsmount *mnt;
553         struct qstr last;
554 };
555
556 #define FASYNC_MAGIC 0x4601
557
558 extern int fasync_helper(int, struct file *, int, struct fasync_struct **);
559
560 #define DQUOT_USR_ENABLED       0x01    /* User diskquotas enabled */
561 #define DQUOT_GRP_ENABLED       0x02    /* Group diskquotas enabled */
562
563 struct quota_mount_options
564 {
565         unsigned int flags;             /* Flags for diskquotas on this device */
566         struct semaphore dqio_sem;      /* lock device while I/O in progress */
567         struct semaphore dqoff_sem;     /* serialize quota_off() and quota_on()
                                               on device */
568         struct file *files[MAXQUOTAS];  /* fp's to quotafiles */
569         time_t inode_expire[MAXQUOTAS]; /* expiretime for inode-quota */
570         time_t block_expire[MAXQUOTAS]; /* expiretime for block-quota */
571         char rsquash[MAXQUOTAS];        /* for quotas threat root as any other
                                               user */
572 };
573
574 /*
575  *      Umount options
576  */
577
578 #define MNT_FORCE       0x00000001      /* Attempt to forcibily umount */
579
580 #include <linux/minix_fs_sb.h>
581 #include <linux/ext2_fs_sb.h>
582 #include <linux/hpfs_fs_sb.h>
583 #include <linux/ntfs_fs_sb.h>
584 #include <linux/msdos_fs_sb.h>
585 #include <linux/iso_fs_sb.h>
586 #include <linux/nfs_fs_sb.h>
587 #include <linux/sysv_fs_sb.h>
```

```
588 #include <linux/affs_fs_sb.h>
589 #include <linux/ufs_fs_sb.h>
590 #include <linux/efs_fs_sb.h>
591 #include <linux/romfs_fs_sb.h>
592 #include <linux/smb_fs_sb.h>
593 #include <linux/hfs_fs_sb.h>
594 #include <linux/adfs_fs_sb.h>
595 #include <linux/qnx4_fs_sb.h>
596 #include <linux/bfs_fs_sb.h>
597 #include <linux/udf_fs_sb.h>
598 #include <linux/ncp_fs_sb.h>
599 #include <linux/usbdev_fs_sb.h>
600
601 extern struct list_head super_blocks;
602
603 #define sb_entry(list)  list_entry((list), struct super_block, s_list)
604 struct super_block {
605         struct list_head        s_list;         /* Keep this first */
606         kdev_t                  s_dev;
607         unsigned long           s_blocksize;
608         unsigned char           s_blocksize_bits;
609         unsigned char           s_lock;
610         unsigned char           s_dirt;
611         struct file_system_type *s_type;
612         struct super_operations *s_op;
613         struct dquot_operations *dq_op;
614         unsigned long           s_flags;
615         unsigned long           s_magic;
616         struct dentry           *s_root;
617         wait_queue_head_t       s_wait;
618
619         struct list_head        s_dirty;        /* dirty inodes */
620         struct list_head        s_files;
621
622         struct block_device     *s_bdev;
623         struct quota_mount_options s_dquot;     /* Diskquota specific options */
624
625         union {
626                 struct minix_sb_info    minix_sb;
627                 struct ext2_sb_info     ext2_sb;
628                 struct hpfs_sb_info     hpfs_sb;
629                 struct ntfs_sb_info     ntfs_sb;
630                 struct msdos_sb_info    msdos_sb;
631                 struct isofs_sb_info    isofs_sb;
632                 struct nfs_sb_info      nfs_sb;
633                 struct sysv_sb_info     sysv_sb;
634                 struct affs_sb_info     affs_sb;
635                 struct ufs_sb_info      ufs_sb;
636                 struct efs_sb_info      efs_sb;
637                 struct romfs_sb_info    romfs_sb;
638                 struct smb_sb_info      smbfs_sb;
639                 struct hfs_sb_info      hfs_sb;
640                 struct adfs_sb_info     adfs_sb;
641                 struct qnx4_sb_info     qnx4_sb;
```

```
642                struct bfs_sb_info      bfs_sb;
643                struct udf_sb_info      udf_sb;
644                struct ncp_sb_info      ncpfs_sb;
645                struct usbdev_sb_info   usbdevfs_sb;
646                void                    *generic_sbp;
647      } u;
648      /*
649       * The next field is for VFS *only*. No filesystems have any business
650       * even looking at it. You had been warned.
651       */
652    struct semaphore s_vfs_rename_sem;        /* Kludge */
653
654      /* The next field is used by knfsd when converting a (inode number based)
655       * file handle into a dentry. As it builds a path in the dcache tree from
656       * the bottom up, there may for a time be a subpath of dentrys which is not
657       * connected to the main tree. This semaphore ensure that there is only ever
658       * one such free path per filesystem. Note that unconnected files (or other
659       * non-directories) are allowed, but not unconnected diretories.
660       */
661      struct semaphore s_nfsd_free_path_sem;
662 };
663
664 /*
665  * VFS helper functions..
666  */
667 extern int vfs_create(struct inode *, struct dentry *, int);
668 extern int vfs_mkdir(struct inode *, struct dentry *, int);
669 extern int vfs_mknod(struct inode *, struct dentry *, int, dev_t);
670 extern int vfs_symlink(struct inode *, struct dentry *, const char *);
671 extern int vfs_link(struct dentry *, struct inode *, struct dentry *);
672 extern int vfs_rmdir(struct inode *, struct dentry *);
673 extern int vfs_unlink(struct inode *, struct dentry *);
674 extern int vfs_rename(struct inode *, struct dentry *, struct inode *, struct
         dentry *);
675
676 /*
677  * This is the "filldir" function type, used by readdir() to let
678  * the kernel specify what kind of dirent layout it wants to have.
679  * This allows the kernel to read directories into kernel space or
680  * to have different dirent layouts depending on the binary type.
681  */
682 typedef int (*filldir_t)(void *, const char *, int, off_t, ino_t);
683
684 struct block_device_operations {
685         int (*open) (struct inode *, struct file *);
686         int (*release) (struct inode *, struct file *);
687         int (*ioctl) (struct inode *, struct file *, unsigned, unsigned long);
688         int (*check_media_change) (kdev_t);
689         int (*revalidate) (kdev_t);
690 };
691
692 struct file_operations {
693         loff_t (*llseek) (struct file *, loff_t, int);
694         ssize_t (*read) (struct file *, char *, size_t, loff_t *);
```

```
695          ssize_t (*write) (struct file *, const char *, size_t, loff_t *);
696          int (*readdir) (struct file *, void *, filldir_t);
697          unsigned int (*poll) (struct file *, struct poll_table_struct *);
698          int (*ioctl) (struct inode *, struct file *, unsigned int, unsigned
                 long);
699          int (*mmap) (struct file *, struct vm_area_struct *);
700          int (*open) (struct inode *, struct file *);
701          int (*flush) (struct file *);
702          int (*release) (struct inode *, struct file *);
703          int (*fsync) (struct file *, struct dentry *);
704          int (*fasync) (int, struct file *, int);
705          int (*lock) (struct file *, int, struct file_lock *);
706          ssize_t (*readv) (struct file *, const struct iovec *, unsigned long,
                 loff_t *);
707          ssize_t (*writev) (struct file *, const struct iovec *, unsigned long,
                 loff_t *);
708 };
709
710 struct inode_operations {
711          int (*create) (struct inode *,struct dentry *,int);
712          struct dentry * (*lookup) (struct inode *,struct dentry *);
713          int (*link) (struct dentry *,struct inode *,struct dentry *);
714          int (*unlink) (struct inode *,struct dentry *);
715          int (*symlink) (struct inode *,struct dentry *,const char *);
716          int (*mkdir) (struct inode *,struct dentry *,int);
717          int (*rmdir) (struct inode *,struct dentry *);
718          int (*mknod) (struct inode *,struct dentry *,int,int);
719          int (*rename) (struct inode *, struct dentry *,
720                          struct inode *, struct dentry *);
721          int (*readlink) (struct dentry *, char *,int);
722          int (*follow_link) (struct dentry *, struct nameidata *);
723          void (*truncate) (struct inode *);
724          int (*permission) (struct inode *, int);
725          int (*revalidate) (struct dentry *);
726          int (*setattr) (struct dentry *, struct iattr *);
727          int (*getattr) (struct dentry *, struct iattr *);
728 };
729
730 /*
731  * NOTE: write_inode, delete_inode, clear_inode, put_inode can be called
732  * without the big kernel lock held in all filesystems.
733  */
734 struct super_operations {
735          void (*read_inode) (struct inode *);
736          void (*write_inode) (struct inode *);
737          void (*put_inode) (struct inode *);
738          void (*delete_inode) (struct inode *);
739          void (*put_super) (struct super_block *);
740          void (*write_super) (struct super_block *);
741          int (*statfs) (struct super_block *, struct statfs *);
742          int (*remount_fs) (struct super_block *, int *, char *);
743          void (*clear_inode) (struct inode *);
744          void (*umount_begin) (struct super_block *);
745 };
```

```
746
747 struct dquot_operations {
748         void (*initialize) (struct inode *, short);
749         void (*drop) (struct inode *);
750         int (*alloc_block) (const struct inode *, unsigned long, char);
751         int (*alloc_inode) (const struct inode *, unsigned long);
752         void (*free_block) (const struct inode *, unsigned long);
753         void (*free_inode) (const struct inode *, unsigned long);
754         int (*transfer) (struct dentry *, struct iattr *);
755 };
756
757 struct file_system_type {
758         const char *name;
759         int fs_flags;
760         struct super_block *(*read_super) (struct super_block *, void *, int);
751         struct module *owner;
752         struct file_system_type * next;
763 };
764
765 #define DECLARE_FSTYPE(var,type,read,flags) \
766 struct file_system_type var = { \
767         name:           type, \
768         read_super:     read, \
769         fs_flags:       flags, \
770         owner:          THIS_MODULE, \
771 }
772
773 #define DECLARE_FSTYPE_DEV(var,type,read) \
774         DECLARE_FSTYPE(var,type,read,FS_REQUIRES_DEV)
775
776 extern int register_filesystem(struct file_system_type *);
777 extern int unregister_filesystem(struct file_system_type *);
778
779 static inline int vfs_statfs(struct super_block *sb, struct statfs *buf)
780 {
781         if (!sb)
782                 return -ENODEV;
783         if (!sb->s_op || !sb->s_op->statfs)
784                 return -ENOSYS;
785         memset(buf, 0, sizeof(struct statfs));
786         return sb->s_op->statfs(sb, buf);
787 }
788
789 /* Return value for VFS lock functions - tells locks.c to lock conventionally
790  * REALLY kosha for root NFS and nfs_lock
791  */
792 #define LOCK_USE_CLNT 1
793
794 #define FLOCK_VERIFY_READ   1
795 #define FLOCK_VERIFY_WRITE 2
796
797 extern int locks_mandatory_locked(struct inode *);
798 extern int locks_mandatory_area(int, struct inode *, struct file *, loff_t,
          size_t);
```

```
799
800 /*
801  * Candidates for mandatory locking have the setgid bit set
802  * but no group execute bit -  an otherwise meaningless combination.
803  */
804 #define MANDATORY_LOCK(inode) \
805         (IS_MANDLOCK(inode) && ((inode)->i_mode & (S_ISGID | S_IXGRP)) ==
S_ISGID)
806
807 static inline int locks_verify_locked(struct inode *inode)
808 {
809         if (MANDATORY_LOCK(inode))
810                 return locks_mandatory_locked(inode);
811         return 0;
812 }
813
814 extern inline int locks_verify_area(int read_write, struct inode *inode,
815                                     struct file *filp, loff_t offset,
816                                     size_t count)
817 {
818         if (inode->i_flock && MANDATORY_LOCK(inode))
819                 return locks_mandatory_area(read_write, inode, filp, offset,
count);
820         return 0;
821 }
822
823 extern inline int locks_verify_truncate(struct inode *inode,
824                                     struct file *filp,
825                                     loff_t size)
826 {
827         if (inode->i_flock && MANDATORY_LOCK(inode))
828                 return locks_mandatory_area(
829                         FLOCK_VERIFY_WRITE, inode, filp,
830                         size < inode->i_size ? size : inode->i_size,
831                         abs(inode->i_size - size)
832                 );
833         return 0;
834 }
835
836
837 /* fs/open.c */
838
839 asmlinkage long sys_open(const char *, int, int);
840 asmlinkage long sys_close(unsigned int);          /* yes, it's really unsigned */
841 extern int do_close(unsigned int, int);           /* yes, it's really unsigned */
842 extern int do_truncate(struct dentry *, loff_t start);
843 extern int get_unused_fd(void);
844 extern void put_unused_fd(unsigned int);
845
846 extern struct file *filp_open(const char *, int, int);
847 extern struct file * dentry_open(struct dentry *, struct vfsmount *, int);
848 extern int filp_close(struct file *, fl_owner_t id);
849 extern char * getname(const char *);
850 #define __getname()       ((char *) __get_free_page(GFP_KERNEL))
```

```
851 #define putname(name)     free_page((unsigned long)(name))
852
853 enum {BDEV_FILE, BDEV_SWAP, BDEV_FS, BDEV_RAW};
854 extern void kill_fasync(struct fasync_struct *, int, int);
855 extern int register_blkdev(unsigned int, const char *,
            struct block_device_operations *);
856 extern int unregister_blkdev(unsigned int, const char *);
857 extern struct block_device *bdget(dev_t);
858 extern void bdput(struct block_device *);
859 extern int blkdev_open(struct inode *, struct file *);
860 extern struct file_operations def_blk_fops;
861 extern struct file_operations def_fifo_fops;
862 extern int ioctl_by_bdev(struct block_device *, unsigned, unsigned long);
863 extern int blkdev_get(struct block_device *, mode_t, unsigned, int);
864 extern int blkdev_put(struct block_device *, int);
865
866 /* fs/devices.c */
867 extern const struct block_device_operations *get_blkfops(unsigned int);
868 extern struct file_operations *get_chrfops(unsigned int, unsigned int);
869 extern int register_chrdev(unsigned int, const char *, struct file_operations *);
870 extern int unregister_chrdev(unsigned int, const char *);
871 extern int chrdev_open(struct inode *, struct file *);
872 extern const char * bdevname(kdev_t);
873 extern const char * cdevname(kdev_t);
874 extern const char * kdevname(kdev_t);
875 extern void init_special_inode(struct inode *, umode_t, int);
876
877 /* Invalid inode operations -- fs/bad_inode.c */
878 extern void make_bad_inode(struct inode *);
879 extern int is_bad_inode(struct inode *);
880
881 extern struct file_operations connecting_fifo_fops;
882 extern struct file_operations read_fifo_fops;
883 extern struct file_operations write_fifo_fops;
884 extern struct file_operations rdwr_fifo_fops;
885 extern struct file_operations read_pipe_fops;
886 extern struct file_operations write_pipe_fops;
887 extern struct file_operations rdwr_pipe_fops;
888
889 extern int fs_may_remount_ro(struct super_block *);
890 extern int fs_may_mount(kdev_t);
891
892 extern int try_to_free_buffers(struct page *);
893 extern void refile_buffer(struct buffer_head * buf);
894
895 #define BUF_CLEAN         0
896 #define BUF_LOCKED        1          /* Buffers scheduled for write */
897 #define BUF_DIRTY         2          /* Dirty buffers, not yet scheduled for write */
898 #define BUF_PROTECTED     3          /* Ramdisk persistent storage */
899 #define NR_LIST           4
900
901 /*
902  * This is called by bh->b_end_io() handlers when I/O has completed.
903  */
```

```
904 extern inline void mark_buffer_uptodate(struct buffer_head * bh, int on)
905 {
906         if (on)
907                 set_bit(BH_Uptodate, &bh->b_state);
908         else
909                 clear_bit(BH_Uptodate, &bh->b_state);
910 }
911
912 #define atomic_set_buffer_clean(bh) test_and_clear_bit(BH_Dirty, &(bh)->b_state)
913
914 extern inline void __mark_buffer_clean(struct buffer_head *bh)
915 {
916         refile_buffer(bh);
917 }
918
919 extern inline void mark_buffer_clean(struct buffer_head * bh)
920 {
921         if (atomic_set_buffer_clean(bh))
922                 __mark_buffer_clean(bh);
923 }
924
925 #define atomic_set_buffer_protected(bh) test_and_set_bit(BH_Protected,
        &(bh)->b_state)
926
927 extern inline void __mark_buffer_protected(struct buffer_head *bh)
928 {
929         refile_buffer(bh);
930 }
931
932 extern inline void mark_buffer_protected(struct buffer_head * bh)
933 {
934         if (!atomic_set_buffer_protected(bh))
935                 __mark_buffer_protected(bh);
936 }
937
938 extern void FASTCALL(__mark_buffer_dirty(struct buffer_head *bh, int flag));
939 extern void FASTCALL(mark_buffer_dirty(struct buffer_head *bh, int flag));
940
941 #define atomic_set_buffer_dirty(bh) test_and_set_bit(BH_Dirty, &(bh)->b_state)
942
943 extern void balance_dirty(kdev_t);
944 extern int check_disk_change(kdev_t);
945 extern int invalidate_inodes(struct super_block *);
946 extern void invalidate_inode_pages(struct inode *);
947 #define invalidate_buffers(dev) __invalidate_buffers((dev), 0)
948 #define destroy_buffers(dev)    __invalidate_buffers((dev), 1)
949 extern void __invalidate_buffers(kdev_t dev, int);
950 extern int floppy_is_wp(int);
951 extern void sync_inodes(kdev_t);
952 extern void write_inode_now(struct inode *);
953 extern void sync_dev(kdev_t);
954 extern int fsync_dev(kdev_t);
955 extern void sync_supers(kdev_t);
956 extern int bmap(struct inode *, int);
```

```
957 extern int notify_change(struct dentry *, struct iattr *);
958 extern int permission(struct inode *, int);
959 extern int get_write_access(struct inode *);
960 extern void put_write_access(struct inode *);
961 extern struct dentry * do_mknod(const char *, int, dev_t);
962 extern int do_pipe(int *);
963
964 extern int open_namei(const char *, int, int, struct nameidata *);
965
966 extern int kernel_read(struct file *, unsigned long, char *, unsigned long);
967 extern struct file * open_exec(const char *);
968
969 /* fs/dcache.c -- generic fs support functions */
970 extern int is_subdir(struct dentry *, struct dentry *);
971 extern ino_t find_inode_number(struct dentry *, struct qstr *);
972
973 /*
974  * Kernel pointers have redundant information, so we can use a
975  * scheme where we can return either an error code or a dentry
976  * pointer with the same return value.
977  *
978  * This should be a per-architecture thing, to allow different
979  * error and pointer decisions.
980  */
981 #define ERR_PTR(err)    ((void *)((long)(err)))
982 #define PTR_ERR(ptr)    ((long)(ptr))
983 #define IS_ERR(ptr)     ((unsigned long)(ptr) > (unsigned long)(-1000))
984
985 /*
986  * The bitmask for a lookup event:
987  *  - follow links at the end
988  *  - require a directory
989  *  - ending slashes ok even for nonexistent files
990  *  - internal "there are more path compnents" flag
991  */
992 #define LOOKUP_FOLLOW              (1)
993 #define LOOKUP_DIRECTORY           (2)
994 #define LOOKUP_SLASHOK             (4)
995 #define LOOKUP_CONTINUE            (8)
996 #define LOOKUP_POSITIVE            (16)
997 #define LOOKUP_PARENT              (32)
998
999 /*
1000  * "descriptor" for what we're up to with a read for sendfile().
1001  * This allows us to use the same read code yet
1002  * have multiple different users of the data that
1003  * we read from a file.
1004  *
1005  * The simplest case just copies the data to user
1006  * mode.
1007  */
1008 typedef struct {
1009         size_t written;
1010         size_t count;
```

```
1011          char * buf;
1012          int error;
1013 } read_descriptor_t;
1014
1015 typedef int (*read_actor_t)(read_descriptor_t *, struct page *, unsigned long,
unsigned long);
1016
1017 extern struct dentry * lookup_dentry(const char *, unsigned int);
1018 extern int walk_init(const char *, unsigned, struct nameidata *);
1019 extern int walk_name(const char *, unsigned, struct nameidata *);
1020 extern struct dentry * lookup_one(const char *, struct dentry *);
1021 extern struct dentry * __namei(const char *, unsigned int);
1022
1023 #define namei(pathname)          __namei(pathname, LOOKUP_FOLLOW)
1024 #define lnamei(pathname)         __namei(pathname, 0)
1025
1026 extern void iput(struct inode *);
1027 extern struct inode * igrab(struct inode *);
1028 extern ino_t iunique(struct super_block *, ino_t);
1029
1030 typedef int (*find_inode_t)(struct inode *, unsigned long, void *);
1031 extern struct inode * iget4(struct super_block *, unsigned long, find_inode_t,
void *);
1032 static inline struct inode *iget(struct super_block *sb, unsigned long ino)
1033 {
1034          return iget4(sb, ino, NULL, NULL);
1035 }
1036
1037 extern void clear_inode(struct inode *);
1038 extern struct inode * get_empty_inode(void);
1039
1040 extern void insert_inode_hash(struct inode *);
1041 extern void remove_inode_hash(struct inode *);
1042 extern struct file * get_empty_filp(void);
1043 extern void file_move(struct file *f, struct list_head *list);
1044 extern void file_moveto(struct file *new, struct file *old);
1045 extern struct buffer_head * get_hash_table(kdev_t, int, int);
1046 extern struct buffer_head * getblk(kdev_t, int, int);
1047 extern void ll_rw_block(int, int, struct buffer_head * bh[]);
1048 extern int is_read_only(kdev_t);
1049 extern void __brelse(struct buffer_head *);
1050 extern inline void brelse(struct buffer_head *buf)
1051 {
1052          if (buf)
1053                  __brelse(buf);
1054 }
1055 extern void __bforget(struct buffer_head *);
1056 extern inline void bforget(struct buffer_head *buf)
1057 {
1058          if (buf)
1059                  __bforget(buf);
1060 }
1061 extern void set_blocksize(kdev_t, int);
1062 extern unsigned int get_hardblocksize(kdev_t);
```

```
1063 extern struct buffer_head * bread(kdev_t, int, int);
1064 extern struct buffer_head * breada(kdev_t, int, int, unsigned int, unsigned
int);
1065 extern void wakeup_bdflush(int wait);
1066
1067 extern int brw_page(int, struct page *, kdev_t, int [], int);
1068
1069 typedef int (*writepage_t)(struct file *, struct page *, unsigned long,
              unsigned long, const char *);
1070 typedef int (get_block_t)(struct inode*,long,struct buffer_head*,int);
1071
1072 /* Generic buffer handling for block filesystems.. */
1073 extern int block_flushpage(struct page *, unsigned long);
1074 extern int block_symlink(struct inode *, const char *, int);
1075 extern int block_write_full_page(struct page*, get_block_t*);
1076 extern int block_read_full_page(struct page*, get_block_t*);
1077 extern int block_prepare_write(struct page*, unsigned, unsigned, get_block_t*);
1078 extern int cont_prepare_write(struct page*, unsigned, unsigned, get_block_t*,
1079                                     unsigned long *);
1080 int generic_block_bmap(struct address_space *, long, get_block_t *);
1081 int generic_commit_write(struct file *, struct page *, unsigned, unsigned);
1082
1083 extern int generic_file_mmap(struct file *, struct vm_area_struct *);
1084 extern ssize_t generic_file_read(struct file *, char *, size_t, loff_t *);
1085 extern ssize_t generic_file_write(struct file *, const char *, size_t, loff_t *);
1086 extern void do_generic_file_read(struct file *, loff_t *, read_descriptor_t *,
              read_actor_t);
1087
1088 extern ssize_t generic_read_dir(struct file *, char *, size_t, loff_t *);
1089
1090 extern struct file_operations generic_ro_fops;
1091
1092 extern int vfs_readlink(struct dentry *, char *, int, const char *);
1093 extern int vfs_follow_link(struct nameidata *, const char *);
1094 extern int page_readlink(struct dentry *, char *, int);
1095 extern int page_follow_link(struct dentry *, struct nameidata *);
1096 extern struct inode_operations page_symlink_inode_operations;
1097
1098 extern int vfs_readdir(struct file *, filldir_t, void *);
1099
1100 extern struct super_block *get_super(kdev_t);
1101 struct super_block *get_empty_super(void);
1102 void remove_vfsmnt(kdev_t dev);
1103 extern void put_super(kdev_t);
1104 unsigned long generate_cluster(kdev_t, int b[], int);
1105 unsigned long generate_cluster_swab32(kdev_t, int b[], int);
1106 extern kdev_t ROOT_DEV;
1107 extern char root_device_name[];
1108
1109
1110 extern void show_buffers(void);
1111 extern void mount_root(void);
1112
1113 #ifdef CONFIG_BLK_DEV_INITRD
```

```
1114 extern kdev_t real_root_dev;
1115 extern int change_root(kdev_t, const char *);
1116 #endif
1117
1118 extern ssize_t char_read(struct file *, char *, size_t, loff_t *);
1119 extern ssize_t block_read(struct file *, char *, size_t, loff_t *);
1120 extern int read_ahead[];
1121
1122 extern ssize_t char_write(struct file *, const char *, size_t, loff_t *);
1123 extern ssize_t block_write(struct file *, const char *, size_t, loff_t *);
1124
1125 extern int file_fsync(struct file *, struct dentry *);
1126 extern int generic_buffer_fdatasync(struct inode *inode, unsigned long
          start_idx, unsigned long end_idx);
1127
1128 extern int inode_change_ok(struct inode *, struct iattr *);
1129 extern void inode_setattr(struct inode *, struct iattr *);
1130
1131 /*
1132  * Common dentry functions for inclusion in the VFS
1133  * or in other stackable file systems. Some of these
1134  * functions were in linux/fs/ C (VFS) files.
1135  *
1136  */
1137
1138 /*
1139  * We need to do a check-parent every time
1140  * after we have locked the parent - to verify
1141  * that the parent is still our parent and
1142  * that we are still hashed onto it..
1143  *
1144  * This is required in case two processes race
1145  * on removing (or moving) the same entry: the
1146  * parent lock will serialize them, but the
1147  * other process will be too late..
1148  */
1149 #define check_parent(dir, dentry) \
1150         ((dir) == (dentry)->d_parent && !d_unhashed(dentry))
1151
1152 /*
1153  * Locking the parent is needed to:
1154  *  - serialize directory operations
1155  *  - make sure the parent doesn't change from
1156  *    under us in the middle of an operation.
1157  *
1158  * NOTE! Right now we'd rather use a "struct inode"
1159  * for this, but as I expect things to move toward
1160  * using dentries instead for most things it is
1161  * probably better to start with the conceptually
1162  * better interface of relying on a path of dentries.
1163  */
1164 static inline struct dentry *lock_parent(struct dentry *dentry)
1165 {
1166         struct dentry *dir = dget(dentry->d_parent);
```

```
1167
1168            down(&dir->d_inode->i_sem);
1169            return dir;
1170  }
1171
1172  static inline struct dentry *get_parent(struct dentry *dentry)
1173  {
1174            return dget(dentry->d_parent);
1175  }
1176
1177  static inline void unlock_dir(struct dentry *dir)
1178  {
1179            up(&dir->d_inode->i_sem);
1180            dput(dir);
1181  }
1182
1183  /*
1184   * Whee.. Deadlock country. Happily there are only two VFS
1185   * operations that does this..
1186   */
1187  static inline void double_down(struct semaphore *s1, struct semaphore *s2)
1188  {
1189            if (s1 != s2) {
1190                    if ((unsigned long) s1 < (unsigned long) s2) {
1191                            struct semaphore *tmp = s2;
1192                            s2 = s1; s1 = tmp;
1193                    }
1194                    down(s1);
1195            }
1196            down(s2);
1197  }
1198
1199  /*
1200   * Ewwwwwwww... _triple_ lock. We are guaranteed that the 3rd argument is
1201   * not equal to 1st and not equal to 2nd - the first case (target is parent of
1202   * source) would be already caught, the second is plain impossible (target is
1203   * its own parent and that case would be caught even earlier). Very messy.
1204   * I _think_ that it works, but no warranties - please, look it through.
1205   * Pox on bloody lusers who mandated overwriting rename() for directories...
1206   */
1207
1208  static inline void triple_down(struct semaphore *s1,
1209                                  struct semaphore *s2,
1210                                  struct semaphore *s3)
1211  {
1212            if (s1 != s2) {
1213                    if ((unsigned long) s1 < (unsigned long) s2) {
1214                            if ((unsigned long) s1 < (unsigned long) s3) {
1215                                    struct semaphore *tmp = s3;
1216                                    s3 = s1; s1 = tmp;
1217                            }
1218                            if ((unsigned long) s1 < (unsigned long) s2) {
1219                                    struct semaphore *tmp = s2;
1220                                    s2 = s1; s1 = tmp;
```

```
1221                              }
1222                      } else {
1223                              if ((unsigned long) s1 < (unsigned long) s3) {
1224                                      struct semaphore *tmp = s3;
1225                                      s3 = s1; s1 = tmp;
1226                              }
1227                              if ((unsigned long) s2 < (unsigned long) s3) {
1228                                      struct semaphore *tmp = s3;
1229                                      s3 = s2; s2 = tmp;
1230                              }
1231                      }
1232                      down(s1);
1233              } else if ((unsigned long) s2 < (unsigned long) s3) {
1234                      struct semaphore *tmp = s3;
1235                      s3 = s2; s2 = tmp;
1236              }
1237              down(s2);
1238              down(s3);
1239 }
1240
1241 static inline void double_up(struct semaphore *s1, struct semaphore *s2)
1242 {
1243              up(s1);
1244              if (s1 != s2)
1245                      up(s2);
1246 }
1247
1248 static inline void triple_up(struct semaphore *s1,
1249                              struct semaphore *s2,
1250                              struct semaphore *s3)
1251 {
1252              up(s1);
1253              if (s1 != s2)
1254                      up(s2);
1255              up(s3);
1256 }
1257
1258 static inline void double_lock(struct dentry *d1, struct dentry *d2)
1259 {
1260              double_down(&d1->d_inode->i_sem, &d2->d_inode->i_sem);
1261 }
1262
1263 static inline void double_unlock(struct dentry *d1, struct dentry *d2)
1264 {
1265              double_up(&d1->d_inode->i_sem,&d2->d_inode->i_sem);
1266              dput(d1);
1267              dput(d2);
1268 }
1269
1270 #endif /* __KERNEL__ */
1271
1272 #endif /* _LINUX_FS_H */
```

APPENDIX A

Bibliography

Corbató, F. J., and V. A. Vyssotsky, "Introduction and overview of the Multics system," (54K).

Glaser, E. L., J. F. Couleur, and G. A. Oliver, "System design of a computer for time-sharing applications," (26K).

Vyssotsky, V. A., F. J. Corbató, and R. M. Graham, "Structure of the Multics Supervisor," (45K).

Daley, R. C., and P. G. Neumann, "A general-purpose file system for secondary storage," (66K, 3 figures).

Ossanna, J. F., L. Mikus, and S. D. Dunten, "Communications and input-output switching in a multiplexed computing system," (39K, 3 figures).

Many other papers followed. Here are the ones available online.

Andre Bensoussan, Charlie Clingen, and Bob Daley presented the paper "The Multics virtual memory: concepts and design" at the Second ACM Symposium on Operating systems Principles in Princeton NJ, in October 1969; the paper was subsequently reprinted in the Communications of the ACM in 1972. (54K, 6 figures).

Corby, Charlie Clingen, and Jerry Saltzer presented our experience as of 1972 in "Multics—the first seven years," at the 1972 Spring Joint Computer Conference. (59K, 3 figures).

Charlie Clingen and I described "The Multics system programming process" in an invited paper for COMPCON 78. This paper describes how system changes were managed and controlled, and what we did to make the system high quality. (17K, 1 figure).

Paul Green has written a detailed description of the *Multics Virtual Memory*, and made it available online.

Papers and Books

N. Adleman, *Effects of Producing a Multics Security Kernel*, Honeywell Information Systems Inc., McLean, VA, Federal Systems Operations (NTIS AD-A031 220/7), October 1975.

N. Adleman, *Engineering Investigations in Support of Multics Security Kernel Software Development*, Honeywell Information Systems Inc.,

McLean, VA, Federal Systems Operations (NTIS AD-A040 329/5), October 19, 1976.

N. Adleman, J. R. Gilson, R. J. Sestak, and R. J. Ziller, *Security Kernel Evaluation for Multics and Secure Multics Design, Development and Certification, Semi-annual Progress Report, 1 Jan–30 June 76*, Honeywell Information Systems Inc., McLean, VA, Federal Systems Operations (NTIS AD-A038 261/4), August 1976.

N. Adleman, J. R. Gilson, R. J. Sestak, and R. J. Ziller, *Semi-Annual Progress Report July 1975 to December 1975*. Honeywell Information Systems Inc., McLean, VA, Federal Systems Operations (NTIS AD-A037 501/4), January 1976.

N. Adleman, R. J. Ziller, and J. C. Whitmore, *Multics Security Integration Requirements, 1 January 1976–31 December 1980*, Honeywell Information Systems Inc., McLean, VA, Federal Systems Operations (NTIS AD-A041 514/1), March 1976.

S. R. Ames, Jr. and D. K. Kallman, *Multics Security Kernel Validation: Proof Description*, Vol. 1, Mitre Corp., Bedford, MA (NTIS AD-A056 901/2), July 1978.

S. R. Ames, Jr. and J. G. Keeton-Williams, "Demonstrating security for trusted applications on a security kernel base," *IEEE Comp. Soc. Proc 1980 Symposium on Security and Privacy*, April 1980.

S. R. Ames, Jr. and J. K. Millen, *Interface Verification for a Security Kernel, System Reliability and Integrity*, Vol. 2, Infotech State of the Art report, 1-21, 1978.

A. Bensoussan, C. T. Clingen, and R. C. Daley, "The multics virtual memory: concepts and design," *Proc Second ACM SOSP*, Princeton, NJ, October 1969; *Commun. ACM* 15, 5, pp. 308–318, May 1972.

D. E. Bell, and L. J. LaPadula, *Computer Security Model: Unified Exposition and Multics Interpretation*, ESD-TR-75-306, Hanscom AFB, Bedford, MA, 1975 (also available as DTIC AD-A023588).

D. E. Bell, and L. J. LaPadula, *Secure Computer Systems: Unified Exposition and Multics Interpretation*, Mitre Technical Report MTR-2997, rev 2, March 1976 (also available as NTIS AD-A023 588/7).

J. Berstel, and J.-F. Perrot, *MULTICS: guide de l'usager*, Manuels Informatiques Masson, Paris, 1986.

K. J. Biba, S. R. Ames, Jr., E. L. Burke, P. A. Karger, W. R. Price, R. R. Schell, W. L. Schiller, *The Top Level Specification of a Multics Security Kernel*, WP-20377, Mitre Corp, Bedford, MA, August 1975.

D. Birnbaum, J. J. Cupak, J. D. Dyar, R. Jackson, *Multics Remote Data Entry System*. Volume I, Pattern Analysis and Recognition Corp., Rome, NY, Rome Air Development Center, Griffiss AFB, NY, NTIS, Oct. 1979.

I.I. Bisbey, L. Richard, J. Carlstedt, D. M. Chase, D. Hollingworth, *Data Dependency Analysis*, ISI-RR-76-45, USC Information Sciences Institute, February 1976 (NTIS: ADA 022017).

R. L. Bisbey and D. Hollingworth, *Protection Analysis: Final Report*, ISI-SR-78-13, USC Information Sciences Institute, July 1978 (NTIS: ADA 056816).

Bull HN Information Systems Inc., *Multics Data Security and Data Privacy*.

E. L. Burke, et al., *Emulating a Honeywell 6180 Computer System*, Mitre Corporation, AD 787 218, June 1974, 1–73.

C. T. Clingen, *Program Naming Problems in a Shared Tree-structured Hierarchy*, Proc. Conf. on Techniques in Software Engineering, October 1969.

A. W. Colijn, A note on the Multics command language, *Software—Practice and Experience* 11, 6, pp. 741–744, July 1981.

F. J. Corbató, *A Paging Experiment with the Multics System (In Honor of P. M. Morse)*, MIT Press, Cambridge, MA, 217–228, 1969.

F. J. Corbató, and C. T. Clingen, *A Managerial View of the Multics System Development*, in *Research Directions in Software Technology* (ed.), P. Wegner, M.I.T. Press, 1979, and in *Tutorial: Software Management*, D. J. Reifer, (ed), IEEE Computer Society Press, 1986.

F. J. Corbató, and J. H. Saltzer, "Some considerations of supervisor program design for multiplexed computer systems," *Proc. IFIP 4th Global Conf.*, Edinburgh, August 1968.

F. J. Corbató, and V. A. Vyssotsky, "Introduction and overview of the Multics system," *AFIPS Conf Proc 27*, 185–196, 1965.

F. J. Corbató, C. T. Clingen, and J. H. Saltzer, "Multics—the first seven years," *Proc SJCC*, 571–583, May 1972.

F. J. Corbató, M. M. Daggett, and R. C. Daley, "An experimental time-sharing system," *AFIPS Conf Proc 21*, 335–344, 1962.

F. J. Corbató, "PL/I as a tool for system programming," *Datamation 15*, 68–76, May 6, 1969.

F. J. Corbató, *Sensitive Issues in the Design of Multi-use Systems*, MIT Project MAC MAC-M-383, December 1968.

F. J.Corbató, "On building systems that will fail" (A. M. Turing Award lecture), *Commun. ACM 34* No. 9, September 1991.

J. F. Couleur and E. L. Glaser, US Patent No 3,412,382, Shared-access data processing system, filed November 26, 1965, awarded November 19, 1968.

J. F. Couleur, and R. F. Montee, US Patent No 4,300,192, Method and means for storing and accessing information in a shared access multi-programmed data processing system, ("New System Architecture" patent) filed November 14, 1978, awarded November 10, 1981.

J. F. Couleur, "The Core of the Black Canyon Computer Corporation," in *IEEE Annals of the History of Computing* 17, 4, Winter 1995, 56–60.

P. A. Crisman, (ed.), *The Compatible Time-sharing System: A Programmer's Guide*, 2nd ed., MIT Press, 1965.

R. C. Daley, and J. B. Dennis, "Virtual memory, processes, and sharing in Multics," *Commun. ACM 11*, 306–312, May 1968.

R. C. Daley, and P. G. Neumann, "A general-purpose file system for secondary storage," *AFIPS Conf Proc 27*, 212–230, 1965.

Datapro, *An Overview of Operating Systems Security*, Datapro IS56-001, *Datapro Reports on Information Security*, June 1986.

Datapro, *Bull HN Information Systems Inc: Security Capabilities of Multics*. Datapro IS56-115-101, *Datapro Reports on Information Security*; Vol 3, April 1989.

E. E. David, Jr. and R. M. Fano, "Some thoughts about the social implications of accessible computing," *AFIPS Conf Proc 27*, 243–248, 1965.

R. C. Davis, *A Security Compliance Study of the Air Force Data Services Center Multics System*, Mitre Corp., Bedford, MA, NTIS, December 1976.

P. J. Denning, "The working set model for program behavior," *Commun. ACM 11*, 5, 323–333, May 1968.

P. J. Denning, "Virtual memory," *Computing Surveys 2*, 3, 153–189, September 1970.

J. B. Dennis, "A multiuser computation facility for education and research," *Commun. ACM 7*, 521–529, September 1964.

J. B. Dennis, "Segmentation and the design of multiprogrammed computer systems," *IEEE Intl. Conv. Rec. 3*, 214–225, 1965.

L. P. Deutsch, and B. W. Lampson, "An online editor," (QED) *Commun. ACM 10*, 12, 793–799, December 1967.

D. S. Diamond, and L. L. Selwyn, "Considerations for computer utility pricing policies," *Proc. ACM 23d Natl. Conf.*, 189–200, 1968.

P. J. Downey, *Multics Security Evaluation: Password and File Encryption Techniques*, US Air Force, Electronic Systems Div., Hanscom AFB, Bedford, MA (NTIS AD-A045 279/7), June 1977.

R. M. Fano, and P. Elias, *Project MAC 25th Anniversary*, MIT LCS, 1989.

R. M. Fano, "The computer utility and the community," *IEEE Int. Conv. Rec. 12*, 30–37, 1967.

R. M. Fano, "The MAC system: The computer utility approach," *IEEE Spectrum 2*, 56–64, January 1965.

R. M. Fano, and F. J. Corbató, "Time-sharing on computers," *Scientific American 215*, 3, 129–140, September, 1966; also in *Information, A Scientific American Book*, W. H. Freeman & Co., 1966, 76–95.

R. M. Fano, "Project MAC," in *Encyclopedia of Computer Science and Technology*, Vol. 12, Marcel Dekker, Inc., New York and Basel, 1979.

R. J. Feiertag, and E. I. Organick, The Multics input/output system, *Proc. ACM Third SOSP*, 35–41, October 1971.

R. J. Feiertag, K. N. Levitt, and L. Robinson, "Proving multilevel security of a system design," *ACM Operating Systems Rev. 11*, 5; *Proc ACM 6th SOSP*, West Lafayette, IN, November 1977.

R. R. Fenichel, and J. C. Yochelson, "A LISP garbage collector for virtual memory computer systems," *Commun. ACM 12*, 611–612, 1969.

R. M. Frankston, *A Limited Service System on Multics* (S.B. thesis), MIT, June 1970.

R. M. Frankston, "Nonhistory of IBM Time-Sharing," (letter), *IEEE Ann. His. Computing 18*, 3: 72–73 Fall 1996.

R. A. Freiburghouse, A user's guide to the Multics FORTRAN compiler implementation, CISL, October 1969.

R. A. Freiburghouse, "The Multics PL/I compiler," *Proc. 1969 FJCC*, 187–199, 1969.

K. A. Frenkel, "An interview with Fernando José Corbató," *Commun. ACM 34,* 9, September 1991.

O. D. Friesen and J. A. Weeldreyer, "Multics integrated data store: an implementation of a network data base manager utilizing relational data base methodology," *Proc 11th Hawaii Intl. Conf. on System Sciences*, Vol. 1, 67–84, 1978.

O. D. Friesen, N.S. Davids, and R. E. Brinegar, *MRDS/LINUS: System Evaluation*, in *Relational Database Systems: Analysis and Comparison*, J. W. Schmidt and M. L. Brodie, (eds.), Springer-Verlag, Berlin 1983.

M. Gasser, *A Random Word Generator for Pronounceable Passwords*, MTR-3006, Mitre Corp., Bedford, MA, ESD-TR-75-97; HQ Electronic Systems Division, Hanscom AFB, MA.

M. Gasser, S. R. Ames, and L. J. Chmura, *Test Procedures for Multics Security Enhancements*, Mitre Corp., Bedford, MA, NTIS, December 1976.

D. Gifford, "Hardware estimation of a process's primary memory requirements," *Commun. ACM*, September 1977.

E. L. Glaser, "A brief description of privacy measures in the Multics operating system," *Proc AFIPS 1967 SJCC*, 303–304.

E. L. Glaser, J. F. Couleur, and G. A. Oliver, "System design of a computer for time-sharing applications," *AFIPS Conf Proc 27*, 197–202, 1965.

R. M. Graham, "Protection in an information processing utility," *Commun. ACM 11*, 5, 365–369, May 1968.

B. S. Greenberg, and S. H. Webber, "The Multics multilevel paging hierarchy," *Proc. 1975 IEEE Intercon.*, 1975.

J. M. Grochow, "MOO in Multics," *Software—Practice and Experience 2*, 303–308, 1972.

J. M. Grochow, "Real-time graphic display of time-sharing system operating characteristics," *AFIPS Conf. Proc. 35*, pp. 379–385, 1969.

H. Henderson and E. I. Organick, *Considerations in the Design of an Xds Sigma 7 Multics*, University of Texas, Department of Computer Science, NTIS, September, 1969.

K. B. Henningan, *Hardware Subverter for the Honeywell 6180*, ESD-TR-76-352, MTR-3280, Dec. 1976, 1–222.

J. Whitmore, A. Bensoussan, P. Green, D. Hunt, A. Kobziar, and J. Stern, *Design for Multics Security Enhancements*, ESD-TR-74-176, ESD AFSC Hanscom AFB, Bedford, MA, 1974.

Honeywell, *Multics Security Kernel Certification Plan*, Honeywell Information Systems Inc. McLean, VA Federal Systems Operations (NTIS AD-A055 171/3), July 1976.

K. Ikeda, *Structure of a Computer Utility: Anatomy of Multics* (in Japanese), 2nd ed., Shokoda Co. Ltd., Tokyo, 1976.

D. M. Jordan, "Multics Data Security," *Scientific Honeyweller 2*, 2, June 1981.

J. King, and W. A. Shelly, "A family history of honeywell's large-scale computer systems," *IEEE Annals of the History of Computing*, Vol. 19, No. 4, October/ December 1997.

R. D. Lackey, "Penetration of computer systems, an overview," *Honeywell Computer Journal 8*, 2, 1974.

C. E. Landwehr, "The best available technologies for computer security," *IEEE Computer 16*(7) 86–100, July 1983.

J. McCarthy, "A time-sharing operator program for our projected IBM 709," MIT Computation Center memo, 1959.

W. A. Montgomery, "Measurements of Sharing in Multics," *ACM Operating Systems Review 11*, 5; *Proc ACM 6th SOSP*, West Lafayette, IN, November 1977.

NCSC staff, *Department of Defense Trusted Computer System Evaluation Criteria*, DOD 5200.28-STD (the "Orange Book"), December 1985.

P. G. Neumann, "The role of motherhood in the pop art of system programming," *Proc. Second ACM SOSP*, October 1969.

M. M. Pozzo, "Life cycle assurance for trusted computer systems: a configuration management strategy for Multics," *7th DOD/NBS Computer Security Conf.*, September 1984.

E. Pugh, et al., IBMs 360 and early 370 systems.

D. M. Ritchie, "The evolution of the UNIX time-sharing system," *Bell System Technical Journal 63*, 8, Oct. 1984.

D. M. Ritchie, "The development of the C language," *ACM SIGPLAN Notices 28*, 3, 201–208 (ACM HOPL-II Conf.), March 1993.

T. Rus, *Data Structures and Operating Systems*, John Wiley & Sons, Chichester, 1979.

J. H. Saltzer, P. A. Janson, and D. H. Hunt, "Some Multics security holes which were closed by 6180 hardware," in *Patterns of Security Violations: Multiple References to Arguments*, H. C. Forsdick and D. P. Reed, (eds.), MIT, Cambridge, MA, 1975.

J. H. Saltzer, "A simple linear model of demand paging performance," Project MAC memo M0131, November 1972; also *Commun. ACM 17*, 4, April 1974.

J. H. Saltzer and J. F. Ossanna, "Remote terminal character stream processing in Multics," *AFIPS Conf Proc 36* (1970 SJCC), 621–627, 1970.

J. H. Saltzer, "Naming and Binding of Objects," in R. Bayer, R. M. Graham, and G. Seegmuller (eds.), *Operating Systems: An Advanced Course*, Springer Verlag, New York, 1979, 99–208. [Appendix A: Case Study of Naming in Multics, 193–208.]

J. H. Saltzer, "On the modeling of paging algorithms," ACM Forum, *Commun. ACM 19*, 5, May 1976.

P. H. Salus, *A Quarter Century of UNIX*, Addison Wesley, 1994.

M. D. Schroeder and J. H. Saltzer, "A hardware architecture for implementing protection rings," *Proc. ACM Third SOSP*, 42–54, October 1971; *Commun. ACM 15*, 3, 157–170, March 1972.

M. D. Schroeder, "Engineering a security kernel for Multics," *ACM Operating Systems Rev. 9*, 5, 25–32, *Proc. ACM 5th SOSP*, November, 1975.

M. D. Schroeder, "Performance of the GE-645 associative memory while Multics is in operation," *Proc. ACM SIGOPS Workshop on System Performance Evaluation*, Harvard, Cambridge, MA, April 1971.

M. D. Schroeder, D. D. Clark, and J. H. Saltzer, "The Multics kernel design project," *ACM Operating Systems Rev. 11, 5; Proc. ACM 6th SOSP*, West Lafayette, IN, November 1977.

M. J. Spier and E. I. Organick, "The Multics inter-process communication facility," *Proc ACM Second SOSP*, 83–91, October 1969.

J. A. Stern, *Multics Security Kernel Top Level Specification*, Honeywell Information Systems Inc. McLean, VA, Federal Systems Operations (NTIS AD-A060 000/7), November 1976.

T. H. Van Vleck, "An example of industry-university cooperation: Multics," *IRIA Tenth Anniversary Conf.*, Paris, June 1978.

T. H. Van Vleck and C. T. Clingen, "Implementation of security concepts in a large-scale operating system," *Honeywell Security Symposium*, Monaco, December 1980.

T. H. Van Vleck and C. T. Clingen, "The Multics system programming process," *Proc. IEEE COMPCON 78*, Atlanta, May 1978; reprinted in *IEEE Tutorial on Software Maintenance*, 1981.

T. H. Van Vleck, "Control of access to computer system resources," *Proc. IEEE COMPCON 74*, San Francisco, February 1974.

T. H. Van Vleck, "The administration and management of Multics," *Project MAC Multics Symposium*, January 1971.

D. R. Vinograd, "What's a system to do?—Assuring system data integrity," *Proc. IEEE Conf.*, September 1971.

V. A. Vyssotsky, F. J. Corbató, and R. M. Graham, "Structure of the Multics supervisor," *AFIPS Conf. Proc. 27*, 203–212, 1965.

R. Watson, *Time-Sharing System Concepts*, McGraw-Hill, 1970.

J. A. Weeldreyer and O. D. Friesen, "Multics relational data store: an implementation of a relational data base manager," *Proc. 11th Hawaii Intl. Conf. on System Sciences*, Vol. 1, 52–66. 1978.

J. Whitmore, A. Bensoussan, P. Green, D. Hunt, and A. Kobziar, *Design for Multics Security Enhancements*, Honeywell Information Systems Inc., Cambridge, MA, (NTIS AD-A030 801/5), December 1973.

T. Whiteside, *Computer Capers*. Published as a book and in the New Yorker as a two-part series in late 1977 or early 1978.

P. T. Withington, *Design and Abstract Specification of a Multics Security Kernel*. Vol. 2, Mitre Corp., Bedford, MA (NTIS AD-A053 148/3), March 1978.

P. T. Withington, *A Secure Flat File System for Multics*, Mitre Corp., Bedford MA.

B. L. Wolman, "Debugging PL/I programs in the Multics environment," *AFIPS Conf. Proc. 41*, Part I (1972 FJCC), 507–514, AFIPS Press, 1972.

J. P. L. Woodward, *Design and Abstract Specification of a Multics Security Kernel*, Vol. 3, Mitre Corp., Bedford, MA (NTIS AD-A053 149/1), March 1978.

D. B. Yntema, *The Cambridge Project: Computer Methods for Analysis and Modeling of Complex Systems*, Massachusetts Institute of Technology, AD-783 626, Feb. 1974, 1–29.

The GNU License

Linux is written and distributed under the GNU General Public License which means that its source code is freely distributed and available to the general public.

GNU General Public License

Version 2, June 1991
Copyright (C) 1989, 1991 Free Software Foundation, Inc. 675 Mass Ave, Cambridge, MA 02139, USA Everyone is permitted to copy and distribute verbatim copies of this license document, but changing it is not allowed.

Preamble

The licenses for most software are designed to take away your freedom to share and change it. By contrast, the GNU General Public License is intended to guarantee your freedom to share and change free software— to make sure the software is free for all its users. This General Public License applies to most of the Free Software Foundation's software and to any other program whose authors commit to using it. (Some other Free Software Foundation software is covered by the GNU Library General Public License instead.) You can apply it to your programs, too.

When we speak of free software, we are referring to freedom, not price. Our General Public Licenses are designed to make sure that you have the freedom to distribute copies of free software (and charge for this service if you wish), that you receive source code or can get it if you want it, that you can change the software or use pieces of it in new free programs; and that you know you can do these things.

To protect your rights, we need to make restrictions that forbid anyone to deny you these rights or to ask you to surrender the rights. These restrictions translate to certain responsibilities for you if you distribute copies of the software, or if you modify it.

For example, if you distribute copies of such a program, whether gratis or for a fee, you must give the recipients all the rights that you have. You must make sure that they, too, receive or can get the source code. And you must show them these terms so they know their rights.

We protect your rights with two steps: (1) copyright the software, and (2) offer you this license which gives you legal permission to copy, distribute and/or modify the software.

Also, for each author's protection and ours, we want to make certain that everyone understands that there is no warranty for this free software. If the software is modified by someone else and passed on, we want its recipients to know that what they have is not the original, so that any problems introduced by others will not reflect on the original authors' reputations.

Finally, any free program is threatened constantly by software patents. We wish to avoid the danger that redistributors of a free program will individually obtain patent licenses, in effect making the program proprietary. To prevent this, we have made it clear that any patent must be licensed for everyone's free use or not licensed at all.

The precise terms and conditions for copying, distribution and modification follow.

GNU GENERAL PUBLIC LICENSE TERMS AND CONDITIONS FOR COPYING, DISTRIBUTION AND MODIFICATION

0. This License applies to any program or other work which contains a notice placed by the copyright holder saying it may be distributed under the terms of this General Public License. The "Program", below, refers to any such program or work, and a "work based on the Program" means either the Program or any derivative work under copyright law: that is to say, a work containing the Program or a portion of it, either verbatim or with modifications and/or translated into another language. (Hereinafter, translation is included without limitation in the term "modification".) Each licensee is addressed as "you".

Activities other than copying, distribution and modification are not covered by this License; they are outside its scope. The act of running the Program is not restricted, and the output from the Program is covered only if its contents constitute a work based on the Program (independent of having been made by running the Program). Whether that is true depends on what the Program does.

1. You may copy and distribute verbatim copies of the Program's source code as you receive it, in any medium, provided that you conspicuously and appropriately publish on each copy an appropriate copyright notice and disclaimer of warranty; keep intact all the notices that refer to this License and to the absence of any warranty; and give any other recipients of the Program a copy of this License along with the Program.

You may charge a fee for the physical act of transferring a copy, and you may at your option offer warranty protection in exchange for a fee.

2. You may modify your copy or copies of the Program or any portion of it, thus forming a work based on the Program, and copy and distribute such modifications or work under the terms of Section 1 above, provided that you also meet all of these conditions:

a) You must cause the modified files to carry prominent notices stating that you changed the files and the date of any change.

b) You must cause any work that you distribute or publish, that in whole or in part contains or is derived from the Program or any part thereof, to be licensed as a whole at no charge to all third parties under the terms of this License.

c) If the modified program normally reads commands interactively when run, you must cause it, when started running for such interactive use in the most ordinary way, to print or display an announcement including an appropriate copyright notice and a notice that there is no warranty (or else, saying that you provide a warranty) and that users may redistribute the program under these conditions, and telling the user how to view a copy of this License. (Exception: if the Program itself is interactive but does not normally print such an announcement, your work based on the Program is not required to print an announcement.)

These requirements apply to the modified work as a whole. If identifiable sections of that work are not derived from the Program, and can be reasonably considered independent and separate works in themselves, then this License, and its terms, do not apply to those sections when you distribute them as separate works. But when you distribute the same sections as part of a whole which is a work based on the Program, the distribution of the whole must be on the terms of this License, whose permissions for other licensees extend to the entire whole, and thus to each and every part regardless of who wrote it. Thus, it is not the intent of this section to claim rights or contest your rights to work written entirely by you; rather, the intent is to exercise the right to control the distribution of derivative or collective works based on the Program.

In addition, mere aggregation of another work not based on the Program with the Program (or with a work based on the Program) on a volume of a storage or distribution medium does not bring the other work under the scope of this License.

3. You may copy and distribute the Program (or a work based on it, under Section 2) in object code or executable form under the terms of Sections 1 and 2 above provided that you also do one of the following:

a) Accompany it with the complete corresponding machine-readable source code, which must be distributed under the terms of Sections 1 and 2 above on a medium customarily used for software interchange; or,

b) Accompany it with a written offer, valid for at least three years, to give any third party, for a charge no more than your cost of physically performing source distribution, a complete machine-readable copy of the corresponding source code, to be distributed under the terms of Sections 1 and 2 above on a medium customarily used for software interchange; or,

c) Accompany it with the information you received as to the offer to distribute corresponding source code. (This alternative is allowed only for noncommercial distribution and only if you received the program in object code or executable form with such an offer, in accord with Subsection b above.)

The source code for a work means the preferred form of the work for making modifications to it. For an executable work, complete source code means all the source code for all modules it contains, plus any associated interface definition files, plus the scripts used to control compilation and installation of the executable. However, as a special exception, the source code distributed need not include anything that is normally distributed (in either source or binary form) with the major components (compiler, kernel, and so on) of the operating system on which the executable runs, unless that component itself accompanies the executable.

If distribution of executable or object code is made by offering access to copy from a designated place, then offering equivalent access to copy the source code from the same place counts as distribution of the source code, even though third parties are not compelled to copy the source along with the object code.

4. You may not copy, modify, sublicense, or distribute the Program except as expressly provided under this License. Any attempt otherwise to copy, modify, sublicense or distribute the Program is void, and will automatically terminate your rights under this License. However, parties who have received copies, or rights, from you under this License will not have their licenses terminated so long as such parties remain in full compliance.

5. You are not required to accept this License, since you have not signed it. However, nothing else grants you permission to modify or distribute the Program or its derivative works. These actions are prohibited by law if you do not accept this License. Therefore, by modifying or

distributing the Program (or any work based on the Program), you indicate your acceptance of this License to do so, and all its terms and conditions for copying, distributing or modifying the Program or works based on it.

6. Each time you redistribute the Program (or any work based on the Program), the recipient automatically receives a license from the original licensor to copy, distribute or modify the Program subject to these terms and conditions. You may not impose any further restrictions on the recipients' exercise of the rights granted herein. You are not responsible for enforcing compliance by third parties to this License.

7. If, as a consequence of a court judgment or allegation of patent infringement or for any other reason (not limited to patent issues), conditions are imposed on you (whether by court order, agreement or otherwise) that contradict the conditions of this License, they do not excuse you from the conditions of this License. If you cannot distribute so as to satisfy simultaneously your obligations under this License and any other pertinent obligations, then as a consequence you may not distribute the Program at all. For example, if a patent license would not permit royalty-free redistribution of the Program by all those who receive copies directly or indirectly through you, then the only way you could satisfy both it and this License would be to refrain entirely from distribution of the Program.

If any portion of this section is held invalid or unenforceable under any particular circumstance, the balance of the section is intended to apply and the section as a whole is intended to apply in other circumstances.

It is not the purpose of this section to induce you to infringe any patents or other property right claims or to contest validity of any such claims; this section has the sole purpose of protecting the integrity of the free software distribution system, which is implemented by public license practices. Many people have made generous contributions to the wide range of software distributed through that system in reliance on consistent application of that system; it is up to the author/donor to decide if he or she is willing to distribute software through any other system and a licensee cannot impose that choice.

This section is intended to make thoroughly clear what is believed to be a consequence of the rest of this License.

8. If the distribution and/or use of the Program is restricted in certain countries either by patents or by copyrighted interfaces, the original copyright holder who places the Program under this License may add an explicit geographical distribution limitation excluding those countries,

so that distribution is permitted only in or among countries not thus excluded. In such case, this License incorporates the limitation as if written in the body of this License.

9. The Free Software Foundation may publish revised and/or new versions of the General Public License from time to time. Such new versions will be similar in spirit to the present version, but may differ in detail to address new problems or concerns.

Each version is given a distinguishing version number. If the Program specifies a version number of this License which applies to it and "any later version", you have the option of following the terms and conditions either of that version or of any later version published by the Free Software Foundation. If the Program does not specify a version number of this License, you may choose any version ever published by the Free Software Foundation.

10. If you wish to incorporate parts of the Program into other free programs whose distribution conditions are different, write to the author to ask for permission. For software which is copyrighted by the Free Software Foundation, write to the Free Software Foundation; we sometimes make exceptions for this. Our decision will be guided by the two goals of preserving the free status of all derivatives of our free software and of promoting the sharing and reuse of software generally.

NO WARRANTY

11. BECAUSE THE PROGRAM IS LICENSED FREE OF CHARGE, THERE IS NO WARRANTY FOR THE PROGRAM, TO THE EXTENT PERMITTED BY APPLICABLE LAW. EXCEPT WHEN OTHERWISE STATED IN WRITING THE COPYRIGHT HOLDERS AND/OR OTHER PARTIES PROVIDE THE PROGRAM "AS IS" WITHOUT WARRANTY OF ANY KIND, EITHER EXPRESSED OR IMPLIED, INCLUDING, BUT NOT LIMITED TO, THE IMPLIED WARRANTIES OF MERCHANTABILITY AND FITNESS FOR A PARTICULAR PURPOSE. THE ENTIRE RISK AS TO THE QUALITY AND PERFORMANCE OF THE PROGRAM IS WITH YOU. SHOULD THE PROGRAM PROVE DEFECTIVE, YOU ASSUME THE COST OF ALL NECESSARY SERVICING, REPAIR OR CORRECTION.

12. IN NO EVENT UNLESS REQUIRED BY APPLICABLE LAW OR AGREED TO IN WRITING WILL ANY COPYRIGHT HOLDER, OR ANY OTHER PARTY WHO MAY MODIFY AND/OR REDISTRIBUTE THE PROGRAM AS PERMITTED ABOVE, BE LIABLE TO YOU FOR DAMAGES, INCLUDING ANY GENERAL, SPECIAL, INCIDENTAL OR CONSEQUENTIAL DAMAGES ARISING OUT OF THE USE OR

INABILITY TO USE THE PROGRAM (INCLUDING BUT NOT LIMITED TO LOSS OF DATA OR DATA BEING RENDERED INACCURATE OR LOSSES SUSTAINED BY YOU OR THIRD PARTIES OR A FAILURE OF THE PROGRAM TO OPERATE WITH ANY OTHER PROGRAMS), EVEN IF SUCH HOLDER OR OTHER PARTY HAS BEEN ADVISED OF THE POSSIBILITY OF SUCH DAMAGES.

END OF TERMS AND CONDITIONS

Appendix: How to Apply These Terms to Your New Programs

If you develop a new program, and you want it to be of the greatest possible use to the public, the best way to achieve this is to make it free software which everyone can redistribute and change under these terms.

To do so, attach the following notices to the program. It is safest to attach them to the start of each source file to most effectively convey the exclusion of warranty; and each file should have at least the "copyright" line and a pointer to where the full notice is found.

<one line to give the program's name and a brief idea of what it does.> Copyright (C) 19yy <name of author>

This program is free software; you can redistribute it and/or modify it under the terms of the GNU General Public License as published by the Free Software Foundation; either version 2 of the License, or (at your option) any later version.

This program is distributed in the hope that it will be useful, but WITHOUT ANY WARRANTY; without even the implied warranty of MERCHANTABILITY or FITNESS FOR A PARTICULAR PURPOSE. See the GNU General Public License for more details.

You should have received a copy of the GNU General Public License along with this program; if not, write to the Free Software Foundation, Inc., 675 Mass Ave, Cambridge, MA 02139, USA.

Also add information on how to contact you by electronic and paper mail.

If the program is interactive, make it output a short notice like this when it starts in an interactive mode:

Gnomovision version 69, Copyright (C) 19yy name of author Gnomovision comes with ABSOLUTELY NO WARRANTY; for details type 'show w'. This is free software, and you are welcome to redistribute it under certain conditions; type 'show c' for details.

The hypothetical commands 'show w' and 'show c' should show the appropriate parts of the General Public License. Of course, the commands you use may be called something other than 'show w' and 'show c'; they could even be mouse-clicks or menu items—whatever suits your program.

You should also get your employer (if you work as a programmer) or your school, if any, to sign a "copyright disclaimer" for the program, if necessary. Here is a sample; alter the names:

> Yoyodyne, Inc., hereby disclaims all copyright interest in the program 'Gnomovision' (which makes passes at compilers) written by James Hacker.
> <signature of Ty Coon>, 1 April 1989
> Ty Coon, President of Vice

This General Public License does not permit incorporating your program into proprietary programs. If your program is a subroutine library, you may consider it more useful to permit linking proprietary applications with the library. If this is what you want to do, use the GNU Library General Public License instead of this License.

Logical Volume Manager Abstract

Logical Volume Manager Abstract   2/02/2000

Goals:

Implement a very flexible virtual disk subsystem to handle disk storage.
Online allocation and relocation of storage.
Online extension and reduction of storage.

Function:

The Logical Volume Manager (LVM) adds an additional layer between
the physical peripherals and the i/o interface in the kernel to
get a logical view of disks.

This allows the concatenation of several disks (so-called physical volumes
or PVs) to form a storage pool (so-called Volume Group or VG) with
allocation units called physical extents (called PE).

Parts out of this VG then can be allocated in form of
so-called Logical Volumes or LVs in units called logical extents or LEs.
Each logical extent is mapped to a corresponding physical extent
of equal size. These physical extents are mapped to offsets and blocks
on the disk(s).

The LVs can then be used through device special files similar to
/dev/sd[a-z]* or /dev/hd[a-z]* named /dev/VolumeGroupName/LogicalVolumeName.

But going beyond this, you are able to extend or reduce VGs AND LVs at runtime.

Concept:

The configuration information for the physical volume, volume group and
logical volume(s) is stored on each physical volume and in automatically
created backup files, which are stored in the /etc/lvmtab.d directory.

The config area on the disk(s) is called Volume Group Descriptor Area or VGDA.

A LVM driver holds mapping tables between the LEs of LVs and the PEs of PVs.
These tables are created/updated/deleted by super user LVM commands.

The main mapping function of the driver is called with a logical block
in a LV from functions in /usr/src/linux/drivers/block/ll_rw_blk.c
(in functions ll_rw_block() and ll_rw_swap_file()) and looks up the
corresponding physical block/disk pair in a table.
Then it returns this pair to the calling ll_rw_*() function causing a
physical i/o request to the disk block(s) to be queued.

Example:

If the capacity of a LV gets too small and your VG containing this LV is full,
you could add another PV to that VG and simply extend the LV afterwards.

If you reduce or delete a LV you can use the freed capacity for different
LVs of the same VG.

The above scenario looks like this:

```
    /-----------------------------------------\
    |   /--------\      VG 1      /--------\   |
    |   |        |                |        |   |
    |   |  PV 1  |    ......       |  PV n  |   |
    |   |     /----------------------\     |   |
    |   |     \-------LV 1-----------/     |   |
    |   \--------/                \--------/   |
    \-----------------------------------------/
```

PV 1 could be /dev/sdc1
PV n could be /dev/sde1
VG 1 could be vg00
LV 1 could be /dev/test_vg/test_lv

Configuration steps for getting the above scenario:

1. after installing LVM do an "insmod lvm" or
   setup kerneld/kmod to load it automatic (see INSTALL)

2. set up partitions (#1) on both disks with partition type 0x8e
   (i used this type to avoid using LINIX primary partitions etc.)

3. do a "pvcreate /dev/sd[ce]1"
   For testing purposes you can use more than one
   primary and/or extended partition on a disk.
   Don't do that for normal LVM operation for performance reasons.
   If you have to, don't stripe logical volumes over physical volumes
   associated to partitions on the same disk.

4. do a "vgcreate test_vg /dev/sd[ce]1"
   (vgcreate activates the volume group too)

5. do a "lvcreate -L100 -ntest_lv test_vg" to get a 100MB linear LV
   or a "lvcreate -i2 -I4 -l100 -nanother_test_lv test_vg" to get a
   100 LE large logical volume with 2 stripes and stripesize 4 KB.

6. use created LVs as you like to.
   For example generate a file system in one with "mke2fs /dev/test_vg/test_lv"
   and mount it.

Overview and concept of commands:

I grouped and named LVM commands analog to HP's.
So the commands for physical volume handling all start with pv,
those for volume group handling start with vg and the ones for

```
logical volumes start with lv.


e2fsadm        - administration wrapper for logical volume including file system
                 resizing for lvextend, lvreduce, e2fsck and resize2fs

lvchange       - change attributes of a logical volume
lvcreate       - create a logical volume
lvdisplay      - display logical volume config data
lvextend       - extend a logical volume in size
lvreduce       - reduce a logical volume in size
lvremove       - remove a logical volume
lvrename       - renames an inactive logical volume
lvscan         - find all existing logical volumes

lvmchange      - emergency program to change attributes of the LVM
lvmdiskscan    - scan all disks / partitions and multiple devices and list them
lvmsadc        - statistic data collector
lvmsar         - statistic data reporter

pvchange       - change attributes of physical volumes
pvcreate       - create a physical volume
pvdata         - debug list physical volume group descriptor area
pvdisplay      - display physical volume config information
pvmove         - move logical extents to a different physical volume
pvscan         - find all existing physical volumes

vgcfgbackup    - backup all volume group descriptor areas
vgcfgrestore   - restore volume group descriptor area(s) to disk(s)
vgchange       - activate/deactivate volumr group(s)
vgck           - check volume group descriptor area for consistency
vgcreate       - create a volume group from physical volume(s)
vgdisplay      - display volume group config information
vgexport       - export volume group (make it unknown to the system)
vgextend       - extend a volume group by one or more physical volumes
vgimport       - import a volume group (make it known to the/another system)
vgmerge        - merge two volume groups into one
vgmknodes      - creates volume group directory with all logical volume specials
vgreduce       - reduce a volume group by one or more empty physical volume(s)
vgremove       - remove an empty volume group
vgrename       - renames an inactive volume group
vgscan         - scan for volume groups
vgsplit        - split one volume group into two



Example LVM session output:
--------------------------

# create physical volumes on 9 SCSI disk primary partition 1
pvcreate /dev/sd[b-eg-k]1
pvcreate -- /dev/sdb1 has an invalid physical volume identifier
pvcreate -- physical volume on /dev/sdb1 successfully created
pvcreate -- reinitializing physical volume
```

```
pvcreate -- physical volume on /dev/sdc1 successfully created
pvcreate -- reinitializing physical volume
pvcreate -- physical volume on /dev/sdd1 successfully created
pvcreate -- reinitializing physical volume
pvcreate -- physical volume on /dev/sde1 successfully created
pvcreate -- reinitializing physical volume
pvcreate -- physical volume on /dev/sdg1 successfully created
pvcreate -- reinitializing physical volume
pvcreate -- physical volume on /dev/sdh1 successfully created
pvcreate -- reinitializing physical volume
pvcreate -- physical volume on /dev/sdi1 successfully created
pvcreate -- reinitializing physical volume
pvcreate -- physical volume on /dev/sdj1 successfully created
pvcreate -- reinitializing physical volume
pvcreate -- physical volume on /dev/sdk1 successfully created


# create a volume group with default physical extent size
# from these physical volumes
vgcreate my_first_vg /dev/sd[b-eg-k]1
vgcreate -- INFO: using default physical extent size 4096 KB
vgcreate -- INFO: maximum logical volume size is 256 GB
vgcreate -- doing automatic backup of vg05
vgcreate -- volume group my_first_vg successfully created


# Oops ;-)
# Don't like the limitations caused by default physical extent size
# --> deactivate and delete volume
vgchange -an my_first_vg
vgchange -- my_first_vg successfully deactivated

vgremove my_first_vg
vgremove -- volume group my_first_vg successfully removed


# create a volume group with physical extent size of 8192 KB
# from these physical volumes
vgcreate -s 8192 my_first_vg /dev/sd[b-eg-k]1
vgcreate -- INFO: maximum logical volume size is 512 GB
vgcreate -- doing automatic backup of my_first_vg
vgcreate -- volume group my_first_vg successfully created


# display volume group config
vgdisplay my_first_vg
--- Volume group ---
VG Name                my_first_vg
VG Write Access        read/write
VG Status              available
VG #                   1
```

```
MAX LV                    31
Cur LV                    0
Open LV                   0
MAX LV Size               512 GB
Max PV                    256
Cur PV                    9
Act PV                    9
VG Size                   12636 MB
PE Size                   8192 KB
Total PE                  1579
Alloc PE / Size           0 / 0 KB
Free  PE / Size           1579 / 12632 MB


# do it again Sam but verbose
vgdisplay -v my_first_vg
--- Volume group ---
VG Name                   my_first_vg
VG Write Access           read/write
VG Status                 available
VG #                      1
MAX LV                    31
Cur LV                    0
Open LV                   0
MAX LV Size               512 GB
Max PV                    256
Cur PV                    9
Act PV                    9
VG Size                   12636 MB
PE Size                   8192 KB
Total PE                  1579
Alloc PE / Size           0 / 0 KB
Free  PE / Size           1579 / 12636 MB


--- No logical volumes defined in my_first_vg ---


--- Physical volumes ---
PV Name (#)               /dev/sdb1 (1)
PV Status                 available / allocatable
Total PE / Free PE        131 / 131

PV Name (#)               /dev/sdc1 (2)
PV Status                 available / allocatable
Total PE / Free PE        131 / 131

PV Name (#)               /dev/sdd1 (3)
PV Status                 available / allocatable
Total PE / Free PE        131 / 131

PV Name (#)               /dev/sde1 (4)
PV Status                 available / allocatable
Total PE / Free PE        131 / 131
```

```
PV Name (#)            /dev/sdg1 (5)
PV Status              available / allocatable
Total PE / Free PE     131 / 131

PV Name (#)            /dev/sdh1 (6)
PV Status              available / allocatable
Total PE / Free PE     131 / 131

PV Name (#)            /dev/sdi1 (7)
PV Status              available / allocatable
Total PE / Free PE     131 / 131

PV Name (#)            /dev/sdj1 (8)
PV Status              available / allocatable
Total PE / Free PE     125 / 125

PV Name (#)            /dev/sdk1 (9)
PV Status              available / allocatable
Total PE / Free PE     537 / 537



# create a linear physical volume with all space of the volume group
lvcreate -l1579 my_first_vg
lvcreate -- doing automatic backup of my_first_vg
lvcreate -- logical volume /dev/my_first_vg/lvol1 successfully created



# create an ext2fs on newly created logical volume
mke2fs /dev/my_first_vg/lvol1
mke2fs 1.10, 24-Apr-97 for EXT2 FS 0.5b, 95/08/09
Linux ext2 file system format
File system label=
3235840 inodes, 12939264 blocks
646963 blocks (5.00%) reserved for the super user
First data block=1
Block size=1024 (log=0)
Fragment size=1024 (log=0)
1580 block groups
8192 blocks per group, 8192 fragments per group
2048 inodes per group
Superblock backups stored on blocks:
                8193, 16385, 24577, 32769, 40961, 49153, 57345, 65537, 73729,
                81921, 90113, 98305, 106497, 114689, 122881, 131073, 139265,
147457,

Writing superblocks and file system accounting information: done
0.66user 26.55system 3:06.62elapsed 14%CPU (0avgtext+0avgdata 0maxresident)k
0inputs+0outputs (97major+522minor)pagefaults 0swaps


# and mount it (not very exiting :-) )
mount /dev/my_first_vg/lvol1 /mnt
```

Kernel Parameters v2.2.9

The following is a consolidated list of the kernel parameters as defined in the file init/main.c and sorted into English Dictionary order (defined as ignoring all punctuation and sorting digits before letters in a case insensitive manner), and with descriptions where known.

The text in square brackets at the beginning of the description state the restrictions on the kernel for the said kernel parameter to be valid. The restrictions referred to are that the relevant option is valid if:

APIC	APIC support is enabled.
APM	Advanced Power Management support is enabled.
AX25	Appropriate AX.25 support is enabled.
CD	Appropriate CD support is enabled.
EIDE	EIDE/ATAPI support is enabled.
FB	The frame buffer device is enabled.
HW	Appropriate hardware is enabled.
ISDN	Appropriate ISDN support is enabled.
JOY	Appropriate joystick support is enabled.
LP	Printer support is enabled.
LOOP	Loopback device support is enabled.
MCA	MCA bus support is enabled.
MDA	MDA console support is enabled.
MOUSE	Appropriate mouse support is enabled.
NET	Appropriate network support is enabled.
NFS	Appropriate NFS support is enabled.
PARIDE	The ParIDE subsystem is enabled.
PCI	PCI bus support is enabled.
PCMCIA	The PCMCIA subsystem is enabled.
PNP	Plug & Play support is enabled.
PPT	Parallel port support is enabled.
PS2	Appropriate PS/2 support is enabled.
RAM	RAM disk support is enabled.
SCSI	Appropriate SCSI support is enabled.

SERIAL	Serial support is enabled.
SMP	The kernel is an SMP kernel.
SOUND	Appropriate sound system support is enabled.
VGA	The VGA console has been enabled.
VT	Virtual terminal support is enabled.
XT	IBM PC/XT MFM hard disk support is enabled.

In addition, the following text indicates that the option:

BUGS=	Relates to possible processor bugs on the said processor.
KNL	Is a kernel start-up parameter.

Note that *all* kernel parameters listed below are *case sensitive*, and that a trailing = on the name of any parameter states that that parameter will be entered as an environment variable, whereas its absence indicates that it will appear as a kernel argument readable via /proc/cmdline by programs running once the system is up.

```
53c7xx=             [HW,SCSI] Amiga SCSI controllers.
adb_buttons=        [HW,MOUSE]
advansys=           [HW,SCSI]
aha152x=            [HW,SCSI]
aha1542=            [HW,SCSI]
aic7xxx=            [HW,SCSI]
AM53C974=           [HW,SCSI]
apm=                [APM] Advanced Power Management.
arcrimi=            [HW,NET]
ataflop=            [HW, M68k]
atamouse=           [HW,MOUSE] Atari Mouse.
atascsi=            [HW,SCSI] Atari SCSI.
aztcd=              [HW,CD] Aztec CD driver.
baycom_par=         [HW,AX25] BayCom Parallel Port AX.25 Modem.
baycom_ser_fdx=     [HW,AX25] BayCom Serial Port AX.25 Modem in
                              Full
                    Duplex Mode.
baycom_ser_hdx=     [HW,AX25] BayCom Serial Port AX.25 Modem in
                              Half
                    Duplex Mode.
bmouse=             [HW,MOUSE,PS2] Bus mouse.
BusLogic=           [HW,SCSI]
cdu31a=             [HW,CD]
cm206=              [HW,CD]
com20020=           [HW,NET]
com90io=            [HW,NET]
com90xx=            [HW,NET]
console=            [KNL] output console + comm spec (speed,
                          control, parity).
```

```
cyclades=          [HW,SERIAL] Cyclades multi-serial port adapter.
debug              [KNL] Enable kernel debugging (events log
                        level).
decnet=            [HW,NET]
digi=              [HW,SERIAL] io parameters + enable/disable
                        command.
digiepca=          [HW,SERIAL]
dmascc=            [HW,AX25,SERIAL] AX.25 Z80SCC driver with DMA
                        support available.
dmasound=          [HW,SOUND] (sound subsystem buffers).
dtc3181e=          [HW,SCSI]
eata=              [HW,SCSI]
eda=               [HW,PS2]
edb=               [HW,PS2]
ether=             [HW,NET] Ethernet cards parameters (iomem, irq,
                        dev_name).
fd_mcs=            [HW,SCSI]
fdomain=           [HW,SCSI]
floppy=            [HW]
ftape=             [HW] Floppy Tape subsystem debugging options.
gdth=              [HW,SCSI]
gscd=              [HW,CD]
gvp11=             [HW,SCSI]
hd=                [EIDE] (E)IDE hard drive subsystem geometry
                        (Cyl/heads/sectors) or tune parameters.
hfmodem=           [HW,AX25]
HiSax=             [HW,ISDN]
hisax=             [HW,ISDN]
in2000=            [HW,SCSI]
init=              [KNL]
ibmmcascsi=        [HW,MCA,SCSI] IBM MicroChannel SCSI adapter.
icn=               [HW,ISDN]
ide?=              [HW] (E)IDE subsystem : config (iomem/irq),
                        tuning or debugging
                        (serialize,reset,no{dma,tune,probe}) or
                        chipset specific parameters.
idebus=            [HW] (E)IDE subsystem : VLB/PCI bus speed.
in2000=            [HW,SCSI]
init=              [KNL] Default init level.
ip=                [PNP]
isp16=             [HW,CD]
js_14=             [HW,JOY]
js_am=             [HW,JOY]
js_an=             [HW,JOY]
js_as=             [HW.JOY]
js_console=        [HW,JOY]
js_console2=       [HW,JOY]
js_console3=       [HW,JOY]
js_db9=            [HW,JOY]
js_db9_2=          [HW,JOY]
js_db9_3=          [HW,JOY]
js_tg=             [HW,JOY]
js_tg_2=           [HW,JOY]
js_tg_3=           [HW,JOY]
```

```
kbd-reset           [VT]
load_ramdisk=       [RAM] List of ramdisks to load from floppy.
lp=0                [LP] Specify parallel ports to use, e.g,
lp=port[,port...]   lp=none,parport0 (lp0 not configured, lp1 uses
lp=reset            first parallel port). 'lp=0' disables the
lp=auto             printer driver. 'lp=reset' (which can be
                       specified in addition to the ports) causes
                       attached printers to be reset. Using
                       lp=port1,port2,... specifies the parallel
                       ports to associate lp devices with, starting
                       with lp0. A port specification may be 'none'
                       to skip that lp device, or a parport name
                       such as 'parport0'. Specifying 'lp=auto'
                       instead of a port specification list means
                       that device IDs from each port should be
                       examined, to see if an IEEE 1284-compliant
                       printer is attached; if so, the driver will
                       manage that printer.
ltpc=               [HW]
mac5380=            [HW,SCSI]
max_loop=[0-255]    [LOOP] Set the maximum number of loopback
                       devices that can be mounted.
maxcpus=            [SMP] States the maximum number of processors
                       that an SMP kernel should make use of.
max_scsi_luns=      [SCSI]
mca-pentium         [BUGS=ix86]
mcd=                [HW,CD]
mcdx=               [HW,CD]
md=                 [HW] RAID subsystems devices and level.
mdacon=             [MDA]
mem=                [KNL] force use XX Mb of memory when the kernel
                       is not able to see the whole system
                       memory or for test.
msmouse=            [HW,MOUSE] Microsoft Mouse.
ncr5380=            [HW,SCSI]
ncr53c400=          [HW,SCSI]
ncr53c400a=         [HW,SCSI]
ncr53c406a=         [HW,SCSI]
ncr53c8xx=          [HW,SCSI]
nfsaddrs=           [NFS]
nfsroot=            [NFS] nfs root filesystem for disk-less boxes.
nmi_watchdog=       [KNL, BUGS=ix86] debugging features for SMP
                       kernels.
no387               [BUGS=ix86] Tells the kernel to use the 387
                       maths emulation library even if a 387
                       maths coprocessor is present.
noapic              [SMP,APIC] Tells the kernel not to make use of
                       any APIC that may be present on the
                       system.
noasync             [HW, M68K] Disables async and sync negotiation
                       for all devices.
nodisconnect        [HW,SCSI, M68K] Disables SCSI disconnects.
no-halt             [BUGS=ix86]
```

noinitrd	[RAM] Tells the kernel not to load any configured initial RAM disk.
no-scroll	[VGA]
nosmp	[SMP] Tells an SMP kernel to act as a UP kernel.
nosync	[HW, M68K] Disables sync negotiation for all devices.
optcd=	[HW,CD]
panic=	[KNL] kernel behaviour on panic.
parport=0	[HW,PPT] Specify parallel ports. 0 disables.
parport=auto	Use 'auto' to force the driver to use
parport=0xBBB	any IRQ/DMA settings detected (the
[,IRQ[,DMA]]	default is to ignore detected IRQ/DMA settings because of possible conflicts). You can specify the base address, IRQ, and DMA settings; IRQ and DMA should be numbers, or 'auto' (for using detected settings on that particular port), or 'nofifo' (to avoid using a FIFO even if it is detected). Parallel ports are assigned in the order they are specified on the command line, starting with parport0.
pas16=	[HW,SCSI]
pcbit=	[HW,ISDN]
pcd.	[PARIDE]
pci=	[PCI]
pd.	[PARIDE]
pf.	[PARIDE]
pg.	[PARIDE]
pirq=	[SMP,APIC] mp-table.
plip=	[PPT,NET] Parallel port network link.
profile=	[KNL] enable kernel profiling via /proc/profile (param:log level).
prompt_ramdisk=	[RAM] List of RAM disks to prompt for floppy disk before loading.
pt.	[PARIDE]
ramdisk=	[RAM] Sizes of RAM disks in kilobytes [deprecated].
ramdisk_size=	[RAM] New name for the ramdisk parameter.
ramdisk_start=	[RAM] Starting block of RAM disk image (so you can place it after the kernel image on a boot floppy).
reboot=	[BUGS=ix86]
reserve=	[KNL,BUGS] force the kernel to ignore some iomem area.
riscom8=	[HW,SERIAL]
ro	[KNL] Mount root device read-only on boot.
root=	[KNL] roct filesystem.
rw	[KNL] Mount root device read-write on boot.
S	[KNL] run init in single mode.
sbpcd=	[HW,CD] Soundblaster CD adapter.
scsi_logging=	[SCSI]
sjcd=	[HW,CD]

```
sonycd535=          [HW,CD]
sound=              [SOUND]
soundmodem=         [HW,AX25,SOUND] Use sound card as packet radio
                            modem.
specialix=          [HW,SERIAL] Specialix multi-serial port
                            adapter.
st=                 [HW] SCSI tape parameters (buffers, etc.).
st0x=               [HW,SCSI]
stram_swap=         [HW]
switches=           [HW, M68K]
sym53c416=          [HW,SCSI]
sym53c8xx=          [HW,SCSI]
t128=               [HW,SCSI]
tmc8xx=             [HW,SCSI]
tmscsim=            [HW,SCSI]
tp720=              [HW,PS2]
u14-34f=            [HW,SCSI]
video=              [FB] frame buffer configuration.
vga=                [KNL] on ix386, enable to choose a peculiar
                            video mode (use vga=ask for menu).
wd33c93=            [HW,SCSI]
wd7000=             [HW,SCSI]
wdt=                [HW]
xd=                 [HW,XT] Original XT pre-IDE (RLL encoded) disks.
xd_geo=             [HW,XT]
```

INDEX

Note: Boldface numbers indicate illustrations; italic t indicates a table; italic f indicates a footnote reference.

SOFTWARE AND INFORMATION LICENSE

The software and information on this diskette (collectively referred to as the "Product") are the property of The McGraw-Hill Companies, Inc. ("McGraw-Hill") and are protected by both United States copyright law and international copyright treaty provision. You must treat this Product just like a book, except that you may copy it into a computer to be used and you may make archival copies of the Products for the sole purpose of backing up our software and protecting your investment from loss.

By saying "just like a book," McGraw-Hill means, for example, that the Product may be used by any number of people and may be freely moved from one computer location to another, so long as there is no possibility of the Product (or any part of the Product) being used at one location or on one computer while it is being used at another. Just as a book cannot be read by two different people in two different places at the same time, neither can the Product be used by two different people in two different places at the same time (unless, of course, McGraw-Hill's rights are being violated).

McGraw-Hill reserves the right to alter or modify the contents of the Product at any time.

This agreement is effective until terminated. The Agreement will terminate automatically without notice if you fail to comply with any provisions of this Agreement. In the event of termination by reason of your breach, you will destroy or erase all copies of the Product installed on any computer system or made for backup purposes and shall expunge the Product from your data storage facilities.

LIMITED WARRANTY

McGraw-Hill warrants the physical diskette(s) enclosed herein to be free of defects in materials and workmanship for a period of sixty days from the purchase date. If McGraw-Hill receives written notification within the warranty period of defects in material or workmanship, and such notification is determined by McGraw-Hill to be correct, McGraw-Hill will replace the defective diskette(s). Send request to:

Customer Service
McGraw-Hill
Gahanna Industrial Park
860 Taylor Station Road
Blacklick, OH 43004-9615

The entire and exclusive liability and remedy for breach of this Limited Warranty shall be limited to replacement of defective diskette(s) and shall not include or extend to any claim for or right to cover any other damages, including but not limited to, loss of profit, data, or use of the software, or special, incidental, or consequential damages or other similar claims, even if McGraw-Hill has been specifically advised as to the possibility of such damages. In no event will McGraw-Hill's liability for any damages to you or any other person ever exceed the lower of suggested list price or actual price paid for the license to use the Product, regardless of any form of the claim.

THE McGRAW-HILL COMPANIES, INC. SPECIFICALLY DISCLAIMS ALL OTHER WARRANTIES, EXPRESS OR IMPLIED, INCLUDING BUT NOT LIMITED TO, ANY IMPLIED WARRANT OF MERCHANTABILITY OR FITNESS FOR A PARTICULAR PURPOSE. Specifically, McGraw-Hill makes no representation or warranty that the Product is fit for any particular purpose and any implied warranty of merchantability is limited to the sixty day duration of the Limited Warranty covering the physical diskette(s) only (and not the software or information) and is otherwise expressly and specifically disclaimed.

This Limited Warranty gives you specific legal rights, you may have others which may vary from state to state. Some states do not allow the exclusion of incidental or consequential damages, or the limitation on how long an implied warranty lasts, so some of the above may not apply to you.

This Agreement constitutes the entire agreement between the parties relating to use of the Product. The terms of any purchase order shall have no effect on the terms of this Agreement. Failure of McGraw-Hill to insist at any time on strict compliance with this Agreement shall not constitute a waiver of any rights under this Agreement. This Agreement shall be construed and governed in accordance with the laws of New York. If any provision of this Agreement is held to be contrary to law, that provision will be enforced to the maximum extent permissible and the remaining provisions will remain in force and effect.